THE COLLECTED COURSES OF
THE ACADEMY OF EUROPEAN LAW

VOLUME XXIV/3

The Emergence of European Society through Public Law

A Hegelian and Anti-Schmittian Approach

THE COLLECTED COURSES OF THE ACADEMY OF EUROPEAN LAW

Edited by: Professor Neha Jain, Professor Claire Kilpatrick, Professor Sarah Nouwen, and Professor Joanne Scott

Assistant Editor: Joyce Davies

The Academy of European Law is housed at the European University Institute in Florence, Italy. The Academy holds annual advanced-level summer courses focusing on topical, cutting-edge issues in Human Rights Law and The Law of the European Union. The courses are taught by highly qualified scholars and practitioners in a highly interactive environment. General courses involve the examination of the field as a whole through a particular thematic, conceptual, or philosophical lens or look at a theme in the context of the overall body of law. Specialized courses bring together a number of speakers exploring a specific theme in depth. Together, they are published as monographs and edited volumes in the Collected Courses of the Academy of European Law series. The Collected Courses series has been published by Oxford University Press since 2000. The series contains publications on both foundational and pressing issues in human rights law and the law of the European Union.

OTHER TITLES IN THE SERIES INCLUDE:

Revisiting the Fundamentals of the Free Movement of Persons in EU Law
Edited by Niamh Nic Shuibhne

Data at the Boundaries of European Law
Edited by Deirdre Curtin and Mariavittoria Catanzariti

Legal Mobilization for Human Rights
Edited by Gráinne de Búrca

The UK's Withdrawal from the EU
A Legal Analysis
Michael Dougan

Justifying Contract in Europe
Political Philosophies of European Contract Law
Martijn W. Hesselink

Contemporary Challenges to EU Legality
Edited by Claire Kilpatrick and Joanne Scott

Reframing Human Rights in a Turbulent Era
Gráinne de Búrca

New Legal Approaches to Studying the Court of Justice
Revisiting Law in Context
Edited by Claire Kilpatrick and Joanne Scott

The Emergence of European Society through Public Law

A Hegelian and Anti-Schmittian Approach

ARMIN VON BOGDANDY

Translated by
NAOMI SHULMAN

Revised by
THEODOR SHULMAN

OXFORD
UNIVERSITY PRESS

OXFORD
UNIVERSITY PRESS

Great Clarendon Street, Oxford, OX2 6DP,
United Kingdom

Oxford University Press is a department of the University of Oxford.
It furthers the University's objective of excellence in research, scholarship,
and education by publishing worldwide. Oxford is a registered trade mark of
Oxford University Press in the UK and in certain other countries

Published in the United States of America by Oxford University Press
198 Madison Avenue, New York, NY 10016, United States of America

British Library Cataloguing in Publication Data
Data available

Library of Congress Control Number: 2023951177

ISBN 978–0–19–890934–7

DOI: 10.1093/oso/9780198909347.001.0001

Dedicated to the Tuesday Roundtable and the Ius Constitutionale Commune en América Latina Network

Foreword

This book reconstructs the transformation of public law in Europe after 1945. It focuses on how this transformation mirrors, and even furthers, the emergence and democratization of European society. To make its case, it compares the European transformation with that in Latin America. In terms of positive law, it centres on Article 2 of the European Union (EU) Treaty.

I should note that I write as a German public-law scholar (*Staatsrechtslehrer*) who has been greatly influenced by Eberhard Grabitz and Claus-Dieter Ehlermann, two great jurists of the European cause. Since kites rise highest against the wind, my analysis engages, in an intellectual tradition founded by Georg Wilhelm Friedrich Hegel, with Carl Schmitt, Ernst-Wolfgang Böckenförde, Joseph H. Weiler, and the Second Senate of the *Bundesverfassungsgericht*.

This book takes up—and identifies—thoughts from earlier texts, some of which were co-authored with Jürgen Bast, Sergio Dellavalle, Matthias Goldmann, Laura Hering, Stephan Hinghofer-Szalkay, Michael Ioannidis, Christoph Krenn, Davide Paris, Luke Dimitrios Spieker, René Urueña, and Ingo Venzke. I thank Sabino Cassese, Philipp Dann, Rainer Forst, Klaus Günther, Reinhard Mehring, Alexander Somek, and the Polish Deputy Ombudsman Maciej Taborowski, an exemplary and courageous legal scholar, for critical readings of the manuscript. I owe many suggestions to the *Ius Constitutionale Commune en América Latina* (ICCAL) network, organized by Mariela Morales Antoniazzi, as well as to our Tuesday roundtable. I gratefully acknowledge the support from Michael Ioannidis, Eva Neumann, Giacomo Rugge, Dana Schmalz, Desirée Schmitt, Luke Dimitrios Spieker, Silvia Steininger, Benedict Vischer, and especially Lea Berger, Ben Fridrich, Yvonne Klein, Joshua Puhze, Philipp Sauter, Jasper Siegert, Effi Spiegel, and Catharina Ziebritzki, who braved the struggle with EndNote.

This book elaborates on my General Course at the Florentine Academy of European Law. It was written as part of the Frankfurt Cluster of Excellence named *Normative Orders*, which was led by Rainer Forst and Klaus Günther. Funding from the Deutsche Forschungsgemeinschaft's Leibniz Programme allowed the expansion of the ICCAL network. Suhrkamp published the German version of this book in early 2022.

The book captures developments until September 2021. Since that time, significant events have occurred in the realm of European public law that corroborate its central argument. On 16 February 2022, the Court of Justice of the European Union's Plenary ruled that the values enumerated in Article 2 of the Treaty on European Union (TEU) 'define the very identity of the European Union as a common legal order' (Case C-156/21, *Hungary v. Parliament and Council* and Case C-157/21, *Poland v. Parliament and Council*). On 27 July 2022, the General Court's Grand Chamber affirmed that the democratic integrity of European society serves as a legitimate aim deserving protection (Case T-125/22, *RT France v. Council*). On 8 June 2023, the European Commission contested Poland's 'Lex Tusk' as violating the principle of democracy outlined in Articles 2 and 10 of the TEU (IP/23/3134). In academia, Loïc Azoulai has framed EU law in terms similar to those used in this book, describing it as 'The Law of European Society' (*Common Market Law Review*, Special Issue 59 (2022), 203). The genie of European democratic society is out of the bottle: may this book contribute to its flourishing.

Heidelberg, August 2023

A Note to the Reader

Cross-references are indicated by a series of numbers and letters. For example, 'see 3.3.C' refers the reader to Chapter 3, section 3, part C, and 'see 4.2' refers to Chapter 4, section 2.

Table of Contents

Table of Cases

For the benefit of digital users, table entries that span two pages (e.g. 52–53) may, on occasion, appear on only one of those pages.

EUROPEAN UNION CASES

Court of Justice of the European Union

General Court Cases

INTERNATIONAL CASES

European Court on Human Rights (ECtHR)

INTER-AMERICAN COURT OF HUMAN RIGHTS (IACTHR)

NATIONAL CASES

Costa Rica

Czechia

France

Germany

Hungary

Italy

Poland

United Kingdom

United States

1
Outline

1. Idea and Programme

Many Europeans struggle to understand where European Union (EU)-centred Europeanization has led them. The standard response—that their situation is *sui generis*, one of a kind—no longer holds. Thus, Brexit, disappointments such as in the fight against COVID-19 and conflicts over European financial transfers, immigration, or dubious judicial reforms in some Member States, demand a more substantial answer. With this in mind, I reconstruct European integration by reconstructing European public law in the light of Article 2 of the Treaty on European Union (TEU).[1]

According to Article 2 TEU, all Europeans are today part of *one* society. European integration may not have produced a European state or people, but it has helped create a European society. This society is intimately interwoven with European public law, for the Treaty legislator—that is, the 27 Member States' political systems in cooperation with EU institutions—avails itself of constitutional principles to characterize it. Thus, Article 2 TEU states that European society is one 'in which pluralism, non-discrimination, tolerance, justice, solidarity and equality between women and men prevail' and in which the values of 'respect for human dignity, freedom, democracy, equality, the rule of law and respect for human rights, including the rights of persons belonging to minorities' apply.

I interpret this statement as the manifesto, identity, and constitutional core of a *democratic* society. This take is not mere academic speculation. According to the German government's Memorandum on the Lisbon Treaty, the values of Article 2 TEU 'constitute the essence of a democratic society'.[2] Thus, Europeans should understand that European integration has ushered in a European democratic society. This approach takes the bull by the horns because democracy represents the key concept in the struggle to understand and develop our society.

Some will question whether Article 2 TEU can serve as the constitutional core of European society. Its conceptual potpourri appears to reflect woolly compromise. And indeed, it mediates between many ideas, identities, interests, traditions, and

[1] For a psychological reconstruction, see O. Angelucci von Bogdandy, *Zur Ökologie einer Europäischen Identität. Soziale Repräsentationen von Europa und dem Europäer-Sein in Deutschland und Italien* (2003).

[2] Memorandum on the Treaty of Lisbon of 13 December 2007, Bundestag publication BT-Drucks, 16/8300, 153.

The Emergence of European Society through Public Law. First Edition. Armin von Bogdandy, Oxford University Press.
 DOI: 10.1093/oso/9780198909347.003.0001

world views. But in the Hegelian tradition in which I write, this is an asset, not a shortcoming.[3] Indeed, Hegel considers a well-functioning constitution as a system of mediations.[4] On this view, Article 2 TEU establishes the standards by which European society must seek its compromises. While compromises (i.e. mediations) characterize true democracies,[5] immediacy represents the promise of hybrid or authoritarian regimes.[6]

The spirit of compromise expressed in Article 2 TEU lies at the democratic heart of European society. In Hegelian terms, the haggling in Brussels is desirable if it engenders mediations that meet the standards of Article 2 TEU. As compromises, these mediations will always meet criticism for the most diverse reasons. However, such criticism is a valuable asset in itself for it feeds European society's self-critical attitude.

European public law, I hold, thus provides the normative structure of European democratic society. This take is not universally shared. For the public law scholar Christoph Schönberger, it represents 'constitutional science fiction'.[7] The political scientist Philip Manow's view is even more sombre: 'Anyone who invokes Europe wants to cheat.'[8]

To be sure, European institutions, public law, and society exhibit manifold deficiencies.[9] A democratic compromise may even compromise a democratic society for not every compromise is valuable.[10] In reconstructing the democratic features of European public law, this book does not, therefore, glorify the status quo. To the contrary, it suggests further transformations.

Although I write in the Hegelian tradition, I do not believe that progress is a foregone conclusion. Future transformations may take many directions, as may the interpretation of the standards of Article 2 TEU. Thus, transformative constitutionalism for a more European democratic society (see 2.6.D) is one option—but so is a European concert of powerful states, one country's hegemony, executive federalism, national withdrawal, and—last but not least—the ideas personified by Viktor Orbán.[11] A European democratic society exists, but it does not seem to be consolidated.

[3] G. W. F. Hegel, *Lectures on the History of Philosophy*, Vol. 1 (1995 [1837]) 35.

[4] G. W. F. Hegel, *Elements of the Philosophy of Right* (1991 [1821]) para. 302, addition.

[5] D. Innerarity, *Democracy in Europe. A Political Philosophy of the EU* (2018) 61 ff.

[6] G. Frankenberg, *Autoritarismus. Verfassungstheoretische Perspektiven* (2020) 255 ff.

[7] Schönberger, 'Hegemon wider Willen. Zur Stellung Deutschlands in der Europäischen Union', 66 *Merkur* (2012) 1, at 5 f., 8.

[8] Manow, 'Ach, Europa—Ach, Demokratie', 66 *Merkur* (2012) 20, at 26.

[9] In novel form, R. Menasse, *The Capital* (2019); in greater detail see 2.4.A.

[10] Thus, on the policies of the European Council vis-à-vis Poland and Hungary, Editorial comments, 'Compromising (on) the General Conditionality Mechanism and the Rule of Law', 58 *Common Market Law Review* (2021) 267; see 3.5.B.

[11] For an overview, see G. Levi and D. Preda (eds), *Euroscepticisms. Resistance and Opposition to the European Community/European Union* (2019).

2. European Society

This book presents European public law as the law of European society. This is not science fiction but a scholarly reconstruction. Article 2 TEU provides its legal anchor as it explicitly refers to *society*.[12]

There are many European societies. Consider the more than 3,000 European companies in the legal form of *Societas Europaea* (such as Airbus, BASF, and Dior) and thousands of civil society organizations, ranging from the European Society of International Law, to the European Society of Cardiology, to the European Society for Spiritual Regression. The term 'society' in Article 2 TEU encompasses all of these, but it refers to much more—namely, the social whole constituted by the EU Treaty.

To clarify this concept of society, I show that it takes on the role of Hegel's concept of the state. The latter includes all public institutions, with their staff, procedures, instruments, and practices, but also all citizens with all their social relationships.[13] Over the course of the nineteenth century, the concept of society increasingly came to designate this social whole as well.[14] That links German thought with a tradition famously expressed by Article 16 of the French Declaration of the Rights of Man and Citizen of 1789, one of the most important provisions of European constitutionalism. It states: 'Any society in which no provision is made for guaranteeing rights or for the separation of powers, has no Constitution.'

Since the beginning of the twentieth century, that broad understanding of society is safely established. Max Weber wrote quite naturally about public authority, bureaucracy, government, and the state in his seminal book *Economy and Society*.[15] The European Convention on Human Rights (ECHR) illustrates how common this understanding is in Europe today. Many of its provisions feature the words 'a democratic society', for example, Article 6(1), Article 8(2), Article 9(2), Article 10(2), and Article 11(2) ECHR. In doing so, they mainly refer to the Convention states' public institutions as Article 16 Declaration of the Rights of Man and Citizen.

If society and state designate the same social whole, that does not mean that choosing one or the other is immaterial. To mark one difference: the concept of society conceives the social whole rather from the vantage point of interacting individuals, whereas the concept of state conceives it rather from the vantage point

[12] The term has received little attention from legal scholars; see Calliess, 'Art. 2 EUV', in C. Calliess and M. Ruffert (eds), *EUV/AEUV. Das Verfassungsrecht der Europäischen Union mit Europäischer Grundrechtecharta. Kommentar* (2016) para. 30; Klamert and Kochenov, 'Article 2 TEU', in M. Kellerbauer, M. Klamert, and J. Tomkin (eds), *The EU Treaties and the Charter of Fundamental Rights. A Commentary* (2019) para. 5; Fumagalli, 'Commento Art. 2 TUE', in A. Tizzano (ed.), *Trattati dell'Unione europea* (2014) 11, at 14; but see also Mangiameli, 'Article 2', in H.-J. Blanke and S. Mangiameli (eds), *The Treaty on European Union (TEU): A Commentary* (2013) paras 35–41.

[13] von Bogdandy, 'Hegel und der Nationalstaat', 30 *Der Staat* (1991) 513.

[14] P. Vogel, *Hegels Gesellschaftsbegriff und seine geschichtliche Fortbildung durch Lorenz von Stein, Marx, Engels und Lassalle* (1925).

[15] M. Weber, *Economy and Society* (2002) 52 ff., 212 ff., 635 ff.

of public authority. Society is also more open on possible forms of public authority that provide for political unity. Focusing on society might help overcome statist thinking.

Moreover, European society provides for a new understanding of conflicts in the European Union. Whereas today many conflicts are conceived as conflicts *between* Member States, the new approach frames them as conflicts *within* one society. For example, the crisis over the rule of law is mostly understood as one between liberal Western Member States and some illiberal Eastern ones. The new frame brings to the fore that quite a number of citizens and parties in Western Europe share the views of Viktor Orbán and Jarosław Kaczyński. A similar point can be made for policies of solidarity, today mostly framed as a conflict between Northern and Southern European Member States.

Of course, the question remains whether European society—a society that does not form a state—is a viable democratic entity. Many believe it is not (see 3.2.C, 3.4.B, 3.5.B). This book endeavours to prove the opposite.

While Article 2 TEU envisions a European society without a European state, it does not picture a stateless society. Instead, it posits the Member States, including all their public institutions, as essential parts of European society. The *society* of Article 2 TEU is not limited to the sphere that Hegel calls *civil* (*bürgerliche*) society, that is, to the web of economic relations. Article 3 para. 3 TEU uses the term 'internal market' to designate this web.[16] The term 'civil society' (*Zivilgesellschaft*), moreover, usually refers to the sphere of social engagement or non-profit organizations, as does the term in Article 11(2) of the EU Treaty.[17] Article 2 TEU's *society*, by contrast, denotes the social whole, which encompasses all the institutions of the Union and its Member States as well as all their citizens and other residents. Under Article 2 TEU, society thus represents the ultimate social reference of European law.

Article 2 refers to *European* society[18]—and not to the societies of the Member States[19]—because it uses the singular 'society'. It does not allude to the global (or world) society because it refers to the EU Member States and to democratic values.[20] The reference to values also underscores that Article 2 does not conceive of society in opposition to the concept of *community*: the German dichotomy between society and community, which goes back to Ferdinand Tönnies, is irrelevant when it comes to Article 2 TEU.

[16] Hegel, *Elements of the Philosophy of Right* (n. 4) para. 182.

[17] Mendes, 'Participation and the Role of Law after Lisbon. A Legal View on Article 11 TEU', 48 *Common Market Law Review* (2011) 1849.

[18] CJEU, Case C-574/12, *Centro Hospitalar de Setúbal and SUCH*, Opinion of AG Mancini (EU:C:2014:120), para. 40; groundbreaking Mangiameli (n. 12).

[19] Thus Monjal, 'Le projet de traité établissant une Constitution pour l'Europe. Quels fondements théoriques pour le droit constitutionnel de l'Union européenne?', 40 *Revue trimestrielle de droit européen* (2004) 443, at 453 f.

[20] On the scarcity of values in world society, see Luhmann, 'Die Weltgesellschaft', 57 *Archiv für Rechts- und Sozialphilosophie* (1971) 1.

Ferdinand Tönnies distinguished between society and community by emphasizing the specific significance that values hold for a community.[21] Following Tönnies, society is often understood as a group that is only integrated in market terms, whereas community is taken to mean a more cohesive group, one integrated through values. Thus, a society's bonds are rather thin and transactional, whereas a community's bonds are thick and normative. The European Treaties' path and terminology exhibit an almost opposite logic. In 1958, the Treaty-makers started with the *Community* of the European Economic Community (EEC) Treaty; in 2007, after half a century of integration, they postulated a society based on values (see 3.1.D).

The factual statement in Article 2 TEU—namely, that there is a European society—is sociologically robust.[22] Of course, numerous questions remain as to how to conceptualize European society and how to observe it. As a basic concept of European thought, society has been theorized in many different ways, and the relevant data can be reconstructed in similarly various forms. To interpret Article 2 TEU, it suffices to understand society as social interaction or communicative practice.[23] Legal scholars observe such interaction or practice mainly through the study of certain texts: constitutions, treaties, laws, decrees, directives, judgments, and scholarly publications. These texts provide the empirical basis for my reconstruction of European society.

Lawyers concentrate on juridical disputes, which are an especially intense form of social interaction and communicative practice. Accordingly, European society becomes a reality in the many conflicts involving the terms of Article 2 TEU, conflicts in which *European* rights, *European* justice, *European* solidarity, *European* democracy, or the *European* rule of law become disputatious. Indeed, European society creates itself in these disputes.[24] European law plays a constitutive role inasmuch as it conceptualizes the conflicts as European conflicts, civilizes them, and renders their legal outcomes valid, effective, and legitimate.

Is addressing all Union citizens as part of a European society a merely external ascription, or can we also understand European society as European citizens' self-description? Sceptics will point out that Article 2 TEU was concocted by a small group of people in the Brussels bubble surrounding the Rue de la Loi. However, most constitutions emerged in even smaller bubbles. Many drafting processes were less public, less dramatic, and less political than that of the Lisbon Treaty from 2003 to 2009. The latter involved a convention staged to maximize publicity,

[21] Riedel, 'Gesellschaft, Gemeinschaft', in O. Brunner, W. Conze, and R. Koselleck (eds), *Geschichtliche Grundbegriffe. Historisches Lexikon zur politisch-sozialen Sprache in Deutschland* (1975) 801, esp. at 830 ff.

[22] See W. Outhwaite, *European Society* (2008).

[23] Müller, 'Auf dem Weg in eine europäische Gesellschaft? Begriffsproblematik und theoretische Perspektiven', 17 *Berliner Journal für Soziologie* (2007) 7, at 24.

[24] Přibáň, 'Introduction: On Europe's Crises and Self-Constitutions', in J. Přibáň (ed.), *Self-Constitution of European Society. Beyond EU politics, law and governance* (2016) 1, at 3.

a first dramatic failure in the French and Dutch referendums, two Irish referendums, a series of Member State ratifications with qualified majorities, and some spectacular court cases.[25]

In 1987, Hartmut Kaelble's pioneering study had identified a European society but saw scant evidence of self-reflexive processes.[26] For him, then, the concept represented a merely external ascription. In 2020, however, Kaelble noted that the national societies have continued to coalesce 'substantively'.[27] Accordingly, I interpret the singular *society* posited in Article 2 TEU in 2007 as European citizens' self-description (see 2.2.B, 3.2.A–C).

3. Transformation

It is common to understand European law as characterized by transformations.[28] The concept of *structural transformation* deepens this understanding. *Structural transformation* is a theoretical concept with a practical purpose, as I now show with the help of the pioneering studies of Leibholz, Habermas, and Friedmann.

In 1952, the public law scholar and judge Gerhard Leibholz delivered a seminal lecture entitled 'The Structural Transformation of Modern Democracy'. He had a chequered history. In 1933, he wanted to reconcile fascism and democracy;[29] in 1938, he fled from the National Socialists to England; and in 1951, after returning, he became one of the initial members of the *Bundesverfassungsgericht*'s Second Senate. In the latter capacity, he wrote the famous memorandum that has undergirded the *Bundesverfassungsgericht*'s powerful role in the Federal Republic.[30] Leibholz's lecture in Karlsruhe shed light on what the Senate planned to do: advance democracy through judge-made law in response to a structural transformation. In other words, Leibholz bet on the court's potential to democratize societies.

For over two decades, Leibholz was the mastermind of a case law that assigned the political parties a leading role in the Federal Republic. Ingeniously, he reversed

[25] J.-C. Piris, *The Lisbon Treaty. A Legal and Political Analysis* (2010) 25–63; D. Phinnemore, *The Treaty of Lisbon. Origins and Negotiation* (2013) esp. at 16 ff., 148 ff., 178 ff.

[26] H. Kaelble, *Auf dem Weg zu einer europäischen Gesellschaft. Eine Sozialgeschichte Westeuropas 1880–1980* (1987).

[27] H. Kaelble, *Eine europäische Gesellschaft? Beiträge zur Sozialgeschichte Europas vom 19. bis ins 21. Jahrhundert* (2020) 185 ff., at 200.

[28] See, e.g. Stein, 'Lawyers, Judges, and the Making of a Transnational Constitution', 75 *American Journal of International Law* (1981) 1; Weiler, 'The Transformation of Europe', 100 *Yale Law Journal* (1991) 2403; Ioannidis, 'Europe's New Transformations. How the EU Economic Constitution Changed during the Eurozone Crisis', 53 *Common Market Law Review* (2016) 1237.

[29] G. Leibholz, *Die Auflösung der liberalen Demokratie in Deutschland und das autoritäre Staatsbild* (1933) 79.

[30] On the memorandum, see Schönberger, 'Karlsruhe: Notes on a Court', in M. Jestaedt *et al.* (eds), *The German Federal Constitutional Court: The Court Without Limits* (2020) 1, at 9.

the Weimar Republic's criticism of the party state and propagated an interpretation of the constitution whereby West Germany almost turned into a *particracy*. At the same time, he committed the parties to democratic principles.[31] Leibholz legitimized the idea of this case law by asserting that a structural transformation had occurred. The mass democracy of modern societies in post-war Europe, as recognized by the Basic Law, was 'entirely different […] in its fundamental structure' from the liberal democracy inscribed in many constitutions until the Second World War.[32] This change was so 'weighty' that it appeared 'transformative'.[33] In Leibholz's view, this transformation charted a course towards a democratic society.

By highlighting the structural transformation, Leibholz overcame the German Empire and Weimar Republic's distrust of political parties. Ever forward-looking, he discarded this doctrine as a conceptual zombie and, with gravitas, called on legal scholarship to identify and support the delineation of such transformations.[34]

The transformation of German society has moved on since Leibholz. Today, German society is embedded in a European society for which the democratic question arises in a different form. Thus, Europe does not have major parties that shape the political views of a few relevant social milieus. Accordingly, Leibholz does not help us understand that the 190 parties represented in the European Parliament in 2021 can provide true democracy.[35] Incidentally, the Second Senate (of which he was once a part) is deeply sceptical of the European Parliament's democratic potential.[36]

Leibholz's model has always been criticized for being overly narrow.[37] Today, a model that focuses on a few major parties is outdated. Instead, we ought to conceptualize a democratic society as a far more complex system of mediation. In Article 2, the Treaty legislator has set out the standards for such a system (see 3.5).

We can readily identify one aspect: a propensity for compromise. Compromise explains the potpourri of standards in Article 2 TEU (see 1.1). It also characterizes a parliament made up of 190 parties. European democracy thus follows a different path to that in the British or US democracies, where two parties determine the citizens' fate. Despite their chagrin about their own democracy, few EU citizens would maintain that Europe should take those democracies as an example.

The democratic idea is also the fulcrum of Jürgen Habermas' habilitation thesis *Strukturwandel der Öffentlichkeit* (*The Structural Transformation of the Public*

31 A.-B. Kaiser (ed.), *Der Parteienstaat. Zum Staatsverständnis von Gerhard Leibholz* (2013).

32 G. Leibholz, *Der Strukturwandel der modernen Demokratie. Vortrag, gehalten in der Juristischen Studiengesellschaft in Karlsruhe am 30. April 1952* (1952) 16.

33 Ibid. 8.

34 Ibid. 7.

35 European Parliament, 'Constitution of the 9th Legislature of the European Parliament', press release 2 July 2019.

36 See part 4.

37 W. Hennis, *Die mißverstandene Demokratie* (1973) 81 ff.; Hennis, 'Der "Parteienstaat" des Grundgesetzes. Eine gelungene Erfindung (1992)', in W. Hennis (ed.), *Auf dem Weg in den Parteienstaat. Aufsätze aus vier Jahrzehnten* (1998) 107.

Sphere), which was published 10 years after Leibholz's book. The work transcends Leibholz's focus on parties. It develops the concept of a politically active public sphere, which—many decades later—would become central to the discussions on European democracy.[38] The notion of democracy that undergirds Articles 9–12 TEU owes much to these discussions. Indeed, almost half a century later, Habermas came to champion the European democratic cause as a truly European public intellectual.[39]

Habermas' book of 1962 suggests a method that I will follow here. It promotes 'a systematic comprehension of our own society from the perspective of one of its central categories'.[40] As shown in his later study *Between Facts and Norms*, public law is one of these categories. Accordingly, studying the transformation of public law should be as illuminating as inquiring into the transformation of the public sphere: 'Nowhere is Europe more real than in the law.'[41]

In 1962, Habermas, like Leibholz in 1952, still focused on transformations occurring within the confines of the Hegelian state. Both considered this framework of a democratic society so self-evident that they hardly addressed transnational structures. A focus on the latter emerged with Wolfgang Friedmann's *The Changing Structure of International Law* of 1964. The former Berlin labour court judge, who had fled the Nazis, became a key scholar of the progressive Manhattan School of international law, not least because of that book.[42]

Friedmann's book contends that international law has various structures. The first are those of traditional international law; as the law of diplomacy, they primarily serve to make or maintain peace between competing powers. Friedmann designates these structures the international law of *coexistence*. But he also argues that there is more to the international realm than the competition between great powers. Thus, new structures supplement and overlie the old ones. Friedmann makes out an additional, more constructive layer of international law that allows states to pursue common interests by means of common institutions. He calls it the international law of *cooperation*.

And then, Friedmann maintains, there is an avant-garde beyond the international law of cooperation. He identifies it as the law of *integration*, heralded by the three European communities: the European Coal and Steel Community (ECSC), the European Economic Community (EEC), and the European Atomic

[38] All the way to the Second Senate; see, e.g. BVerfGE 123, 267, *Lisbon*, paras 249, 251; U. Di Fabio, *Staat im Recht* (2020) 38 f.

[39] See his contributions in J. Habermas, *The Divided West* (2014) 39 ff.; Habermas, 'The Crisis of the European Union in the Light of a Constitutionalization of International Law', 23 *European Journal of International Law* (2012) 335, at 339, 345.

[40] J. Habermas, *The Structural Transformation of the Public Sphere: An Inquiry into a Category of Bourgeois Society* (1989) 5.

[41] Comité de Réflexion sur le Préambule de la Constitution, *Redécouvrir le Préambule de la Constitution. Rapport du comité présidé par Simone Veil* (2008) 41.

[42] On the Manhattan School, see Kennedy, 'Tom Franck and the Manhattan School', 35 *New York University Journal of International Law & Politics* (2003) 397, esp. at 420 ff.

Energy Community. Friedmann presents it as part of the transformation towards a European confederation.[43] In doing so, he foreshadows what the Treaty legislator would enshrine in Article 2 TEU four decades later.

4. European Hegelianism and Anti-Schmittianism

Scholarly research should be conscious of its positionality. This book will develop European public law in the tradition that Georg Wilhelm Hegel established 200 years ago with his *Elements of the Philosophy of Right*. As distant as the Age of Metternich is, the Hegelian tradition can, nevertheless, help us better understand our society.[44] This positioning should serve to locate my book in the thicket of contemporary European thought.

What do I take from Hegel? His scholarship focused on a transformational project, namely, the Prussian reforms after the Napoleonic wars. These reforms held out the promise of freedom, progress, and overcoming outdated structures. This book likewise seeks to understand a transformational project with great promise, as stated in Articles 1, 2, and 3 TEU. Hegel's writing posits an ambitious understanding of freedom that goes far beyond mere liberty and is, instead, based on intersubjectivity; I share this understanding.[45] Hegel presents constitutions and legislation as forms of mediation; this offers a key to understanding the democratic nature of European law. His theory largely consists of the elaboration of concepts, and so does this book. As with Hegel, my elaboration is not abstract and deductive but historical and institutionalist.[46] Hegel calls such an approach 'reconstruction'.[47] This study follows that method.[48]

One of Hegel's fundamental insights is that we must trace the development of social phenomena if we wish to understand them. I do so with a focus on transformations. *Transformation* is a perspective that takes an evolutionary approach but attends to discontinuities, threshold phases, and metamorphoses; it does not stress continuity. Transformations in the sense of *structural transformation*

[43] W. G. Friedmann, *The Changing Structure of International Law* (1964) 18 f.

[44] Münkler, 'Hegel und wir', 14 *Zeitschrift für Ideengeschichte* (2020) 5; A. Honneth, *Das Recht der Freiheit. Grundriß einer demokratischen Sittlichkeit* (2011) esp. at 14 ff.; Schmalz, 'Social Freedom in a Global World: Axel Honneth's and Seyla Benhabib's Reconsiderations of a Hegelian Perspective on Justice', 26 *Constellations* (2019) 301.

[45] On Hegel's concept of freedom, see E.-W. Böckenförde, *Der Staat als sittlicher Staat* (1978) 23 ff.; Habermas, 'Noch einmal: Zum Verhältnis von Moral und Sittlichkeit', in R. Forst and K. Günther (eds), *Normative Ordnungen* (2021) 25.

[46] Fulda, 'Zum Theorietypus der Hegelschen Rechtsphilosophie', in D. Heinrich and R.-P. Horstmann (eds), *Hegels Philosophie des Rechts: Die Theorie der Rechtsformen und ihre Logik* (1982) 393.

[47] Hegel, 'Vorlesungen über die Geschichte der Philosophie III (1819–1831)', in E. Moldenhauer and K. M. Michel (eds), *Werke in zwanzig Bänden mit Registerband, Bd. 20* (1970) 505.

[48] For details, see Goldmann, 'Dogmatik als rationale Rekonstruktion. Versuch einer Metatheorie am Beispiel völkerrechtlicher Prinzipien', 53 *Der Staat* (2014) 373; Patberg, 'Suprastaatliche Verfassungspolitik und die Methode der rationalen Rekonstruktion', 53 *Der Staat* (2014) 401.

denote fundamental changes, as the books by Leibholz, Habermas, and Friedmann illustrate.

Research on structural transformation includes the question of driving forces. Hegel refers to the march of God in the world, but that is hardly convincing today. Friedmann points to power, values, ideologies, and interests, yet leaves their relationship open.[49] Scholars have identified the following forces as crucial to the structural transformation of European law: the governments of the nation states,[50] the logic of transnational socialization,[51] the dynamics of capitalism,[52] the internal dynamics of the juridical field,[53] and the discursive power of a good idea.[54]

The instruments of legal scholarship do not help us determine the relationship between these forces. But, at the same time, I believe that the law is not simply a dependent variable of external forces (see 4.1.A, 5.1.A). Accordingly, the title of this book, *The Transformation of European Public Law*, contains both an objective and a subjective genitive.[55] There are two sides to the *transformation of public law*.[56] On the one hand, the transformation of public law signifies that law itself is transformed by the complex forces of European society (*genetivus obiectivus*). On the other hand, the law can itself bring forth social change (*genetivus subiectivus*), not least due to its transcendental normativity.[57] This is one interpretation of Hegel's famous—and, to some, infamous—argument that the real is rational.

In many respects, Hegel's concepts help reconstruct our world. In others, however, his thought is hopelessly outdated. Hegel describes the academic and administrative Berlin elite of his time as the avant-garde of the world spirit. Today, with all due respect, nobody views the actors in Berlin, Brussels, Budapest, Karlsruhe, Luxembourg, Paris, Strasbourg, Warsaw, or any other European city in this way. For Hegel, the project of transformation is rational and legitimate precisely because it is the march of God on Earth. Today, only the idea of democracy can justify a transformational project, an idea largely absent in Hegel's thought.[58] Hegel understands the legal order as an *objective spirit*, whereas this book deals with *legal*

[49] Friedmann (n. 43) 45.

[50] A. Moravcsik, *The Choice for Europe. Social Purpose and State Power from Messina to Maastricht* (1998).

[51] E. B. Haas, *The Uniting of Europe. Political, Social and Economical Forces, 1950–1957* (1958); de Búrca, 'Rethinking Law in Neofunctionalist Theory', 12 *Journal of European Public Policy* (2005) 310, at 317.

[52] J. Galtung, *Europe in the Making* (1989); Negri, 'Faire l'Europe dans la mondialisation', 14 *Multitudes* (2003) 51, at 52 f.

[53] A. Vauchez, *L'Union par le droit. L'invention d'un programme institutionnel pour l'Europe* (2013).

[54] A. Wiener, *'European' Citizenship Practice. Building Institutions of a Non-State* (1998) 49 f.

[55] G. Mohr and M. Willaschek, *Immanuel Kant, Kritik der reinen Vernunft* (1998) 14.

[56] D. Schindler, *Verfassungsrecht und soziale Struktur* (1932).

[57] J. Habermas, *Between Facts and Norms: Contributions to a Discourse Theory of Law and Democracy* (2008 [1992]) 1 ff.

[58] V. Hösle, *Hegels System. Der Idealismus der Subjektivität und das Problem der Intersubjektivität* (1998) 576 f.

structures in light of principles.[59] And while Hegel claims to reconcile all antagonisms, this book relies on compromises that are justifiable in light of Article 2 TEU.

The title's singular form of *transformation* is not a synonym for Hegel's *system*. I do not interpret the diverse conceptual histories (see 2.2–6), the formation of European principles (see 3.1–6), the development of the Court of Justice of the European Union (CJEU) and the European Court of Human Rights (ECtHR) with their manifold lines of case law (see 4.3, 4.6), the strengthening of constitutional courts and their networking (see 4.1–2, 4.4–5), or the Europeanization of legal scholarship (see 5.1–3) as necessary facets of one and the same phenomenon. Nevertheless, I embed this book in one epistemic context by organizing the material to speak to one idea, namely, the transformation of European public law from the *state-centred law of the European powers* to the normative structure of a *democratic European society*.

This project rests on the premise that legal structures express social structures. This premise is ingrained in a Hegelian theory because of the latter's institutionalist penchant. It is supported by sociological theories that conceive of social structures as patterns for human interactions.[60] Since such patterns often have a legal dimension, the law is part of many social structures.[61] Article 2 TEU posits a very close relationship between European law and European society inasmuch as it proclaims that European legal standards 'prevail' in European society. The French version of Article 2 TEU, like most of the other versions, is even more explicit for it states that legal principles *characterize* European society.

Hegel's theory provided a powerful narrative, and hence legitimation, for the Prussian transformative project. The European transformation lacks such a narrative, and many consider this a serious shortcoming (see 3.2.A–B, 3.5.A). Albrecht Koschorke, a scholar of narratives, argues the opposite, however. He argues that, in contrast to Hegel's Prussia, European society does not require a legitimating narrative because it is far more integrated and because its legal network is much more tightly woven.[62] Accordingly, European society can spare the tremendous costs of establishing a general narrative (see 3.2.B–C).[63]

Many will consider this take misguided because it entails a European democracy without a European common identity (see 3.2.C, 3.5.A) as well as a European public law without European statehood (see 2.3.A). Hegel's thinking supports such scepticism since his philosophy of law argues that society requires statehood in order to function.[64] In doing so, it established the most important German

[59] On the conceptual history, see Kross, 'Struktur', in J. Ritter and K. Gründer (eds), *Historisches Wörterbuch der Philosophie, Bd. 10* (1998) columns 303–334.

[60] Habermas, *The Structural Transformation of the Public Sphere* (n. 40) 31 ff.

[61] U. Di Fabio, *Herrschaft und Gesellschaft* (2018) 139 ff.

[62] A. Koschorke, *Hegel und wir* (2015) 202–206; Koschorke, 'Auf der Suche nach dem verlorenen Europa-Narrativ', in C. Franzius, F. C. Mayer, and J. Neyer (eds), *Die Neuerfindung Europas. Bedeutung und Gehalte von Narrativen für die europäische Integration* (2019) 21, at 29–31.

[63] Koschorke, *Hegel und wir* (n. 62) 149, 189.

[64] Hegel, *Elements of the Philosophy of Right* (n. 4) para. 182 addition, para. 258.

tradition of state-centred thought. Since I consider Carl Schmitt the most thought-provoking and influential exponent of this current,[65] this book will engage his writings more than those of any other author, thereby helping clarify my position within European legal thought.

One might question whether a study on the transformation towards a European democratic society should discuss—and thereby recognize and even honour—such a compromised author. We must recall Schmitt's connection to authoritarianism in general and to national socialism in particular.[66] Yet, one can reject an author's positions and nevertheless engage with his or her work.[67] Schmitt introduced influential concepts that have opened up fruitful perspectives. They can serve legal scholars who reject his premises, approach, positions, and ethos but, like Schmitt, think in a Hegelian tradition.[68]

Above all, however, I engage with Schmitt as an adversary. He posited the centrality of the nation state.[69] For him and his thought, relying on society as the basic concept (see 1.2) is misconceived.[70] On Schmitt's view, then, the promises of the EU cannot hold true. Philip Manow alludes to Schmitt when he claims that '[a]nyone who invokes Europe wants to cheat' (see 1.1).

It bears emphasizing that I am only marginally interested in Schmitt as an influential author of the European right,[71] which abhors political compromise, celebrates ethnic identities, and distrusts international institutions. Rather, Schmitt's writings allow me to engage democratic, liberal scholars who focus on the nation state. Ernst-Wolfgang Böckenförde is a key author in this regard. Writing in the Hegelian tradition,[72] Böckenförde introduced Schmitt's thinking into liberal constitutional discourse and, in doing so, brought it to a new level. Thus, Böckenförde

[65] On Schmitt as a Hegelian, see R. Mehring, *Pathetisches Denken. Carl Schmitts Denkweg am Leitfaden Hegels. Katholische Grundstellung und antimarxistische Hegelstrategie* (1989); R. Mehring, *Denker im Widerstreit. Werk-Wirkung-Aktualität* (2017) 201 ff.

[66] For further details, see R. Mehring, *Carl Schmitt: A Biography* (2014); Tomuschat, 'Carl Schmitt's Diagnosis of the Situation of European Jurisprudence Reconsidered', 80 *Zeitschrift für ausländisches öffentliches Recht und Völkerrecht* (2020) 709.

[67] Habermas, *The Divided West* (n. 39) 135 ff., 188 ff.; Koskenniemi, 'Global Governance and Public International Law', 37 *Kritische Justiz* (2004) 241, at 494.

[68] C. Schmitt, *Verfassungsrechtliche Aufsätze aus den Jahren 1924–1925. Materialien zu einer Verfassungslehre* (1958) 427 ff.

[69] J.-W. Müller, *A Dangerous Mind. Carl Schmitt in Post-War European Thought* (2003) 49 ff.; Libin and Patapan, 'Schmitt Fever. The Use and Abuse of Carl Schmitt in Contemporary China', 18 *International Journal of Constitutional Law* (2020) 130.

[70] C. Schmitt, *Der Begriff des Politischen. Mit einer Rede über das Zeitalter der Neutralisierungen und Entpolitisierungen* (1932) 24 f.; C. Schmitt, *Hugo Preuß. Sein Staatsbegriff und seine Stellung in der deutschen Staatslehre* (1930) 20.

[71] De Benoist, 'Die Aktualität Carl Schmitts', 42 *Sezession* (2011) 14; P. Lendvai, *Orbán. Hungary's Strongman* (2018) 179.

[72] Volkmann, 'Gespräche mit Hegel', 59 *Der Staat* (2020) 489. On the relationship, see R. Mehring, *"Welch gütiges Schicksal": Ernst-Wolfgang Böckenförde/Carl Schmitt: Briefwechsel 1953–1984* (2022).

adapted Schmitt's dangerous thought for the democratic Federal Republic just as Hans-Georg Gadamer did with Martin Heidegger's.[73]

Writing in the tradition of Hegel and Schmitt, Böckenförde formulates the theorem of necessary homogeneity, which culminates in what is probably the most famous sentence of German constitutional theory after 1945: 'The liberal, secularized state is sustained by conditions it cannot itself guarantee.'[74] This observation became a core concern for numerous theories of public law. Many believe that Böckenförde identified a real problem; the societal prerequisites they suggest in response include the nation, a people, We-ness, Christianity, welfare state redistribution, or one inclusive public sphere.

There are other theoretical schools that have sought to articulate what holds society together. For a few decades, North American communitarianism did so with great success.[75] Yet, I see no real added value in communitarianism compared to the Hegelian tradition. And indeed, this approach is now withering.[76] In my opinion, the same verdict applies to the school of thought that replaced communitarianism as the most fashionable: neorepublicanism.[77]

This book would not exist without Hegel, Schmitt, and Böckenförde. I have spent many years with their texts. And yet, I argue that the transformation of European public law has altered nation states in the sense of a Hegelian suppression (*Aufhebung*).[78] While nation states endure as evolutionary achievements, they are transformed and improved as they join in the democratic European society invoked by Article 2 TEU.

[73] Habermas, 'Urbanisierung der Heideggerischen Provinz. Laudatio auf Hans Georg Gadamer aus Anlaß der Verleihung des Hegel-Preises der Stadt Stuttgart', in H.-G. Gadamer and J. Habermas (eds), *Das Erbe Hegels* (1979) 9.

[74] Böckenförde, 'The Rise of the State as a Process of Secularization (1967)', in E.-W. Böckenförde *et al.* (eds), *Religion, Law, and Democracy: Selected Writings* (2017) 152, at 167.

[75] A. MacIntyre, *After Virtue: A Study in Moral Theory* (1984); Hegel is important to many communitarian thinkers.

[76] Dellavalle, 'Per un concetto pluridimensionale di libertà. Il contributo della filosofia politica hegeliana al superamento della controversia tra liberalismo e comunitarismo', 4 *Filosofia e Questioni Pubbliche* (1998) 31.

[77] For an application to the EU, see R. Bellamy, *A Republican Europe of States: Cosmopolitanism, Intergovernmentalism and Democracy in the EU* (2019).

[78] G. W. F. Hegel, *Phenomenology of Spirit* (2013 [1807]) para. 113.

2
Concepts

1. The Old *Jus Publicum Europaeum*

Let me illustrate my approach with a joke. An academy offers a prize for the best study on camels. The French scholar goes to the Jardin des Plantes, sits on a bench next to the camels, observes the animals for an afternoon, and, that night, writes a reflective essay entitled 'Le chameau et moi' ('The Camel and I').[1] The English scholar spends six months travelling through Arabia, where she collects abundant data and publishes, in *Nature*, 'The Camel in Numbers'. The German scholar spends two lonely years among piles of books to present the 400-page study 'Der Begriff des Kamels' ('The Concept of the Camel').

One of Hegel's key insights is that precise understanding requires the efforts of abstraction. Embedded as I am in this scholarly tradition, I trace the transformation of European public law by attending to the transformation of its basic concepts. This is more than a terminological exercise. Since law is a social construct, its basic concepts fulfil an ontological function. Concepts are not simply words that denote something. Instead, they establish meaning and create knowledge.[2] Sociologically, concepts such as public law, society, or democracy are considered a 'frame', that is, shared patterns of perception and interpretation that allow social groups to organize discourse.[3] For this reason, we must understand the transformation *of* fundamental concepts as both an objective and a subjective genitive (see 1.1, 5.1.A): While the transformation of a legal concept follows social transformation, it is itself, at the same time, a force in such a social process.

I delve into the transformation of European public law beginning with the state-centred law of the Concert of Europe (see 2.1). Against this backdrop, I discuss the emergence of a new European public law, based on decisions reacting to the Second World War (see 2.2). I then liberate this public law from its statist embrace and ground it in one of modernity's fundamental differentiations, the dualism of *public versus private* (see 2.3).

Public law comes in one of two guises: administrative or constitutional law. The conceptual moves that allow for a European administrative law and a European

[1] This style of scholarship has now arrived in Germany, for good reason. See Haltern, 'Europarecht und ich', 68 *Jahrbuch des öffentlichen Rechts* (2020) 439.

[2] R. Koselleck, *Vergangene Zukunft. Zur Semantik geschichtlicher Zeiten* (3rd edn, 1995) XXIII.

[3] Vliegenthart and van Zoonen, 'Power to the Frame. Bringing Sociology Back to Frame Analysis', 26 *European Journal of Communication* (2011) 101.

The Emergence of European Society through Public Law. First Edition. Armin von Bogdandy, Oxford University Press.
 DOI: 10.1093/oso/9780198909347.003.0002

constitutional law thus shed further light on the overall transformation of European public law. The concept of a European administrative law never sparked much controversy, but it allows us to discuss the ever-present challenge of an overbearing bureaucracy (see 2.4). The concept of European constitutional law proved much more controversial (see 2.5). To conclude this section, I introduce the concept of transformative constitutionalism to frame what appears to be European public law's answer to its greatest challenge (see 2.6).

According to Hegel, it is the 'Peace of Westphalia which secured this independent status for the parts', that is, the incipient modern states.[4] This perception still holds. In the West's self-description, the Peace of 1648 represents the threshold to a great transformation. Now, the leading idea was no longer the political unity of the Christian world but the sovereign state.[5] In these processes of state formation, modern public law emerged, together with the autonomization of the political, the *raison d'état*, theories of sovereignty, and an increasingly voluntaristic concept of law.[6] Hegel's philosophy of law synthesizes these developments, thus framing legal thinking up to the twenty-first century.[7]

The concept of European public law developed in the wake of this transformation. The following pages focus on Hagemeier's *Jus Publicum Europaeum* as well as Mably and Talleyrand's *droit public de l'Europe*, which Ernst Rudolf Huber and Carl Schmitt called the *Jus Publicum Europaeum*. They form the backdrop against which the transformation after 1945 took place.

A. A Response to the Thirty Years' War

The final disintegration of Christianity's political unity entailed grave consequences for its legal unity. That is particularly true if one focuses on public law and not, as most legal historians do, on private law. Since private law mostly rested on Roman *jus commune*, some legal unity persisted until the era of codifications.[8] Public law had no such basis, which is why it turned to comparative law.

Joachim Hagemeier's *Juris Publici Europaei* is probably the first European comparativist monograph. It consists of eight volumes, published between 1677

[4] Hegel, 'The German Constitution (1798–1802)', in H. B. Nisbet and L. Dickey (eds), *Hegel: Political Writings* (1999) 6, at 75.

[5] D. Croxton, *Westphalia. The Last Christian Peace* (2013). The following section is based on von Bogdandy and Hinghofer-Szalkay, 'European Public Law—Lessons from the Concept's Past', in A. von Bogdandy, P. M. Huber, and S. Cassese (eds), *The Max Planck Handbooks in European Public Law, Vol. I. The Administrative State* (2017) 30.

[6] M. Stolleis and T. Dunlap, *Public Law in Germany. A Historical Introduction from the 16th to the 21st Century* (2017); M. Loughlin, *Foundations of Public Law* (2010).

[7] A. Koschorke, *Hegel und wir* (2015) 47, 82 f.

[8] Basedow, 'Hundert Jahre Rechtsvergleichung. Von wissenschaftlicher Erkenntnisquelle zur obligatorischen Methode der Rechtsanwendung', 71 *JuristenZeitung* (2016) 269, at 270.

and 1680. They contain reports on the 'status' of various countries and polities.[9] The work provided an extensive overview of public laws in Europe.[10]

Hagemeier does not specify the purpose of his endeavour, but his life offers a clue. His interest was certainly not purely academic. Born in Hamburg, he acted as councillor for the count of Oldenburg, later as an imperial councillor, and finally as vice chancellor and syndic of the Wetterau College of Imperial Counts. As an envoy to the Imperial Diet in Regensburg, he gained intimate knowledge of the German and European structures and politics.[11] In this context, his *Jus Publicum Europaeum* promoted mutual understanding that was necessary to create a new, post-unitary order.

Scholarship on European public law began inductively, with country reports, by presenting its diversity in different legal systems. There was certainly an alternative approach: the much more influential *Jus Publicum Universale*.[12] The latter was deduced from abstract principles in the tradition of Aristotelian natural law. Hagemeier did not give in to the temptation of such abstract thinking. Instead, his approach was institutionalist, as is that of my book.

Hagemeier's *Jus Publicum Europaeum* foreshadows another of this book's pillars: the distinction between private and public law (2.3.D). His *Jus Publicum Europaeum* is far removed from the *jus commune*, which constituted private law in most of early modern Europe. Thus, the uniform *jus commune* was the very opposite of the diverse *Jus Publicum Europaeum*. Hagemeier consequently contributed to public law's independence.

Hagemeier's books supported negotiations for a new order, but it prefigured neither it nor its legal form. What we today call international law hardly played a role in Hagemeier's *Jus Publicum Europaeum*. It only came into being in the eighteenth century, when it became known as the *droit public de l'Europe*.

[9] On the methodology used, see Mohnhaupt, '"Europa" und "ius publicum" im 17. und 18. Jahrhundert', in C. Bergfeld *et al.* (eds), *Aspekte europäischer Rechtsgeschichte. Festgabe für Helmut Coing zum 70. Geburtstag* (1982) 207, esp. at 219–224.

[10] The title reads *Juris Publici Europaei* and not *Jus Publicum Europaeum* because it is the genitive to *Epistola*: J. Hagemeier, *Juris Publici Europaei de Trium Regnorum Septentrionalium Daniae, Norvvegiae & Sveciae Statu, Epistola Prima* (1677); J. Hagemeier, *Juris Publici Europaei de Statu Galliae, Epistola II* (1678); J. Hagemeier, *Juris Publici Europaei de Statu Angliae, Scotiae Et Hiberniae, Epistola III* (1678); J. Hagemeier, *Juris Publici Europaei de Statu Imperii Germanici, Epistola IV* (1678); J. Hagemeier, *Juris Publici Europaei de Statu Provinciarum Belgicarum, Epistola V* (1679); J. Hagemeier, *Juris Publici Europaei de Statu Italiae, Epistola VI* (1679); J. Hagemeier, *Juris Publici Europaei de Statu Regnorum Hungariae et Bohemiae, Epistola VII* (1680); J. Hagemeier, *Juris Publici Europaei de Statu Regni Poloniae et Imperii Moscovitici, Epistola VIII* (1680).

[11] H. Schröder, *Lexikon der hamburgischen Schriftsteller bis zur Gegenwart, Bd. 3. Günther-Kleye* (1857). The spelling of the name varies; the spelling Hagemeyer was also common.

[12] On this issue, see M. Stolleis, *Geschichte des öffentlichen Rechts in Deutschland, Bd. 1. Reichspublizistik und Policeywissenschaft 1600–1800* (1988) 267 ff., 291 ff.

B. The *Droit Public de l'Europe*

The dominant narrative today is that a new *international law* enshrined the Westphalian order of Europe.[13] While I do not contest this account, I add some nuances for the purposes of this book and focus on the historical *droit public de l'Europe* (or *droit public européen*). Today, that *droit public* may be relevant in two opposite ways. According to Christoph Schönberger, today's European public law reflects the same logic as the historical *droit public*.[14] In my understanding, by contrast, our European public law has overcome the old *droit public de l'Europe*.

The term *droit public de l'Europe* identifies the international law of the 'French' era.[15] It encompassed not only international but also some domestic law, in particular principles of public authority as well as dynastic orders of succession, dynastic marriage contracts, and courtly conventions.[16] Thus, the legal side of the European order of the seventeenth and eighteenth centuries consisted of 'interstate law' as well as of dynastic law between royal families.[17] After the French Revolution, the dynastic elements lost importance. In consequence, the term '*droit public de l'Europe*' increasingly centred on elements that today are considered international law.

It was the Abbé Gabriel Bonnot de Mably who, particularly in his work *Le droit public de l'Europe fondé sur les traités*, introduced the most influential understanding of the concept.[18] Mably was an important French political author. He gained diplomatic experience as secretary to Cardinal de Tencin and compiled a collection of all European treaties since 1648. This collection became the foundation for his work on the *droit public de l'Europe*.[19] It became a standard work even though—or perhaps because—its publication was initially prohibited.[20]

Mably placed intergovernmental treaties at the centre of his *droit public*, thereby detaching international law from Christian natural law. He began, as later did Hegel, with the Treaties of Münster and Osnabrück in 1648. He considered these treaties 'laws for Europe',[21] which, for that reason, provide a form of European unity. Mably described these and further important treaties and both contextualized

[13] On its contested history, see Koskenniemi, 'A History of International Law Histories', in B. Fassbender and A. Peters (eds), *The Oxford Handbook of the History of International Law* (2012) 215.

[14] Schönberger, 'Hegemon wider Willen. Zur Stellung Deutschlands in der Europäischen Union', 66 *Merkur* (2012) 1, at 5 f.

[15] W. Grewe, *The Epochs of International Law* (2000) 27.

[16] Ibid.

[17] C. Schmitt, *The Nomos of the Earth in the International Law of the Jus Publicum Europaeum* (2006 [1950]) 235.

[18] G. B. de Mably, *Le droit public de l'Europe, fondé sur les traitez conclus jusqu'en l'année 1740* (1746). On the importance of Mably, see Koskenniemi, 'The Public Law of Europe. Reflections on a French 18th Century Debate', in H. Lindemann *et al.* (eds), *Erzählungen vom Konstitutionalismus* (2012) 43.

[19] E. A. Whitfield, *Gabriel Bonnot de Mably* (1930).

[20] See G. B. de Mably, *Collection complète des œuvres de l'abbé de Mably* (1794/1795) 237.

[21] Ibid. 239.

and evaluated them, generally from a French perspective. Overall, his *droit public* supported the notion that the European powers, and thus powerful France, could shape this European legal order. And indeed, Mably's *droit public* did not provide for transnational institutions.

After the French Revolution, Charles Maurice de Talleyrand-Périgord, one of the deftest statesmen of his time, further expanded the concept of a *droit public européen*, with a more constitutional and markedly restorative note. After the Holy Alliance had defeated the French revolutionary transformation of Europe, Talleyrand advocated monarchical legitimacy as the guiding principle of a *droit public européen*. It thus offered an alternative to the principle that might is right, which was feared in all European capitals.[22] Talleyrand argued that the *droit public européen* protected monarchical sovereignty just as the domestic *droit public* protected private property.

Talleyrand used the term legitimistically. Previously an ardent advocate of the Revolution and then of Bonaparte, he now stood for the interests of the restored French monarchy. The traditionalist conception of monarchical legitimacy, which he declared the basic principle of the *droit public européen* and, hence, of the European order, suited the interests of all rulers. The geostrategist's trick was to propagate a principle of great interest to all monarchs in their struggle with progressive ideas and thereby to advance the interests of defeated France.

After the Second World War, the public law scholar Ernst Rudolf Huber deepened this legitimistic notion. He obtained his doctorate, which was supervised by Carl Schmitt, in 1926 and later wrote the textbook *Verfassungsrecht des Großdeutschen Reiches* (*Constitutional Law of the Greater German Reich*),[23] a standard work of National Socialist constitutional law. Classified as a mere 'sympathizer' after the war, he turned to constitutional history. His groundbreaking *Deutsche Verfassungsgeschichte seit 1789* (*German Constitutional Law after 1789*) renewed his academic prominence in the young Federal Republic. Its Volume I assigned the *Jus Publicum Europaeum* a function for both domestic *and* international law under the *Ancien Régime*. In Huber's view, the *Jus Publicum Europaeum* of that time consisted of the law of interstate relations as well as of 'inviolable' elements of a common European constitutional law.[24]

Huber, like Talleyrand, maintained that the *Jus Publicum Europaeum* had a legitimist thrust. Consequently, he considered the European monarchies' intervention in revolutionary France justified for the revolutionary overthrow and execution of Louis XVI had violated the European constitutional principle of monarchical

[22] P.-L. Couchoud and J.-P. Couchoud (eds), *Mémoires de Talleyrand. Tome II* (1957) 436 ff.; Grewe, *The Epochs of International Law* (n. 15) 430 f.; D. Cooper, *Talleyrand* (1955) 232 f.

[23] E. R. Huber, *Verfassungsrecht des Großdeutschen Reiches* (1939).

[24] E. R. Huber, *Deutsche Verfassungsgeschichte seit 1789, Bd. 1. Reform und Restauration. 1789 bis 1830* (1957) 16 ff.

legitimacy. In Huber's reconstruction, this common European constitution limited state sovereignty.[25]

Although *droit public européen* mostly denoted a conservative order, there were also some progressive conceptions. In 1856, the journalist and politician Francisque Bouvet published his *Introduction à l'établissement d'un droit public européen*, which expressed a European vision of peace similar to William Penn's. Bouvet was 'une sorte d'abbé de Saint-Pierre républicain' ('a kind of republican Abbé de Saint-Pierre').[26] He had espoused democratic ideals during the reign of the French king Louis-Philippe and even went to prison in 1832 for his work *République et Monarchie*.[27] In 1848 and 1849, the years of the Revolution, he served as a deputy in the *assemblée nationale constituante* and the *assemblée nationale législative*.[28] During these years, he participated in the International Congresses of the Friends of Peace in Brussels and Paris.[29] As early as 1849, he was known as a proponent of perpetual peace, envisioning a permanent congress of all peoples as a means to resolve conflicts between nations. After the Bonapartist coup d'état in December 1851, he initially withdrew from the public eye but later became the Empire's consul in Mosul.

His study, published in 1856, addresses the idea of lasting peace. It is divided into two parts. The first part focuses on the historical functions of war. In the second part, Bouvet argues for his idea of a *droit public européen*. Against the backdrop of the Crimean War, he calls for a confederative European system, modelled on the German Confederation.[30] At its centre, he envisaged a parliamentary assembly (*diète ou congrès*) that would settle all matters that could lead to conflict. Presenting Napoleon I as the harbinger of this order, he counted on Napoleon III to implement his ideas.[31] For Bouvet, the European and the cosmopolitan dimension did not contradict one another. Like Wolfgang Friedmann 100 years later, Bouvet believed that a Europe structured according to liberal principles would inspire the whole world, which would grow together through technological progress.[32] His European public law is progressive, but it is merely a political vision and not a legal reconstruction. It thus represents the opposite of Carl Schmitt's *Jus Publicum Europaeum* in almost every respect.

[25] Ibid.

[26] P. Larousse, *Grand dictionnaire universel du XIXe siècle. Tome II* (1867) 1165.

[27] F. Bouvet, *République et monarchie, ou Principes d'ordre social* (1832).

[28] See the entry on Bouvet in Deux Journalistes, *Biographie des 750 représentants à l'Assemblée législative, élus le 13 mai 1849* (1849) 10 and the page of the Assemblée Nationale, http://www.assemblee-nationale.fr (last visited 31 August 2022).

[29] N. N., *Congrès des amis de la paix universelle, Réuni à Bruxelles en 1848* (1849) 21, 55; Granier, 'Le mouvement en faveur de la paix', in *Congrès des amis de la paix universelle, Réuni à Paris en 1849* (1850) 1.

[30] F. Bouvet, *Introduction à l'établissement d'un droit public européen* (1856) XII, 189 f.

[31] Ibid. 176 ff.

[32] Ibid. 187.

C. Schmitt's *Jus Publicum Europaeum*

Of all the books on the *Jus Publicum Europaeum*, none is as famous as Schmitt's *The Nomos of the Earth in the International Law of the Jus Publicum Europaeum.*[33] In fact, the term owes its prominence to him: because of Schmitt's influence, Huber writes on the *Jus Publicum Europaeum* and not on the *droit public de l'Europe*. Schmitt's concept—like Talleyrand's and Huber's—encompasses international law as well as the constitutional orders of the European states, both of which undergirded the international order.[34] Schmitt presents the *Jus Publicum Europaeum* as a grand civilizational achievement owed to the wisdom of European statesmen, diplomats, philosophers, and jurists.

In Schmitt's view, the supremacy of the United States has annihilated this order. Schmitt's *Jus Publicum Europaeum* is thus an obituary as well as a defence.[35] On 5 September 1948, Schmitt, the only important German public law scholar who refused to be 'denazified', noted, 'I will lay down the "Nomos of the Earth" as a flowering branch of my discrimination at the grave of European international law.'[36]

War's lawfulness is a core issue in his *Nomos*. Schmitt claimed that the Allied *ex post* criminalization of the *waging of a war of aggression* was as illegitimate as using the atomic bomb and even worse than Hitler's crimes.[37] He insisted on the lawfulness of war between states. In addition, he claimed that criminalizing war does not eliminate wars but, instead, makes them all the more violent.[38] Given the elementary fact of enmity in international relations (see 2.3.C), the old international law (the *Jus Publicum Europaeum*) at least prevented a declaration of the enemy as *hors-la-loi* ('outside the law') and hence the sort of inhumanity that a 'just' war in the name of humankind can entail.[39]

Schmitt's *Jus Publicum Europaeum* describes a state-centred system that seeks to cabin, not overcome, war. To do so, Schmitt argues, it establishes a specific and binding spatial order that, in his view, represents the international equivalent of a *pouvoir constituant*'s decisions.[40] This order is managed by states for Schmitt's *Jus Publicum* leaves no room for supranational institutions.[41]

[33] Hoock, 'Jus Publicum Europaeum. Zur Praxis des europäischen Völkerrechts im 17. und 18. Jahrhundert', 50 *Der Staat* (2011) 422.

[34] C. Schmitt, *Staat, Großraum, Nomos. Arbeiten aus den Jahren 1916–1969* (1995) 592 ff.

[35] M. Stolleis, *Geschichte des öffentlichen Rechts in Deutschland, Bd. 1. Reichspublizistik und Policeywissenschaft 1600–1800* (2012) 204.

[36] C. Schmitt, *Glossarium. Aufzeichnungen der Jahre 1947–1951* (1991) 196.

[37] Ibid. 191.

[38] C. Schmitt, *The Concept of the Political* (1996 [1932]) 36 f.

[39] See M. Koskenniemi, *The Gentle Civilizer of Nations. The Rise and Fall of International Law 1870–1960* (2001) 426.

[40] Schmitt, *The Nomos of the Earth* (n. 17) 147.

[41] On Schmitt's polemic against Georges Scelle and his international constitutionalism, see P. P. Portinaro, *La crisi dello jus publicum europaeum. Saggio su Carl Schmitt* (1982) 202.

In many ways, the order of Schmitt's *Jus Publicum Europaeum* represents the opposite of that envisioned in the Treaty of the European Union (TEU). In Article 2 TEU, present-day European public law pledges a European democratic society that features institutions of its own and abides by principles such as pluralism, human rights, and tolerance, including those of the Charter of the United Nations, with its prohibition of the use of force (Article 21 TEU). Schmitt's writing helps underscore these features of today's European public law and the discontinuity between the old and the new law.

At the same time, our European public law realizes some of the features that Schmitt considered crucial to the old *Jus Publicum Europaeum*. They include a legal order based on a geographical idea, a *particular* rather than *universal* community of states, admission criteria according to a specific European understanding of statehood, and—last but not least—comparable constitutional structures.[42]

Schmitt's *Jus Publicum Europaeum* also confronts current European law with the thorny question of its impact on European relations with the rest of the world. While Schmitt's *Jus Publicum* cabins inner-European conflict, it does not bound the appropriation and exploitation of other world regions: What is at stake is 'push[ing] both of these dangerous forms of war and enmity [civil war and colonial war] to the margins'.[43] The *Jus Publicum Europaeum* is thus complicit in European colonialism and imperialism, including their bestiality.

This latter dimension of the old European public law has become an important topic,[44] and the new European public law also merits attention in this respect. On the one hand, it is committed to universal international law, global solidarity, and mutual respect among all peoples (Article 3(5) TEU). On the other hand, one motive for European integration was maintaining colonial domination.[45] Crucially, this motive is not alien to today's European foreign trade law and development aid either.[46]

Schmitt's concept of a *Jus Publicum*, though problematic and outdated in many respects, remains topical. The term gained traction when the West's conception of order moved eastward after the fall of the Iron Curtain. In 1991, Peter Häberle, speaking of a new *Jus Publicum Europaeum*, postulated the advent of a common European constitutional law.[47] Various projects on common constitutional

[42] Goldmann, 'Hopes of Progress. European Integration in the History of International Law', 26 *MPIL Research Paper Series* (2018) 11.

[43] Schmitt, *Glossarium* (n. 36) 250.

[44] Goldmann (n. 42).

[45] B. Olivi, *L'Europa difficile. Storia politica dell'integrazione europea 1948–2000* (2000) 30 ff.

[46] P. Dann and A. Hammel, *The Law of Development Cooperation. A Comparative Analysis of the World Bank, the EU and Germany* (2013) 43 ff.

[47] Häberle, 'Gemeineuropäisches Verfassungsrecht', 18 *Europäische Grundrechte-Zeitschrift* (1991) 261, at 263.

structures of this sort have co-opted this label, for instance, the *Societas Iuris Publici Europaei* and the *Ius Publicum Europaeum* (IPE) project.[48]

Already in 1954, Paul Guggenheim, a Swiss scholar of international law was articulating the problems as well as the potential of a new European public law.[49] 'Concerning its substantive content', he denounced the *Jus Publicum Europaeum* as 'an ideological interpretation of numerous rules of general international law'. Although he does not mention Carl Schmitt, he is evidently responding to his *Nomos*. At the same time, Guggenheim projected that the European Coal and Steel Community (ECSC) of 1952 could lead to a true *Jus Publicum Europaeum* that stands between universal international law and the domestic legal systems of Europe. Guggenheim's concluding sentence prophesies the transformative potential of this European public law: 'It would be no small irony in world history if the sovereign state [. . .], which [. . .] remains the most important factor in the political structure [. . .] of international law, were to undergo a structural transformation due to the blossoming of the Jus publicum europaeum.'[50] This is what occurred.

2. New Concepts for the New Law

To portray transformations, it helps define ruptures and transitions.[51] Historical institutionalism conceptualizes the latter as *critical junctures*.[52] I share that take, but instead of using the term 'critical junctures', I employ Koselleck's notion of a *Sattelzeit*, literally 'saddle time', which I translate as a *threshold phase* (*période charnière*). It stands in the Hegelian tradition and closely links the history of events with the history of concepts, as does this book.[53]

The years following Germany's defeat in 1945 constitute the first threshold phase for the new European public law. The end of the Second World War led to the founding treaties, which ushered in the first era of this new public law under the iconic concept of a *community of law* (*Rechtsgemeinschaft*). The second threshold phase began with the collapse of socialism in 1989 and culminated in the

[48] Schäffer, 'Gründung einer Societas Iuris Publici Europaei (SIPE)', 58 *Zeitschrift für öffentliches Recht* (2003) 405, at 405 f.; on the IPE project, see A. von Bogdandy, *Ius Publicum Europaeum* (Max Planck Institut), https://www.mpil.de/de/pub/forschung/nach-rechtsgebieten/oeffentliches-recht/ius-publicum-europaeum.cfm (last visited 31 August 2022).

[49] Guggenheim, 'Das Jus publicum europaeum und Europa', 3 *Jahrbuch des öffentlichen Rechts* (1954) 1.

[50] Ibid. 14.

[51] In detail, see Diggelmann, 'The Periodization of the History of International Law', in Fassbender and Peters (n. 13) 997.

[52] Capoccia, 'Critical Junctures', in O. Fioretos, T. G. Falleti, and A. Sheingate (eds), *The Oxford Handbook of Historical Institutionalism* (2016) 89.

[53] Koselleck, 'Einleitung', in O. Brunner, W. Conze, and R. Koselleck (eds), *Geschichtliche Grundbegriffe. Historisches Lexikon zur politisch-sozialen Sprache in Deutschland, Bd. 1* (1972) XIII, at XV.

Maastricht Treaty, which reorganized Europe. This era elevated the legal community to a political union, which, in 2007, asserted the existence of a European society in accordance with the standards of Article 2 TEU. Finally, the financial crisis in 2008 and Viktor Orbán's victory in 2010 may have constituted a third threshold phase.[54]

A. The First Threshold Phase

Schmitt teaches us that the German defeat revolutionized the geopolitical constellation and ended the old European public law. Since 1945, international law's most important institutions have operated out of New York and Washington. For decades, the defining conflict involved the President of the United States and the General Secretary of the Communist Party of the Soviet Union. From the 1960s on, decolonization further reduced the international relevance of European states. Today, it seems anachronistic that France and the United Kingdom hold a permanent seat in the United Nations Security Council.[55] Martti Koskenniemi's *Gentle Civilizer of Nations*—arguably the most acclaimed history of international law penned by a European—presents the transformation of international law after the Second World War as a decline.[56]

When old structures decline, new ones emerge. The decline of the old European public law enabled the transition to the new European public law. Koskenniemi's book does not claim that Europe has seen no further activity in the field of international law. Rather, the geopolitical change and some gentle pressure from the United States led to innovative European institutions that transcended the horizon of pre-war international law.[57] The United Nations Economic Commission for Europe began its work in 1947, while the Organisation for European Economic Cooperation (OEEC) did so in 1948 and the Council of Europe in 1949.[58] On 9 May 1950, the French Foreign Minister Robert Schuman demanded '*efforts créateurs*' for European unification, which brought about the ECSC Treaty, the nucleus of today's European Union.[59] In essence, Schuman relied on a common bureaucracy

[54] Madsen, 'From Boom to Backlash? The European Court of Human Rights and the Transformation of Europe', in H. Aust and E. Demir (eds), *The European Court of Human Rights: Current Challenges in Historical and Comparative Perspective* (2020) 21; P. Rosanvallon, *Le siècle du populisme. Histoire, théorie, critique* (2020) esp. at 227–241.

[55] Zimmermann, 'Article 27', in B. Simma *et al.* (eds), *The Charter of the United Nations. A Commentary* (2012) 871, at para. 278.

[56] Koskenniemi, *The Gentle Civilizer of Nations* (n. 39) 413–480.

[57] L. V. Majocchi, *La difficile costruzione dell'unità europea* (1996) 168 ff.

[58] Convention on European Economic Cooperation of 16 April 1948, Treaties of the Federal Republic of Germany Vol. 1 (1955) 2; Statute of the Council of Europe of 5 May 1949, Federal Law Gazette 1950 I, 263; Convention for the Protection of Human Rights and Fundamental Freedoms of 4 November 1950, Federal Law Gazette 1952 II, 685, 953.

[59] R. Schuman, *Déclaration du 9 mai* (1950), https://www.robert-schuman.eu/fr/declaration-du-9-mai-1950 (last visited 31 August 2022).

and a common market. Max Weber teaches us that these are, indeed, two powerful mechanisms of creating a society.[60]

Until the 1970s, it remained open which of the various organizations, if any, would play the leading role that the European Union plays today. 'There was no master plan for any of this', writes a prominent historian of European integration. 'The developments ensued from diverse historical processes with the typical twists and turns, learning processes, dead ends and new beginnings.'[61] This is not how we imagine a history of the *Weltgeist* to read.

There have certainly been attempts to create such a narrative.[62] Thus, the European Union (EU) Member State governments decided to celebrate Europe Day on the anniversary of Schuman's declaration (Article I-8 sub-para. 5 of the failed Treaty establishing a Constitution for Europe (TCE) of 2004). The commemoration was supposed to establish a rite of European society and give rise to a sense of identity, comparable to Bastille Day in France, the Day of Liberation from the Germans in the Czech Republic, France, Italy, the Netherlands, or Slovakia, the Day of Polish Independence, and the Day of German Unification. In each case, societies are meant to remember their unity and celebrate a defining transition.

Schuman's initiative had a complex background: the idea of a lasting European peace order certainly played an important role, explaining Article I-8 sub-para. 5 TCE and even the project to beatify Schuman.[63] But protecting French colonial possessions was also on his mind:[64] Then, as now, the motives for transforming European society were not always noble. Moreover, it was clear at the time that the United States would not accept France's initial strategy of weakening Germany permanently.

With this American blessing, the (European) Treaties inaugurated a transformation that emancipated European law from international law. Of course, some legal scholars still interpret the EU through the lens of international law. By no means does this only include scholars caught in the past; some more forward-looking authors do so, too.[65] As foreshadowed by Friedmann (see 1.3), European integration may be the most significant proof that the democratic rule of law beyond the

[60] M. Weber, *Economy and Society* (2002) 43, 978 f.

[61] K. K. Patel, *Project Europe: A History* (2020) 13–49, quote at 48; likewise T. Judt, *Postwar. A History of Europe since 1945* (2005) 8.

[62] Koschorke (n. 7) 162–169.

[63] See Vatican News, 'Robert Schuman, Father of European Unity, on Path to Sainthood' (19 June 2021), https://www.vaticannews.va/en/pope/news/2021-06/robert-schuman-father-of-european-unity-on-path-to-sainthood.html (last visited 31 August 2022).

[64] Olivi (n. 45) 30 ff.

[65] J. Klabbers, *An Introduction to International Organizations Law* (4th edn, 2022) 14 ff.; de Witte, 'The European Union as an International Legal Experiment', in G. de Búrca and J. H. H. Weiler (eds), *The Worlds of European Constitutionalism* (2012) 19.

state is not a utopia but indicative of a possible general transformation of international law.[66]

In any event, the transformation of European law depends on its emancipation from international law. Again, Koskenniemi hits the nail on the head when he argues that US foreign policy after 1945 severely limited the autonomy of international law. However, European law's autonomy became central to the European community of law, the first defining concept of the new European public law.

B. Hallstein's Community of Law

The concept of a European community of law is primarily attributed to Walter Hallstein. Hallstein, a Frankfurt professor of private and comparative law whose dissertation dealt with the Versailles Treaty, was one of Konrad Adenauer's key foreign policy advisers, especially on European integration. As State Secretary in the Foreign Office, he participated in all important negotiations. His commitment culminated in his appointment as the first President of the EEC Commission in 1958.

Hallstein's notion of the 'European community of law', coined in 1962, defined and even created a new legal field.[67] Many lectures on European law begin by stating that Europe is a community of law and then teach European law in this light, thus shaping the students' legal mindset. The juridical term has even reached the general public and found its way into political discourse.[68] I should note that the German term *Rechtsgemeinschaft* has a particularly thick meaning. While the word *communauté/comunità* has no theoretical weight in the Romance languages, *Gemeinschaft* has perhaps too much of it (see 1.2).[69] The concept of a 'community of law' predates Hallstein,[70] but he coined the term for the *European* enterprise.[71] It is his most important scholarly legacy. In terms of conceptual strategy, his move resembles Leibholz's structural transformation, which also created a new field of judicial interpretation and activism (see 1.3).

[66] Goldmann (n. 42) 3; for my thoughts on this issue, see von Bogdandy, Goldmann, and Venzke, 'From Public International to International Public Law. Translating World Public Opinion into International Public Authority', 28 *European Journal of International Law* (2017) 115.

[67] Hallstein, 'Die EWG—eine Rechtsgemeinschaft (1962)', in T. Oppermann (ed.), *Europäische Reden* (1979) 341.

[68] See Stolleis, 'Unsere Rechtsgemeinschaft', *Frankfurter Allgemeine Zeitung* (3 June 2016).

[69] F. Tönnies, *Gemeinschaft und Gesellschaft. Abhandlung des Communismus und des Socialismus als empirischer Culturformen* (1887); on the French understanding, see A. Vauchez, *Brokering Europe. Euro-Lawyers and the Making of a Transnational Polity* (2015) 75.

[70] See, e.g. W. Burckhardt, *Die Organisation der Rechtsgemeinschaft. Untersuchungen über die Eigenart des Privatrechts, des Staatsrechts und des Völkerrechts* (2nd edn, 1944).

[71] Mayer, 'Europa als Rechtsgemeinschaft', in G. F. Schuppert, I. Pernice, and U. Haltern (eds), *Europawissenschaft* (2005) 429, at 430. Claus-Dieter Ehlermann revealed, in an interview, that he had provided academic support in his first years at the Commission.

Hallstein is not a European saint, nor was he the only relevant actor. Antoine Vauchez's pioneering study *L'Union par le droit* introduces us to many other jurists who shaped European public law in the early 1960s.[72] With their doctrinal innovations, these courageous and creative jurists turned the amorphous law of the three founding Treaties into a transformative force. By contrast, the United Nations Economic Commission for Europe, the Organisation for European Economic Co-operation, or the Council of Europe have not undergone comparable processes of legal evolution. This difference has been crucial in turning the EU into the most relevant transformational force[73] as well as the hub of the emerging European society.

Hallstein legitimized this community of law with great pathos: 'For the first time, the rule of law will supplant power and its manipulation, the balance of various forces, quests for hegemony, and the game of alliances.'[74] While Hallstein's European community of law started as a vague concept,[75] a phalanx of lawyers soon thickened it with the help of articles, books, memos, briefings, and judgments. The concept of the community of law came to encompass key achievements: the unity of Community law (irrespective of it serving three different organizations); its autonomy, direct effect, and primacy, market freedoms and fundamental rights; and an ever-growing body of regulatory law, with the Commission and the Court of Justice as guardians of it all. In this way, Community law became a social structure. Hegel would speak of objective spirit, Hauriou of institutions, Schmitt of concrete order, and Bourdieu of a new field of law.

Today, it is beyond question that this body of law has been transformative.[76] Of course, the internal dynamics of the legal field have not transformed social structures on their own. This process required consonant political, economic, and social forces. But it is safe to assume that the legal innovations helped bring about today's European society.

Sixty years later, Hallstein's concept has begun to show its age. This reveals how Community law has developed, indeed transformed, over these decades. Hallstein's community of law primarily refers to the EEC, that is, to a supranational organization. It hardly considers the Member States. Granted, the community of law implies supranational control over the Member States' enforcement of Community law, be it by means of infringement proceedings or preliminary ruling proceedings. Yet, this does not alter the supranational focus.[77] Given the current problems

[72] A. Vauchez, *L'Union par le droit. L'invention d'un programme institutionnel pour l'Europe* (2013); see also the expanded English version: Vauchez, *Brokering Europe* (n. 69).

[73] Patel (n. 61) 40.

[74] Hallstein, 'Die EWG' (n. 67) 344.

[75] W. Hallstein, *Die Europäische Gemeinschaft* (1973) 33.

[76] The canonical texts are American: Stein, 'Lawyers, Judges, and the Making of a Transnational Constitution', 75 *American Journal of International Law* (1981) 1; Weiler, 'The Transformation of Europe', 100 *Yale Law Journal* (1991) 2403.

[77] See Snyder, 'The Effectiveness of European Community Law: Institutions, Processes, Tools and Techniques', 56 *Modern Law Review* (1993) 19.

with the rule of law in Poland and Hungary, this focus appears myopic today (see 2.6.D, 3.6, 4.6).

This is not the only problem. One achievement of Hallstein's community of law is that it conceptualizes the *sui generis* nature of the EU somewhere between a mere international organization and a federal state. The core idea is that, due to its developed law, the EEC is a community of law, as opposed to other transnational organizations, whose law is weaker. Unlike a state, however, the EEC does not have the power of coercion.[78] This significantly reduces the need for democratic legitimacy.

Hallstein's community of law is an ingenious response to the problem of legitimacy. It mobilizes the legitimatory resources of the idea of law without triggering the specific justificatory burden that attends coercion. Who would want to oppose a community of law whose common institutions peacefully organize Europe and refrain from coercion? However, today's Union wields coercive instruments (see 2.3.A).

Politicization is another reason why Hallstein's concept has started to show its age. Since the second threshold phase, Union politics have become politicized in a way that is not captured by Hallstein's community of law.[79] Instead, the latter follows the tradition of David Mitrany, the creator of technocratic functionalism.[80] To be sure, Hallstein's community of law is not opposed to parliamentarism. In fact, the Court of Justice of the European Union (CJEU) even used his concept to strengthen the European Parliament.[81] But for Hallstein, the EEC's political character primarily lies in its regulation of economic processes.[82] In other words, he considers it political because it makes law and determines European policies (see, today, Articles 26–197 Treaty on the Functioning of the European Union (TFEU)), not because these policies are publicly debated, contested, or resisted. Ultimately, Hallstein's concept does not capture the conflictual nature of today's European society.

By the same token, Hallstein's concept exhibits yet another symptom of age because it is premised on the idea that law will always bring Europe together.[83] Yet today, European law is also a divisive force. The prominent examples include European requirements for national budgetary policy, migration law, refugee law, and the UK's withdrawal because of its fundamental aversion to European law.

[78] Hallstein, 'Die EWG' (n. 67) 348; Pernice, 'Begründung und Konsolidierung der Europäischen Gemeinschaft als Rechtsgemeinschaft', in M. Zuleeg (ed.), *Der Beitrag Walter Hallsteins zur Zukunft Europas. Referate zu Ehren von Walter Hallstein* (2003) 56.

[79] For further details, see Zürn, 'Politicization Compared: At National, European, and Global Levels', 26 *Journal of European Public Policy* (2019) 977; Hirschl, 'The Judicialization of Mega-Politics and the Rise of Political Courts', 11 *Annual Review of Political Science* (2008) 93.

[80] Mayer, 'Europa als Rechtsgemeinschaft' (n. 71) 432.

[81] CJEU, Case 294/83, *Les Verts v. Parliament* (EU:C:1986:166) 'community based on the rule of law'; see also this contribution written by one of the protagonists, Zuleeg, 'Die Europäische Gemeinschaft als Rechtsgemeinschaft', 9 *Neue Juristische Wochenschrift* (1994) 545, at 548.

[82] Hallstein, *Die Europäische Gemeinschaft* (n. 75).

[83] Ibid. 33.

Hallstein's community of law suggests that every act of Union law should be celebrated. Today, no one finds this convincing anymore.

Hallstein's community of law thus fails to grasp the current conflictual politicization of European law.[84] Public debates on how to shape European law can decide Member State elections. In fact, such debates have given rise to a defining cleavage in the European party system.[85] One key question is whether European law can cabin this conflictual politicization and give it a constructive turn.

The concept of the community of law suggests answering politicization with legalism.[86] However, this path is strongly contested.[87] Indeed, the German invocation of the community of law is often interpreted elsewhere as a smokescreen for German interests.[88]

Today, Hallstein's community of law does not convey an adequate understanding of European law.[89] This does not mean that we should abandon it. The doctrinal concept of the community of law (or, as the CJEU calls it today, the *union* of law) should be reduced to the requirement that all public power be subject to judicial review (Article 19 TEU, Article 47 Charter of Fundamental Rights (CFR)).[90] This is, indeed, a characteristic of the EU,[91] but only one of many. Apart from that, Hallstein's concept should be historicized, indicating a period that the process of Europeanization has left behind.

This proposal conforms with the law. The Treaty legislator never enshrined the concept of the *community* of law but instead posited a much richer concept at the next critical juncture in the second threshold phase: the *rule* of law (Article 2 TEU). The English terminology obscures the magnitude of the step taken. The French, Italian, German, and Greek versions use a term that refers to statehood: *État de droit, Stato di diritto, Rechtsstaat, κράτος δικαίου*. While there might be an international rule of law or an international legal community, there is certainly no international *État de droit*.

[84] Dehousse, 'Constitutional Reform in the European Community. Are There Alternatives to the Majoritarian Avenue?', 18 *West European Politics* (1995) 118, at 124; U. Haltern, *Europarecht und das Politische* (2005) 44, 104 ff.

[85] Dawson and de Witte, 'From Balance to Conflict. A New Constitution for the EU', 22 *European Law Journal* (2016) 204, at 207.

[86] Schorkopf, 'Gestaltung mit Recht. Prägekraft und Selbststand des Rechts in einer Rechtsgemeinschaft', 136 *Archiv des öffentlichen Rechts* (2011) 323.

[87] M. K. Brunnermeier, H. James, and J.-P. Landau, *The Euro and the Battle of Ideas* (2016).

[88] Pollicino, 'The European "Market" for Constitutional Ideas. Abuse of a Judicial Dominant Position?', *Verfassungsblog* (9 October 2020); Cassese, 'The Paths of European Legal Scholarship', *Verfassungsblog* (5 October 2020); Sonnevend, 'How Not to Become Hegemonial. Self-Preservation through Verfassungsdogmatik', *Verfassungsblog* (13 October 2020); Sarmiento, 'On the Road to German Hegemony in EU Law?', *Verfassungsblog* (7 October 2020); Halberstam, 'Anti-Hegemony and Its Discontents. On Germany in Europe', *Verfassungsblog* (14 October 2020).

[89] Thus, it does not appear in the book by A. Jakab, *European Constitutional Language* (2016).

[90] CJEU, Case C-362/14, *Schrems* (EU:C:2015:650) para. 60.

[91] M. Kottmann, *Introvertierte Rechtsgemeinschaft. Zur richterlichen Kontrolle des auswärtigen Handelns der Europäischen Union* (2014) 25 ff., 79 ff., 235 ff., 296 ff.

C. Mosler's European Law

European law is more than Union law. The legal structure of European society rests on various legal orders. It is the common achievement of Union law, the law of the Council of Europe (in particular, the European Convention on Human Rights (ECHR)) and, importantly, the national legal orders.[92] This suggests a holistic concept of European law,[93] one that Hermann Mosler formulated.

For many, the term 'European law' denotes either the law of the EU or both EU law and the law of the Council of Europe.[94] Mosler's concept of European law is much broader because it also includes part of the Member States' domestic law. This is a transformational definition because the distinction between domestic law and international law constitutes a conceptual foundation of public law.[95] Of course, there were holistic theories before Mosler, such as Kelsen's monism and Schmitt's *Jus Publicum Europaeum*.[96] But Mosler articulates a holistic understanding that is tailored to the European law of the post-war order.[97]

As a legal architect of Germany's *Westbindung*, Mosler was an important lawyer in terms of both scholarship and practice. The Frankfurt law professor served as legal adviser to Adenauer and Hallstein and later as the director of the Max Planck Institute for Comparative Public Law and International Law. In recognition of his achievements, he became the first German judge at the European Court of Human Rights (ECtHR) in 1959 and the first German judge at the International Court of Justice in 1976.[98] His international career symbolizes the Federal Republic's successful integration into the West.

Mosler developed his concept in the context of a massive conflict personified by the sovereigntist Charles de Gaulle and the federalist Walter Hallstein. Hallstein's early successes led defenders of national sovereignty to oppose him. The French

[92] This is the central insight of European legal pluralism. See Halberstam, 'Systems Pluralism and Institutional Pluralism in Constitutional Law. National, Supranational and Global Governance', in M. Avbelj (ed.), *Constitutional Pluralism in the European Union and Beyond* (2012) 94 ff.

[93] The attribute 'holistic' describes the character of European law as encompassing different legal orders; it does not refer to a holistic understanding of society. See von Bogdandy and Dellavalle, 'Universalism and Particularism. A Dichotomy to Read Theories on International Order', in S. Kadelbach, T. Kleinlein, and D. Roth-Isigkeit (eds), *System, Order, and International Law* (2017) 482.

[94] In this sense, see B. Stirn and Y. Aguila, *Droit public français et européen* (2021) 371.

[95] H. Triepel, *Völkerrecht und Landesrecht* (1899) 12–22; Dupuy, 'International Law and Domestic (Municipal) Law', in R. Wolfrum (ed.), *Max Planck Encyclopedia of Public International Law (online)* (2011).

[96] H. Kelsen, *Pure Theory of Law* (1967 [1934]) 320 ff.; on Schmitt, see 2.1.C.

[97] Mosler, 'Begriff und Gegenstand des Europarechts', 28 *Zeitschrift für ausländisches öffentliches Recht und Völkerrecht* (1968) 481; Mosler, 'European Law—Does it Exist?', 19 *Current Legal Problems* (1966) 168. The following discussion is based on von Bogdandy, 'Ways to Frame the European Rule of Law: Rechtsgemeinschaft, Trust, Revolution, and Kantian Peace', 14 *European Constitutional Law Review* (2018) 675.

[98] On Mosler, see Lange, 'Between Systematization and Expertise for Foreign Policy: The Practice-Oriented Approach in Germany's International Legal Scholarship (1920–1980)', 28 *European Journal of International Law* (2017) 535.

chaise vide policy from 30 May 1965 to 30 January 1966, which the French government used to block the transition to majority voting in the Council, is the most famous example of this opposition.[99]

The conflict between the visions of Hallstein and de Gaulle has many aspects. Here, I focus on Mosler's mediating concept of European law. As stated, the latter encompasses Community law (now Union law) and the ECHR, as well as domestic law. Mosler's approach was inductive and cautious. Consequently, he included not the entire body of domestic law but only the domestic acts of implementation, as well as autonomous Member State acts 'issued with a view to the objectives of European integration'.[100] Despite being inductive and cautious, this approach is nevertheless transformational because it posits a body of law that spans different legal orders. Mosler admitted that his concept was radical, writing that '[i]t explodes the boundaries between international and domestic law'.[101]

How does this relate to the aforementioned political conflict? Hallstein's vision of federal European institutions stood against de Gaulle's *Europe des patries*. Mosler's concept mediates between these two because it stresses that both levels are important and serve a common purpose. In other words, Mosler anticipated what would transpire during the next decades. In 1992, the framers of the Maastricht Treaty would proclaim a 'union of the peoples of Europe' (Article A(2) TEU, now Article 1(2) TEU: in detail, see 2.2.D). In 1996, Ingolf Pernice's concept of constitutional union (*Verfassungsverbund*) developed Mosler's notion and turned it into a cornerstone of the European constitutional debate of the 1990s and 2000s.[102] One of the CJEU's most important doctrines developed along these lines, too. Thus, every Member State court is a Union court (*Unionsgericht*) or, as the CJEU puts it in the more timid English version, an '"ordinary" [court] within the European Union legal order'.[103]

Mosler's holistic concept encompassed a body of law that transcends the individual legal orders. In terms of actors, it conjoined representatives of Member State law, Union law, and the ECHR, in particular the judges of the national apex courts, the constitutional courts, the CJEU, and the ECtHR. Thirty years later, Andreas Voßkuhle, then the President of the German Federal Constitutional Court, coined the English term of constitutional courts' multilevel cooperation to capture this understanding.[104] Since Voßkuhle speaks of a *Verbund*

[99] In detail, see L. van Middelaar, *The Passage to Europe. How a Continent Became a Union* (2014) 54 ff.

[100] Mosler, 'Begriff und Gegenstand des Europarechts' (n. 97) 500.

[101] Ibid.

[102] Pernice, 'Die Dritte Gewalt im europäischen Verfassungsverbund', 31 *Europarecht* (1996) 27; Pernice, 'Multilevel Constitutionalism and the Treaty of Amsterdam: European Constitution-Making Revisited?', *Common Market Law Review* (1999) 703.

[103] CJEU, Opinion 1/09, *Accord sur la création d'un système unifié de règlement des litiges en matière de brevets* (EU:C:2011:123) para. 80; Rosas, 'The National Judge as EU Judge: Opinion 1/09', in P. Cardonnel, A. Rosas, and N. Wahl (eds), *Constitutionalising the EU Judicial System. Essays in Honour of Pernilla Lindh* (2012) 105.

[104] Voßkuhle, 'Multilevel Cooperation of the European Constitutional Courts', 6 *European Constitutional Law Review* (2010) 175.

(*Verfassungsgerichtsverbund*), we should instead translate the German original as 'union of constitutional courts', however. Regardless of the translation, Voßkuhle's concept highlights that the actors of the various legal orders have a common responsibility. Of course, they are first and foremost committed to the legal order that established their institution. For that reason, their responsibility is differentiated, which means that all judges carry a common but differentiated responsibility. The holistic concept of European law helps grasp and fulfil this complex task (see 4.5).

The holistic concept articulates what occurs in countless legal operations every day throughout European society. Union law depends on national law for a myriad of reasons, not least in order to become effective in millions of legal relationships. At the same time, many legal operations under the Member States' legal orders depend on European law's transnational components. Legal education increasingly reflects this interdependence, thus transforming the socialization of future lawyers.[105] Some professors even fuse the domestic and the transnational in their courses.[106]

For a long time, scholars observed this transformation primarily between the individual Member States and the EU, that is, in the vertical dimension. Yet, by now it has become clear that the horizontal interweaving of Member States' legal orders is also transformative.[107] Even apex courts, once lonely by definition, are integrating into horizontal European networks (see 4.2, 4.4). At the same time, courses on comparative European law are newly popular (see 5.2.C).[108]

D. The Union and the union

The holistic concept of European law reveals the meaning of *union* and thus some of the finality of European integration. In EU law, we find the *Union* and *union*. The two are related, but they are not identical. The Treaty legislator carefully distinguishes between the word's capitalized and uncapitalized form.

While the capitalized word represents a name, the uncapitalized one denotes a concept.[109] The Member States 'establish [. . .] the Union' (Article 1(1) TEU), 'creating an ever closer union' (Article 1(2) TEU). The Union (i.e. the EU) is just an

[105] Schorkopf, 'Selbstverständnis und Perspektiven der Europarechtswissenschaft. Eine Rechtswissenschaft für das organisierte Europa', 68 *Jahrbuch des öffentlichen Rechts* (2020) 527, at 540 f.

[106] Sydow, 'Die Europarechtswissenschaft europäisieren? Überlegungen zur Strukturentwicklung der juristischen Fakultäten und zur Lehre des Europarechts', 68 *Jahrbuch des öffentlichen Rechts* (2020) 545, at 553, 557.

[107] Pernice, 'La Rete Europea di Costituzionalità. Der Europäische Verfassungsverbund und die Netzwerktheorie', 70 *Zeitschrift für ausländisches öffentliches Recht und Völkerrecht* (2010) 51.

[108] C. Grewe and H. Ruiz Fabri, *Droits constitutionnels européens* (1995); A. Weber, *European Constitutions Compared* (2019); C. D. Classen, *Nationales Verfassungsrecht in der Europäischen Union. Eine integrierte Darstellung von 27 Verfassungsordnungen* (2021); E. Di Salvatore (ed.), *Sistemi costituzionali europei* (2021).

[109] Clearly distinguished in CJEU, Case C-216/18 PPU, *LM* (EU:C:2018:586) para. 49.

element, and indeed an instrument, of an 'ever closer union among the peoples of Europe'. This concept of union corresponds to the holistic concept of European law and provides the setting for European society.

The French and Italian versions have used the concept since 1957, with the French preamble to the EEC Treaty declaring its objective to be '*une union sans cesse plus étroite*'. 'Union' is a weighty term that is used by other continental polities such as the union of the US Constitution, the Soviet Union, or the Indian Union. Perhaps that is why the German version of the EEC Treaty uses a less weighty term, *Zusammenschluss*. Only in 1992 did the German version of the Union Treaty also opt for *Union*. The word is capitalized in the German, but for being a German noun, not a name. Indeed, the Dutch Article 1(2) TEU does not use '*Unie*' but '*verbond*'. The following discussion is not concerned with the name of the legal subject designated in Article 47 TEU. Rather, it engages with the concept, with the 'union'.

The concept denotes a 'union among the peoples of Europe'. As these are the Member States' peoples, the union embraces the Member States. Accordingly, the union denotes the compound, or totality, of all Member States and the EU. Today, many use this broad concept to address that totality, in particular in public or political communication.[110] By contrast, political science and legal doctrine have created various neologisms for the union, often featuring the term 'multilevel' or 'network'. German doctrine has settled on the concept of '*Verbund*' to articulate a totality of domestic and EU law and institutions and is very concerned with its translation into other languages. Switching to *union* can put this concern to rest and promote a common discourse.

The word 'union' in Article 1(2) TEU has a meaning similar to that of the German term *Gesamtstaat*, which articulates the totality composed of the federal level and the federated entities (*Länder*). European law is the law of such a totality in the European dimension, with this totality comprising Union and Member State law.

The union of Article 1(2) TEU transcends the EU just as European law extends beyond Union law. At the same time, the union must be conceptualized from the vantage point of Union law. Union law is as constitutive for the union as it is for European law, which is not the case for the Member States' legal orders. As Brexit has shown, the union does not fall apart when a Member State leaves. By contrast, a European union without the EU would be an entirely different polity. The same holds for European society.

Mosler's European law conceptualizes a union of different legal orders and articulates their strong interdependence and close interaction. Although from 1968, it helps delineate how most legal fields have transformed over the following five decades.[111] Today, there is a European public law spanning various legal orders (see

[110] Charlemagne, 'Ever Farther Union', *The Economist* (27 February 2016).

[111] Ackermann, 'Eine "ungeheure Jurisprudenz"? Die Europarechtswissenschaft und die Europäisierung des Rechts', 68 *Jahrbuch des öffentlichen Rechts* (2020) 471.

2.3–2.5) as well as a European private law of obligations,[112] family and inheritance law,[113] civil procedure,[114] labour and social law,[115] and criminal law.[116] Many state institutions are integrated into networks shaped by Union law. Institutional self-conceptions have Europeanized.[117] Only the crowned heads of states have avoided integration, with dynastic marriage policy in charge of their European identity.

Numerous theories conceptualize this phenomenon.[118] They have produced concepts of *Verbund*, of European legal pluralism and network theories, liberal intergovernmentalism, multilevel constitutionalism, and European federalism.[119] Scholars of administrative law employ concepts such as *Verwaltungsverbund*, *Verwaltungsunion*, *administration mixte*, *coadministration*, or *integrated administration*.[120] While these concepts differ in many ways, most consider the legal orders interconnected to such an extent that the interconnection shapes their very structure.

Mosler's concept of European law encompasses not only Community and Member State law but also the ECHR, including its Court. This acknowledges that the ECtHR is essential to the union because it subjects all power relations to the respect for human rights. The human rights dimension is crucial to the European society of Article 2 TEU (see 4.3.C).

Many national constitutions align the protection of individual rights with the ECHR's requirements.[121] The Convention, as interpreted by the ECtHR, is key to the democratic transformation of the Central and Eastern European EU Member States.[122] As foreshadowed by Mosler's concept, Article 6(2 and 3) TEU translates

[112] L. Díez-Picazo y Ponce de Léon, A. M. Morales Moreno, and E. Roca Trias, *Los principios del derecho europeo de contratos* (2002).

[113] K. Boele-Woelki *et al.*, *Principles of European Family Law Regarding Property, Maintenance and Succession Rights of Couples in de facto Unions* (2019).

[114] A. de la Oliva Santos and F. Gascón Inchausti, *Derecho procesal civil europeo. Competencia judicial internacional, reconocimiento y ejecución de resoluciones extranjeras en la Unión Europea* (2011).

[115] M. Schlachter and H. M. Heinig, *Europäisches Arbeits- und Sozialrecht* (2nd edn, 2020).

[116] A. Klip, *European Criminal Law. An Integrative Approach* (3rd edn, 2016).

[117] Grabenwarter, 'Zusammenfassung der Ergebnisse der vorangegangenen Sitzungen für den XVI. Kongress der Konferenz der Europäischen Verfassungsgerichte', in Verfassungsgerichtshof der Republik Österreich (ed.), *Die Kooperation der Verfassungsgerichte in Europa. Aktuelle Rahmenbedingungen und Perspektiven* (2014) 174.

[118] On the German debate, see Weber, 'Formen Europas. Rechtsdeutung, Sinnfrage und Narrativ im Rechtsdiskurs um die Gestalt der Europäischen Union', 55 *Der Staat* (2016) 151.

[119] von Bogdandy, 'The European Union as a Supranational Federation: A Conceptual Attempt in the Light of the Amsterdam Treaty', 6 *Columbia Journal of European Law* (2000) 27; R. Schütze, *From Dual to Cooperative Federalism: the Changing Structure of European Law* (2009); C. Möllers, *Die Europäische Union als demokratische Föderation* (2019).

[120] E. Schmidt-Aßmann and B. Schöndorf-Haubold (eds), *Der Europäische Verwaltungsverbund. Formen und Verfahren der Verwaltungszusammenarbeit in der EU* (2005); Franchini, 'Les notions d'administration indirecte et de coadministration', in J.-B. Auby and J. Dutheil de la Rochère (eds), *Droit administratif européen* (2007) 245, at 252 ff.

[121] Stone Sweet and Keller, 'The Reception of the ECHR in National Legal Orders', in A. Stone Sweet and H. Keller (eds), *A Europe of Rights. The Impact of the ECHR on National Legal Systems* (2008) 3.

[122] I. Motoc and I. Ziemele (eds), *The Impact of the ECHR on Democratic Change in Central and Eastern Europe. Judicial Perspectives* (2016).

the ECHR's relevance for Union law into positive law.[123] Accordingly, this book presents the CJEU and the ECtHR as two facets of one transformation (see 4.4.A).

My holistic understanding, which follows that of Mosler, differs from other holistic conceptions that seek to overcome the divide between international and domestic law, such as Kelsen's monism or Jessup's transnational law[124] as well as visions of a global law,[125] a law of humanity,[126] a cosmopolitan law, a world law,[127] or a world domestic law.[128] Mosler's concept has far greater reconstructive potential than these approaches, thanks to the spectacular development of its subject. Only European law has developed from an abstract conceptual sketch to a concrete legal field.

Two further demarcations deepen this understanding of the union and European law. On the one hand, it opposes the traditional approach that explains all legal phenomena through the lens of state sovereignty.[129] On the other hand, it rejects viewing the European developments as an instance of global governance, comparable to international regimes such as those of the World Trade Organization, the United Nations (UN), the Organisation for Economic Co-operation and Development (OECD), the Association of Southeast Asian Nations, or Mercosur. True, interdependence is not a purely European phenomenon but a key concept of international relations.[130] However, nowhere do we find an institutional and legal union that resembles European society. Thus, projections of a 'global community of courts'[131] have not materialized.[132]

Yet, while this concept of European law presents the legal regimes as closely interwoven, it does not conceive of them as parts of one European legal order.[133] Some scholars advocate such a monistic approach,[134] according to which European law would integrate the law of the Union and that of the Member States similarly to how German law integrates federal and regional (*Länder*) law in Germany.[135] The

[123] F. J. García Roca, *La transformación del Convenio Europeo de Derechos Humanos* (2019) 139 f.

[124] P. C. Jessup, *Transnational Law* (1956); Kingsbury, Krisch, and Stewart, 'The Emergence of Global Administrative Law', 68 *Law and Contemporary Problems* (2005) 15.

[125] C. W. Jenks, *The Common Law of Mankind* (1958).

[126] Benhabib, 'The Philosophical Foundations of Cosmopolitan Norms', in S. Benhabib and R. Post (eds), *Another Cosmopolitanism. The Berkeley Tanner Lectures* (2006) 13.

[127] M. Delmas-Marty, *Trois défis pour un droit mondial* (1998).

[128] J. Habermas, *The Divided West* (2014) 144 f., 160 ff.

[129] Hillgruber, 'Souveränität—Verteidigung eines Rechtsbegriffs', 57 *JuristenZeitung* (2002) 1072.

[130] R. O. Keohane and J. S. Nye, *Power and Interdependence. World Politics in Transition* (1977).

[131] A.-M. Slaughter, *A New World Order* (2004) 100.

[132] Wiener and Liste, 'Lost without Translation? Cross-Referencing and a New Global Community of Courts', 21 *Indiana Journal of Global Legal Studies* (2014) 263, at 263.

[133] On the concept of the legal order, see D. Burchardt, *Die Rangfrage im europäischen Normenverbund. Theoretische Grundlagen und dogmatische Grundzüge des Verhältnisses von Unionsrecht und nationalem Recht* (2015) 15–20, 220–243.

[134] Grussmann, 'Grundnorm und Supranationalität', in T. von Danwitz *et al.* (eds), *Auf dem Wege zu einer europäischen Staatlichkeit* (1993) 47, at 58 ff.; Letsas, 'Harmonic Law. The Case against Pluralism', in J. Dickson and P. Eleftheriadis (eds), *Philosophical Foundations of European Union Law* (2012) 77.

[135] Ossenbühl, 'Rechtsquellen. § 28', in H. Kube *et al.* (eds), *Leitgedanken des Rechts. Paul Kirchhof zum 70. Geburtstag* (2013) 311, at 317.

domestic insistence on legal autonomy vis-à-vis Union law speaks against a fusion of this sort.[136] Moreover, Union law is jealous of its autonomy, too.[137]

Daily practice constitutes another argument against fusing the different legal orders. In European legal practice, every legal act must be assigned to a specific legal order to determine its validity, lawfulness, legal effects, or legitimacy. In the German Federal Republic, any such act is firmly embedded in the federal legal order, which is shaped by the Basic Law. Article 2 TEU is not advanced enough to suggest a similar reconstruction of an overarching European legal order. Phenomena of further fusion, above all in the European System of Central Banks (Articles 282–283 TFEU), have, thus far, remained an exception.

Thus, my holistic concept of European law does not eliminate differentiation. Rather, it develops a new complexity to substantiate the union of Article 1(2) TEU. As a result, it helps articulate the pluralistic structure of European union and society.

3. Public Law without Statehood

A. A Dogma and a Breakthrough

European public law organizes European society but not a European state. Europeanization has ushered in powerful European public institutions, but they are not considered state bodies. Thus, it has severed the tie that inextricably linked publicness to statehood. This cut implies a deep conceptual transformation.

To begin with, it is noteworthy that the EU is not considered a state. European statehood has been on the European mind for centuries, and many voices have propagated European integration as a state-building process. Churchill advocated a European federal state in his Zurich speech of 1947, one of the most celebrated events of the first threshold phase.[138] And a European federal state was certainly more than simply the British conservative's project. Instead, it inspired the programme of the Italian Left and the young German Christian Democratic Union (CDU) in equal measure,[139] mobilized society,[140] and was soon institutionalized (see 2.2.A). Already in the 1950s, Jean Monnet declared, with regard to his ECSC,

[136] On autonomy, see Nic Shuibhne, 'What Is the Autonomy of EU Law, and Why Does That Matter?', 88 *Nordic Journal of International Law* (2019) 9.

[137] CJEU, Opinion 2/13, *ECHR Accession II* (EU:C:2014:2454).

[138] Churchill, 'European Unity. "Something That Will Astonish You", Zurich, 19 September 1946', in D. Cannadine (ed.), *The Speeches of Winston Churchill* (1990) 309.

[139] For an overview, see Bance, 'The Idea of Europe: From Erasmus to ERASMUS', 22 *Journal of European Studies* (1992) 1, esp. at 10 ff.

[140] Losano, 'Una "rivoluzione federale europea" alla fine della Seconda guerra mondiale', in U. Campagnolo (ed.), *Verso una costituzione federale per l'Europa. Una proposta inedita del 1943* (2003) 3.

that '[t]he United States of Europe has begun'.[141] And in 1969, Walter Hallstein asserted that a European federal state had emerged, albeit an 'unfinished' one.[142]

Since Europe integrated spectacularly over the following decades, we ought to be surprised at how much the idea of European statehood faded.[143] There is much to be said for classifying today's EU as a federal state if we employ the established concept of statehood. European public law would then be the law of that state; it would be state law, or *Staatsrecht*, to use a charged German concept.

The EU meets all the conventional elements of statehood: territory, citizens, and authority.[144] Of course, the Union is different from the United States, the Indian Union, the Soviet Union, or the Federal Republic of Germany. But the criteria for statehood are flexible, as the Federal Republic of Bosnia and Herzegovina demonstrates. The latter is considered a state although it was founded in an international treaty and is both supervised by an international administration and divided into hostile constituent republics and peoples.[145] In all three respects, the EU resembles a state to a much greater degree.

Already in 1968, the EEC had established a European customs territory.[146] Since then, all goods must cross a physical and administered external border that delimits a single space (Article 29 TFEU, Article XXIV General Agreement on Tariffs and Trade (GATT)). This distinguishes the European space from concepts of a global legal space, from virtual spaces, or from spaces of deterritorialized private law.[147] The next step, in 1987, was the establishment of an internal market as one economic space (Article 26(2) TFEU).

The Amsterdam Treaty of 1997 extended this logic to the movement of people,[148] and the Treaty of Lisbon of 2007 established an internal area (space, *espace*, *Raum*) of freedom, security, and justice. The Schengen Borders Code, a piece of EU legislation, regulates the entry of third-state nationals.[149] Even during the COVID-19

[141] J. Monnet, *Les États-Unis d'Europe ont commencé: La communauté européenne du charbon et de l'acier. Discours et allocutions 1952–1954* (1955).

[142] W. Hallstein, *Der unvollendete Bundesstaat. Europäische Erfahrungen und Erkenntnisse* (1969).

[143] But it never disappeared, as evidenced by German Foreign Minister Fischer's famous Humboldt speech: J. Fischer, 'Vom Staatenverbund zur Föderation—Gedanken über die Finalität der europäischen Integration', 29-1 *Bulletin der Bundesregierung* (vom 24. Mai 2000).

[144] G. Jellinek, *Die Lehre von den Staatenverbindungen (1882). Herausgegeben und eingeleitet von Walter Pauly* (1996) 179 f., 183.

[145] On Bosnia and Herzegovina, see Grewe, 'Constitutional Jurisdiction in Ex-Yugoslavia in the Perspective of the European Legal Space', in A. von Bogdandy, P. M. Huber, and C. Grabenwarter (eds), *The Max Planck Handbooks in European Public Law, Vol. IV. Constitutional Adjudication: Common Themes and Challenges* (2023) 51, 74–75.

[146] In the current Customs Code, this is Art. 4 of Regulation 952/2013 of the European Parliament and of the Council of 9 October 2013 laying down the Union Customs Code, OJ 2013 L 269/1.

[147] Günther and Kadelbach, 'Recht ohne Staat?', in K. Günther and S. Kadelbach (eds), *Recht ohne Staat? Zur Normativität nichtstaatlicher Rechtsetzung* (2011) 9, at 10 ff.

[148] Communication from the Commission on a New Pact on Migration and Asylum, COM(2020) 609 final, 23 September 2020.

[149] Regulation 2016/399 of the European Parliament and of the Council of 9 March 2016 establishing a Community Code on the rules governing the movement of persons across borders (Schengen Borders Code), OJ 2016 L 77/1.

pandemic, when EU Member States reactivated border control (and some of Germany's federated states instituted checkpoints at their state lines), the principle of a borderless space remained,[150] with all impediments deemed exceptional and transitory.

This European territoriality has transformed the Member States' territoriality. Their borders have become common constructs of the associated legal orders, and their protection now represents a common responsibility (Article 7 Frontex Regulation 2019/1896).[151] Europeans in Haarlem, Helsinki, Heidelberg, or Huelva now perceive the Evros in Greece as their external border and as quite an effective one at that, compared to many state borders.[152]

Overall, European territoriality has been achieved, and Union territory constitutes a legal term (Article 153(1)(g) TEFU). The latter must be defended (Article 42(7) TEU). Of course, it is a big question as to whether the Union can do so on its own if faced with Russian aggression. But if that were the criterion for statehood, no state in Europe would have enjoyed statehood between 1945 and 1991 except the Union of Soviet Socialist Republics (USSR) (see 2.3.C).

Statehood requires citizens, subjects, nationals, people. European citizenship has been around from the very beginning. As early as 1951, Walter Hallstein used that concept to describe the free movement of workers.[153] In 1964, Ipsen and Nicolaysen coined the concept of market citizenship,[154] though many lambasted this apolitical form of citizenship. Europeans became political citizens in 1979, when the first direct elections to the European Parliament were held. Since 1993, the Treaty has defined these electors as EU citizens following a suggestion by Altiero Spinelli, a pioneering federalist.[155]

At that time, some viewed EU citizenship with scepticism.[156] Soon, however, its effects became visible. Visionary scholars[157] and the CJEU made EU citizenship socially relevant, with new doctrines treating Europeans as true citizens, not just as actors in the common market. The Treaty of Lisbon then placed EU citizenship in

[150] Müller, 'Die Auswirkungen der Covid-19-Pandemie', in W. Weidenfeld and W. Wessels (eds), *Jahrbuch der Europäischen Integration 2020* (2020) 59.

[151] D. Fernández-Rojo, *EU Migration Agencies. The Operation and Cooperation of FRONTEX, EASO and EUROPOL* (2021).

[152] V. Moreno-Lax, *Accessing Asylum in Europe: Extraterritorial Border Controls and Refugee Rights under EU Law* (2017) 38; J. Oltmer, *Die Grenzen der EU. Europäische Integration, 'Schengen' und die Kontrolle der Migration* (2021) 1.

[153] W. Hallstein, *Der Schuman-Plan. Nachschrift des am 28. April 1951 in der Aula der Johann-Wolfgang-Goethe-Universität Frankfurt am Main gehaltenen Vortrags* (1951) 18.

[154] Ipsen and Nicolaysen, 'Haager Kongreß für Europarecht und Bericht über die aktuelle Entwicklung des Gemeinschaftsrechts', 17 *Neue Juristische Wochenschrift* (1964) 339, at 340.

[155] EP Resolution of 14 February 1984 on the draft Treaty establishing the European Union, OJ 1984 C 77/33, 33; Pistone, 'Altiero Spinelli and the Strategy for the United States of Europe', in L. Levi (ed.), *Altiero Spinelli and Federalism in Europe and in the World* (1990) 133.

[156] Weiler, 'Citizenship and Human Rights', in J. A. Winter *et al.* (eds), *Reforming the Treaty on European Union. The Legal Debate* (1996) 57, at 65.

[157] Shaw, 'Citizenship of the Union. Towards a Post-National Membership?', in Academy of European Law (ed.), *Collected Courses of the Academy of European Law, Vol. 6, Book 1* (1998) 237.

the centre of European democracy (Article 9 TEU; see 3.5.A). It even postulated a corresponding collective: the European society of Article 2 TEU (see 1.2).

EU citizenship is not free-standing. It follows Member State nationality (Article 9(2) TEU). Since citizenship works similarly in other federations, this dependence does not vitiate European statehood.[158] The same is true for the lack of a European people (see 3.5.A). Even in the United States, some interpret the term 'people' in the federal constitution as referring to the peoples of the individual states; for them, the Union itself does not have a people.[159]

The third conventional element of statehood is authority. This, too, is highly developed at the European federal level. The European Treaties establish an active legislature, powerful executive bodies (namely, the Commission, the European Central Bank (ECB), and various agencies), and a strong court. These institutions can impose their will using an arsenal of sanctions.[160] Since 2021, there are even European public prosecutors,[161] and violations of EU law can result in colossal financial loss.[162] Greek citizens can attest to EU institutions' power after the ECB caused a financial 'near-death experience' in 2015.[163] At the international level, nearly all of the world's governments treat the chief diplomat of the EU delegation as an ambassador.[164] An ambassador is usually the envoy of a sovereign, of a state.

What the Union authority lacks is its own means of physical coercion: there are neither EU police officers nor EU soldiers. There is, however, the border management agency, Frontex.[165] The agency establishes border management teams (Article 2 No. 18 Frontex Regulation), migration management support teams (Article 2 No. 19, Article 40 Frontex Regulation), and return teams (Article 2 No. 29, 52 Frontex Regulation), which can use 'force, including the carrying and use of

[158] Jackson, 'Citizenship and Federalism', in T. A. Aleinikoff and D. Klusmeyer (eds), *Citizenship Today. Global Perspectives and Practices* (2010) 127, at 182.

[159] USSC, *US Term Limits, Inc. v. Thornton*, 514 U.S. 779, 846 n 1 (1995) (Thomas, J, dissenting). See also Mahoney, 'Preamble', in L. W. Levy, K. L. Karst, and D. J. Mahoney (eds), *Encyclopedia of the American Constitution* (1986) 1435 (noting that the word 'people' stood in for the peoples of the individual states because it was unclear, at the time of the Constitution's drafting, which states would be part of the Union when the Constitution became effective).

[160] S. Bitter, *Die Sanktion im Recht der Europäischen Union. Der Begriff und seine Funktion im europäischen Rechtsschutzsystem* (2011) 121 ff.

[161] Council Regulation 2017/1939 of 12 October 2017 implementing enhanced cooperation on the establishment of the European Public Prosecutor's Office, OJ 2017 L 283/1.

[162] Regulation 2020/2092 of the European Parliament and of the Council of 16 December 2020 on a general regime of conditionality for the protection of the Union budget, OJ 2020 LI 433/1; Łacny, 'The Rule of Law Conditionality under Regulation No 2092/2020—Is It All About the Money?', 13 *The Hague Journal on the Rule of Law* (2021) 1.

[163] ECB Press Release, *ELA to Greek Banks Maintained at Its Current Level* (28 June 2015), https://www.ecb.europa.eu/press/pr/date/2015/html/pr150628.en.html (last visited 6 April 2022); ECB Press Release, *ELA to Greek Banks Maintained* (6 July 2015), https://www.ecb.europa.eu/press/pr/date/2015/html/pr150706.en.html (last visited 6 April 2022).

[164] Wouters and Duquet, 'The EU and International Diplomatic Law: New Horizons?', 7 *Hague Journal of Diplomacy* (2012) 31, at 44 f.

[165] Regulation 2019/1896 of the European Parliament and of the Council of 13 November 2019 on the European Border and Coast Guard and repealing Regulations (EU) No. 1052/2013 and (EU) No. 2016/1624, OJ 2019 L 295/1.

service weapons, ammunition and equipment' (Article 82(8) Frontex Regulation). More generally, Article 4(3) TEU tasks Member States with enforcing Union law like their domestic law. For the individual, Union law is thus as authoritative (and coercive) as domestic law.

In conclusion, there are good reasons to conceive of the EU as a federal state.[166] The idea of a European state has faded not for lack of evidence but because of a dogma that contains a great truth. This dogma reflects that there is no general will to found a European federal state.[167]

Whatever the evidence for European statehood, there has not been a majority of Europeans ready to conceive of it in that way.[168] The Constitutional Treaty of 2004, which might have been read as expressing such a will,[169] failed. Reconstructive legal scholarship should take this into account. In a democratic society, statehood by stealth is not desirable.

Terminology matters. The current Treaties do not begin with 'We, the people' but with the King of the Belgians. Pursuant to Article 1(1) TEU, 'the High Contracting Parties establish among themselves' a European Union. The Treaties thus respect the red lines established to prevent the Union's statehood,[170] as also shown by the provisions on amending the Treaties (see Article 48 TEU, which leaves the Member States' competence-competence principle untouched), the rigid and stingy financial constitution, and the lack of federal coercion vis-à-vis the Member States.[171]

Renouncing European statehood has good normative reasons beyond respecting the democratic process. It avoids continental nation-building, with all its likely costs and possible dangers, not least violence. It seems better to read Europeanization as a Hegelian overcoming, that is, as preserving the achievements of the nation states while taming their deficiencies.[172] The concept of European society—despite being a collective singular similar to state, people, or nation—requires less homogeneity or identity (see 3.2.A–3.2.C). That is a monumental civilizational achievement. And it is liberating for it means that the Union does not require a grand narrative or shared ideology.[173]

[166] F. Schorkopf, *Der europäische Weg. Geschichte und Gegenwart der Europäischen Union* (3rd edn, 2020) 223.

[167] J.-M. Ferry, *La question de l'État européen* (2000) esp. at 277 ff.

[168] European Commission, *Standard Eurobarometer 79—Public Opinion on the European Union* (Spring 2013) 79; V. Giscard d'Estaing, *Rapport oral présenté au conseil européen de Thessalonique, le 20 juin 2003* (2003).

[169] von Bogdandy, 'The Prospect of a European Republic. What European Citizens Are Voting For', 42 *Common Market Law Review* (2005) 913.

[170] BVerfGE 123, 267, *Lisbon*, paras 179, 232 ff., 244 ff.

[171] For a protagonist's analysis, see Amato, 'From the Years of the Convention to the Years of Brexit. Where Do We Go from Here?', in N. W. Barber, M. Cahill, and R. Ekins (eds), *The Rise and Fall of the European Constitution* (2019) 11, at 13 f.

[172] Weiler, 'In Defence of the Status Quo: Europe's Constitutional *Sonderweg*', in J. H. H. Weiler and M. Wind (eds), *European Constitutionalism beyond the State* (2003) 7.

[173] Koschorke (n. 7) 197.

European public law thus operates on the basis of a conceptual differentiation. Only the Member States are states, while the EU (see 2.2.D) is not. Thus, European public law needs to be conceptualized without European statehood.

This need not remain the case forever. We cannot foresee the reactions to grave economic crises, civil strife, ecological catastrophes, or military aggressions. Drafts of continental statehood are on the table.[174] They are not just read by dreamy academic federalists, as Emmanuel Macron showed with his Sorbonne speech of 2017.[175]

B. The Transformation of Sovereignty

The concept of sovereignty transformed together with that of the state. For a long time, it substantiated the traditional understanding of the state as well as of the international order, of domestic public law as well as of public international law. Both Hegel and Jellinek maintained that all of the foregoing can be 'explained by sovereignty and on the basis of sovereignty'.[176] On this view, sovereignty premises all law on the will of the state and posits the state's supreme power over all other domestic social spheres.[177] As sovereignty *of the people*, it justifies all law with the democratic principle.[178] Turned outwards, as sovereignty under *international law*, it protects the state and bases all international obligations on the will of the latter. This conception of sovereignty thus shapes both domestic public law and public international law, but it does so in opposite ways: Domestic public law supports a vertical structure of authority, while international law allows for a horizontal structure of cooperation.

The developments described in 2.3.A undermined the traditional understanding of sovereignty. The 2009 Lisbon judgment of the *Bundesverfassungsgericht*'s Second Senate provides good evidence. The Senate places sovereignty front and centre and certainly asserts German sovereignty. Yet, to make a meaningful argument, the Senate limits German sovereignty to the protection of only the most essential aspects of the German constitutional order. Now, sovereignty denotes issues that

[174] U. Guérot, *Warum Europa eine Republik werden muss! Eine politische Utopie* (2016) 81 ff.; G. Verhofstadt, *Europe's Last Chance. Why the European States Must Form a More Perfect Union* (2017) 229 ff.

[175] On this speech, see Jacqué, 'Deux discours, une vision?', 53 *Revue trimestrielle de droit européen* (2017) 629, at 629; Vieilledent, 'Deux voix pour l'Europe. Pour une relance de l'Union européenne', 423 *Futuribles* (2018) 5, at 7; Eijsbouts and Reestman, 'European Sovereignty', 14 *European Constitutional Law Review* (2018) 1.

[176] Jellinek (n. 144) 36; G. W. F. Hegel, *Elements of the Philosophy of Right* (1991 [1821]) para. 278.

[177] Randelzhofer, 'Staatsgewalt und Souveränität', in J. Isensee and P. Kirchhof (eds), *Handbuch des Staatsrechts der Bundesrepublik Deutschland Band II. Verfassungsstaat* (2004) 143, at § 17 paras 25 ff., 35 ff.

[178] H. Heller, *Die Souveränität. Ein Beitrag zur Theorie des Staats- und Völkerrechts* (1927) 70 ff; D. Grimm, *Souveränität. Herkunft und Zukunft eines Schlüsselbegriffs* (2009) 35 ff.

can never be left to European politics. This very narrow understanding of sovereignty is a far cry from the sweeping concepts of Hegel and Jellinek.

Though transformed, the concept of sovereignty remains essential, in particular to articulate fears of foreign domination. Many societies, especially in Central and Eastern Europe, vividly and painfully recall eras of Ottoman, Habsburg, Russian, German, and Soviet domination. Exploiting such memories, some governments resist EU obligations by denouncing them as instruments of foreign rule, unacceptable to national sovereignty.[179] To counter such portrayals, the Union needs to demonstrate its democratic credentials and how it seeks to protect Europe against the dominance of the United States, China, Russia, or any Member State.

The concept of sovereignty, like that of identity (see 3.1.A), often characterizes projects commonly considered populist.[180] Conceptually speaking, Macron may thus have been smart to claim this concept for the European project.[181] As with identity, however, this attempt might give credit to Schmittian thinking and Schmittian doubts about European public law and society.

C. Schmitt's *The Concept of the Political*

For Schmitt, public law without a state (and sovereignty) is either impossible or dystopian. This follows from the prerequisites he postulates for a viable public law. Schmitt elaborates on the popular theorem that the nation state alone provides the consensus and loyalty necessary for a stable social order. According to this view, my book seems a futile, and even dangerous, undertaking. Here, I will show that Schmitt's theorem is insightful but unpersuasive.

Schmitt articulates this theorem prominently in his *The Concept of the Political*.[182] The booklet represents one of the most influential texts of any legal scholar.[183] It argues that a political community requires social homogeneity in order to function well, that every political community is in conflict with other communities, and that a normative order that extends beyond a homogeneous community will be precarious. These kinds of assumptions do not necessarily advocate authoritarian models of order (see 1.4). However, they always imply that any European public law is to be conceived from a national perspective unless a European state has formed.[184]

[179] On the accusations, see Kaczyński, 'Is the European Union Truly Like the Soviet Union?', *Euractiv* (8 February 2021).

[180] Rosanvallon (n. 54) esp. at 10.

[181] Jacqué (n. 175) 629; Vieilledent (n. 175) 7; Eijsbouts and Reestman (n. 175).

[182] Schmitt, *The Concept of the Political* (n. 38).

[183] The central idea can already be found in H. Morgenthau, *Die internationale Rechtspflege, ihr Wesen und ihre Grenzen* (1929) 69; see Koskenniemi, *The Gentle Civilizer of Nations* (n. 39) 436.

[184] C. Schmitt, *Hugo Preuß. Sein Staatsbegriff und seine Stellung in der deutschen Staatslehre* (1930) esp. at 14–17.

This crucial issue also surfaces in the context of collective identity (see 3.2.B) and European democracy (see 3.4.B–3.5.B). Here, I confront Schmitt's core argument.

Schmitt's *The Concept of the Political* radicalizes the approach centred on the nation state by postulating hard conflict as the vanishing point of public law: 'The concept of the state presupposes the concept of the political.'[185] This famous sentence means that domestic public law (like public international law) must be understood, interpreted, and applied from the perspective of conflict. Schmitt describes the state as only one of the possible institutionalizations of political relations. In an almost Copernican turn, he upends the conventional relationship between the two key concepts (state and politics). Schmitt then defines the concept of the political in *modal* and *phenomenal* terms, namely, as the *most intense* of all human relationships.[186] In politics, the other is either friend or enemy.[187]

Schmitt first makes an anthropological argument to support the primacy of violent conflict: the innate aggressiveness of humans[188]—or, more precisely, of men, since women play no role in his theory. According to *The Concept of the Political*, 'what remains is the remarkable and, for many, certainly disquieting diagnosis that all genuine political theories presuppose man to be evil.'[189] But aggressiveness is not only an ontic premise; its creative dynamic also makes it valuable.

Schmitt's second argument is of an epistemic nature: only by analysing exceptional situations, it states, do we gain real insights. He admits that life-and-death struggles are not omnipresent, that they are, in fact, rare. Nevertheless, they are what matters: 'That the extreme case appears to be an exception does not negate its decisive character but confirms it all the more.'[190]

This approach has far-reaching consequences for the understanding of public law. The authority to govern is central to domestic public law, on which this text from 1932 focuses. Schmitt advocates an interpretation of the Weimar Constitution that allows for a strong executive with potentially dictatorial powers. He claims that pluralism belongs in the international sphere, not in domestic politics. Indeed, he holds that domestic pluralism—be it of a social or political nature—endangers the state's existence.

Schmitt's text is similarly consequential for international law. International organizations can provide a useful opportunity for interstate negotiations but no more than that.[191] In Schmitt's view, there can be no international, transnational, or European public law that empowers international, transnational, or European

[185] Schmitt, *The Concept of the Political* (n. 38) 19.

[186] Böckenförde, 'Der Begriff des Politischen als Schlüssel zum staatsrechtlichen Werk Carl Schmitts', in H. Quaritsch (ed.), *Complexio Oppositorum. Über Carl Schmitt. Vorträge und Diskussionsbeiträge des 28. Sonderseminars 1986 der Hochschule für Verwaltungswissenschaften Speyer* (1988) 283, at 284 f.

[187] Schmitt, *The Concept of the Political* (n. 38) 28 f., 32, 46.

[188] Ibid. 61.

[189] Ibid.

[190] Ibid. 35; the central text is C. Schmitt, *Political Theology* (2005 [1922]) 1 f.

[191] Schmitt, *The Concept of the Political* (n. 38) 56.

institutions to advance the international, transnational, or European common good. He considers such institutions, such as the League of Nations at the time, the foreign policy instruments of powerful states.[192] This is how Marine Le Pen and Matteo Salvini, France's and Italy's most powerful opposition politicians, have described the EU in recent years: as an instrument of German politics and interests.[193]

Thus, Schmitt renews the old world view of particularism for an era characterized by mass democracy and international interdependence. He reformulates particularist assumptions gleaned from 2,000 years of political ideas: the primacy of foreign policy, the weakness of a rules-based international order, the omnipresence of conflict, the necessity of leadership, and homogeneity as a precondition of domestic order; the call of heroism, sacrifice, and community; and (last but not least) the discontent with a commodified and mechanized society.[194] Schmitt's *Concept of the Political* helps better comprehend such notions, which, in 1932, played the same role in shaping the law and legal practices as they would in 2020. Many hold similar views, albeit only rarely as radically as Schmitt.

Schmitt's *The Concept of the Political* does not address the question of a European order. He certainly noted the end of the 'Westphalian' order later (see 2.1.C). During the Second World War, at the time of the German conquests, he articulated an international order based on *Großräume*. After Germany's defeat, these disappeared from his writings. After 1945, Schmitt had no constructive idea for Europe.

This lack of constructive answers diminishes Schmitt's thought. For my argument, however, the weakness of its foundations is even more important than its strengths. Contrary to Schmitt's anthropological premises, an abundance of psychological, sociological, and anthropological research has demonstrated that cooperative behaviour is just as common as conflictual.[195] The same applies to Schmitt's epistemic argument that only the exceptional case reveals the 'core of the matter'.[196] Of course, the study of exceptional circumstances, of threshold phases or critical junctures, offers an opportunity for great insight. But Schmitt's argument overlooks that there is no exception without normality and that there can be no epistemic primacy in a mutually dependent relationship.

Schmitt's thinking in irreconcilable dualisms is likewise unconvincing. I recognize that dualisms structure knowledge and generate intellectual dynamics. In a

[192] Ibid. 55 f.

[193] Le Pen, 'L'Union européenne est dirigée par l'Allemagne […] L'euro, la monnaie européenne, est calquée pour l'Allemagne. Elle a été fabriquée par l'Allemagne et pour l'Allemagne', television report on France 2 (Télé Matin, 15 May 2014); Salvini, 'L'euro è stato un errore, si è avvantaggiata solo la Germania', television report on Rete 4 (26 May 2020).

[194] Schmitt, 'Der Begriff des Politischen. Vorwort von 1971 zur italienischen Ausgabe', in Quaritsch (n. 186) 269, at 269–274, 271 f.

[195] Parks, Joireman, and Van Lange, 'Cooperation, Trust, and Antagonism. How Public Goods Are Promoted', 14 *Psychological Science in the Public Interest* (2013) 119. This objection had already been formulated by Strauss, 'Anmerkungen zu Carl Schmitt, Der Begriff des Politischen', 67 *Archiv für Sozialwissenschaft und Sozialpolitik* (1932) 732.

[196] Schmitt, *The Concept of the Political* (n. 38) 35.

Hegelian tradition, however, dualisms that are conflicts can be used to contribute to understanding and developing law, politics, and society.[197] Schmitt's thought largely lacks this dimension. For him, dualisms that are conflicts are to be fought out.[198]

Last but not least, the European experience refutes Schmitt's uncompromising insistence on the nation state. The recent crises are telling in this regard. At first, the euro, sovereign debt, refugee, Brexit, and COVID-19 crises seemed to validate Schmitt:[199] while the state took the centre stage, the EU and its law appeared sidelined. However, the European institutions then developed a European response.[200] Of course, they did so in cumbersome procedures, through lambasted compromises, and in a piecemeal fashion. Nevertheless, elaborate a European response they did. European public law is not a fair-weather phenomenon, then. It allows Europe to deal with—or at least tame—even the most challenging conflicts.

I find nothing in Schmitt's *The Concept of the Political* that makes my idea of a European public law untenable. At the same time, I accept the importance of many phenomena crucial to Schmitt's thought: the heterogeneity of world views, interests, and identities; the danger of biased public institutions and alienating bureaucratization; and the inevitability of hard conflict, of winners and losers. These are insights to guide the analysis of the European institutions, procedures, and standards (see 2.3–2.5).

D. Public versus Private Law

Since European public law cannot be defined in relation to a European state, I define it through its difference from private law.[201] This builds on the dualism of public and private law, which, in turn, mirrors a fundamental differentiation of modern societies. Private and public action belong to two different social spheres because they operate by different logics and require different justifications.[202] The

[197] Brunkhorst, 'The Co-evolution of Cosmopolitan and National Statehood. Preliminary Theoretical Considerations on the Historical Evolution of Constitutionalism', 47 *Cooperation and Conflict* (2012) 176.

[198] Schmitt, *Political Theology* (n. 190) 45 f., 51 f.

[199] See Joerges, 'Europe's Economic Constitution in Crisis and the Emergence of a New Constitutional Constellation', 15 *German Law Journal* (2014) 985; Thym, 'The "Refugee Crisis" as a Challenge of Legal Design and Institutional Legitimacy', 53 *Common Market Law Review* (2016) 1545.

[200] See Biermann *et al.*, 'Political (Non-)Reform in the Euro Crisis and the Refugee Crisis. A Liberal Intergovernmentalist Explanation', 26 *Journal of European Public Policy* (2017) 1; Alemanno, 'The European Response to COVID-19: From Regulatory Emulation to Regulatory Coordination?', 11 *European Journal of Risk Regulation* (2020) 307; M. Ludwigs and S. Schmahl (eds), *Die EU zwischen Niedergang und Neugründung. Wege aus der Polykrise* (2020).

[201] B. Stirn, *Towards a European Public Law* (2017) 155 ff. This paragraph draws on von Bogdandy, Goldmann, and Venzke (n. 66).

[202] Hegel, *Elements of the Philosophy of Right* (n. 176) paras 182 ff.; A. Honneth, *Das Recht der Freiheit. Grundriß einer demokratischen Sittlichkeit* (2011) 317 ff.

President of the French Republic, of the EU Commission, or of the ECtHR are bound by public interests, while the Chief Executive Officer (CEO) of the German software company SAP, the Editor-in-Chief of *The Economist*, or the Chair of the International Board of Amnesty International act under the auspices of private freedom. This distinction between public and private appears in almost all legal systems and societies.

Hegel's philosophy of law is central to that distinction because it overcomes the Enlightenment thinking that grounded public law in a contract, a legal form that originates in private law. Hegel's philosophy thus propels the development of autonomous public law theories. The distinction is important analytically but also normatively. In Habermas' view, it is constitutive of a democratic society.[203] Indeed, Schmitt had declared it defunct in the National Socialist *Führerstaat*.[204]

The private and the public sphere are not incommunicado. They are constitutive of each other because they acquire substance only in their dialectic; indeed, they produce each other.[205] Of course, the processes of globalization and digitalization have watered down this distinction. But it has already survived manifold challenges and vigorous criticism. Its persistence and resilience demonstrate that it is both important and practical. I will discuss some challenges and criticisms to clarify the distinction and, in doing so, specify this book's conception of public law.

For Kant and Kelsen, all law enacted by public institutions is public.[206] Accordingly, the French *code civil*, the German Stock Corporation Act, or the European Regulation (EC) No. 2157/2001 on the Statute for a European Company belong to public law. This conception of public law is synonymous with positive law and, in democratic societies, with democratic law. Accordingly, it is too broad for the purposes of this study. More, it undervalues a differentiation that is crucial to modern societies.

Another criticism of the distinction between the public and the private is based on the existence of hybrid actors. An example are *public–private partnerships*, which the EU uses to promote scientific research.[207] On closer inspection,

[203] J. Habermas, *The Structural Transformation of the Public Sphere: An Inquiry into a Category of Bourgeois Society* (1989) 1 f., 141; E.-W. Böckenförde, *Die verfassungstheoretische Unterscheidung von Staat und Gesellschaft als Bedingung der individuellen Freiheit. 178. Sitzung am 12. Juli 1972 in Düsseldorf* (1973).

[204] Schmitt, 'Die geschichtliche Lage der deutschen Rechtswissenschaft', 41 *Deutsche Juristen-Zeitung* (1936) 15, at 21.

[205] Mende, 'Privatheit und Global Governance in der Internationalen Politischen Theorie', 6 *Zeitschrift für Politische Theorie* (2015) 207.

[206] Kant, 'Die Metaphysik der Sitten', in W. Weischedel (ed.), *Werkausgabe, Bd. VIII* (1977) 303, at 427 ff.

[207] See Art. 25 of Regulation 1291/2013 of the European Parliament and of the Council of 11 December 2013 concerning the Framework Programme for Research and Innovation Horizon 2020 (2014–2020) and repealing Decision No. 1982/2006/EC, OJ 2013 L 347/104; the individual partnerships are listed at European Commission, *European Partnerships in Horizon Europe*, https://ec.europa.eu/info/research-and-innovation/funding/funding-opportunities/funding-programmes-and-open-calls/horizon-europe/european-partnerships-horizon-europe_en (last visited 17 August 2022).

however, hybrid actors reinforce, not undercut, the distinction: to identify a hybrid entity, we require the *private* and the *public* as meaningful concepts. A hybrid vehicle is a vehicle with a combustion engine *and* an electric motor, and a mule is a cross between a horse and a donkey. That some phenomena may be difficult to qualify does not make a distinction any less valuable.

Another point of criticism is that the *public–private* distinction may serve as an argument to prevent democratic law from penetrating certain spheres of society. It is, indeed, possible that the distinction is used ideologically in order to protect private power.[208] For instance, it might be used to fight the democratic regulation of asymmetrical relationships, be they in families, companies, a value chain, or an established market.[209]

Yet, the phenomenon of private power does not render the distinction between public and private law useless. To the contrary, it confirms its importance: it throws into relief the difference between public, parliamentary legislation and rule-making by companies like Facebook,[210] between the European Commission and private standard-setters like Moody's, between the ECB and Deutsche Bank, or between Frontex officials and the employees of a private security firm. Reconstructive legal scholarship cannot dismiss the fact that private and public institutions are subject to different legal regimes. Although some aspects of human rights apply directly to private actors, the two spheres continue to operate by a different logic.[211] Eliminating the distinction would essentially require equating, in legal terms, private power with public authority.[212] There are no indications thereof in European law, notwithstanding its considerable antidiscrimination legislation. The adequate response to abuses is to regulate private power in accordance with the standards of Article 2 TEU—as has occurred with EU antidiscrimination law—but not to abandon the public–private distinction.

Some private actors use private law to escape such regulation, creating a body of law that Gunther Teubner calls a new *lex mercatoria*, a transnational private law tailored to corporate interests.[213] It is largely autonomous from public regulation because it exploits the differences and the competition between different

[208] Kelsen (n. 96) 280 ff.

[209] Kennedy, 'The Stages of the Decline of the Public/Private Distinction', 130 *University of Pennsylvania Law Review* (1982) 1349, at 1352; J. Mende, *Global Governance und Menschenrechte. Konstellationen zwischen Privatheit und Öffentlichkeit* (2020) 17.

[210] Schweitzer, 'Digitale Plattformen als private Gesetzgeber. Ein Perspektivwechsel für die europäische "Plattform-Regulierung"', 31 *Zeitschrift für europäisches Privatrecht* (2019) 1.

[211] Human Rights Council, Report of the Special Representative of the Secretary-General on the Issue of Human Rights and Transnational Corporations and Other Business Enterprises, John Gerard Ruggie, *Guiding Principles on Business and Human Rights: Implementing the United Nations 'Protect, Respect and Remedy' Framework*, UN Doc. A/HRC/17/31 (21 March 2011); Ruggie, 'Business and Human Rights. The Evolving International Agenda', 101 *American Journal of International Law* (2007) 819.

[212] B. Sordi, *Diritto pubblico e diritto privato. Una genealogia storica* (2020) 240.

[213] Teubner, 'Breaking Frames. Economic Globalization and the Emergence of lex mercatoria', 5 *European Journal of Social Theory* (2002) 199.

legal orders. This private law causes serious problems.[214] It is no small success of European public law that it succeeds in regulating part of such private power.[215] European society has set up public institutions that help reproduce the dialectic of public and private in a transnational field.

On this basis, the classification of a norm as either public or private depends on the social sphere to which it belongs. Making this determination can be challenging. The abstraction of two social spheres does not translate easily into legal doctrine, which operates in the concreteness of social relations. However, doctrine has established criteria that succeed in tracing the distinction. These criteria ask whether a norm mainly addresses a public or a private legal entity, establishes a vertical relationship (i.e. one of subordination) or a horizontal one, and focuses on public interests or the private structuring of relationships.[216] Traditional understandings can help, too.[217] While these criteria do not always help distinguish public from private regulations beyond reasonable doubt, the distinction persists and characterizes most legal orders.

There are private actors, such as Amnesty International or Transparency International, that pursue a general interest. But their mandates stem solely from the members of their association, not from society as a whole. They are subject to different standards of lawfulness and legitimacy than public institutions. Rankings by Transparency International constitute free speech. By contrast, the European Commission's rankings—such as the EU Justice Scoreboard (see 3.3.D), which evaluates the Member States' judiciary—require a specific legal basis.

Using this distinction, public law can thus be constructed without a state. On this basis, I will now reconstruct the most significant differentiation in public law, that between administrative and constitutional law. These two concepts are foundational because they divide the world of public law. Though they share a common basis, their differences, not least in their Europeanization, illuminate the transformation of European public law.

4. Administrative Law without a State

A. On the Ambivalence of Europeanization

For a long time, public administration was synonymous with state administration. Accordingly, administrative law was just a part of state law (*Staatsrecht*). Today, the European Treaty legislator uses this term to address the Union's administrative

[214] K. Pistor, *The Code of Capital. How the Law Creates Wealth and Inequality* (2019).

[215] A. Bradford, *The Brussels Effect. How the European Union Rules the World* (2020).

[216] Ruffert, 'Perspektiven des Internationalen Verwaltungsrechts', in C. Möllers, A. Voßkuhle, and C. Walter (eds), *Internationales Verwaltungsrecht* (2007) 394, at 402.

[217] BVerfGE 11, 192, *Beurkundungswesen*, para. 33.

bodies and activities (e.g. in Article 298 TFEU and Article 41 CFR). The terms 'European administrative law' and 'EU administrative law' are firmly established, even though there is no European state to administer them. This raises the question of how the concept of administrative law transformed and what this says about European society. In short, the development thus far gives rise to both hope and concern.

On the one hand, the Europeanization of administrative law may help institutionalize rationality beyond the states, thus serving a transnational common good. Here, public administration designates bodies and actions that are firmly in the hands of dedicated, educated, and farsighted civil servants. The administration they oversee is somewhat autonomous from politics' irrationalities, both national and international. This benevolent perception of administration can rely on Hegel.[218] Responding to the two world wars, David Mitrany's functionalism elaborated this vision for the international sphere.[219] Ernst B. Haas, a Frankfurt-born US political scientist, presented a custom-tailored application of it at the very moment the EEC Treaty entered into force; in doing so, he provided the first major model of European integration.[220]

On the other hand, the concern is that European administrative law means European rule by bureaucrats. Some critics argue that European bodies designated as public administration may instead set up a secretive, remote, and insensitive bureaucracy that disenfranchises citizens and undermines the achievements of the post-war social settlements. Already in 1954, Severo M. Giannini, a founder of democratic Italian administrative law, surmised that European integration would bring about a 'unione amministrativa' in form but a 'dittatura federale' in substance.[221]

The metaphor of the European administration as a bureaucratic monster articulates this worry.[222] It has two different meanings. The more harmless one is linked to Samuel von Pufendorf, who provided what is probably the most influential description of the Holy Roman Empire of the German Nation. Pufendorf, the very first professor of international law and Hagemeier's contemporary (see 2.1.A), described the Empire as a monster-like body because its structure could not be conceptualized.[223] Here, monstrosity reflects a lack of concepts to grasp a particular body politic, one best considered *sui generis*.

[218] Hegel, *Elements of the Philosophy of Right* (n. 176) paras 287, 297; Koschorke (n. 7) 174–178.

[219] D. Mitrany, *A Working Peace System* (1943); Mitrany, 'The Functional Approach to World Organization', 24 *International Affairs* (1948) 350.

[220] E. B. Haas, *The Uniting of Europe. Political, Social and Economical Forces, 1950–1957* (1958).

[221] Giannini, 'Brevi osservazioni sul Trattato per la Comunità europea di difesa', 10 *Società* (1954) 523, at 527.

[222] H. M. Enzensberger, *Gentle Monster Brussels: Or the Disenfranchisement of Europe* (2011).

[223] F. Salomon, *Severinus de Monzambano (Samuel von Pufendorf). De statu Imperii Germanici* (1910) ch. VI, para. 9, at 126.

However, most critics of the Union's powers have more serious concerns than it being *sui generis*. Ernst-Wolfgang Böckenförde views European administrative law as 'a technical and pragmatic construct of economic rationality', completely subservient to the logic of the European market.[224] According to Aldo Sandulli, the regulatory law of European monetary union strangles European society.[225] Here, the structural transformation of public law is moving not towards a European democratic society but towards almost dystopian constellations.[226]

The advent of EU administration is not the only cause for concern. The Europeanization of domestic administrations and domestic administrative law presents a delicate matter, too. European administrative law loosens a domestic administration's ties to 'its' state, people, and parliament. Under German public law, as under many other Member States', the statute is an administration's most important source of democratic legitimation. Under European administrative law, however, domestic administrations must implement Union regulations, adapt their organization and procedures to Union law, and execute other Member States' measures.[227] From a domestic perspective, the weakening of the domestic administration's democratic legitimacy appears all too evident.

To advance on a critical issue, it is often helpful to take a step back by conceptualizing the phenomenon. How, then, can we understand European administrative law? Like any administrative law, it is hard to define.[228] Some see European administrative law as 'the enforcement of the provisions of Community law in concrete situations'.[229] But this definition is too narrow because it does not, for instance, encompass administrative law-making under Article 290 TFEU. Eberhard Schmidt-Aßmann and Thomas von Danwitz contend that European administrative law also includes administrative law-making and the law of cooperation between administrative bodies across legal orders.[230] They thus convey an understanding of European administrative law's complexity but not why so many are weary of it. It is Sabino Cassese, Severo M. Giannini's master student, who hits the nail on the head when he describes administrative law as an all-powerful law (*un droit tout puissant*).[231]

[224] Böckenförde, 'Kennt die europäische Not kein Gebot?', in E.-W. Böckenförde (ed.), *Wissenschaft, Politik, Verfassungsgericht* (2011) 299, at 302.

[225] A. Sandulli, *Il ruolo del diritto in Europa. L'integrazione europea dalla prospettiva del diritto amministrativo* (2018) 59 ff.

[226] W. Streeck, *Buying Time. The Delayed Crisis of Democratic Capitalism* (2017) 165–189.

[227] L. De Lucia, *Amministrazione transnazionale e ordinamento europeo. Saggio sul pluralismo amministrativo* (2009) 245 ff.

[228] E. Forsthoff, *Lehrbuch des Verwaltungsrechts, Bd. 1. Allgemeiner Teil* (10th edn, 1973) 1.

[229] Mager, 'Entwicklungslinien des europäischen Verwaltungsrechts', in P. Axer *et al.* (eds), *Das Europäische Verwaltungsrecht in der Konsolidierungsphase. Systembildung—Disziplinierung—Internationalisierung* (2010) 11, at 13 f.

[230] Schmidt-Aßmann, 'Strukturen des Europäischen Verwaltungsrechts. Einleitende Problemskizze', in E. Schmidt-Aßmann and W. Hoffmann-Riem (eds), *Strukturen des Europäischen Verwaltungsrechts* (1999) 9, at 32; T. von Danwitz, *Europäisches Verwaltungsrecht* (2008) 4 ff.

[231] Cassese, '"Le droit tout puissant et unique de la société". Paradossi del diritto amministrativo', 59 *Rivista trimestrale di diritto pubblico* (2009) 879.

B. Cassese's All-Powerful Law

Cassese's characterization of administrative law as a *droit tout puissant* presents it as a powerful instrument of executive authority to implement political decisions.[232] Cassese describes its development through the French example.[233] From the seventeenth century on, the French monarchy developed a hierarchical and centralized administration that used a special law to implement its leaders' political goals vis-à-vis society. The law was special because it suspended the ordinary, the common, law as well as the courts' power in favour of state administration.

The French development became the model for much of the continent in the eighteenth century. Palaces modelled on Versailles were built throughout Continental Europe, demonstrating the triumph of this idea. England, where early parliamentarization and the Glorious Revolution of 1688 prevented the development of a special law that privileges public authority, constitutes an important exception.[234]

On the continent, many monarchies ventured into building state bureaucracies and a corresponding special law. As Alexis de Tocqueville maintained, the French Revolution did not hinder but, to the contrary, propelled the development of the state apparatus's special law.[235] With the Constitution of the Year VIII (1799), Napoleon established the *Conseil d'État* to strengthen his rule. The French *Conseil d'État* became the paradigmatic institution of administrative law, and, indeed, of the public law of the nineteenth and much of the twentieth centuries.[236]

Executing the special law fell to a dedicated expertocratic group that imbued the state with a specific model of administrative rationality.[237] This group, led by the members of the *Conseil d'État*, had considerable autonomy even from everyday politics.[238] Neither parliament nor the government but the members of the *Conseil d'État* shaped administrative law's structures through their decisions and scholarship. Until today, French administrative law is taught using books that teach the leading decisions,[239] not the structures of the relevant legislation.

232 Auby and Dutheil de la Rochère, 'Introduction générale', in Auby and Dutheil de la Rochère (n. 120) 1, at 4.

233 Cassese, 'The Administrative State in Europe', in von Bogdandy, Huber, and Cassese (n. 5) 57; della Cananea, 'Verwaltungsrechtliche Paradigmen im europäischen Rechtsraum. § 52', in A. von Bogdandy, S. Cassese, and P. M. Huber (eds), *Handbuch Ius Publicum Europaeum, Bd. III. Verwaltungsrecht in Europa: Grundlagen* (2010) 447.

234 Auby, 'The Transformation of the Administrative State and Administrative Law', in von Bogdandy, Huber, and Cassese (n. 5) 601, at 605.

235 A. de Tocqueville, *L'Ancien Régime et la Révolution* (1856).

236 Auby and Morabito, 'Evolution and Gestalt of the French State', in von Bogdandy, Huber, and Cassese (n. 5) 165, at 176, 178 ff., 186 f.

237 Chrétien, 'Frankreich. § 59', in A. von Bogdandy, S. Cassese, and P. M. Huber (eds), *Handbuch Ius Publicum Europaeum, Bd. IV. Verwaltungsrecht in Europa: Wissenschaft* (2011) 81, at para. 7.

238 See K. Marx, *Der achtzehnte Brumaire des Louis Bonaparte (1852). Kommentar von Hauke Brunkhorst* (2007) on the role of the administration at 142 and 172 f.

239 F. Colin, *L'essentiel des grands arrêts du droit administratif* (2018).

Indeed, when the Third Republic abolished the authoritarianism of the Second Empire in 1870, it left untouched the understanding of administrative law as a special law and the position of the *Conseil d'État*. Herein lies the essence of the *Blanco* judgment of the *Tribunal des Conflits*, remembered today as the beginning of democratic French administrative law.[240] This Tribunal, established by a Republican law of 1872 and composed in equal parts of judges of the *Cour de cassation* and members of the *Conseil d'État*, affirmed that administrative law was a special law entrusted to the *Conseil d'État*.[241]

This special law seemed paradigmatic of the administration of a strong nation state, to which many nineteenth- and twentieth-century legal scholars were committed, not just in France. The concept of *puissance publique* was the linchpin. Léon Duguit's progressively inspired attempt to replace the concept of *puissance publique* with that of *service public* failed to gain traction even among his followers.[242] The state's democratization certainly did not end bureaucratic rule.

The French development was paradigmatic, with 'Paris play[ing] the same role for administrative law that Rome plays for private law'.[243] That the *Conseil d'État* served as an example for the European Court of Justice and the French led the European bureaucracy for decades attests to this fact.[244] Thus, Émile Noël, a graduate of the *École Normale Supérieure*, the institution of higher education synonymous with the French state, shaped the European Commission more than anyone else, serving as its first Secretary General from 1958 to 1987.[245]

The dominance of French administrative law in the nineteenth and twentieth centuries did not lead to harmonization; administrative law followed different national paths.[246] Consider that Otto Mayer, often extolled as the founder of German administrative law, followed the French example in constructing an administrative law for Germany but opted for a clearly more authoritarian version than the Third Republic's in line with the overall outlook of the newly founded German Empire.

Accordingly, administrative law gained a reputation as an instrument of anti-democratic tendencies. In 1924, now under the democratic Weimar Constitution, Otto Mayer prefaced the third edition of his seminal textbook on administrative law with the statement that '[c]onstitutions come and go, but administrative law is

[240] Tribunal des conflits, 'Arrêt Blanco du 8 février 1873', in M. Long *et al.* (eds), *Les grands arrêts de la jurisprudence administrative* (21st edn, 2017) 1.

[241] Auby and Morabito (n. 236) 180, 184 f.

[242] Heuschling, 'The Complex Relationship between Administrative and Constitutional Law: A Comparative and Historical Analysis', in von Bogdandy, Huber, and Cassese (n. 5) 493, at 510.

[243] Cassese, 'Le droit tout puissant' (n. 231) 882 f.

[244] Ministère des Affaires Etrangères, *Rapport de la Délégation française sur le Traité et la Convention signés à Paris* (1951) 32.

[245] Van Middelaar (n. 99) 271.

[246] Fromont, 'A Typology of Administrative Law in Europe', in von Bogdandy, Huber, and Cassese (n. 5) 579; Schiera, 'Die gemeineuropäische Geschichte des Verwaltungsrechts und seiner Wissenschaft. § 68', in von Bogdandy, Cassese, and Huber, *Handbuch Ius Publicum Europaeum, Bd. IV* (n. 237) 399.

there to stay' ('*Verfassungsrecht vergeht, Verwaltungsrecht besteht*').[247] This became one of administrative law's most famous dicta. It also demonstrates how authoritarian persistence can obstruct a democratic transformation. Mayer's statement reflected how much the civil service resisted the democratic politics under the Weimar Constitution. This is why it was a climactic event for Carl Schmitt when Hermann Göring appointed him to the Prussian Council of State on 11 July 1933.

Against this background, one of the primary objectives of the Federal Republic would be to democratize the administration and administrative law.[248] For that reason, the German Basic Law (i.e. in the Federal Constitutional Court's interpretation) provides that issues considered essential are exclusively the domain of parliamentary legislation. Europeanization and European administrative law undermine this democratization, as becomes apparent in Hans Peter Ipsen's concept of Europe as a *Zweckverband funkioneller Integration*.

C. Ipsen's Supreme Regulatory Agency

Cassese's *droit tout puissant* problematizes European administrative law as that of executive authority. Hans Peter Ipsen's *Zweckverband funkioneller Integration* demonstrates what can follow from that. The concept is hard to translate. Literally, it designates a 'purposive association of functional integration'. In substance, it suggests that we should conceptualize European law as the law of a supreme regulatory agency. This conceptualization substantiates the concern that Union law enables executive policies that circumvent democratic procedures.

Community law has been the vehicle of transformative policies that would have been almost impossible to implement at the national level because of the many checks and balances in the Member States. The European Single Market Programme of 1985 provides a well-known example. With a flood of regulations, directives, and decisions, Council and Commission deeply transformed the Member States' economies,[249] ending the embedded capitalism of the post-war period. Some critics believe that Union law continues to advance neoliberal transformations to this day.[250]

Against this background, the conceptualization of European law as a law of executive authority renders problematic EU law's two most famous doctrines: the principles of direct effect and of the primacy of EU law over Member State law

[247] O. Mayer, *Deutsches Verwaltungsrecht, Bd. 1* (1924) Preface VI; Heuschling, 'The Complex Relationship between Administrative and Constitutional Law' (n. 242) 502 ff.

[248] R. Wahl, *Herausforderungen und Antworten. Das öffentliche Recht der letzten fünf Jahrzehnte* (2006) 16 ff.

[249] Commission of the European Communities, Completing the Internal Market: White Paper from the Commission to the European Council (Milan, 28–29 June 1985), COM(85) 310.

[250] F. W. Scharpf, *Governing in Europe: Effective and Democratic?* (1999); Palombarini, 'L'Italie, un laboratoire politique européen', 66 *Le Monde diplomatique* (2021) 1, at 12 f.

(see 3.3.C, 4.3.B). We commonly celebrate these doctrines as historic achievements. Their effect is to push aside the generally applicable law (i.e. the Member States' law) when it conflicts with Union law. Since EU law for a long time emanated mainly from executive institutions—the Council and the Commission—and, in most cases, superseded a domestic provision based on a parliamentary statute, it makes for a law of executive privilege. Moreover, the ordinary (i.e. the domestic courts) cannot invalidate Union acts; only the CJEU—a court dedicated to the new centre of power, according to Ipsen's concept—can do so.

It adds to the problem that the Treaties provide little explicit ground for the doctrines. Instead, the latter—including that regarding the CJEU's monopoly—are the CJEU's own creation. And until 2020, the Court's primary argument was functional: these doctrines, the Court stated, find their legal justification in the fact that they are necessary for the effective and uniform implementation of Union policies.[251] In this respect, Union law exhibits the characteristics of a special law of the executive to carry out social transformations.[252]

Ipsen's *Zweckverband funktioneller Integration* represents the most famous legal articulation of this understanding in Germany. Ipsen, Schmitt's academic companion of many years, was an influential man, the doyen of German European law and the honorary chairman of the Association of German Public Law Professors (*Vereinigung der Deutschen Staatsrechtslehrer*).[253] He wrote the major German comprehensive treatise on Community law, where he introduced his concept of the EEC as a 'purposive association of functional integration'.[254] Ernst Haas' neofunctionalism underpinned this thinking (see 2.4.A). Schmitt respected Ipsen's work.[255] More than 20 years later, the Florentine political scientist Giandomenico Majone similarly conceptualized the European Community by reflecting on US regulatory agencies.[256]

For Ipsen, the Community law's remove from democratic processes was its very point; consequently, he argued against its parliamentarization. One can see a Schmittian element in the fact that Community law helps the executives retain dominance over society, thus, on this understanding, ensuring its viability. Ipsen's

[251] CJEU, Case 314/85, *Foto-Frost* (EU:C:1987:452) paras 15 ff. In detail, see P. Pescatore, *Le droit de l'intégration. Emergence d'un phénomène nouveau dans les relations internationales selon l'expérience des Communautés européennes* (2005 [1972]) 78. On the change in 2020, see Lenaerts, 'No Member State Is More Equal Than Others. The Primacy of EU law and the Principle of the Equality of the Member States before the Treaties', 43 *MPIL Research Paper Series* (2020) 37, at 42.

[252] Patel (n. 61) 116–145.

[253] On Ipsen's relationship with Schmitt, see Joerges, 'Europe as a Großraum? Shifting Legal Conceptualisations of the Integration Project', in C. Joerges and N. S. Ghaleigh (eds), *Darker Legacies of Law in Europe. The Shadow of National Socialism and Fascism over Europe and its Legal Traditions* (2003) 182 f.

[254] H. P. Ipsen, *Europäisches Gemeinschaftsrecht* (1972) 196 ff., 1055.

[255] Schmitt, 'The Legal World Revolution (1978)', *Télos* (1987) 73, at 85 f.

[256] Majone, 'The European Community as a Regulatory State', in Academy of European Law (ed.), *Collected Courses of the Academy of European Law, Vol. 5, Book 1* (1996) 321, at 357.

thought, and its success, shows that European public law's structural transformation did run the risk of promoting the executive dominance and providing little democratic input and control. This would certainly not have led to a European democratic society.

However, European politics took a different path. The Treaty legislator constitutionalized and parliamentarized Union law and linked it to European society. Therefore, Ipsen's approach (as well as Majone's) cannot capture the basic principles of today's Union law. Nevertheless, their thinking remains influential.[257] Importantly, the *Bundesverfassungsgericht*'s Second Senate ultimately continues to conceptualize Union law in administrative law categories (see 3.2.C, 3.4.B).

Certain European policies towards Greece, refugees, or university reform demonstrate the persistent dangers of a bureaucratic rule for which hardly anyone takes responsibility.[258] Yet, Union law has become the democratic law of European society (see 3.5) and not the special law of a supreme European regulatory agency.

This is not to deny the existence of a European administrative law, of which the Treaties conceive broadly. Articles 197 and 291 TFEU do not use the narrow concept of *application* but the broader concept of *implementation* to define administrative tasks. Administration thus refers to the implementation of political decisions.[259] Beyond the application of rules in individual cases, this also includes implementing legislation and the performance of services, as well as governance through information, rankings, or best practices. The Research Network on EU Administrative Law (ReNEUAL) model rules on European administrative law contain an entire book each on administrative rule-making, contracts, and administrative information management.

Cassese's *droit tout puissant* encompasses diverse instruments of bureaucratic implementation. All seek to help bureaucracies deal effectively and uniformly with the *administrés* (the administered persons), as an evocative French term calls the citizens.[260] The problem that this attitude bespeaks remains: even if European law has not developed as the law of a supreme regulatory agency, many *administrés* face a vast, possibly alienating complex of Union and state bureaucracies.[261] Aligning

[257] P. L. Lindseth, *Power and Legitimacy. Reconciling Europe and the Nation-State* (2010) 251 ff.; Schorkopf, 'Value Constitutionalism in the European Union', 21 *German Law Journal* (2020) 956, at 957 f.

[258] Ioannidis, 'Debt Restructuring in the Light of Pringle and Gauweiler—Flexibility and Conditionality', in European Central Bank (ed.), *ESCB Legal Conference 2016* (2017) 78; Ziebritzki, 'The Integrated EU Hotspot Administration and the Question of the EU's Liability', in M. Kotzur *et al.* (eds), *The External Dimension of EU Migration and Asylum Policies. Border Management, Human Rights and Development Policies in the Mediterranean Area* (2020) 253.

[259] Pioneering R. Mayntz (ed.), *Implementation politischer Programme. Empirische Forschungsberichte* (1980).

[260] On this concept, see Chrétien (n. 237) paras 16 and 52.

[261] Bovens, Curtin, and 't Hart, 'Studying the Real World of EU Accountability. Framework and Design', in M. A. P. Bovens, D. Curtin, and P. 't Hart (eds), *The Real World of EU Accountability. What Deficit?* (2010) 31.

European administrative law with the principles of Article 2 TEU and reconstructing it in their light continues to be a daunting task.

D. Democratic Administrative Law

A European democratic society needs administrative law to be democratic, too. To that end, administrative law must be parliamentarized. In other words, its legal bases must stem from a democratic majority. But that is not enough for a fully democratic administrative law requires more than its parliamentarization. To understand what else is needed, it helps to inquire into the historical development of the term *administrative law*.

While some authors already consider the special law of eighteenth-century executive authority administrative law,[262] most date its beginning to the nineteenth century. They do so to mark a desirable transformation of the law of executive authority. At the core of this transformation are legal innovations that recognized the administration's counterpart as rights holders.[263] Accordingly, many scholars started reconstructing the special law of executive authority also from the citizens' perspective (*ex parte civium*) and not just from the executive's (*ex parte principis*).

Though eighteenth-century public law scholarship drew on the Enlightenment, it mostly referred to strands that considered a strong executive indispensable to state building (see 2.1.A). In consequence, it typically served the expansion of monarchical authority.[264] As was shown by the French Revolution, this process met with resistance from a new group of actors that Hegel conceptualized as civil society (see 1.2). The successes of these groups were enshrined in new constitutional settlements in France and beyond.

In the nineteenth century, the new term 'administrative law' signalled scholars' efforts to support the implementation of these settlements, to bring them to life in everyday dealings with executive power.[265] Robert von Mohl (1799–1875), a leading German jurist as well as an influential liberal politician, provides a good example. In fact, he became an obligatory reference for the concept of *Rechtstaat*, that is, a state under the rule of law.[266] Mohl conceptualized the legal material as

[262] Leitl-Staudinger, 'Österreich. § 62', in von Bogdandy, Cassese, and Huber, *Handbuch Ius Publicum Europaeum, Bd. IV* (n. 237) 195, paras 1 ff.; Jakab, 'Ungarn. § 67', in von Bogdandy, Cassese, and Huber, *Handbuch Ius Publicum Europaeum, Bd. IV* (n. 237) 365, paras 1 ff.; Wasilewski, 'Polen. § 63', in von Bogdandy, Cassese, and Huber, *Handbuch Ius Publicum Europaeum, Bd. IV* (n. 237) 229, paras 1 ff.

[263] Auby (n. 234) 603.

[264] Stolleis, 'Entwicklungsstufen der Verwaltungsrechtswissenschaft', in W. Hoffmann-Riem, E. Schmidt-Aßmann, and A. Voßkuhle (eds), *Grundlagen des Verwaltungsrechts, Bd. 1* (2006) § 2, paras 18 ff.

[265] In detail, see Santamaría Pastor, 'Spanien. § 66', in von Bogdandy, Cassese, and Huber, *Handbuch Ius Publicum Europaeum, Bd. IV* (n. 237) 323, para. 3; Zacharias, 'Der Begriff des Verwaltungsrechts in Europa. § 72', in von Bogdandy, Cassese, and Huber, *Handbuch Ius Publicum Europaeum, Bd. IV* (n. 237) 541, paras 58 ff.

[266] M. Stolleis, *Public Law in Germany, 1800–1914* (2001).

administrative law instead of *police law* (*Policeyrecht*) in order to herald a progressive development: the transformation of a relationship of pure executive authority into a legal relationship. The administration's counterpart turned from mere subordinate into legal subject, a person. To be a person, a rights holder, is a huge normative achievement. Hegel's philosophy of law highlights its importance. His *Elements of the Philosophy of Right* contains only one outright duty, namely, to 'be a person and respect others as persons'.[267]

Patrice Chrétien even holds that French administrative law only came into being under the liberal constitution of the Third Republic, that is, in 1873. The *Conseil d'État*, which had advised two authoritarian rulers, Napoleon Bonaparte as well as Louis Napoleon, found itself in a crisis of legitimacy after the latter's fall in 1870. Its response was to liberalize its jurisprudence under the guidance of Edouard Laferrière.[268] To this end, it developed legal principles that protected the citizens and gave them legal standing. The CJEU would pursue a similar path 100 years later.[269]

This is not to argue that administrative scholarship focused exclusively on civic emancipation, either in the nineteenth century or today. Otto Mayer, who some remember as the true founding figure of German administrative law, was very supportive of the executive; Reimund Schmidt-De Caluwe, his main biographer, even concludes that his work proposed 'legalizing the police state'.[270] When state building is not yet far advanced, many scholars emphasize the authoritative component of administrative law. Thus, administrative law in Italy in the late nineteenth and early twentieth centuries recognized the subordinate as a legal subject but focused on strengthening authority.[271] Again, this parallels the development of European administrative law: in the conflict between the interests of the citizen concerned and the European institutions, the CJEU gave preference to the latter for a long time.[272]

Administrative law in the nineteenth century was emancipatory inasmuch as it created and fleshed out legal institutions that operationalized the compromises between liberal and authoritarian forces.[273] That remained a plausible programme for the twentieth century, particularly in difficult circumstances. Thus, beginning in the 1950s, accomplished administrative law scholarship developed in Franco's

[267] Hegel, *Elements of the Philosophy of Right* (n. 176) para. 36.

[268] Chrétien (n. 237) paras 13 ff.

[269] Thus, for instance, Jürgen Schwarze considers the general principles of administrative law as the core of the discipline: J. Schwarze, *European Administrative Law* (rev. 1st edn, 2006) CX ff., CXIV ff.

[270] R. Schmidt-De Caluwe, *Der Verwaltungsakt in der Lehre Otto Mayers. Staatstheoretische Grundlagen, dogmatische Ausgestaltung und deren verfassungsbedingte Vergänglichkeit* (1999) 49, 262.

[271] Mattarella, 'Evolution and Gestalt of the Italian State', in von Bogdandy, Huber, and Cassese (n. 5) 329, at 332 ff., esp. at 338 ff.; Fraenkel-Haeberle and Galetta, 'Verwaltungsgerichtsbarkeit in Italien. § 131', in A. von Bogdandy, P. M. Huber, and L. Marcusson (eds), *Handbuch Ius Publicum Europaeum, Bd. VIII. Verwaltungsgerichtsbarkeit in Europa: Institutionen und Verfahren* (2019) 269, at paras 9 ff., 14.

[272] A. Ward, *Judicial Review and the Rights of Private Parties in EC Law* (2000) 318 ff.

[273] Schiera (n. 246) paras 1 ff.

Spain around Eduardo García de Enterría. It reconstructed the few areas of freedom and thereby established the foundations for a democratic administrative law under the 1978 Constitution.[274] In socialist Poland, a remarkable scholarship likewise developed during periods of cautious liberalization;[275] it flourished when the country adopted a democratic constitution in 1992. Summing up, a democratic administrative law is characterized by the fact that it stems from the will of the majority and recognizes the individual whom it addresses.

It is mostly new constitutional law that provides the impetus to democratize administrative law in this twofold sense. This leads to a question that represents the most contested conceptual issue in European public law: has its transformation after 1945 produced a European and, in particular, an EU constitutional law? To me, it has. Indeed, no concept shows the transformation of European public law better than that of EU constitutional law.

5. Constitutional Law without a Constitutional Text

A. The Second Threshold Phase

The development of an EU constitutional law represents the defining achievement of the second period of European law. The transition from the first to the second period is well illustrated by the doctoral thesis of Joseph H. Weiler. Born in South Africa, raised in Israel, and educated in England, Weiler worked at the European University Institute from 1978 to 1985, where he organized the seminal Florence Integration Project Series for Mauro Cappelletti.[276] He later held positions at Michigan, Harvard, and New York universities. His dissertation, which he wrote at the European University Institute, proposed an equilibrium model to explain Community law's success. This work revealed to me like no other Europe's legal transformation during the first period.[277]

Weiler showed how the crisis between Hallstein and de Gaulle (see 2.2.B) triggered a settlement that led to the successes of the next two decades. The crisis abated when the Council agreed, in the famous (or, to some, infamous) Luxembourg compromise of 1966, to refrain from deciding by majority decision.[278] This supposedly

[274] Santamaría Pastor (n. 265) paras 67 ff.

[275] Wróbel, 'Polen. § 47', in von Bogdandy, Cassese, and Huber, *Handbuch Ius Publicum Europaeum, Bd. III* (n. 233) 229, at paras 49 ff.

[276] M. Cappelletti, M. Seccombe, and J. H. H. Weiler (eds), *Integration through Law. Europe and the American Federal Experience* (1985–1988).

[277] Weiler, 'The Community System. The Dual Character of Supranationalism', 1 *Yearbook of European Law* (1981) 267; in monograph form, J. H. H. Weiler, *Il sistema comunitario europeo. Struttura giuridica e processo politico* (1985).

[278] Ziller, 'Defiance for European Influence—The Empty Chair and France', in A. Jakab and D. Kochenov (eds), *The Enforcement of EU Law and Values. Ensuring Member States' Compliance* (2017) 422.

gave rise to a paradox: when considering the EEC, most lawyers saw an autonomous legal order emancipated from international law thanks to its direct effect, primacy, and an authoritative Court of Justice (see 2.2.B, 3.3.C, 4.3.B), and some even saw a proto-federal polity. By contrast, most political scientists saw the EEC as only one of many regulatory international organizations, not least because of the unanimity requirement in the Council. Yet, Weiler maintained that this was not a paradox at all but rather the key to deeper understanding: He argued that unanimity in the Council provided the political backing to autonomize Community law. Thanks to this autonomization, Community law enabled policymakers to pursue entirely new possibilities of regulatory policymaking (see 2.4).

The requirement of political unanimity assured every Member State government that the EEC only pursued policies that it could live with and that the former might, in fact, have a keen interest in the latter's policies. Therefore, all governments had a strong interest in enforcing their arduously negotiated decisions; the community of law (see 2.2.B) provided the instruments for this task. In this configuration, the EEC became the centre of European coordination, shaping many fields of law. Weiler's model makes plausible why the heads of state and government chose the EEC as the central forum for intra-European policy coordination in the early 1970s.[279] This coordination then connected the various legal orders in the manner described by Mosler's concept of European law (see 2.2.C).

Yet, unanimity came at a high—often too high—price, even for the sovereigntist Margaret Thatcher, Britain's prime minister.[280] The Single European Act of 1986 expressed the Member States' common will to overcome the Luxembourg Compromise and to allow majority decisions in the Council in important policy areas. It thus became politically possible to overrule individual Member States. This upset the balance of Weiler's equilibrium model and prompted a new wave of structural transformation, with constitutional issues—in particular, the question of democratic legitimacy—becoming explosive.

The fall of the Iron Curtain in 1989 required a far deeper reorganization of Europe. It resulted in further propelling the ongoing transformation. This was certainly not the only option. It is easy to overlook that very different options were propagated during those years.[281] But, with the blessing of the United States, the Member States eventually agreed on deepening and expanding their union.[282] The

[279] Report by the Foreign Ministers of the Member States on the problems of political unification (Davignon Report), Bull. EC 11-1970, 9.

[280] Of course, the details of the entire story are much more complex. See van Middelaar (n. 99) 73 ff., 100 ff.

[281] G. J. Ikenberry, *After Victory. Institutions, Strategic Restraint, and the Rebuilding of Order after Major Wars* (2001) 215 ff.

[282] In detail, see van Middelaar (n. 99) 181 ff. From the contemporaries' perspective, this was far less clear. One need only recall the famous formulation of 'constitutional chaos'. See Curtin, 'The Constitutional Structure of the Union. A Europe of Bits and Pieces', 30 *Common Market Law Review* (1993) 17, at 67.

Treaty of Maastricht of 1992 represented a momentous step: among many things, it transformed the Community into the Union[283] and opted for a monetary union. In doing so, European politics finally exited the realm of purely low politics. New controversies politicized Europe and helped the European society emerge by processing them. In parallel, the Council of Europe and the ECHR took on new roles that complemented the EU (see 2.6.D, 3.1.C, 3.5.C).

Trust theory helps understand this transition. Hegel had already argued that public institutions are only viable if one can 'trust' that one's 'substantial and particular interest is preserved and contained in the interest and end of an other'.[284] Many considered the generation of such trust the very business of the nation state. Carl Schmitt speaks of the friendship between citizens of a state (see 2.3.C). This is not a proto-fascist idea: For Alexander Somek, too, civic friendship is a key for a democratic community.[285]

Trust beyond the nation state is a fairly recent topic,[286] as is the related question of transnational identity (see 3.2.C). Scholarship distinguishes between *confidence* and *trust*. Not every form of cooperative conduct constitutes an expression of trust. In a political context, one should speak of trust only if someone allows themselves to be vulnerable by voluntarily granting someone else, the trustee, power over their essential interests, such as their life or well-being. This also explains why disappointments often lead to vehement reactions.[287]

The concept of trust illuminates what is new about the second period of European public law. In the first period, European regulatory policies did not require much from European citizens; they demanded their permissive consensus rather than their trust.[288] But this is no longer enough in the second period, as demonstrated by the controversies over the European responses to the financial crisis, the sovereign debt crisis, the refugee crisis, the crisis of the rule of law, and the COVID-19 crisis.[289] This also explains, to some extent, why the CJEU has made protecting mutual trust between all public institutions a core concern in its recent jurisprudence.[290]

[283] Which was a convoluted process. See von Bogdandy and Nettesheim, 'Die Verschmelzung der Europäischen Gemeinschaften in der Europäischen Union', *Neue juristische Wochenschrift* (1995) 2324.

[284] Hegel, *Elements of the Philosophy of Right* (n. 176) para. 268; Volkmann, 'Gespräche mit Hegel', 59 *Der Staat* (2020) 489, at 490.

[285] Somek, 'Postnational European Democracy. Aristotelian Caveats', in H. Krunke, H. Petersen, and I. Manners (eds), *Transnational Solidarity. Concept, Challenges and Opportunities* (2020) 229, esp. at 235–239.

[286] Ruzicka and Keating, 'Going Global. Trust Research and International Relations', 5 *Journal of Trust Research* (2015) 8; Genna, 'Images of Europeans. Transnational Trust and Support for European Integration', 20 *Journal of International Relations and Development* (2017) 358.

[287] Michel, 'Time to Get Emotional. Phronetic Reflections on the Concept of Trust in International Relations', 19 *European Journal of International Relations* (2012) 869, at 870.

[288] Zürn (n. 79) 978 f.

[289] Schorkopf, 'Wertesicherung in der Europäischen Union. Prävention, Quarantäne und Aufsicht als Bausteine eines Rechts der Verfassungskrise?', 51 *Europarecht* (2016) 147, at 156.

[290] *ECHR Accession II* (n. 137) paras 168, 191; *LM* (n. 109) paras 35 ff.; Lenaerts, 'La vie après l'avis. Exploring the Principle of Mutual (Yet Not Blind) Trust', 54 *Common Market Law Review* (2017) 805;

Today, Eurobarometer tracks citizens' trust. The results are sobering. According to Eurobarometer 2019, only 44 per cent of EU citizens trust the EU's institutions. While this is not good, it is not an argument in favour of the nation state since the respondents' average trust in their national government and parliament is, at 34 per cent each, 10 percentage points lower still.[291] Today, people trust the Union more than the average Member State.

Since the 1990s, the controversies on the trustworthiness of European and national institutions have mostly centred on the concepts codified in Article 2 TEU. Most Europeans believe that a trustworthy order must respond to the principles established in that provision: justice, solidarity, human dignity, freedom, democracy, equality, rule of law, and the protection of minorities. Yet, for a period to be considered a threshold phase in Koselleck's sense, it must show proof of conceptual adjustments, not simply novel phenomena. In European public law, the issue was if and how Union primary law should be conceptualized as constitutional law.[292]

This question became profoundly relevant in the early 2000s. Consider the *Humboldt Speeches on Europe*, organized by Ingolf Pernice and, later, by Matthias Ruffert. There, top-tier politicians addressed this question in an attempt to convey their vision for Europe's future.[293] Rarely has legal scholarship orchestrated such a major political debate.

B. The Long March of the Constitutionalist Approach

At first glance, it seems rather easy to reconstruct fundamental norms of European public law as constitutional law. Constitutional approaches to international law have a long and impressive pedigree.[294] Wolfgang Friedmann built on this tradition when he interpreted the EEC Treaty as *international constitutional law* as early as 1964.[295] This is no academic flight of fancy. After all, Hermann Mosler and

E. M. Kullak, *Vertrauen in Europa. Entwicklung und Funktion als Verfassungsgrundsatz des Unionsrechts* (2020) 199 f.

[291] European Commission, *Standard Eurobarometer 91—Public Opinion on the European Union* (Spring 2019) 5. On the robustness of the data, see Bläser, 'Europa im Spiegel der öffentlichen Meinung. Bilanz und Perspektiven des Eurobarometers nach 40 Jahren', 41 *Leviathan* (2013) 351; critically Höpner and Jurczyk, 'Kritik des Eurobarometers. Über die Verwischung der Grenze zwischen seriöser Demoskopie und interessengeleiteter Propaganda', 40 *Leviathan* (2012) 326.

[292] For a protagonist's view, see J.-C. Piris, *Does the European Union Have a Constitution? Does It Need One?* (2001).

[293] I. Pernice (ed.), *Europa-Visionen* (2007); M. Ruffert (ed.), *Europa-Visionen. Perspektiven auf Europa vor, während und nach der Krise* (2019). On the European debate, R. Dehousse, *Une Constitution pour l'Europe?* (2002).

[294] T. Kleinlein, *Konstitutionalisierung im Völkerrecht. Konstruktion und Elemente einer idealistischen Völkerrechtslehre* (2012) esp. at 5 ff.

[295] W. G. Friedmann, *The Changing Structure of International Law* (1964) 153 ff., 158. For a contemporary appraisal of Inter-American law, see M. A. Gómez de la Torre, *Derecho Constitucional Interamericano, Vol. 1* (1964) 225 ff.

Carl Friedrich Ophüls, the legal architects of Adenauer's policy, also interpreted the Treaties using constitutional categories.[296] Indeed, the German federal government, when presenting the EEC Treaty to the *Bundestag*, claimed that it 'brought into being a European entity of constitutional genus'.[297]

In 1981, Eric Stein, a Czech émigré and professor at the University of Michigan, introduced what became the first paradigmatic constitutional understanding of Community law. He reconstructed the CJEU's case law as the *Making of a Transnational Constitution*.[298] His piece was so convincing that the *American Journal of International Law* published hardly any article on the EEC's internal law afterwards. The constitutional terminology was judicially consecrated in 1986, when the CJEU called the EEC Treaty a 'constitutional charter of the Community'.[299]

However, Stein and the Court of Justice operated with a thin concept as it focused mainly on the authority of Community law and the Court of Justice's operation. It described a system of federal execution rather than one of legitimate mediation between interests, values, and ideas. As the continent reorganized in the 1990s, this understanding crumbled. Above all, the expansion of powers in the Maastricht Treaty raised the issue of democratic legitimacy.

The thrust of the conceptual debate changed profoundly. The integrationists had hitherto claimed that the fundamental norms of Community law bore a constitutional quality in order to legitimize it.[300] Now, the defenders of the nation state argued that Community law *lacked* constitutional character to support the primacy of domestic constitutional law, on which all democratic legitimacy was said to rest.

Constitutional law and administrative law are a part of public law, but they have very different foci. In short, administrative law executes public authority, whereas constitutional law constitutes and legitimizes it. In its most audacious form, constitutional law transforms rule into an exercise of self-determination ('We, the People').

There are two versions of this argument. One was articulated by Paul Kirchhof, the rapporteur of the Second Senate's *Maastricht* judgment, which identified the question of European democracy as the core issue of European transformation (see 3.4.B). 'In a democracy', Kirchhof writes, 'the free citizen determines the decisions of the community. Within the community of a nation [*Staatsvolk*], he is equally a ruler and not just a subject.'[301] On this view, a constitution is only conceivable as the

[296] For a historical reconstruction, see Boerger and Rasmussen, 'Transforming European Law. The Establishment of the Constitutional Discourse from 1950 to 1993', 10 *European Constitutional Law Review* (2014) 199, at 201 ff.

[297] Bundestag publication BT-Drucks. 2/3340, 108.

[298] Stein (n. 76). On Stein, see Boerger, 'At the Cradle of Legal Scholarship on the European Union. The Life and Early Work of Eric Stein', 62 *American Journal of Comparative Law* (2014) 859.

[299] *Les Verts v. Parliament* (n. 81) para. 23.

[300] CJEU, Case 6/64, *Costa v. E.N.E.L.*, Opinion of AG Lagrange (EU:C:1964:51) 605.

[301] Kirchhof, 'The European Union of States', in A. von Bogdandy and J. Bast (eds), *Principles of European Constitutional Law* (2011) 735, at 737.

constitution of a state. Ernst-Wolfgang Böckenförde, another justice of the Second Senate who also participated in the decision, presented a famous legal theory on this issue, one that follows the Hegelian and Schmittian tradition (see 3.2.B).[302]

Christoph Möllers has formulated the other, less state-centred version of the argument. He maintains that the concept of a constitution, to respect its emancipatory thrust, must be interpreted in the tradition of the American and French revolutions. Thus, Möllers claims, a constitution does not necessarily require statehood or a *demos*, but it does demand a process of collective self-determination that enables the 'democratic politicisation of law-making through the founding of an entirely new system of government'.[303]

From the vantage point of these two paradigmatic approaches, the concept of European constitutional law seems reductionist or outright ideological. Any claim of a structural transformation towards a European constitutional law would be shallow, futile, or misguided. What is lacking is either a European nation, people, or *demos* (Kirchhof) or an act that could be understood as Europeans' collective self-determination (Möllers).

Both positions find support in the fact that the 2004 Treaty establishing a Constitution for Europe was derailed in 2005. It was replaced by the less ambitious Reform Treaty of Lisbon.[304] Following the will of the heads of state and government, it dispensed with the 'constitutional concept'.[305] The failure of the Constitutional Treaty in 2005 was such a defining experience that political leaders decided to avoid the constitutional question altogether, even in 2020, when they once again discussed Europe's future.[306]

However, that failure does not impede an EU constitutional law for a variety of reasons. The European Council, a gubernative body that lacks any legislative power (Article 15(1) TEU) cannot have the final say over whether the Treaties have a constitutional character.[307] Furthermore, the European Council's opinion on what makes up the 'constitutional concept' is legally flimsy. According to the Presidency's conclusions, the constitutional concept 'consisted in repealing all existing treaties and replacing them by a single text called "Constitution"'.[308] This

302 Böckenförde, 'Die Entstehung des Staates als Vorgang der Säkularisation', in his *Säkularisation und Utopie. Ebracher Studien. Ernst Forsthoff zum 65. Geburtstag* (1967) 75, at 75–94.

303 Möllers, 'Pouvoir Constituant—Constitution—Constitutionalisation', in von Bogdandy and Bast (n. 301) 169, at 171. He has changed his position since then: Möllers, *Die Europäische Union als demokratische Föderation* (n. 119).

304 In detail, see de Búrca, 'General Report', in H. F. Köck and M. M. Karollus (eds), *Vorbereitung der Europäischen Union für die Zukunft. Notwendige Änderungen des Primärrechts nach der Nicht-Ratifizierung des Vertrags über eine Verfassung für Europa* (2008) 385, at 391 ff.

305 European Council of 21/22 June 2007, Presidency Conclusions (11177/1/07 REV 1), Annex I: Mandate for the IGC, para. 1.

306 De la Baume, 'Conference on the Future of Europe: Don't Mention the T Word', *Politico* (21 January 2020); Council of the European Union, Joint Declaration on the Conference on the Future of Europe of 5 March 2021 (6796/21).

307 European Council of 21/22 June 2007, Presidency Conclusions (n. 305) para. 3.

308 Ibid. para. 1; Memorandum of the Federal Government on the Treaty of Lisbon of 13 December 2007, Bundesrat publication BR-Drucks. 928/07, 134.

would mean that neither Germany (whose constitution is named the *Basic Law*) nor Austria, with its more than 100 Federal Constitutional Laws, would have a constitution.[309] Moreover, the European Council has never called into question the CJEU's case law on the matter.[310] Last but not least, legal concepts are autonomous and independent of any official blessing.

But how can we reconstruct EU primary law as EU constitutional law? In my view, the most important argument is that the European Treaty legislator founded the Union, and with it European society, on the basic concepts of democratic constitutionalism. It started with the Treaty of Amsterdam (1997), in particular its Article 6(1) TEU. In 2007, with the Treaty of Lisbon, the Treaty legislator continued along this path, in particular in Article 2 TEU, placing human dignity, freedom, democracy, equality, the rule of law, and respect for human rights (including the rights of persons belonging to minorities) front and centre, together with justice, solidarity, equality between women and men, pluralism, non-discrimination, and tolerance.

This provision does not consist of empty words. Nowadays, many major debates in European society employ these terms, be it regarding the Euro crisis, the migration crisis, the rule-of-law crisis, or the COVID-19 crisis. The basic concepts of democratic constitutionalism always play a central role when it comes to determining the best response to these crises. The fact that their meaning for the issue at stake is disputed only emphasizes their importance as these controversies help constitute and integrate European society.

This constitutionalist reading relies on the positivization of constitutional principles and their relevance for European controversies, but not exclusively. It can also point to structural aspects. Thus, the Union's primary law establishes public authority; institutes a hierarchy of norms and legitimizes legal acts; creates a citizenry; grants actionable fundamental rights; and regulates the relationship between legal orders, between public authority and the economy as well as between law and politics.[311] In short, it establishes a system of mediation, which is the core function of a constitution in a Hegelian tradition.[312]

The political processes related to the Amsterdam and Lisbon Treaties do not meet all expectations of democratic self-determination. But neither does the US Constitution, some of whose founding fathers were slave owners, nor the Basic Law of the Federal Republic, which was not even sovereign at the time. Indeed, most constitutions probably fail the test of self-determination, if strictly applied.

[309] Wiederin, 'Österreich. § 7', in A. von Bogdandy, P. Cruz Villalón, and P. M. Huber (eds), *Handbuch Ius Publicum Europaeum, Bd. I. Grundlagen und Grundzüge staatlichen Verfassungsrechts* (2007) 389, paras 44 f.

[310] Dougan, 'The Treaty of Lisbon 2007. Winning Minds, Not Hearts', 45 *Common Market Law Review* (2008) 617, at 698.

[311] Comparatively, see Frankenberg, 'The Return of the Contract. Problems and Pitfalls of European Constitutionalism', 6 *European Law Journal* (2000) 257.

[312] Hegel, *Elements of the Philosophy of Right* (n. 176) para. 302.

Not least the political mobilization in the European constitutional process between 2001 and 2009 has probably been greater than the mobilization in most of the EU Member States' processes of constitutional framing or amendment.

Crises sometimes help advance the essential. In the crises of the 2010s, the CJEU's jurisprudence—including decisions such as Opinion 2/13[313], *Associação Sindical dos Juízes Portugueses* (*ASJP*),[314] *Achmea*,[315] *LM*,[316] *Commission/Poland*,[317] *Wightman*,[318] and *CETA*[319]—gave the project of constitutional reconstruction a tremendous boost. The CJEU now also conceptualizes the EU as a Union of values, not least in order to defend its foundations against authoritarian developments.[320] Today, the substance of Article 2 TEU goes far beyond constitutional aesthetics[321] or empty pathos.[322]

This jurisprudence added a genuinely constitutional logic to the previous functional logic of Union law, that is, the logic of practical effectiveness (*effet utile*), of which the doctrines of direct effect and of the primacy of EU law are the most famous examples. More than anything else, these two doctrines embodied, for a long time, what is specific about Union law.[323] Today, these doctrines are reconsidered in the light of the constitutional principle of equality—both of Union citizens and of the Member States.[324]

In the second period of European public law, the debates concerning European society are framed in constitutional categories more and more often. One of the most prominent European journals today is the *European Constitutional Law Review*, which is headquartered in the Netherlands and published in England. Spanish scholars run the *Revista de derecho constitucional europeo*, and all constitutional law journals I know feature a wealth of articles on EU primary law. Correspondingly, the outright opposition to a constitutional reconstruction of Union primary law is fading. Regardless of how the various positions re-emerge (albeit transformed), the new discursive field is now shaped by constitutional concepts.

313 *ECHR Accession II* (n. 137) para. 168.

314 CJEU, Case C-64/16, *Associação Sindical dos Juízes Portugueses* (EU:C:2018:117) paras 30–32.

315 CJEU, Case C-284/16, *Achmea* (EU:C:2018:158) para. 34.

316 *LM* (n. 109) paras 35, 48, 50.

317 CJEU, Case C-619/18, *Commission v. Poland* (EU:C:2019:531) paras 42, 47.

318 CJEU, Case C-621/18, *Wightman* (EU:C:2018:999) paras 62 f.

319 CJEU, Opinion 1/17, *CETA* (EU:C:2019:341) para. 110.

320 Martín y Pérez de Nanclares, 'La Unión Europea como comunidad de valores. A vueltas con la crisis de la democracia y del Estado de Derecho', 43 *Teoría y Realidad Constitucional* (2019) 121, at 126 f.

321 Weiler, 'On the Power of the Word. Europe's Constitutional Iconography', 3 *International Journal of Constitutional Law* (2005) 173.

322 Haltern, 'Pathos and Patina. The Failure and Promise of Constitutionalism in the European Imagination', 9 *European Law Journal* (2003) 14.

323 Pescatore (n. 251) 84 ff.; in greater detail, see 3.3.C, 4.3.B.

324 Lenaerts, Gutiérrez Fons, and Adam, 'Exploring the Autonomy of the European Legal Order', 81 *Zeitschrift für ausländisches öffentliches Recht und Völkerrecht* (2021) 47.

Any constitutional approach should reconstruct primary law as a framework for politics, systematize it in light of constitutional theories and doctrines, explore its legitimatory foundations, mediate between social and legal discourses, and strive for a corresponding disciplinary self-understanding.[325] The constitutional approach allows for different perspectives, corresponding to the different views that circulate in European society. In doing so, it should help European society articulate the different positions, resolve its controversies, and adopt legitimate decisions.

Hegel's theory supports this approach. It presents a constitution as an evolutionary achievement, as opposed to a voluntaristic act.[326] It accords little significance to concepts such as constituent power or founding moments. Instead, it stresses historical processes and embedded practices, like most institutionalist theories. This helps us understand the constitutionalization of many European practices that only became part of primary law once they had proven successful: the European Council, the understanding of the Assembly as a parliament, the expansion into many policy fields, fundamental rights, the primacy of EU law, and the fusion of different organizations in one single Union.

At the same time, the European constitutionalizing process appears incomplete, not least because of the Constitutional Treaty's failure. This important feature can be illustrated by speaking only of constitutional law and not of a European constitution. Thus, while the CJEU speaks of constitutional principles, the concept of a 'constitutional legislator' only appears in an Opinion by a strongly federalist Advocate General[327] and in a few decisions of the General Court.[328] Currently, the neutral term *auteurs des traités* or *du traité* (*authors of the Treaties* or *Treaty*) prevails.[329] However, the German version of some Advocate Generals' opinions features the evocative collective singular *Vertragsgesetzgeber*, *Treaty legislator*, to refer to the united political systems in their constituent role under Articles 48 and 54 TEU.[330] As this collective singular fits well with the collective singular of European society, I will use it throughout this study.

[325] T. Giegerich, *Europäische Verfassung und deutsche Verfassung im transnationalen Konstitutionalisierungsprozeß. Wechselseitige Rezeption, konstitutionelle Evolution und föderale Verflechtung* (2003); R. Schütze, *European Constitutional Law* (2nd edn, 2016); A. Rosas and L. Armati (eds), *EU Constitutional Law. An Introduction* (3rd edn, 2018); S. Besson, *Droit constitutionnel européen. Précis de droit et résumés de jurisprudence* (2019); Y. Gómez Sánchez and C. Elías Méndez, *Derecho constitucional europeo* (2019).

[326] Hegel, *Elements of the Philosophy of Right* (n. 176) para. 271. On the many flaws of Hegel's concept of the constitution, see Bobbio, 'La costituzione in Hegel', in N. Bobbio (ed.), *Studi hegeliani* (1981) 69.

[327] CJEU, Case 34/86, *Council v. Parliament*, Opinion of AG Mancini (EU:C:1986:221) 2161.

[328] CJEU, Joint Cases T-172/98 and T-175/98 to T-177/98, *Salamander and others v. Parliament and Council* (EU:T:2000:168) para. 75 ('founding authority of the Community'; in German: '*Verfassungsgeber der Gemeinschaft*'); Case T-561/14, *One of Us and others v. Commission* (EU:T:2018:210) paras 113 ff. ('founding authority'; in German: '*verfassungsgebende Gewalt*').

[329] CJEU, Case C-583/11, *Inuit Tapiriit Kanatami and others v. Parliament and Council* (EU:C:2013:625) para. 70.

[330] CJEU, Case C-224/98, *D'Hoop*, Opinion of AG Geelhoed, (EU:C:2002:103) para. 28; Case C-583/11, *Inuit Tapiriit Kanatami and others v. Parliament and Council*, Opinion of AG Kokott (EU:C:2013:21) paras 111 f.

C. On the Purview of Primacy

Article 2 TEU sets out the foundations of European public law, much like Article 1 of the Italian Constitution or Articles 1 and 20 of the German Basic Law for their legal orders. This suggests that its standards have primacy over all other law, and this primacy implies a structural transformation.

Until the mid-twentieth century, most European states' constitutions were documents of political rather than strictly legal importance.[331] Only in its second half did the primacy of constitutional law slowly develop as a general feature. The explicit hierarchical subordination of legislation to the constitution, the advent of constitutional adjudication (see 4.1.A), and the strengthening of rights (see 4.3.C) were crucial to this evolution. Fundamental and human rights can become relevant in countless social conflicts. Applying the former to the latter allows constitutionalizing and thus transforming the meaning of statutes, regulations, customary law, and case law.[332] Further elements consisted in conceptualizing constitutional principles as societal values and promoting a constitutionally based ethos among not only lawyers and public officials but also citizens (see 3.1.D).

The latter element corresponds to a central demand of modern constitutionalism. Already in 1791, Talleyrand (see 2.1.B), still a progressive at the time, was demanding that the people learn about the constitution in order to anchor the Republic in the hearts of all citizens.[333] Hegel similarly wrote on political sentiment and patriotism as elementary normative attitudes.[334] In 1970, the political scientist Dolf Sternberger coined the term 'constitutional patriotism', which Jürgen Habermas then popularized.[335]

There are significant differences between the EU Member States' constitutionalization processes (see 4.1.B). Nevertheless, all Member State legal orders have developed in this way, not least thanks to Europeanization (see 4.2). In fact, Article 4(2) TEU only makes sense with this commonality for it reflects domestic constitutional law's substantive role in expressing the Member States' identity.

331 For Germany, see Wahl, 'Der Vorrang der Verfassung', 20 *Der Staat* (1981) 485, esp. at 502 ff.

332 G. F. Schuppert and C. Bumke, *Die Konstitutionalisierung der Rechtsordnung. Überlegungen zum Verhältnis von verfassungsrechtlicher Ausstrahlungswirkung und Eigenständigkeit des 'einfachen' Rechts* (2000).

333 Heuschling, 'Frankreich. § 28', in A. von Bogdandy, P. Cruz Villalón, and P. M. Huber (eds), *Handbuch Ius Publicum Europaeum, Bd. II. Offene Staatlichkeit—Wissenschaft vom Verfassungsrecht* (2008) 491, at para. 4.

334 Hegel, *Elements of the Philosophy of Right* (n. 176) para. 268.

335 D. Sternberger, *Verfassungspatriotismus* (1990) esp. at 17 ff., 24, 30 f.; Habermas, 'Historical Consciousness and Post-Traditional Identity: Remarks on the Federal Republic's Orientation to the West', 31 *Acta Sociologica* (1988) 3, at 9; for the EU, see Weiler, 'Federalism without Constitutionalism. Europe's Sonderweg', in K. Nicolaïdis and R. Howse (eds), *The Federal Vision. Legitimacy and Levels of Governance in the United States and the European Union* (2001) 54, at 63.

Article 2 TEU is indebted to this school of thought as well. It joins the constitutional standards meant to form European society.[336] Kris Grimonprez shows how this provision can be the vanishing point of European society's democratic education.[337] For that reason, Article 2 TEU's standards undergird Europe's transformative constitutionalism.

6. Transformative Constitutionalism

Many citizens believe—albeit for different, even contradictory, reasons—that neither European law nor European society fully meet the ideal of a democratic society in accordance with the standards of Article 2 TEU. The debate about where the deficits lie and how to address them constitutes an essential element of European society. European law provides a framework for it, but it can also be a force of change (see 1.4). Its most combative form is transformative constitutionalism.

European law has always been a transformative force. For a long time, the transformation was thought to consist of harmonization and centralization. This understanding is no longer timely and should be replaced by one centred on Article 2 TEU (see 2.6.A). On this view, European law can use transformative constitutionalism to tackle what is perhaps Europe's most serious problem: Member States that endanger European society's democratic character (see 2.6.B). To explain what that might mean, I present Latin American transformative constitutionalism (see 2.6.C). On that basis, I reflect on the European path of the past three decades as well as on options for the future (see 2.6.D).

A. Democratic Society Instead of *Ever Closer Union*

The language of the European Treaties is dry. But there is one motto that has shaped the European project's public imagination: the 'ever closer union'.[338] Its transformational impetus is tremendous. The idea already informed Article 1 of the Statute of the Council of Europe, which, since 1949, mandates the latter, albeit timidly, 'to achieve greater unity between its members'. The EEC's formula then caught Europe's imagination and turned into a true motto: since 1957, the Member States avow, in the first recital of the Preamble to the EEC Treaty (now the TFEU Treaty), that they are 'determined to lay the foundations of an ever closer union among the peoples of Europe'. This transformational impetus has borne fruit: 27

[336] P. Ridola, *Diritto comparato e diritto costituzionale europeo* (2010) 8 ff; C. Pinelli, *Alla ricerca dell'autenticità perduta. Identità e differenze nei discorsi e nei progetti di Europa* (2017) 40.

[337] K. Grimonprez, *The European Union and Education for Democratic Citizenship. Legal Foundations for EU Learning at School* (2020) esp. at 339 ff.

[338] On the distinction between *union* and *Union*, see 2.2.D.

Member States, many of which defined themselves for centuries by their mutual antipathies,[339] now consider themselves part of one society, as they proclaim in Article 2 TEU (see 1.2).

The 1957 declaration is alive and not an outdated relic. In 1992, the EU Treaty even reinforced the objective first spelled out in 1957. Its preamble expresses the resolution to 'mark a new stage in the process of European integration' and to 'continue the process of creating an ever closer union among the peoples of Europe'. Moreover, that Treaty introduced the 'ever closer union' as a legal objective in the operative part of the Treaties in Article 1 (2) TEU. In the turmoil of the European debt crisis, the plenary of the CJEU stressed this by stating that 'the implementation of the process of integration […] is the raison d'être of the EU itself'.[340] Of course, some argue that there has been enough of becoming 'ever closer'.[341] The United Kingdom even wanted to remove these words from the Treaties.[342] Yet, the British government failed to get its way and subsequently left the union.

For a long time, the ever closer union was understood as ever more unification and centralization. Hallstein presented the EEC as the path to a European federal state.[343] The bicycle metaphor, according to which the Union falls over if it does not move forward, expresses this understanding of 'ever closer' particularly well.[344] 'European law', Matthias Ruffert wrote in 2015, 'has always been the law designed to deepen […] European integration.'[345]

This understanding of the transformative thrust is no longer convincing. It cannot explain important legal innovations that counteract ever further unification and centralization, such as the subsidiarity principle, the protection of a Member State's national identity, the fortified limits on the Union's competences (Articles 4 and 5 TEU), and the possibility of withdrawal (Article 50 TEU). Moreover, European law also contains domestic law (see 2.2.C), which is even more explicit when it comes to limiting harmonization and defending a Member State's national identity (see 3.2.C). Today, public debates often focus on whether addressing a societal problem requires more or less 'Europe'. Sometimes, such questions can

[339] Deutsch, 'The Growth of Nations. Some Recurrent Patterns of Political and Social Integration', 5 *World Politics* (1953) 168.

[340] *ECHR Accession II* (n. 137) para. 172. Classen, 'Unionsrecht als Integrationsrecht verstehen! Zu Selbstverständnis und Perspektiven der Europarechtswissenschaft', 68 *Jahrbuch des öffentlichen Rechts* (2020) 489.

[341] Charlemagne (n. 110); Klein, 'Integration und Verfassung', 139 *Archiv des öffentlichen Rechts* (2014) 165, at 192 f.

[342] Miller, '"Ever Closer Union" in the EU Treaties and Court of Justice Case Law', *House of Commons Briefing Papers* (2015) 1, at 13 ff.; Cameron and Ross, 'David Cameron: the EU Is Not Working and We Will Change It', *The Telegraph* (15 March 2014).

[343] Hallstein, *Die Europäische Gemeinschaft* (n. 75) 36.

[344] On Hallstein's stance, see Hallstein, 'Mitten auf dem Weg zur Einheit Europas. Zum zehnten Jahrestag der Unterzeichnung des EWG-Vertrags in Rom am 25. März 1957', 22 *Europa-Archiv* (1967) 195.

[345] M. Ruffert, *Europäische Währungspolitik als Herausforderung für das Recht* (2015) 37.

decide a Member State's elections.[346] More versus less 'Europe' has hardened into a political cleavage as important as the old right versus left cleavage.

The core purpose of European law should not lie on one side of that cleavage. There is a lively debate over alternative understandings of the ever closer union.[347] I have suggested that the concept of a European legal space might provide such an understanding.[348] In this book, I go a step further and posit the standards of Article 2 TEU as the purpose of European law. These standards are crucial to what the ever closer union is about (see 3.1.C). The union is ever closer when it is *ever more perfect* in complying with its principles.

B. The Emergence of a New Concept

The Constitution of the United States of America has been aiming for a 'more perfect Union' since 1789. In the 1950s, it became clear even to the Supreme Court Justices that this required addressing, and eventually overcoming, undemocratic social structures. The US Supreme Court's *Brown v. Board of Education* decision showed the country, and the world, that apex courts can play a role in this process. It addressed the most serious deficiency in US society: racially motivated discrimination against citizens.[349] *Brown v. Board of Education* became the most famous transformative decision in legal history and perhaps the most celebrated of all judicial decisions worldwide.

Brown v. Board of Education and the ensuing case law inspired what would emerge as transformative constitutionalism in Latin America a generation later: many of its protagonists had studied the US Rights Revolution.[350] Because it is evident that systemic racial discrimination persists in the United States, it is clear to all that judgments alone cannot transform society. But they can contribute to such transformation.[351] In other words, courts can transcend their customary role of settling individual cases and stabilizing the *status quo*. *Brown v. Board of Education* highlights that the law, with its many actors and institutions, can play its own role in social transformations, notwithstanding its limits, paradoxes, and failures.

[346] Dawson and de Witte (n. 85) 207.

[347] For the German debate, see Haltern, 'On Finality', in von Bogdandy and Bast (n. 301) 205; S. Kadelbach (ed.), *Die Europäische Union am Scheideweg. Mehr oder weniger Europa?* (2015); G. Kirchhof, H. E. Kube, and R. Schmidt (eds), *Von Ursprung und Ziel der Europäischen Union. Elf Perspektiven* (2016).

[348] See n. 97.

[349] USSC, *Brown v. Board of Education*, 347 U.S. 483 (1954); Seigenthaler, 'Brown v. Board of Education: Making a More Perfect Union', 34 *Stetson Law Review* (2005) 457.

[350] Y. Dezalay and B. G. Garth, *The Internationalization of Palace Wars. Lawyers, Economists and the Contest to Transform Latin American States* (2002) 110 ff.

[351] S. Moyn, *Not Enough. Human Rights in an Unequal World* (2018) esp. at 173 ff.; S. Levitsky and D. Ziblatt, *How Democracies Die* (2019) 251 ff.

The US Constitution is not alone in its transformative thrust. Many constitutions aim for democratic transformation far more explicitly. The Mexican Constitution of 1917 and the Weimar Constitution of 1919 were pioneering in that regard.[352] They clearly aimed to transform not only public authority but also society as a whole. Today, many constitutions articulate such ambitious objectives.

Yet, transformative constitutionalism involves far more than demanding objectives. It requires, above all, a legal practice that embeds the law in society. Such a legal practice, and with it the concept of transformative constitutionalism, only emerged in the 1990s, when Soviet socialism was failing, human rights discourse was flourishing, and constitutional jurisdiction was gaining strength as a global phenomenon. The Washington consensus on economic policy, as well as the United States' hegemony during those years, played a role, too.[353]

Transformative constitutionalism blazed a trail in the Global South. The jurisprudence of the Colombian Constitutional Court and the South African Constitutional Court, established in 1991 and 1993, respectively, is iconic in this respect.[354] Both courts opted for novel ways of constitutional interpretation to address massive systemic deficiencies. In Colombia, these deficiencies resulted from civil war and organized crime; in South Africa, their cause lay in apartheid.

Karl Klare, an exponent of US critical legal studies, coined the term 'transformative constitutionalism' for the Constitutional Court of South Africa's jurisprudence. Klare defines it as a long-term process of drafting, interpreting, and enforcing a constitution in order to transform political and social institutions and power relations so as to make them more democratic, inclusive, and equal.[355] Thus, a great concept was born.

What are the politics of this concept? Klare portrays South African transformative constitutionalism as a decidedly post-liberal law.[356] By contrast, the South African constitutional scholar Theunis Roux contends that the South African constitution aligns with liberal constitutionalism from the Global North.[357] Roux's understanding finds support in Latin America, where a similar phenomenon is called *neo-constitucionalismo*. Essentially, it seeks to realize a truly democratic

[352] Grote, 'The Mexican Constitution of 1917: An Early Example of Radical Transformative Constitutionalism', in A. von Bogdandy *et al.* (eds), *Transformative Constitutionalism in Latin America. The Emergence of a New Ius Commune* (2017) 149; R. Voigt (ed.), *Aufbruch zur Demokratie. Die Weimarer Reichsverfassung als Bauplan für eine demokratische Republik* (2020).

[353] Kahn, 'Speaking Law to Power. Popular Sovereignty, Human Rights, and the New International Order', 1 *Chicago Journal of International Law* (2000) 1.

[354] D. Bonilla Maldonado, *Constitutionalism of the Global South. The Activist Tribunals of India, South Africa, and Colombia* (2013).

[355] Klare, 'Legal Culture and Transformative Constitutionalism', 14 *South African Journal on Human Rights* (1998) 146, at 150.

[356] Ibid. 150 ff.

[357] Roux, 'Transformative Constitutionalism and the Best Interpretation of the South African Constitution. Distinction without a Difference?', 20 *Stellenbosch Law Review* (2009) 258; Roux, 'A Brief Response to Professor Baxi', in O. Vilhena Vieira, B. Upendra, and F. Viljoen (eds), *Transformative Constitutionalism: Comparing the Apex Courts of Brazil, India and South Africa* (2013) 48, at 51.

society despite difficult circumstances.[358] Following this line of thought, I conceptualize strategies to realize Article 2 TEU in systemically deficient European contexts as transformative constitutionalism.

How does this fit a Hegelian approach? Hegel was profoundly sceptical of the idea that a new constitution could revolutionize society.[359] At the same time, however, he recognized the transformative potential of a new constitution.[360] Again, Hegel laid the groundwork for very different paths.[361]

This study pursues a trail that the liberal Hegel school blazed in the German *Vormärz* period (1815–1848), which includes Eduard Gans (see 5.2.B), Rudolf Haym, and Lorenz von Stein. This school contributed much to the German Constitution of 1849, a milestone of progressive constitutionalism.[362] Since that constitution failed, the school shared its fate. For decades, the works of liberal Hegelianism sat in libraries gathering dust, with right- and left-wing Hegelianism,[363] as well as constitutional positivism, calling the shots.

But then, from the end of the nineteenth century onwards, a group of Americans sought to tackle the crises of US society. To do so, they advocated liberating US public law from the eighteenth-century constitutional concepts that had characterized it up until then. They dusted off the works of the liberal Hegel school and updated its mediations between individual rights and general welfare, society and state, and law and morality. John Dewey, Frank Goodnow, and many others[364] democratized these mediations and rejuvenated them with the vitality of American society. Their thinking led to American pragmatism, the New Deal, and the beginnings of a democratic welfare state. It also informed critical legal studies.[365]

For European public law, engaging with pragmatism and progressive US constitutional law means reappropriating the liberal Hegelian school. Jürgen Habermas personifies the return of this reformed Hegelianism to Europe.[366] This thinking

358 Comanducci, 'Formas de (neo) constitucionalismo. Un análisis metateórico', in M. Carbonell Sánchez (ed.), *Neoconstitucionalismo(s)* (2003) 75; on the various meanings, see Klug, 'Transformative Constitutionalism as a Model for Africa?', in P. Dann, M. Riegner, and M. Bönnemann (eds), *The Global South and Comparative Constitutional Law* (2020) 141.

359 Hegel, *Elements of the Philosophy of Right* (n. 176) para. 273; following this path, see K. Marx, *Critique of Hegel's 'Philosophy of Right'* (1970 [1843/1844]) 112; K. Marx, *On the Jewish Question* (2019 [1844]).

360 Hegel, 'On the English Reform Bill (1831)' in L. Dickey and H. Nisbet (eds), *Hegel: Political Writings* (1999) 234–279.

361 See, e.g. H. Ottmann, *Individuum und Gemeinschaft bei Hegel. Bd I. Hegel im Spiegel der Interpretationen* (1977).

362 Stolleis, *Public Law in Germany, 1800–1914* (n. 266) 248 ff.

363 K. Löwith, *Von Hegel zu Nietzsche. Der revolutionäre Bruch im Denken des neunzehnten Jahrhunderts* (1995) 65 ff.; H. Kiesewetter, *Von Hegel zu Hitler. Die politische Verwirklichung einer totalitären Machtstaatstheorie in Deutschland (1815–1945)* (1995) 135 ff.

364 B. Emerson, *The Public's Law. Origins and Architecture of Progressive Democracy* (2019).

365 Kennedy, 'The Structure of Blackstone's Commentaries', 28 *Buffalo Law Review* (1979) 205, at 210; P. Hamburger, *Is Administrative Law Unlawful?* (2014); E. Schmidt-Aßmann, *Das Verwaltungsrecht der Vereinigten Staaten von Amerika. Grundlagen und Grundzüge aus deutscher Sicht* (2021) 51 ff.

366 J. Habermas, *The Theory of Communicative Action* (2007 [1981]); J. Habermas, *Between Facts and Norms: Contributions to a Discourse Theory of Law and Democracy* (2008 [1992]).

became a true force, shaping domestic and European public opinion on major domestic, European, and international questions. It allows for optimism. My interpretation of Hegel, concluded in 1986 in the shadow of the Berlin Wall, instilled in me the confidence that this wall would fall.[367]

Transformative constitutionalism is not a philosophy of history, nor does it represent a theory of modernization (see 1.4). It is a legal concept to interpret and apply constitutional rules with the objective of contributing to social transformation. We can distinguish two understandings. The first, which is less demanding, finds transformative constitutionalism in any constitutional jurisprudence that promotes democratic transformations (see 2.3.B).[368] The second combines the first with the attempt to address systemic deficiencies, although these deficits need not have the magnitude of racial discrimination in the United States, South African apartheid, or the Colombian state's collapse. Because it is more instructive, I use the more demanding (i.e. narrower) understanding.

Transformative constitutionalism seeks to remedy systemic deficiencies. When it comes to European society, I primarily see such deficiencies in certain Member States, be it because of weak public institutions or defects in their democracy. While the current circumstances are not comparable to the situation of many African American citizens in the United States, South African apartheid, or precarious statehood in Colombia, they do pose a threat to European society (see 2.6.D, 3.6, 4.6). The Latin American experience helps operationalize transformative constitutionalism in European society.

C. Latin American Innovations

Some scholars perceive Europe as being Latin Americanized.[369] This is not the subject of my reflections, which focus on Latin American constitutional innovations (synthesized as transformative constitutionalism) in dealing with systemic deficiencies. In doing so, I hope to illuminate how the CJEU and the ECtHR, the EU Commission and the Venice Commission, activists and legal scholars, and national courts and ombudspersons counteract systemic deficiencies in European society, such as those under the Polish Prawo i Sprawiedliwość (PiS, *Law and Justice*) government.

The Latin American experience is instructive because it, too, uses a common law and common institutions to address systemic deficiencies. Though there is

[367] A. von Bogdandy, *Hegels Theorie des Gesetzes* (1989) 250.

[368] Hailbronner, 'Transformative Constitutionalism. Not Only in the Global South', 65 *American Journal of Comparative Law* (2017) 527.

[369] A. Tausch, *The City on the Hill? The Latin Americanization of Europe and the Lost Competition with the U.S.A.* (2007); Fotopoulos, 'The Latin-Americanization of Greece and the Lessons for the European South', 6 *International Journal of Inclusive Democracy* (2010) 1.

no regional organization like the European Union to provide political unity,[370] there are regional processes that advance constitutional principles. Thus, Latin American transformative constitutionalism operates at two levels: the state and the regional level.

Two institutions stand out at the regional level: the Inter-American Commission and the Inter-American Court of Human Rights (IACtHR).[371] Furthermore, there is a horizontal network of transformative domestic institutions—particularly courts, ombudspersons, public prosecutors' offices, and dedicated bureaucracies—as well as grassroots and non-governmental organizations, all of which generate much of the system's dynamics. These institutions and groups turn transformative constitutionalism into a social practice far beyond the black letter of legal sources. The following discussion will focus on the Inter-American Court's groundbreaking contribution.

The Court's legal basis is the American Convention on Human Rights of 1969, which has been in force since 1978. The Convention did not intend to bring about transformative constitutionalism.[372] Less than half of the 11 initial Convention States had democratically elected governments, and none expected the Convention to have much effect. This seems paradoxical, but we must bear in mind that the Convention was mostly a symbolic gesture against the Cuban Revolution. The governments probably assumed that it would be just as ineffective as the European Convention on Human Rights of that time, which served as its model.[373]

However, the Court found its role by interpreting the Convention as a means to accompany the Latin American democratization that started in the early 1980s. This democratization rested on monumental political decisions, much like the Central and Eastern European one a decade later. For Latin America, the 1980s were a threshold phase, a critical juncture, comparable to that in Europe after the fall of the Iron Curtain.

Latin America has a tradition of constitutionalism that reaches back to the early nineteenth century. For a long time, however, fundamental rights played a largely decorative role. That changed profoundly because of government oppression in the 1970s. Claiming rights became a tool of resistance, which means that they gained political clout and social traction. The titles of reports on that oppression read 'Nunca más'. 'Never again' to allow grave human rights violations became a

[370] On this issue, see the contributions by A. Alegrett Salazar, A. D. de Klor, J. E. Durán Lima, T. Fischer, R. Grote, A. Fuentes Hernández, E. I. Highton, A. Malamud, H. G. Preusse and R. Vigil Toledo, in A. von Bogdandy, C. Landa Arroyo, and M. Morales Antoniazzi (eds), *Integración suramericana a través del derecho? Un análisis interdisciplinario y multifocal* (2009).

[371] Uprimny, 'Las transformaciones constitucionales recientes en América Latina: Tendencias y desafíos', in C. A. Rodríguez-Garavito (ed.), *El derecho en América Latina. Un mapa para el pensamiento jurídico del siglo XXI* (2011) 109, at 114.

[372] In that respect, it is similar to the CJEU, the ECtHR, and many constitutional courts; see 4.1, 4.3.

[373] See in detail X. Soley Echeverría, *The Transformation of the Americas. The Rise of Human Rights and the Inter-American System* (2020) ch. 1 C., ch. 2 A.3.; Ragone, 'The Inter-American System of Human Rights. Essential Features', in von Bogdandy *et al.* (n. 352) 279, at 281 ff.

lodestar of constitutional reform and practice.[374] In the transition to democracy, the concepts wrought in the experience of oppression articulated transformative necessities. Human rights and democratization became intimately intertwined, and courts started to address structural problems accordingly.

Such court cases were part of a broad process of constitutional reform. We may recall the new constitution of Brazil, in 1988, or the Colombian one of 1991, which gave rise to the most visible transformative constitutional jurisprudence in the region. Like many of the other new or amended constitutions, the two were designed to overcome a dark legacy, including that of repressive law. Both constitutions contain comprehensive fundamental rights catalogues and improve the citizens' democratic participation. In addition, they strengthen independent institutions, above all the courts.[375]

These reforms reflected a new understanding of law. Before the 1980s, many people in the region believed that the law primarily served to consolidate the elite's power and prevent social change.[376] After 1980, many started to recognize its potential for *supporting* social transformation, that is, for effectively guaranteeing rights in daily life and strengthening democratic participation.[377] The Colombian President César Gaviria's opening speech at the Constituent Assembly in 1991 stressed the law's (i.e. the lawyers') responsibility for the country's transition to a democratic society.[378] This implied a new professional self-understanding, new doctrines, and new techniques of legal reasoning.[379] Traditional legal formalism was considered a major obstacle, which explains the enthusiasm with which Robert Alexy's work was received.[380] His formalization of the principle of proportionality offered a way for formalistic legal culture to become more socially responsive.

This transformative thrust could have remained a phenomenon of domestic constitutional law, as it did in South Africa. However, it became a regional phenomenon for the new or reformed Latin American constitutions opted to incorporate human rights. The ensuing doctrine of the constitutional bloc ('*bloque de constitucionalidad*') links national constitutions with the American Convention

[374] Soley Echeverría (n. 373) ch. 2 B., ch. 4. The most famous report is probably by the Comisión Nacional sobre la Desaparición de Personas, *Nunca más: Informe Final de la Comisión Nacional sobre la Desaparición de Personas* (1984).

[375] C. Rodríguez-Garavito and D. Rodríguez-Franco, *Radical Deprivation on Trial. The Impact of Judicial Activism on Socioeconomic Rights in the Global South* (2015) 5, 12.

[376] E. Novoa Monreal, *El derecho como obstáculo al cambio social* (1975).

[377] Uprimny (n. 371).

[378] C. Gaviria Trujillo, 'Informe al Congreso' (1 December 1991) quoted in M. J. Cepeda Espinosa, *Introducción a la constitución de 1991. Hacia un nuevo constitucionalismo* (1993) 335.

[379] C. S. Nino, *Fundamentos de derecho constitucional. Análisis filosófico, jurídico y politológico de la práctica constitucional* (1992); Couso, 'The Transformation of Constitutional Discourse and the Judicialization of Politics in Latin America', in J. A. Couso, A. Huneeus, and R. Sieder (eds), *Cultures of Legality. Judicialization and Political Activism in Latin America* (2010) 141, at 152 ff.

[380] R. Alexy, *A Theory of Constitutional Rights* (2002); R. Alexy, *A Theory of Legal Argumentation: the Theory of Rational Discourse as Theory of Legal Justification* (1989).

on Human Rights.[381] On this basis, the domestic constitution mandates the Inter-American System of Human Rights to participate in the transformation towards a democratic society.[382]

Latin American transformative constitutionalism is the joint product of national constitutional law and international human rights. This multilevel constitutionalism formalizes a key experience gleaned from repressive times: as Keck and Sikkink observed in Argentina, Chile, and Mexico, many Latin American actors strongly relied on international and foreign institutions to counter oppression.[383] The constitutional incorporation of human rights validated this strategy.[384]

The Court's jurisprudence offers a useful lens for transformative constitutionalism. One strand centres on removing repressive forces from power in order to stabilize democratic regimes. The Court imposes on states the obligation to prosecute serious human rights violations such as disappearances, executions, and torture. Those responsible must be found, prosecuted, and punished, and the victims and their families must be compensated. In 1988, in its very first judgment, the Court ruled that the Honduran government was accountable for the disappearance of Angel Manfredo Velásquez Rodríguez, a student, in 1981.[385] A ban on sweeping amnesty laws followed. Thus, Peru's democratic transitional government practically demanded the decision in *Barrios Altos v. Perú*, where the Court declared two amnesty laws of the Fujimori regime contrary to international law and even null and void.[386] That helped the new government battle the repressive forces.

Much in the IACtHR's judgments is unprecedented. Neither the ECtHR nor the CJEU have yet declared any domestic law null and void.[387] The IACtHR's jurisprudence on reparations is similarly innovative. Its judgments go beyond merely declaring a violation or awarding financial compensation. The Court also orders collective reparations, demands specific legislation, and prioritizes victims' needs.[388] Some reparations aim to consolidate democracy by strengthening public

[381] Binder, 'Hacia una Corte Constitucional Latinoamericana? La jurisprudencia de la Corte Interamericana de Derechos Humanos con un enfoque especial sobre las amnistías', in A. von Bogdandy, E. Ferrer Mac-Gregor, and M. Morales Antoniazzi (eds), *La justicia constitucional y su internacionalización. Hacia un ius constitutionale commune en América Latina?* (2010) 159.

[382] M. E. Góngora Mera, *Inter-American Judicial Constitutionalism on the Constitutional Rank of Human Rights Treaties in Latin America through National and Inter-American Adjudication* (2011).

[383] M. E. Keck and K. Sikkink, *Activists beyond Borders. Advocacy Networks in International Politics* (1998) 79 ff.

[384] Soley Echeverría (n. 373) 209 ff.

[385] IACtHR, *Velásquez Rodríguez v. Honduras*, Decision (Merits), 29 July 1988, Series C, No. 4. All IACtHR decisions are available online at http://www.corteidh.or.cr/index.php/en/jurisprudencia (last visited 8 September 2022).

[386] IACtHR, *Barrios Altos v. Peru*, Decision (Merits), 14 March 2001, Series C, No. 75. See also *Almonacid Arellano et al. v. Chile*, Decision (Preliminary Objections, Merits, Reparations and Costs), 26 September 2006, Series C, No. 154; *La Cantuta v. Peru*, Decision (Merits, Reparations and Costs), 29 November 2006, Series C, No. 162.

[387] Skordas and Spieker, 'Supranational Law', in A. Peters (ed.), *Max-Planck-Encyclopedia of Public International Law* (2021) para. 30.

[388] IACtHR, *Claude Reyes et al. v. Chile*, Decision (Merits, Reparations and Costs), 19 September 2006, Series C, No. 151.

memory. For example, they mandate public ceremonies designed to teach society historical truths, demand that streets or schools be named after victims or that memorial sites be established, and require high-ranking state officials to acknowledge human rights violations.

By no means does the Court solely address state terrorism. It also supports democracy, that is, the separation of powers, judicial independence, freedom of expression, and the right to access information and to a fair trial.[389] Another cornerstone concerns the protection of vulnerable persons, enabling them also to participate in the democratic rule of law. The IACtHR imposes state obligations to adopt protective measures for youth, women, older persons, indigenous persons, persons with disabilities, communities of African descent, persons from the LGBTQI community, persons in detention, internally displaced persons, and journalists. One case concerned accountability for femicides. The IACtHR obligated Mexico, in the *González y otras* case ('*Campo Algodonero*'), to investigate the disappearance and murder of women in Ciudad Juarez from a gender perspective and to adopt preventative measures to combat discrimination against women.[390] It is telling that this was probably the first international judgment by a bench predominantly composed of women.

The latest cornerstone of the IACtHR's jurisprudence concerns economic, social, cultural, and environmental rights. In 2017, in *Lagos del Campo v. Perú*, the Court declared that these rights are justiciable. It also emphasized that civil and political rights (on the one hand) and economic, social, cultural, and environmental rights (on the other hand) are interdependent.[391]

In 2006, the Court furthered its impact with the doctrine of conventionality control.[392] This doctrine imposes on national judges the obligation to follow the Convention as interpreted by the IACtHR. At first, it seemed to require that all courts accord the Convention primacy over parliamentary law.[393] In response to immense criticism,[394] the Court clarified that conventionality control should be exercised only within the parameters of the domestic courts' jurisdiction under

[389] IACtHR, *Apitz Barbera et al. ('First Court of Administrative Disputes') v. Venezuela*, Decision (Preliminary Objections, Merits, Reparations and Costs), 5 August 2008, Series C, No. 182; *Reverón Trujillo v. Venezuela*, Decision (Preliminary Objections, Merits, Reparations and Costs), 30 June 2009, Series C, No. 197; *Chocrón Chocrón v. Venezuela*, Decision (Preliminary Objections, Merits, Reparations and Costs), 1 July 2011, Series C, No. 227.

[390] IACtHR, *González et al. ('Cotton Fields') v. Mexico*, Decision (Preliminary Objections, Merits, Reparations, and Costs), 16 November 2009, Series C, No. 205.

[391] IACtHR, *Lagos del Campo v. Peru*, Decision (Preliminary Objections, Merits, Reparations and Costs), 31 August 2017, Series C, No. 340.

[392] *Almonacid-Arellano et al. v. Chile* (n. 386); Ferrer Mac-Gregor, 'The Conventionality Control as a Core Mechanism of the Ius Constitutionale Commune', in von Bogdandy *et al.* (n 352) 321.

[393] *Almonacid-Arellano et al. v. Chile* (n. 386).

[394] D. García-Sayán, *Cambiando el Futuro. Testimonios* (2017). García-Sayán was a justice at the IACtHR from 2004 to 2015 and the President of the Court from 2010 to 2014.

domestic law.[395] Its transformative constitutionalism is thus principled but tactically flexible.

I will discuss later what Europeans can take from the Court's jurisprudence to further the principles of Article 2 TEU (see 4.6.A). To conclude these conceptual reflections, I discuss them in the light of two structural issues: the relationship between juridification and politicization and the prerequisites of transformative constitutionalism.

Some claim that juridification entails depoliticization, which would hinder successfully addressing entrenched social problems.[396] But the juridification of social issues in Latin America demonstrates the opposite. Juridification helps create a new language and new fora for publicly identifying structural deficiencies as well as for articulating possible solutions. These are features of politicization rather than depoliticization. Moreover, the IACtHR, like other courts, does not just adjudicate concrete disputes. It also explicitly tackles deficient structures and provides transformative impulses for society as a whole, thereby generating political processes. In other words, there can be a constructive link between juridification and politicization.

Latin America helps understand the prerequisites for linking juridification and politicization and for court-driven transformative constitutionalism. The 'hardware' consists of a democratic state's elementary institutions under the rule of law: an operative constitution that includes fundamental rights, meaningful elections, and a largely independent judiciary, possibly supported by like-minded international institutions. The 'software' requires a supportive public as well as a group of innovative and persistent legal actors, who use seminal cases to address their society's systemic deficiencies.[397] Transformations require both agency *and* structure.

D. European Transformative Constitutionalism

1. Transformative Law and Transformative Constitutionalism

A transformative dynamic characterizes European public law. As early as 1983, Ipsen interpreted the Community Treaties as a constitution with a transformative

[395] IACtHR, *Cabrera García and Montiel-Flores v. Mexico*, Decision (Preliminary Objections, Merits, Reparations and Costs), 26 November 2010, Series C, No. 220, para. 225; *Gelman v. Uruguay*, Decision (Merits and Reparations), 24 February 2011, Series C, No. 221, para. 193; Urueña, 'Domestic Application of International Law in Latin America', in C. A. Bradley (ed.), *The Oxford Handbook of Comparative Foreign Relations Law* (2019) 565.

[396] Hirschl (n. 79).

[397] García Villegas, 'El constitucionalismo aspiracional y las estrategias políticas de transformación social', in M. García Villegas and M. A. Ceballos Bedoya (eds), *Democracia, justicia y sociedad. Diez años de investigación en Dejusticia* (2016) 83.

mandate (a *Wandelverfassung*).[398] Weiler even claims that the Treaties have a messianic character.[399] Giuliano Amato, one of the most prominent constitutional scholars of his generation as well as Italian prime minister, vice-president of the European Convention, and current president of the Italian Constitutional Court, goes even further, interpreting the history of European integration as *Constructing Utopia*.[400]

These are not hopeless dreamers' baseless speculations but examples of reconstructive legal scholarship. The Treaties mandate transformation, as I have elaborated in discussing the 'ever closer union' (see 2.6.A). The Preamble to the EU Treaty substantiates its transformative thrust. Its objective is a Europe marked by solidarity, economic and social progress, peace, and security.[401] The Preamble to the TFEU adds 'the constant improvements of the living and working conditions', 'reducing the differences existing between the various regions' and 'the development of the highest possible level of knowledge'. The Treaties promise citizens that their lives will always improve (see 3.4.C). This transformative teleology is meant to guide the interpretation of the Treaties' provisions as well as of Union policies.

Nevertheless, we should not conceive of the development of European law in its first period as transformative constitutionalism. After the European Defence Community failed before the French National Assembly on 30 August 1954, integration opted for the path of market integration. Constitutionalist aspects were secondary compared to the dominant logic of establishing one European market, although they were relevant for questions of enlargement, identity, and fundamental rights. As early as 1962, the European Parliament used constitutionalist arguments to prevent an association with Franco's Spain.[402] But it was only well into the second period of European public law, in the late 1990s, that the Union began to fully engage in meaningful constitutionalism (see 2.5). The same applies to the Council of Europe. Since 1949, its mandate has been to 'achieve a greater unity between its members for the purpose of safeguarding and realising the ideals and principles which are their common heritage'. But only in the second threshold phase did this mandate gain true traction (see 4.3.C). Transformative constitutionalism addresses systemic deficiencies. Such transformations under constitutional law are a phenomenon of the second period of European public law. It began when

[398] Ipsen, 'Die Verfassungsrolle des Europäischen Gerichtshofs für die Integration', in J. Schwarze (ed.), *Der Europäische Gerichtshof als Verfassungsgericht und Rechtsschutzinstanz. Referate und Diskussionsberichte der Tagung des Arbeitskreises Europäische Integration e.V. in Hamburg vom 2.-4. Juni 1983* (1983) 29, at 29, 32, 51.

[399] Weiler, 'Deciphering the Political and Legal DNA of European Integration. An Exploratory Essay', in Dickson and Eleftheriadis (n. 134) 137, at 146 ff.

[400] Amato *et al.*, 'Introduction', in G. Amato *et al.* (eds), *The History of the European Union. Constructing Utopia* (2019) 1.

[401] Kadelbach, 'Präambel EUV', in H. von der Groeben, J. Schwarze, and A. Hatje (eds), *Europäisches Unionsrecht* (2015).

[402] Patel (n. 61) 155 ff.; Janse, 'The Evolution of the Political Criteria for Accession to the European Community, 1957–1973', 24 *European Law Journal* (2018) 57.

Central and Eastern European societies decided to overcome their authoritarian structures by transforming themselves in the light of the values now established by Article 2 TEU. These societies mandated their constitutions, but also Union law and the law of the Council of Europe, to bring about a corresponding transformation. This constitutionalism yielded true successes, but democratic structures remain frail in some countries. One of the major questions of our time is whether the strengthening of authoritarian forces heralds a new (and much darker) threshold phase or whether a renewed transformative constitutionalism can consolidate the European democratic society. For that reason, I now review the transformation process that began in 1990.

2. The Transformation Governance of the 1990s

In the early 1990s, everything seemed so self-evident. European transformative constitutionalism began with the Central and Eastern European liberation from authoritarian rule, as in Latin America in the 1980s. Most citizens demanded a democratic rule of law that complied with common European standards.[403] A broad reception of Western European constitutional law ensued.[404] The reintroduced concept of the *Ius Publicum Europaeum* (see 2.1) got off to a promising start. Finally, European institutions soon supported this transformation.

Most actors and observers were confident that the Central and Eastern European societies to the West of the former Soviet Union would become liberal democracies. Francis Fukuyama's 'end of history' or Jürgen Habermas' dictum of the 'catch-up revolution' expressed this zeitgeist.[405] At the same time, it was clear that the zeitgeist depended on transnational institutions. Initially, this was mainly the Conference on Security and Co-operation in Europe (CSCE).[406] But soon, it became clear that the zeitgeist required more institutionality than the CSCE could offer.[407]

In 1993, the united Western European governments agreed on European *governance*, which would reorganize Europe by joining the resources of the various European organizations. One manifestation of this agreement was the European

[403] Halmai, 'Ungarn. § 12', in von Bogdandy, Cruz Villalón, and Huber, *Handbuch Ius Publicum Europaeum, Bd. I* (n. 309) 687, at paras 9–28; Tuleja, 'Polen. § 8', in von Bogdandy, Cruz Villalón, and Huber, *Handbuch Ius Publicum Europaeum, Bd I* (n. 309) 451, paras 6–21; on a conceptualization in the sense of transformative constitutionalism, see Sonnevend, 'Preserving the *Acquis* of Transformative Constitutionalism in Times of Constitutional Crisis. Lessons from the Hungarian Case', in von Bogdandy *et al.* (n. 352) 123.

[404] Hartwig, 'Staatslegitimation durch Verfassungsrezeption in Mittel- und Osteuropa', 59 *Zeitschrift für ausländisches öffentliches Recht und Völkerrecht* (1999) 919.

[405] Fukuyama, 'The End of History?', 16 *The National Interest* (1989) 3; J. Habermas, *Die nachholende Revolution* (1990).

[406] See the Concluding Document of the Vienna Follow-Up Meeting of 15 January 1989 (paras 18 f. of the Principles section); also the Charter of Paris of 21 November 1990, at 5 ff.

[407] See, e.g. Moser and Peters, 'Legal Uncertainty and Indeterminacy: Immutable Characteristics of the OSCE?', in M. Steinbrück Platise, C. Moser, and A. Peters (eds), *The Legal Framework of the OSCE* (2019) 3.

Council's decision of 21 and 22 June 1993 that promised the transforming states' accession under the so-called Copenhagen criteria, that is, standards that would later be incorporated into Article 2 TEU.[408] In the same vein, the Council of Europe issued its like-minded Vienna Declaration of the Heads of State and Government of 9 October 1993.[409] These texts laid the political foundation for the path towards transformation.

On this basis, the EU, the Council of Europe, and the CSCE (which became the Organization for Security and Co-operation in Europe (OSCE) in 1994) developed a policy of transformative constitutionalism, albeit without articulating it as such. Here, I will focus on administrative and political actors.[410] Despite there being some tensions between them, these organizations cooperatively formulated and implemented the Western European principles of democratic rule of law vis-à-vis those states. This policy gained traction because it promised accession to the EU, which many Central and Eastern European citizens eagerly desired.

Now, we know that democratic transformations often do not fully live up to democratic rule-of-law standards. The European transformative constitutionalism of those years was marked by Western European hegemony.[411] The Western European states certainly saw this problem. Consequently, the criteria were operationalized in the Council of Europe and the OSCE, that is, in organizations in which the States undergoing transformation soon became members. Yet, it is indicative of hegemony that the EU Member States did not submit to these criteria in equal measure.[412]

The criteria of transformation were concretized in various ways.[413] For instance, the Framework Convention for the Protection of National Minorities, drawn up in the Council of Europe between 1993 and 1995, was key in ensuring the protection of minorities, a particularly sensitive topic.[414] States had to ratify and enforce the Framework Convention in order to fulfil the Copenhagen criteria and Article O TEU (Maastricht Treaty; now Article 49 TEU) on the protection of minorities,[415]

[408] European Council of 21/22 June 1993, Presidency Conclusion (SN 180/1/93 REV 1), at 13. In detail, see Hillion, 'The Copenhagen Criteria and Their Progeny', in C. Hillion (ed.), *EU Enlargement. A Legal Approach* (2004) 1.

[409] Council of Europe, Vienna Declaration of 9 October 1993.

[410] For the ECtHR's contribution, see 4.3.C, 4.6.B.

[411] A first articulation is set out in the Document of the Copenhagen Meeting of the Conference on the Human Rights Dimension of the CSCE of 29 June 1990, point 1.

[412] On the Austrian draft of 26 November 1991 and the Bolzano Draft by the Federal Union of European Nationalities for an Additional Protocol to the ECHR, see R. Hofmann, *Minderheitenschutz in Europa. Völker- und staatsrechtliche Lage in Überblick* (1995) 43.

[413] In detail, see A. Duxbury, *The Participation of States in International Organisations. The Role of Human Rights and Democracy* (2011) esp. at 114–164.

[414] Council of Europe, Framework Convention for the Protection of National Minorities of 1 February 1995. It entered into force on 1 February 1998.

[415] Sasse, 'Minority Rights and EU Enlargement. Normative Overstretch or Effective Conditionality?', in G. N. Toggenburg (ed.), *Minority Protection and the Enlarged European Union: The Way Forward* (2004) 59, at 61, 68, 72.

as concretized by the OSCE's recommendations as well as recommendations by the Committee of Ministers of the Council of Europe and its Parliamentary Assembly. This illustrates how closely the various European institutions cooperated.

A key institution for articulating European constitutional standards, then and now, is the Council of Europe's European Commission for Democracy through Law (Venice Commission), founded in 1990.[416] It is composed mainly of judges and former judges. Initially, its main task was to advise, from a position of great authority, the governments and legislatures of those States undergoing transformation. Since the 2010s, it has the additional task of opposing systemic deficiencies (see 3.6.C, 4.4.C).

The European transformative constitutionalism of the 1990s turned bureaucratic. Many consider this a main cause for later deficiencies.[417] The EU Commission was mainly in charge of transformation.[418] Its so-called progress reports set authoritative standards, as they were important not only for future Member States' eventual accession but also for immediate financial support. Because the Commission's transformative constitutionalism was technocratic, it did little to transform constitutional culture into a living democracy under the rule of law.

No state undergoing transformation, and even less so its citizens, had any true means for challenging the Commission's decisions, some of which were seen as discriminatory or plainly wrong.[419] Thus, the transformation appeared asymmetrical.[420] The citizens of these states were entirely mediatized since they lacked rights as well as possibilities of legal protection. A lot of this inheres in the very structure of an accession process. Nevertheless, we cannot close our eyes to the deficiencies that did exist. In short, the process did not live up to the ideal of 'Democracy through law'.

For some scholars, this transformation ended in failure.[421] This strikes me as a misjudgement. International indices attest that European transformative

416 In detail, see Grabenwarter, 'The Venice Commission: Its Nature, Functioning, and Significance in the Multi-Level Cooperation of Constitutional Courts', in von Bogdandy, Huber, and Grabenwarter (n. 145).

417 Smith, 'Western Actors and the Promotion of Democracy', in J. Zielonka and A. Pravda (eds), *Democratic Consolidation in Eastern Europe, Bd. II. International and Transnational Factors* (2001) 31, at 31.

418 D. Kochenov, *EU Enlargement and the Failure of Conditionality. Pre-accession Conditionality in the Fields of Democracy and the Rule of Law* (2008) 85–295.

419 The Gotovina affair during Croatia's accession procedure offers one example. See M. Rötting, *Das verfassungsrechtliche Beitrittsverfahren zur Europäischen Union und seine Auswirkungen am Beispiel der Gotovina-Affäre im kroatischen Beitrittsverfahren* (2009) 184 ff.

420 Krygier, 'Introduction', in W. Sadurski, A. Czarnota, and M. Krygier (eds), *Spreading Democracy and the Rule of Law? The Impact of EU Enlargement for the Rule of Law, Democracy and Constitutionalism in Post-Communist Legal Orders* (2005) 3, at 12; Kosař, Baroš, and Dufek, 'The Twin Challenges to Separation of Powers in Central Europe. Technocratic Governance and Populism', 15 *European Constitutional Law Review* (2019) 427.

421 I. Krastev and S. Holmes, *The Light That Failed. A Reckoning* (2019); on the problems of this study, Assmann, 'Let's Go East!', 839 *Merkur* (2019) 15.

constitutionalism has delivered a lot of democratic rule of law. Thus, all post-socialist states abandoned many of their authoritarian structures.[422] At the same time, regressions are all too visible, in particular in Hungary and Poland. According to the Freedom House 'Nations in Transit' report, Hungary has turned from a 'consolidated democracy' into a 'hybrid regime' in the past 10 years.[423] V-Dem even lists Hungary as an 'electoral autocracy'.[424] Other indices include Hungary and Poland in the top group of states experiencing the breakdown of democracy.[425] As the two proposals for an Article 7 TEU procedure show, there are reasonable doubts as to whether these states still meet the values of Article 2 TEU.[426]

Many observers agree that these regressions are not solely due to Viktor Orbán and Jarosław Kaczyński's political skills but must also be explained with insufficient transformation.[427] Some argue that the transformation was too elitist and that legal culture could not keep up with it.[428] Others maintain that the transformation disappointed many by unexpectedly resulting in economic hardship rather than prosperity.[429] The subsidies with which the EU supports Orbán's and Kaczyński's governments, the German industry's heavy investments in those countries, and the European People's Party's logic of power also bear mentioning.[430]

As a German legal scholar, I will not presume to identify the regressions' root causes, nor will I offer recommendations for what to do in countries I hardly know. At the same time, I feel certain that the future paths of these societies will shape European public law and society. And there are some aspects that a German legal scholar can address, namely, the legal feasibility of some innovations that might facilitate a second democratic transition (see 3.6). At this point, I discuss the much-debated relationship between transformative constitutionalism and the European economic constitution for a free market economy.

[422] Economist Intelligence Unit, Democracy Index 2010: Democracy in Retreat, 3.

[423] Freedom House, Nations in Transit 2020: Dropping the Democratic Facade, 3.

[424] V-Dem Institute, Autocratization Surges—Resistance Grows: Democracy Report 2020, 16.

[425] Among the 'Top-10 Main Autocratizing Countries', see ibid. See also World Justice Project, Rule of Law Index: 2020 Insights, 20.

[426] European Commission, Reasoned Proposal in accordance with Article 7(1) TEU regarding the rule of law in Poland, COM(2017) 835 final, paras 6 ff.; EP Resolution of 12 September 2018 on a proposal calling on the Council to determine, pursuant to Article 7(1) of the Treaty on European Union, the existence of a clear risk of a serious breach by Hungary of the values on which the Union is founded (2017/2131(INL)), OJ 2019 C 433/66.

[427] Grabbe, 'Six Lessons of Enlargement Ten Years On. The EU's Transformative Power in Retrospect and Prospect', 52 *Journal of Common Market Studies* (2014) 40; Adamski, 'The Social Contract of Democratic Backsliding in the "New EU" Countries', 56 *Common Market Law Review* (2019) 623.

[428] Jakab, 'Institutional Alcoholism in Post-Socialist Countries and the Cultural Elements of the Rule of Law. The Example of Hungary', in A. Bakardjieva Engelbrekt and X. Groussot (eds), *The Future of Europe. Political and Legal Integration Beyond Brexit* (2019) 209.

[429] Sonnevend, 'Preserving the *Acquis* of Transformative Constitutionalism' (n. 403) 132 f.; Kosař, Baroš, and Dufek (n. 420) 427.

[430] Győry, 'Ein Freund, ein guter Freund', *Verfassungsblog* (22 December 2020).

3. Transformative Constitutionalism and the Free Market Economy

The transformation of the 1990s and early 2000s sought to democratize Central and Eastern European societies. It was premised on a constitution that focused on the free market, the better to satisfy the societal demand for prosperity. Many believe that the unexpected hardships of market-based reforms and the new social inequality contributed to the faltering of democratic transformation. This is why this book needs to address the question of how transformative constitutionalism relates to a free market economy.

The EU Treaties establish the standards of democratic constitutionalism in Article 2 TEU and lay down the principles of a decidedly liberal economic constitution in Article 3(3) TEU or Article 119 TFEU. Under this economic constitution, social inequality increased throughout European society, becoming a characteristic of the second phase of European public law.[431] This could militate against applying the concept of transformative constitutionalism to European public law's transformation. Indeed, Karl Klare, who created the concept of transformative constitutionalism, gave it a post-liberal impetus (see 2.6.B).

In my view, this impetus is not convincing. The South African Constitution of 1993 and, to an even greater degree, the Colombian Constitution of 1991 combine transformative constitutionalism with a free market economy. The democratic programme in both states thus does not consider such an economy incompatible with the transformation of society's structure. To the contrary, it is premised on the economy helping it bring about the transformation.[432]

I find the link between transformational constitutionalism and a market-based constitution plausible. Many people associate democracy with prosperity, and social prosperity and democratic stability are closely related (see 3.4.C). Transformative constitutionalism is expensive because it emphasizes solidarity and thus requires huge financial resources. From what we know today, only a free market economy can generate such resources. Of course, there may be tensions between transformative constitutionalism and free market policies.[433] To conceptualize the tensions in legal terms, I suggest conceptualizing them in the light of the European constitutional principles set out in Article 2 TEU. They determine what ultimately defines European society, including its economy.

[431] Eurostat, 'Quality of Life Indicators: Material Living Conditions', 26 May 2020, 3 f.; Bonesmo Fredriksen, 'Income Inequality in the European Union', *OECD Economics Department Working Papers No. 952* (2012).

[432] Álvarez Zárate, 'El derecho económico internacional y el ICCAL frente al constitucionalismo económico latinoamericano', in von Bogdandy *et al.*, El constitucionalismo transformador en América Latina y el derecho económico internacional. De la tensión al diálogo (2018) 289, at 303–307.

[433] Urueña, 'Global Water Governance and the Rise of the Constitutional Regulatory State in Colombia', in N. K. Dubash and B. Morgan (eds), *The Rise of the Regulatory State of the South. Infrastructure and Development in Emerging Economies* (2013) 26; Saffron, 'Can Constitutional Courts be Counterhegemonic Powers vis-à-vis Neoliberalism? The Case of the Colombian Constitutional Court', 5 *Seattle Journal for Social Justice* (2007) 533; H. Brunkhorst, *Das doppelte Gesicht Europas. Zwischen Kapitalismus und Demokratie* (2014).

3
Principles

1. Prolegomena

In European public law, there are few academic societies as influential as the Association of German Teachers of Public Law (*Vereinigung der deutschen Staatsrechtslehrer*). Leading scholars founded it in 1922 to contend with the transformations brought about by the Weimar Constitution. Their objectives were both academic and political and the choice of topics and speakers often programmatic.[1] In 1964, one year after the Court of Justice of the European Union's (CJEU's) landmark judgment in *van Gend en Loos* (see 4.3.B), the Kiel Conference discussed the 'Preservation and Transformation of Democratic Constitutionalism in the International Communities'. The association's board, under Schmitt's disciple Werner Weber, chose the rising star Peter Badura as a speaker.

Badura, probably the youngest speaker in the association's history, set the tone for decades of scholarship. He convinced many scholars that, 'given the inevitable internationalization of economic and military administration, preserving democratic constitutional structures [will] depend [. . .] on whether the ideas of democracy and the rule of law succeed in shattering the confines of the nation state'.[2] The remarks of Badura's co-speaker, Joseph H. Kaiser, went in the same direction (see 3.3.A).

The Kiel Conference initiated the proverbial pro-European Kiel wave, which helped German public law scholars, and even some members of the Schmitt School, overcome their previous Euroscepticism.[3] Their collective effort transformed the ideas of democracy and the rule of law as part of the overall transformation depicted in Chapter 2.

Chapter 3 describes the transformation of the constitutional core or, as many would say, identity. For Badura, in 1964, this core consisted of democracy and the

[1] Heinrich Triepel took the lead. For his stance on liberal democracy, see A. von Bogdandy and R. Mehring (eds), *Heinrich Triepel—Parteienstaat und Staatsgerichtshof. Gesammelte verfassungspolitische Schriften zur Weimarer Republik* (2021).

[2] Badura, 'Bewahrung und Veränderung demokratischer und rechtsstaatlicher Verfassungsstruktur in den internationalen Gemeinschaften', 23 *Veröffentlichungen der Vereinigung der Deutschen Staatsrechtslehrer* (1966) 34, at 38.

[3] F. Günther, *Denken vom Staat her. Die bundesdeutsche Staatsrechtslehre zwischen Dezision und Integration 1949–1970* (2004); A. K. Mangold, *Gemeinschaftsrecht und deutsches Recht. Die Europäisierung der deutschen Rechtsordnung in historisch-empirischer Sicht* (2011). Schmitt himself remained deeply sceptical: Schmitt, 'The Legal World Revolution (1978)', *Télos* (1987) 73, at 85 f.

The Emergence of European Society through Public Law. First Edition. Armin von Bogdandy, Oxford University Press.
 DOI: 10.1093/oso/9780198909347.003.0003

rule of law. Half a century later, the Treaty legislator validated this approach in Article 2 of the Treaty on European Union (TEU). Its take was broader, however, as it used human dignity, freedom, non-discrimination, equality between women and men, and respect for human rights (including the rights of persons belonging to minorities), as well as pluralism, tolerance, justice, and, not least, solidarity to enrich the notion of democracy and the rule of law. Today, almost 60 years after Badura's talk, the transformation of the rule of law, democracy, and the other principles is still ongoing, but much has been achieved.

A. The Promise

Article 2 TEU establishes the ultimate legal grounds of European society. This qualifies its standards as fundamental principles, although the Treaty refers to them as values (see 3.1.B). By engaging with such principles, legal scholarship helps understand, realize, and transform social structures in various ways.[4]

By tracing how principles change over time, we gain a historical understanding of transformations. As stated, the Treaty legislator opted for constitutional principles in the second threshold phase (see 2.5). It took time for this decision to inform the mainstream opinion among legal scholars. For a long time, many continued to refer not to constitutional principles but to general principles, a concept known from private, administrative, and international law (Article 38(1) Statute of the International Court of Justice (ICJ)). Well into the twenty-first century, the two landmark monographs on the topic still focus on general principles.[5] The decision to found the Union on constitutional standards is thus still in the process of implementation.

This lag is significant because doctrines of principles are relevant. The principle of democracy is a good example. Though evidently important, fundamental questions remain unanswered, such as how to interpret a democracy that lacks both a people and electoral equality and in which the executive acts as a democratic representative (see 3.5.A–B). Legal scholarship on these questions reconstructs the principle of democracy and thus participates in the social process of creating meaning and mindsets.[6]

Scholarship on principles organizes the legal material by elaborating structures for the mass of legal provisions and judicial decisions.[7] Such doctrinal structures are particularly significant for European law, which is highly fragmented. In the

[4] On international law, see J. Rauber, *Strukturwandel als Prinzipienwandel. Theoretische, dogmatische und methodische Bausteine eines Prinzipienmodells des Völkerrechts und seiner Dynamik* (2017).

[5] X. Groussot, *General Principles of Community Law* (2006); T. Tridimas, *The General Principles of EU Law* (2009).

[6] R. Koselleck, *Futures Past. On the Semantics of Historical Time* (2004) 84 f.

[7] I. Kant, *Critique of Pure Reason* (1998 [1781]) 358 ff., esp. at 359.

past, under the primacy of private law, legal scholars mainly availed themselves of rigid conceptual pyramids (see 5.3.D). Today, most present the material in flexible systems guided by principles. The CJEU also describes the Union legal order as a 'structured network of principles, rules, and mutually interdependent legal relations'.[8]

Scholarship on principles can likewise serve democracy itself. The aforementioned operations help it constitutionalize the legal order (see 2.5.C), thus radiating fundamental political decisions to all corners of the law. This is significant because law framed by former political regimes persists in some of these corners. This also holds true for Union law, which, for decades, represented the law of pure executive power (see 2.4.A).

From a transformative perspective, moreover, scholarship on principles can also proactively link the law to changing social conditions, interests, and convictions. By advocating new ways to conceive of principles, scholars can articulate new ideas, expectations, and demands voiced in society. Such reconstructions can act as sluices that connect the legal order to societal discourses. At times, reconstructions of principles can even fuel transformative constitutionalism (see 1.4, 3.6, 4.6, 5.4). Consequently, principles can both form the structures of current law and contribute to their transformation.

In addition, constitutional principles allow for a critique that is intrinsic to law. Such criticism differs from general political criticism in that it is based on legal argumentation. For that reason, it can be implemented more easily within the law; no formal legislation is required. Because it resembles a manifesto, Article 2 TEU calls for such criticism (see 5.3.B).

Finally, scholarship on principles can help frame European society. The Treaty legislator expects much from the principles of Article 2 TEU (see 3.2.A), which do not just apply but 'prevail' in European society. The French (and Italian, Spanish, German, etc.) version of the Treaty is even more explicit. According to all these versions, the principles 'characterize' European society. The Treaty legislator assigns these principles a constitutive role for the European legal order and, hence, for the entire European society.

All of these scholarly operations form part of European society. The politicians who made up the Treaty legislators, as well as the scholars conducting the operations, are members of that society. For that reason, these discourses produce European society (see 1.2).

[8] CJEU, Opinion 2/13, *ECHR Accession II* (EU:C:2014:2454) para. 167; Case C-621/18, *Wightman et al.* (EU:C:2018:999) para. 45.

B. Values and Principles

But are the *values* of Article 2 TEU fit for *legal* scholarship? This is by no means evident, precisely because Article 2 TEU refers to its standards as values and not as principles. Often, values are considered ethical convictions, not legal norms.[9] Many categorically distinguish between principles and values, arguing that only the former belong to the law:[10] the law is about legality, they say, whereas values are about what is good and bad. And in 2018, the European Commission stated that, '[t]he Commission, beyond [!] its task to ensure the respect of EU law, is also responsible [...] for guaranteeing the common values of the Union'.[11]

But the distinction between law and values is not convincing, and indeed, the Commission has altered its approach. The standards of Article 2 cl. 1 TEU are part of the law.[12] The Treaty legislator sets them out in the TEU, a legal text;[13] the institutions apply them in legal proceedings (Articles 3, 7, 13, and 49 TEU refer to them); and their violation can lead to sanctions. This makes them binding law, as the deliberations on what is now Article 2 TEU confirm.[14] We have to distinguish the standards of Article 2 TEU from best practices of good governance, ideologies, world views, political morality, and ethics. Their validity, interpretation, and application are subject to juridical reasoning.

Accordingly, I disagree with Frank Schorkopf's concept of a 'constitutionalism of values' for jurisprudence based on Article 2 TEU.[15] His concept blurs the boundaries between the legal and the extra-legal. Schorkopf refers to a *good* order, but what is at stake is the *legal* order. A 'constitutionalism of values' is also problematic, in political terms, for it may support the claim that the measures to enforce Article 2 TEU are ideological or mere party politics.[16]

[9] Müller, 'Auf dem Weg in eine europäische Gesellschaft? Begriffsproblematik und theoretische Perspektiven', 17 *Berliner Journal für Soziologie* (2007) 7, at 17.

[10] J. Habermas, *Between Facts and Norms: Contributions to a Discourse Theory of Law and Democracy* (2008 [1992]); Böckenförde, 'Critique of the Value-Based Grounding of Law', in E.-W. Böckenförde (ed.), *Constitutional and Political Theory* (2017 [1990]) 217. For an overview, see Mezzetti, 'Valori, Principî, Regole', in L. Mezzetti (ed.), *Principî Costituzionali* (2011) 1.

[11] Recital (3) of Commission Recommendation 2018/103 regarding the rule of law in Poland complementary to Recommendations (EU) 2016/1374, (EU) 2017/146 and (EU) 2017/1520, OJ 2018 L 17/50.

[12] In detail, von Bogdandy, 'Principles of a Systemic Deficiencies Doctrine. How to Protect Checks and Balances in the Member States', 57 *Common Market Law Review* (2020) 705, at 716.

[13] G. W. F. Hegel, *Elements of the Philosophy of Right* (1991 [1821]) para. 3; Poscher, 'The Hand of Midas. When Concepts Turn Legal, or Deflating the Hart-Dworkin Debate', in J. C. Hage and D. von der Pfordten (eds), *Concepts in Law* (2009) 99.

[14] Pilette and de Poncis, 'Valeurs, objectives et nature de l'Union', in G. Amato, H. Bribosia, and B. de Witte (eds), *Genèse et destinée de la constitution européenne. Commentaire du Traité établissant une Constitution pour l'Europe à la lumière des travaux préparatoires et perspectives d'avenir* (2007) 287, at 300 f.

[15] Schorkopf, 'Value Constitutionalism in the European Union', 21 *German Law Journal* (2020) 956.

[16] See Cabinet Office of the Prime Minister, *They Want to Make Soros's Man the President of the Commission*, website of the Hungarian Government (2 July 2019), https://2015-2019.kormany.hu/en/the-prime-minister/news/they-want-to-make-soros-s-man-the-president-of-the-commission (last visited 14 August 2022).

Doctrinally, the standards of Article 2 TEU qualify as principles.[17] The Treaty of Amsterdam assigns them this quality (Article 6(1) TEU), and there is no reason to assume that the Treaty legislator diminished their legal relevance with the Treaty of Lisbon. As legal principles, the standards of Article 2 TEU lie within the remit of the CJEU, whose task is to uphold the law (Article 19(1) TEU).[18] What, then, are principles? Like the Treaty legislator, who frequently refers to the concept, I understand principles simply as legal norms of particular significance.[19]

Of course, the standards of Article 2 cl. 1 TEU may still reflect ethical convictions in European society. Distinguishing between legal principles and extra-legal standards does not imply clinical isolation. In most societies, particularly in democratic ones, legal norms and ethical orientations overlap. Indeed, the Treaty legislator, by using the term value, suggests that the Article 2 TEU standards are deeply rooted in European society and the path of European integration (see 2.6.D). In doing so, it linked the standards of Article 2 cl. 1 TEU to over half a century of political discourse, experiences, and decisions. Hence, the standards of Article 2 cl. 1 TEU are more determinate than some critics think.[20]

But what about the standards of Article 2 cl. 2 TEU? The Treaty legislator does not describe them as values. And unlike the standards of Article 2 cl. 1 TEU, they do not serve as a prerequisite for accession, cannot be enforced in the procedures of Article 7 TEU, and do not appear in the mandates of Articles 3(1) and 13(1) TEU. No other provision of the Treaties refers to Article 2 cl. 2 TEU. At the same time, most of its standards reappear throughout the Treaties, for example, non-discrimination in Article 21 of the Charter of Fundamental Rights (CFR) and throughout Part II of the Treaty on the Functioning of the European Union (TFEU) and solidarity, justice, and equality between men and women in Article 3(3) TEU and other provisions. Pluralism is mentioned in Article 11(2) CFR. Only tolerance is not mentioned at all.

When it comes to their legal nature, meaning, justiciability, and scope of application, the standards of Article 2 cl. 2 TEU raise the same doctrinal issues as those of Article 2 cl. 1 TEU (see 4.6.C). While many questions remain open, two aspects seem obvious. First, the Treaty legislator's codification legitimizes political demands for solidarity, pluralism, justice, non-discrimination, and tolerance. The Treaty emboldens citizens to employ these terms in order to articulate and pursue their ideas, interests, and values. Second, the standards of Article 2 cl. 2 TEU serve to interpret Article 2 cl. 1 TEU. If European society shares the values of Article 2

[17] CJEU, Case C-216/18 PPU, *LM* (EU:C:2018:586) paras 70–72.

[18] See, e.g. ibid. para. 50. Sometimes, the CJEU uses the term 'value' as a synonym for legal principle. See ibid. para. 48; Case C-336/19, *Centraal Israëlitisch Consistorie van België and others* (EU:C:2020:1031) paras 41, 47, 77.

[19] Jakab, 'Re-Defining Principles as "Important Rules". A Critique of Robert Alexy', in M. Borowski (ed.), *On the Nature of Legal Principles. ARSP Beiheft 119* (2010) 145.

[20] See C. Möllers and L. Schneider, *Safeguarding Democracy in the European Union. A Study on a European Responsibility* (2018) 79 f.

cl. 1 TEU and, at the same time, is characterized by pluralism, tolerance, solidarity, justice, and non-discrimination, then the standards of Article 2 cl. 2 TEU must inform the values of Article 2 cl. 1 TEU.[21] Consequently, the standards of Article 2 cl. 2 TEU are important legal norms and, thus, legal principles.[22]

Article 2 cl. 2 TEU substantiates the values of Article 2 cl. 1 TEU by imbuing them with considerations of both liberalism and solidarity. Indeed, the European legislator refers to Article 2 TEU in its entirety in its most important act for opposing authoritarian tendencies in European society.[23] Therefore, the 12 principles of Article 2 TEU denote, in their entirety, the European constitutional core.

C. The European Constitutional Core

After the Lisbon Treaty's entry into force, the CJEU, like many scholars, initially attached little importance to Article 2 TEU. Judicial practice and legal scholarship treated Article 2 TEU more like a mere political statement or a recital and not like a provision that reflects the constitutional core. That changed during the multiple crises of the late 2010s. In 2019, the CJEU stated:

> Th[e] autonomy [of the Union legal order] accordingly resides in the fact that the Union possesses a constitutional framework that is unique to it. That framework encompasses the founding values set out in Article 2 TEU, which states that the Union 'is founded on the values of respect for human dignity, freedom, democracy, equality, the rule of law, and respect for human rights', the general principles of EU law, the provisions of the Charter, and the provisions of the EU and FEU Treaties, which include, inter alia, rules on the conferral and division of powers, rules governing how the EU institutions and its judicial system are to operate, and fundamental rules in specific areas, structured in such a way as to contribute to the implementation of the process of integration described in the second paragraph of Article 1 TEU.[24]

This passage acknowledges that Article 2 TEU is central to the Union's constitutional framework. While the latter originates in long-standing case law, Article 2 TEU now gives it a genuinely constitutional bent. This transforms Union law

[21] With regard to pluralism, see CJEU, Case C-623/17, *Privacy International* (EU:C:2020:790) para. 62; Joint Cases C-511/18, C-512/18, and C-520/18, *La Quadrature du Net and others* (EU:C:2020:791) para. 114. With regard to justice, see CJEU, Case C-64/16, *Associação Sindical dos Juízes Portugueses* (EU:C:2018:117) para. 30.

[22] See Article 2 lit. a of Regulation 2020/2092 of the European Parliament and of the Council on a general regime of conditionality for the protection of the Union budget, OJ 2020 LI 433/1; CJEU, Case C-93/19 P, *EEAS v. Hebberecht*, Opinion of AG Kokott (EU:C:2020:305) para. 36.

[23] Recital (1) of the Preamble of Regulation 2020/2092 (n. 22).

[24] CJEU, Opinion 2/17, *CETA* (EU:C:2019:341) para. 110.

because the constitutionalization of Community law began, in the 1960s, with formal, not substantive, principles—namely, autonomy, direct effect, and primacy (see 2.2.B, 3.3.C, 4.3.B).

The values of Article 2 cl. 1 TEU are crucial to European law, as attested by other Treaty provisions (Articles 7, 13, and 49 TEU). Since the Treaty legislator based the Union on them (and only on them), they provide the ultimate grounds for justifying public action.[25] Thus, Article 2 TEU is foundational.[26] Its role somewhat resembles that of the constituent power in some domestic discourses.[27]

The number of principles in Article 2 TEU confirms its foundational status. The provision lists 12 principles. Twelve represents the most symbolic number of all. It designates the closed circle; Israel was made up of 12 tribes; Christ had 12 disciples; celestial Jerusalem has 12 gates; and 12 stars, arranged in the shape of a wreath, form the crown of the woman of the Apocalypse. Article 2 TEU thus takes up the European flag's symbolism, whose 12 golden stars, arranged in a circle against a blue background, promise salvation.[28]

The principles of Article 2 cl. 1 TEU play a leading role beyond Union law, too, because European law in its entirety ultimately depends on Union law (see 2.2.C). Accordingly, Article 2 TEU establishes the constitutional core of the Union as well as Europe. Described in Hegelian terms, Article 2 TEU establishes the 'real ideality', 'the soul', and the 'identity' of European law.[29] That, however, comes with an important caveat: to truly determine European identity, the principles of Article 2 TEU must shape all social relations.

With Article 2 TEU, the Treaty legislator laid down demanding standards. That is fraught with risk because there is an inevitable difference between how the Treaty legislator characterizes European society in Article 2 TEU and what many citizens experience as their social reality. If this difference becomes a gulf, the Union loses its credibility (see 3.6.B). A union of values is even more demanding than a union of money. This highlights the magnitude of the Hungarian and the Polish challenge (see 2.6.D).

The European constitutional core of Article 2 TEU encompasses 12 principles, 6 of which Article 2 cl. 1 TEU singles out as values: 'respect for human dignity, freedom, democracy, equality, the rule of law and respect for human rights, including the rights of persons belonging to minorities'. Article 2 cl. 2 TEU adds six further principles: 'pluralism, non-discrimination, tolerance, justice, solidarity, and equality between women and men'. This prompts the question of their

[25] J. Molinier, *Les principes fondateurs de l'Union européenne* (2005) 24; A. Koschorke, *Hegel und wir* (2015) 21.

[26] Luhmann, 'Are There Still Indispensable Norms in Our Society?', 14 *Soziale Systeme* (2008) 18, at 28.

[27] On relevant theories, see M. Patberg, *Constituent Power in the European Union* (2020) 41 ff.

[28] C. Brütsch, *Die Offenbarung Jesu Christi* (1955) 56 ff.; M. Göldner, *Politische Symbole der europäischen Integration. Fahne, Hymne, Hauptstadt, Pass, Briefmarke, Auszeichnungen* (1988).

[29] G. W. F. Hegel, *The Science of Logic* (2010 [1816]) 643.

relationship. Since they all form part of one Treaty article, they must not be interpreted in isolation from one another. I read them as different aspects of one phenomenon, namely, the constitutional core of European democratic society. A fitting theory comes with Habermas' theory of the co-origin of democracy and human rights: 'The logical genesis of these rights comprises a circular process in which the legal code, or legal form, and the mechanism for producing legitimate law—hence the democratic principle—are co-originally constituted.'[30]

The second recital of the Preamble to the CFR supports this understanding, and so do European institutions, particularly when addressing authoritarian tendencies. The institutions usually focus on the rule of law, which they substantiate with considerations of democracy, pluralism, and fundamental rights. The Venice Commission set this trend with its Rule of Law Checklist.[31] In 2020, the European legislator elevated this understanding to binding law. Article 2 of Regulation 2020/2092 of the European Parliament and of the Council of 16 December 2020 on conditionality, to date the most important legislative act on the European constitutional core, states:

> 'The rule of law' refers to the Union value enshrined in Article 2 TEU. It includes the principles of legality implying a transparent, accountable, democratic and pluralistic law-making process; legal certainty; prohibition of arbitrariness of the executive powers; effective judicial protection, including access to justice, by independent and impartial courts, also as regards fundamental rights; separation of powers; and non-discrimination and equality before the law. The rule of law shall be understood having regard to the other Union values and principles enshrined in Article 2 TEU.

The European constitutional core is not only complex but also pluralistic. The Lisbon Treaty legislator based the Union on human rights (as laid down in the European Convention on Human Rights) and not on fundamental rights (as laid down in its CFR). This makes a difference because fundamental rights constitute a political community's domestic guarantees, while human rights are universal and mostly positivized by international law. This normative pluralism corresponds to the path of European public law, which rests on Union law as well as on the European Convention on Human Rights (see 2.2.A, 2.2.C, 4.4.A).

[30] Habermas, *Between Facts and Norms* (n. 10) 121 f.

[31] European Commission for Democracy through Law (Venice Commission), Rule of Law Checklist, 106th Plenary Session (Venice, 11–12 March 2016). For more, see Fuchs, 'Die Vermessung der Rechtsstaatlichkeit. Die "Rule of Law Checklist" der Venedig-Kommission des Europarates', 45 *Europäische Grundrechtezeitschrift* (2018) 237.

D. From a Society of Private Individuals to a Society of Citizens

These prolegomena converge in the thesis that Article 2 TEU reflects the transformation from a European society of private individuals to a European society of citizens. A comparison of Article 2 TEU of 2007 with Article 2 of the European Economic Community (EEC) Treaty of 1957 demonstrates my point.

Article 2 EEC Treaty of 1957 sought the establishment of a common market, the convergence of national economic policies, the harmonious development of economic life, a continuous and balanced expansion of the economy, greater stability, an accelerated increase in the standard of living, and closer relations between the Member States. Article 2 TEU of 2007 does not refer to any of these things. Now, the issues at hand are pluralism, non-discrimination, tolerance, justice, solidarity, and equality between women and men, as well as human dignity, freedom, democracy, equality, the rule of law, and respect for human rights (including the rights of persons belonging to minorities), all within one society. The categorial transformation is evident. Article 3 TEU, the most important provision on objectives under Union law today, and thus the functional successor to Article 2 EEC Treaty, corroborates this transformation. Article 3(1) TEU determines that the first objective of the Union shall be to promote its values, together with peace and the well-being of its peoples.

Accordingly, the Treaty legislator placed the Union in the republican tradition of the American and French revolutions, of 'life, liberty and the pursuit of happiness', of 'freedom, equality, and fraternity'. Already Kant, and even the monarchist Hegel, considered these principles republican in the sense of a society of citizens.[32] In terms of conceptual history, the heads of state and government thus stood on firm ground when they convened on 29 October 2004 under the words 'Europaeae rei publicae status' after signing the Constitutional Treaty.[33] 'Europaeae rei publicae status' can be translated in various ways, such as 'the condition of the European state'. Given the unwillingness to found a state (see 2.3.A), a more plausible translation would be 'the constitution of the European republic'. True, the Constitutional Treaty failed. But in 2009, the Treaty legislator brought Article I-2 of the Constitutional Treaty into force as Article 2 TEU, changing nothing.

This evolution from Article 2 EEC Treaty to Article 2 TEU corresponds to a transformation in the concept of European society. Article 2 of the EEC Treaty, arguably the first juridical articulation of European society, was interpreted as the

[32] On Kant's republicanism, see Dreier, 'Kants Republik', 59 *JuristenZeitung* (2004) 745. On Hegel, see Vieweg, 'Die Revolution der Freiheit. 250 Jahre Hegel', 8 *Blätter für deutsche und internationale Politik* (2020) 109. On the history of this concept, see T. Thiel, *Republikanismus und die Europäische Union. Eine Neubestimmung des Diskurses um die Legitimität europäischen Regierens* (2012).

[33] See the photo in Das Parlament, *Entwurf eines Vertrags über eine Verfassung für Europa (noch nicht ratifiziert)*, https://www.europarl.europa.eu/about-parliament/de/in-the-past/the-parliament-and-the-treaties/draft-treaty-establishing-a-constitution-for-europe (last visited 14 August 2022).

project of a society of private law, that is, of private individuals. This conception goes back to the ordoliberal school, with which Hallstein was affiliated.[34] Accordingly, some saw a *ius commune* shaped by private law as the heart of European law.[35] In 1964, the Max Planck Society even founded an institute dedicated to this idea, the Frankfurt Max Planck Institute for European Legal History. Its founding director was Helmut Coing, a scholar of private and Roman law, and the Institute's journal bore the programmatic title *Jus Commune*.[36]

According to this understanding, European integration serves to develop a society of private law and individuals. Such a society is less demanding than a society defined by the principles of public law. Turkey, and even Israel, were considered for membership in the early 1960s.[37] The EEC could have developed similarly to the Organisation for European Economic Co-operation (OEEC: now the Organisation for Economic Co-operation and Development, OECD), which today helps connect the economically stronger part of world society. However, the EEC's path took a different direction (see 2.5, 3.2.B, 4.3.B), leading the Treaty legislator to decide, in 2007, to base the Union on standards of public law.

Case law likewise evinces this development. Throughout the first period of European public law, the common (internal) market constituted the dominant objective. In 1987, the CJEU still considered the aim to establish an internal market the 'essential object of the [EEC] Treaty'.[38] In 2017, this aim was but one of several 'fundamental rules in specific areas, structured in such a way as to contribute to the implementation of the process of integration'.[39]

Hegel's philosophy of law, as well as Marx's distinction between *bourgeois* and *citoyen*, flesh out this republican transformation. One of Hegel's core insights is that what he calls *bourgeois* (*bürgerliche*) society (namely, the market economy with its specific institutions) cannot achieve stability on its own. Stability requires further institutional and, in fact, constitutional embedding, which Hegel develops in the state.[40] Karl Marx derives from this his famous distinction between the

[34] Böhm, 'Privatrechtsgesellschaft und Marktwirtschaft', 17 *Jahrbuch für die Ordnung von Wirtschaft und Gesellschaft* (1966) 75; E.-J. Mestmäcker, *Recht in der offenen Gesellschaft. Hamburger Beiträge zum deutschen, europäischen und internationalen Wirtschafts- und Medienrecht* (1993) 60 ff; Riesenhuber, '§ 1. Privatrechtsgesellschaft. Leistungsfähigkeit und Wirkkraft im deutschen und Europäischen Recht', in K. Riesenhuber (ed.), *Privatrechtsgesellschaft. Entwicklung, Stand und Verfassung des Privatrechts* (2009) 1, at 11 ff.

[35] Zimmermann, 'Das römisch-kanonische ius commune als Grundlage europäischer Rechtseinheit', 47 *JuristenZeitung* (1992) 8.

[36] Duve, 'Von der Europäischen Rechtsgeschichte zu einer Rechtsgeschichte Europas in globalhistorischer Perspektive', 20 *Rechtsgeschichte—Legal History* (2012) 18, at 21 ff. The Institute has abandoned this direction, becoming the Max Planck Institute for Legal History and Legal Theory in 2021.

[37] K. K. Patel, *Project Europe: A History* (2020) 41.

[38] CJEU, Case 126/86, *Giménes Zaera* (EU:C:1987:395) para. 10.

[39] *CETA* (n. 24) para. 110.

[40] Hegel, *Elements of the Philosophy of Right* (n. 13) para. 258.

bourgeois, who is guided by business, self-interest, and profit, and the republican-minded *citoyen*.[41]

While the Treaty legislator did not establish a European state (see 2.3.A), it did establish a European citizenship (*citoyenneté*) and public institutions under the constitutional standards of Article 2 TEU. Thus, a comparison between Article 2 TEU and Article 2 EEC Treaty reveals that European society has been transformed from a society of private economic relations into one of citizens. It is not a society in the Marxian sense since the European society recognizes private individuals' economic freedom. The Treaty legislator relied on both the *bourgeois* and *citoyen*. The mediating concept is that of a social market economy, as outlined in Article 3 para. 3 TEU. The tensions between the social and the market are the stuff of European politics, to be mediated under the principles of Article 2 TEU. Article 2 TEU thus provides the vanishing point for the entire European economic constitution (see 3.5.C).[42]

The freedom postulated in Article 2 TEU goes beyond private autonomy. It demands equal freedom for all,[43] as human dignity, equality, and the principles of Article 2 cl. 2 TEU confirm. A terminological development corroborates this understanding: The English version of the Treaty of Amsterdam speaks of liberty, while the English version of the Treaty of Lisbon speaks of freedom. Often, liberty solely designates negative freedom and is conceptualized in the categories of private law. Freedom is a more complex concept in a public law tradition.[44]

The CJEU's case law highlights that freedom fits Union law better. As befits a democratic society, the Court interprets the general prohibition of discrimination as well as Union citizenship, the free movement of workers, or the prohibition of discrimination in association agreements mainly in the light of equal freedom.[45] Article 2 TEU protects the freedom of contract but justifies regulatory interventions if private law entrenches asymmetric social relations (see 2.3.D). The insight that a democratic society must avoid extreme disparities is common to a wide range of approaches, from democratic socialism to ordoliberalism.[46]

[41] K. Marx, *On the Jewish Question* (2020 [1843]).

[42] For a first sketch, see von Bogdandy, 'Founding Principles', in A. von Bogdandy and J. Bast (eds), *Principles of European Constitutional Law* (2011) 9, at 14 ff.

[43] Calliess, 'Die Zukunft der Privatautonomie. Zur neueren Entwicklung eines gemeineuropäischen Rechtsprinzips', in B. Zöchling-Jud *et al.* (eds), *Jahrbuch Junger Zivilrechtswissenschaftler 2000. Prinzipien des Privatrechts und Rechtsvereinheitlichung* (2001) 85, at 90 ff.

[44] E.-W. Böckenförde, *Der Staat als sittlicher Staat* (1978) 23 ff; A. Honneth, *Das Recht der Freiheit. Grundriß einer demokratischen Sittlichkeit* (2011) 232 ff. There are certainly other traditions; see, e.g. A. Kocharov, *Republican Europe* (2017) 77 ff.

[45] CJEU, Case 36/74, *Walrave and Koch v. Association Union cycliste internationale and others* (EU:C:1974:140); Case C-415/93, *Union royale belge des sociétés de football association and others v. Bosman* (EU:C:1995:463); Case C-438/05, *The International Transport Workers' Federation and the Finnish Seamen's Union ('Viking')* (EU:C:2007:772); C-341/05, *Laval un Partneri* (EU:C:2007:809).

[46] Heller, 'Rechtsstaat or Dictatorship?', 16 *Economy and Science* (1987) 127, at 141; D. J. Gerber, *Law and Competition in Twentieth-Century Europe. Protecting Prometheus* (2001) 232 ff.

No one will claim that the transformation into a European democratic society is complete. The deficiencies are there for everyone to see. Scholarship on principles is part of identifying and addressing them.[47]

2. Principles and Identity Politics

A. A Delicate Topic

Perhaps the most sensitive question surrounding constitutional principles is their relationship to identity politics. European integration has never been only about the economy or conflicts that can be calculated and resolved in monetary terms. The concept of identity, like few others, brings together many of the more difficult conflicts, which are then framed as conflicts about principles.

This topic's sensitivity starts with the very concept of identity. It oscillates between what is and what ought to be, between description and prescription.[48] It is often used crypto-normatively, with normative statements being disguised as analytical findings. Furthermore, identity is often bound up with questionable political positions.

Decree No.1, with which, in 1973, Augusto Pinochet justified his military coup, stated that the armed forces would defend the Chilean state's historical and cultural identity.[49] In European society today, so-called identitarian movements similarly seek to defend their state's identity against alleged foreign overpopulation (*Überfremdung*).[50] Orbán's 2011 Basic Law for Hungary, which heralds a new current of constitutional law in European society, assigns the concept a crucial role (Preamble, Article D, Article R(4), Article XVI(1)).[51] In the European Parliament, a political group called 'Identity and Democracy' brings together nationalist parties such as the German *Alternative für Deutschland*, the Italian *Lega*, the French *Rassemblement National*, and the Austrian *Freiheitliche Partei Österreichs*.

[47] Likewise, from the perspective of private law, see Ackermann, 'Eine "ungeheure Jurisprudenz"? Die Europarechtswissenschaft und die Europäisierung des Rechts', 68 *Jahrbuch des öffentlichen Rechts* (2020) 471, at 481 ff.

[48] L. Niethammer, *Kollektive Identität. Heimliche Quellen einer unheimlichen Konjunktur* (2000); also E. Tugendhat, *Self-Consciousness and Self-Determination* (1986) 254 ff.

[49] R. Barros, *Constitutionalism and Dictatorship. Pinochet, the Junta and the 1980 Constitution* (2002) 76 f.

[50] G. Hentges, K. Nottbohm, and H.-W. Platzer (eds), *Europäische Identität in der Krise? Europäische Identitätsforschung und Rechtspopulismusforschung im Dialog* (2017).

[51] On the concept's role in Hungarian case law, see Halmai, 'Abuse of Constitutional Identity', 43 *Review of Central and East European Law* (2018) 23; Bakó, 'The Zauberlehrling Unchained? The Recycling of the German Federal Constitutional Court's Case Law on Identity-, *Ultra Vires*- and Fundamental Rights Review in Hungary', 78 *Zeitschrift für ausländisches öffentliches Recht und Völkerrecht* (2018) 863.

These uses militate against turning the concept of identity into the linchpin of democratic constitutional law.[52] Nevertheless, reconstructive legal scholarship can hardly ignore the concept. After all, identity is crucial to the struggle for a democratic European society. I will show how European public law results from mediations within that struggle.

That the concept of identity is so significant comes down, in part, to a common European initiative by the leaders of the Member States, who assigned it a key role in their 1973 Declaration on European Identity.[53] The Declaration establishes an intimate link between identity and principles, proclaiming that 'the principles of representative democracy, of the rule of law, of social justice—which is the ultimate goal of economic progress—and of respect for human rights' are 'fundamental elements of the European identity'. The Declaration reveals how big a role European principles have played since the early 1960s, for example, in preventing an association with Francoist Spain (see 2.6.D).

Few declarations have left such a mark on the history of European integration. Its backdrop is the diminished role of the United States after the loss of the Vietnam War,[54] the societal expectations leading to the *rights revolution* (see 4.3.C), and the economic difficulties of those years. In these circumstances, the heads of state and government sought a way forward that eventually led to the European society of Article 2 TEU. Identity became a crucial concept both for the European Community's position in the world and for its relations with its citizens. It recalls the American Declaration of Independence.

Since then, forming a European identity has represented an important European policy field.[55] Consider that the current EU Commission began its work in 2019 under the motto 'Promoting our European way of life: Protecting our citizens and our values'.[56] And in 2021, the Parliament, the Council, and the Commission set up the Conference on the Future of Europe with the objective of involving European citizens in the spirit of democratic identity politics.[57]

The concept of identity thus made its European debut to advance European integration. Soon, its role became more complex, with national institutions invoking it as well. Some Member States' constitutional courts have played an especially

[52] von Bogdandy, 'Europäische und nationale Identität. Integration durch Verfassungsrecht?', 62 *Veröffentlichungen der Vereinigung der Deutschen Staatsrechtslehrer* (2003) 156, at 157; M. Polzin, *Verfassungsidentität. Ein normatives Konzept des Grundgesetzes?* (2018) 133 ff., 224 f.

[53] Declaration on European Identity, Bull. EC 12-1973, 118.

[54] Patel (n. 37) 72, 155 ff., 165.

[55] U. Haltern, *Europarecht und das Politische* (2005) 199 ff.

[56] European Commission, *Promoting Our European Way of Life. Protecting Our Citizens and Our Values*, https://ec.europa.eu/info/strategy/priorities-2019-2024/promoting-our-european-way-life (last visited 14 August 2022).

[57] Council of the European Union, Joint Declaration on the Conference on the Future of Europe, Doc. No. 6796/21 (5 March 2021); for a theory, see Habermas, 'Historical Consciousness and Post-Traditional Identity: Remarks on the Federal Republic's Orientation to the West', 31 *Acta Sociologica* (1988) 3, at 11 f.

important role: pointing to the concept of constitutional identity, they claim jurisdiction to review European acts in the light of national principles. Thus, the dialectic of European and national identity was born.

The Second Senate of the German Federal Constitutional Court broke the ground just one year after the Declaration by the heads of state and government. In the *Solange I* decision of 1974, it declared that Article 24(1) of the Basic Law, at that time the basis for Germany's integration, did not authorize 'changing the fundamental structure of the Constitution, on which its identity is based, without amending the Constitution'. Moreover, the Court stated that Article 24 of the Basic Law forbids any amendment to the Treaty 'that would abolish the identity of the current constitution of the Federal Republic of Germany by breaking into the structures that constitute it'.[58]

The *Solange II* decision of 1986 maintained even more categorically that Article 24 of the Basic Law 'does not confer a power to surrender by way of ceding sovereign rights to international institutions the identity of the constitutional order of the Federal Republic by breaking into its basic framework, that is, into the structure which makes it up'.[59] The Second Senate expanded this case law in the Maastricht[60] and Lisbon judgments[61] as well as in its decisions on the sovereign debt and Euro crisis,[62] the European Arrest Warrant,[63] the Outright Monetary Transactions (OMTs) of the European Central Bank (ECB), Public Sector Purchase Programmes (PSPPs),[64] and the Banking Union.[65] In fact, it made it more radical, inasmuch as not even a constitutional amendment may transfer certain competences (see 3.2.C). Some praise the Court as virtually the last defender of democratic constitutionalism.[66]

There is a controversial debate about whether this use of identity endangers the very existence of the Union. The Second Senate does not consider it a problem, for conflicts would occur rarely and the preliminary ruling procedure can serve to alleviate the tension.[67] The CJEU's Advocate General, Pedro Cruz Villalón (previously the President of the Spanish Constitutional Court), takes the opposite position, however:

[58] BVerfGE 37, 271, *Solange I*, para. 43.

[59] BVerfGE 73, 339, *Solange II*, para. 104 (for the translation see 'Wünsche Handelsgesellschaft (Solange II)' (1993) 93 International Law Reports 403).

[60] BVerfGE 89, 155, *Maastricht*, paras 91 ff.

[61] BVerfGE 123, 267, *Lisbon*, paras 216 ff.

[62] BVerfGE 129, 124, *EFSF*, paras 120 ff.; BVerfGE 132, 195, *European Stability Mechanism*, paras 109 f.; BVerfGE 135, 317, *ESM Treaty*, paras *159 ff.*

[63] BVerfGE 140, 317, *Identity Review I.*

[64] BVerfGE 142, 123, *OMT Programme*; BVerfGE 146, 216, *PSPP Preliminary Ruling.*

[65] BVerfGE 151, 202, *European Banking Union.*

[66] See Rupp, 'Ausschaltung des Bundesverfassungsgerichts durch den Amsterdamer Vertrag?', 53 *JuristenZeitung* (1998) 213, at 215, 216 f.; U. Haltern, 'Ultra-vires-Kontrolle im Dienst europäischer Demokratie', 39 *Neue Zeitschrift für Verwaltungsrecht* (2020) 817.

[67] *Identity Review I* (n. 63) paras 40 ff.

> [I]t seems to me an all but impossible task to preserve *this* Union, as we know it today, if it is to be made subject to an absolute reservation, ill-defined and virtually at the discretion of each of the Member States, which takes the form of a category described as 'constitutional identity'. That is particularly the case if that 'constitutional identity' is conceived to be different from the 'national identity' referred to in Article 4(2) TEU.[68]

The Second Senate emphasizes precisely this difference.[69]

Thus, principles are the linchpin of identity conflicts in which powerful actors shape European society. The role of identity is remarkable: a concept introduced to advance European integration also articulates what is crucial for national institutions. Moreover, it helps European discourses that national concerns are defended throughout Europe with a uniform terminology and with a common orientation towards principles. In such disputes, we can observe European society as well as a transformation of public law (see 1.1).

But what exactly is at stake? You need not be a Machiavellian or a public choice theorist to suspect that the parties to the disputes raise, negotiate, and defend their individual interests (see 4.1.D). Yet, there is more to the conflict, as an analysis of the concept shows.

B. Some Identity Theory

Over the decades, identity has emerged as a key concept in European politics and European law. More than any other concept, it now serves to limit Europeanization. A diverse chorus of voices postulates a 'we' (a strong collective identity, a nation state) as a prerequisite for democracy, concluding that European democracy is impossible (see 1.4, 2.3.C).

The issue of a European 'we' almost appears like the litmus test of European public law. I will not dodge it, and my answer has two parts. First, I think it goes too far to link the very possibility of a democratic system of government to a general sense of 'we' among the population. At the same time, I do see the beginnings of a European collective identity.

Let me start with a conceptual clarification. Like any foundational concept, identity has many meanings, which explains much of the vagueness in debates on national or European identity. To understand the link between principles and

[68] CJEU, Case C-62/14, *Gauweiler et al.*, Opinion of AG Cruz Villalón (EU:C:2015:7) paras 59 ff.
[69] BVerfGE 134, 366, *OMT Decision*, para. 29.

identity, one should distinguish between two meanings that stem from the Latin *idem*, the root of the word identity.[70]

The first meaning of identity refers to an ensemble of characteristics that distinguish something or someone. In this sense, a person, group, or constitution has an identity. Carl Schmitt uses the term 'constitutional identity' to describe a constitution's basic features, and many authors have followed suit.[71] Here, constitutional identity is a synonym for the constitutional core (see 3.1.C), mostly conceived of as an ensemble of fundamental principles. Examples include Article 2 TEU, Article 1 of the Italian Constitution, and Article 79(3) of the Basic Law.[72]

The other meaning of the term 'identity' denotes a person's inner attitudes.[73] It refers to a mental process that results in belonging and commitment.[74] For Böckenförde, like many scholars, this process figures among the prerequisites of a democratic state (see 1.4). This stands in a Hegelian tradition: 'A constitution […] is the idea and the consciousness of what is reasonable', 'the kind and character of its [a particular people's] self-consciousness'.[75] *Collective* identity mostly refers to this meaning.

For example, the German Constitutional Court speaks of the 'identification of citizens with the fundamental values symbolized by the flag', on which 'the Federal Republic depends'.[76] This meaning of identity also considers fundamental principles (or values) crucial for identity, but the argument differs from that used for the other meaning. Here, principles are crucial because they allow for the mental processes.

How can principles become relevant to a person's identity? How can citizens develop a constitutional identity? A person's identity is neither directly observable from the outside nor directly accessible to a person's introspection. Any answer requires a conception of what constitutes a person's identity, how it forms, and how it manifests itself.[77]

The question 'Who am I?' is not theoretical but practical for it generally pertains to the individual's own future actions.[78] Imagine A telling B, 'You know me.'

[70] Schmidt, 'Identität. Gebrauch und Geschichte eines modernen Begriffs', 86 *Muttersprache* (1976) 333; Sterck, 'Sameness and Selfhood. The Efficiency of Constitutional Identities in EU Law', 24 *European Law Journal* (2018) 281.

[71] C. Schmitt, *Verfassungslehre* (1928) 103, 205, 215, 235; similarly, P. Häberle, *Europäische Rechtskultur. Versuch einer Annäherung in zwölf Schritten* (1994) 9 ff.; Kirchhof, '§ 19. Die Identität der Verfassung in ihren unabänderlichen Inhalten', in P. Kirchhof and J. Isensee (eds), *Handbuch des Staatsrechts der Bundesrepublik Deutschland Band II. Verfassungsstaat* (2004) 775.

[72] Sommermann, 'Art. 20 GG', in H. von Mangoldt, F. Klein, and C. Starck (eds), *Kommentar zum Grundgesetz, Bd. 2* (2018) para. 3; in detail Polzin (n. 52) 85 ff.

[73] E. H. Erikson, *Psychological Issues. Identity and the Life Cycle* (1959); Erikson, 'Identity, Psychosocial', in D. L. Sills (ed.), *International Encyclopedia of the Social Sciences, Vol. 7* (1968) 61.

[74] Schmidt, 'Identität' (n. 70) 338; J. Habermas, *Zur Rekonstruktion des Historischen Materialismus* (1976) 63 ff., 92 ff.

[75] Hegel, *Elements of the Philosophy of Right* (n. 13) para. 274.

[76] BVerfGE 81, 278, *Bundesflagge*, para. 50; see also BVerfGE 124, 300, *Wunsiedel*, 329, para. 66.

[77] Tugendhat (n. 48) 23 ff.

[78] Ibid. 26, 168.

This usually means, 'You know how I will act in a certain situation.' Since actions are directed towards others, identity is formed in relation to, and with the help of, others. In short, identity depends on intersubjectivity (see 1.4). Hegel formulates this basic philosophical insight (which refutes much of rational choice theory) as '"I" that is "We" and "We" that is "I"'.[79] Today, social psychology describes the sum of the elements by which persons position themselves and act in a society as their social identity.[80]

Because intersubjective contexts are shaped by roles, a person's identity develops through their roles.[81] Roles are normative phenomena since they consist of the social expectations that attach to an individual (see 3.3.C). Since the law shapes many expectations, the constitutionalization of the legal order (see 2.5) can be a path to constitutional identity. Principles are important here because constitutional principles account for much of the legal order's constitutionalization. Principles form identity when they shape provisions (or educational content) relevant to roles.[82] For instance, the fact that both constitutional and Union law require the equality of men and women has probably contributed to the transformation of self-understandings in gender relations over the past decades.[83]

Let us now turn to the question of collective identity. Collective identity consists of consonant psychological processes based on which people perceive themselves as members of a group. A sense of 'we' is the strongest form of this phenomenon. Collective identity is a conscious, reflexive social belonging. But how much of that is needed for a viable democracy?

A democratic society requires some political unity, primarily to accept majority decisions as legitimate.[84] Various concepts articulate this thought, such as homogeneity (see 1.4), legitimacy,[85] community,[86] basic consensus,[87] social trust (see 2.5.A), the public sphere,[88] constitutional patriotism (see 2.5.C), and collective identity. Many approaches, often in a Hegelian tradition, maintain that only a

[79] G. W. F. Hegel, *Phenomenology of Spirit* (2013 [1807]) 110; C. Taylor, *Quellen des Selbst. Die Entstehung der neuzeitlichen Identität* (1994) 639 ff; R. Smend, *Staatsrechtliche Abhandlungen und andere Aufsätze* (3rd edn, 1994) 125, 136, 189, 219 ff; D. Suhr, *Bewußtseinsverfassung und Gesellschaftsverfassung. Über Hegel und Marx zu einer dialektischen Verfassungstheorie* (1975) 302 ff.

[80] O. Angelucci von Bogdandy, *Zur Ökologie einer Europäischen Identität. Soziale Repräsentationen von Europa und dem Europäer-Sein in Deutschland und Italien* (2003) 33 ff.

[81] Tugendhat (n. 48) 235 f., 241; BVerfGE 96, 152, *Parteilehrer*, para. 36.

[82] K. Grimonprez, *The European Union and Education for Democratic Citizenship. Legal Foundations for EU Learning at School* (2020) esp. at 339 ff.

[83] U. Sacksofsky, *Das Grundrecht auf Gleichberechtigung. Eine rechtsdogmatische Untersuchung zu Artikel 3 Absatz 2 des Grundgesetzes* (1996); E. Muir, *EU Equality Law: The First Fundamental Rights Policy of the EU* (2018) 4 ff.

[84] H. Heller, *Europa und der Faschismus* (1929) 10.

[85] Weiler, 'The Transformation of Europe', 100 *Yale Law Journal* (1991) 2403.

[86] C. Taylor, *Wieviel Gemeinschaft braucht die Demokratie? Aufsätze zur politischen Philosophie* (2001) 273 f.

[87] Von Bogdandy, 'Zweierlei Verfassungsrecht. Europäisierung als Gefährdung des gesellschaftlichen Grundkonsenses?', 39 *Der Staat* (2000) 163.

[88] D. Grimm, *The Constitution of European Democracy* (2017) 15 ff., 58 f.

developed collective identity allows for a democratic society (see 1.4). This take explains attempts to forge a European identity. Indeed, already the preamble of the 1952 draft Treaty establishing the European Political Community, which the parliamentary assembly of the European Coal and Steel Community adopted without a single negative vote, projected a European 'We'.

Now, many societies make do with little social legitimacy, community, basic consensus, social trust, a common public sphere, or collective identity. Yet, I do not believe that such societies are incapable of democracy.

The view that a 'we' is essential to democracy strikes me as a postulate more than an irrefutable finding.[89] I have not found compelling arguments in its favour. To the contrary, there are plausible indications that it is false.[90] As Dahrendorf demonstrates from a sociological and Frankenberg from a constitutional perspective, a viable democracy can be premised on difference and conflict, provided there are corresponding processes and procedures of public decision-making.[91] Volkmann even frames this in a Hegelian approach, arguing for a democratic culture of conflict.[92] As for Article 2 TEU, the society invoked in this provision does not require a collective identity (since the authors of the Treaties do not postulate it). However, this provision might be part of a process that generates collective consciousness (see 1.2, 1.4).

The debate on the necessity of 'we-ness' is anything but settled. For the purpose of this book, I rely on some broadly agreed insights to develop my argument. One is that fundamental principles are important, be it in order to establish a collective identity or to provide standards for successful decision-making processes. Moreover, both approaches hold that fundamental principles are vital to processes of societal reflection.

If we look at the European debates through the lens of socio-psychological theories, we see evidence of an emerging collective European consciousness. Again, arguing against Schmitt helps make the point. Schmitt focuses on positive feelings, namely friendship (see 2.3.C). On that view, there is little evidence of a collective European consciousness, considering the many conflicts in European society. However, important theories of social psychology take a different approach. They

[89] On the psychological debate, see Sullivan and Transue, 'The Psychological Underpinnings of Democracy: A Selective Review of Research on Political Tolerance, Interpersonal Trust, and Social Capital', 50 *Annual Review of Psychology* (1999) 625.

[90] Neidhardt, 'Formen und Funktionen gesellschaftlichen Grundkonsenses', in G. F. Schuppert and C. Bumke (eds), *Bundesverfassungsgericht und gesellschaftlicher Grundkonsens* (2000) 15, at 16 f., 26 f.; Koschorke (n. 25) 189 ff., 202 ff.

[91] R. Dahrendorf, *The Modern Social Conflict. An Essay on the Politics of Liberty* (1988) 28 f., 187 ff.; G. Frankenberg, *Die Verfassung der Republik. Autorität und Solidarität in der Zivilgesellschaft* (1996) esp. at 32 ff., 133 ff., 213 ff.

[92] Volkmann, 'Gespräche mit Hegel', 59 *Der Staat* (2020) 489, at 509 f.; A. Farahat, *Transnationale Solidaritätskonflikte. Eine vergleichende Analyse verfassungsgerichtlicher Konfliktbearbeitung in der Eurokrise* (2021) II § 2.

emphasize the cognitive dimension, that is, the perception of belonging to the same social category.

Such theories define social identity, first, through a person's knowledge of group membership.[93] Thus, Schmitt's emotional aspect (friendship) becomes less significant. Of course, emotional processes of valorizing one's own group remain important, but they are not domineering. Contrary to what Schmitt postulates, moreover, attitudes towards foreign groups are not necessarily hostile and can be characterized instead by tolerance and appreciation.[94]

Collective identity often flows from collective memories, which can be seen as entries in a group-specific dictionary with which each member is somehow familiar.[95] It helps greatly if the entries relate to shared experiences of significant events.[96] Those writing in this dictionary shape the social identity and contribute to group formation.[97] For that reason, identity policies as well as politics have been successful in many societies.

Yet, a dictionary for European society cannot resemble too closely those conceived for the European nations in the eighteenth and nineteenth centuries (see 1.2, 1.4). We need not aspire to a strong European 'we' because the transformation of European public law does not amount to a state- and nation-building process (see 2.3.A). The idea is that European and national identity can go well together, provided they communicate with each other.

C. European and National Identity

Section 3.2.B argued that European constitutional law can help European identity emerge. Much has happened in this regard since I first studied this subject in 2002. Let us recall that there were four different organizations at the time, the European Coal and Steel Community (ECSC), the European Community (EC), the European Atomic Energy Community (EAEC), and the European Union (EU), whose status was entirely unclear.[98] European citizens could hardly identify with this confusing

[93] Tajfel and Turner, 'An Integrative Theory of Intergroup Conflict', in W. G. Austin and W. Stephen (eds), *The Social Psychology of Intergroup Relations* (1979) 33; Turner, 'Some Current Issues in Research on Social Identity and Self Categorization Theories', in N. Ellemers, B. Doosje, and R. Spears (eds), *Social Identity. Context, Commitment, Content* (1999) 6; V. Kaina, *Wir in Europa. Kollektive Identität und Demokratie in der Europäischen Union* (2009) esp. at 39 ff.

[94] Mummendey, 'Social Discrimination and Tolerance in Intergroup Relations. Reactions to Intergroup Difference', 3 *Personality and Social Psychology Review* (1999) 158.

[95] F. Cerruti and E. Rudolph (eds), *Un'anima per l'Europa. Lessico di un'identità politica* (2002).

[96] David and Bar-Tal, 'A Sociopsychological Conception of Collective Identity. The Case of National Identity as an Example', 13 *Personality and Social Psychology Review* (2009) 354.

[97] J. Assmann, *Cultural Memory and Early Civilization* (2011) 111 ff.; P. Ricœur, 'Reflections on a New Ethos for Europe', 21 *Philosophy & Social Criticism* (1995) 3, at 6 ff.

[98] Curtin, 'The Constitutional Structure of the Union. A Europe of Bits and Pieces', 30 *Common Market Law Review* (1993) 17; von Bogdandy, 'The Legal Case for Unity. The European Union as a Single Organization with a Single Legal System', 36 *Common Market Law Review* (1999) 887.

institutional landscape. The Treaty of Lisbon overcame this confusion in 2009. Today, virtually all citizens identify the European Union as the organization in charge, which means that the cognitive processes are much easier. Furthermore, the Treaty of Lisbon's Article 2 principles lay down the substance suited to further citizens' identities.[99] The same holds true for the CFR, which has led to CJEU decisions that are widely reported in the media and thus visible to citizens.

The recent crises have also helped the European Union become more relevant and better known (see 2.5.B, 3.6.B). Overall, the Union's politicization (see 2.2.B) has increased its cognitive relevance greatly, and processes of European identity formation are clearly visible. As already mentioned, *Eurobarometer 2019* showed that as many as 73 per cent of respondents—which still included Britons—felt themselves to be citizens of the Union.[100] Union citizens often trust Union institutions more than those of their Member State.[101] The European society postulated by the Treaty legislator in 2007 hence has a concrete socio-psychological dimension.

Handling one problem successfully often gives rise to a new one. Thus, the emergence of European identity might influence, and even harm, national identities, not least because of the Union's fundamental principles. The prohibition of any discrimination on grounds of nationality provides a good example (Article 18 TFEU) as it implies that nationality becomes less salient. The CJEU has even turned European citizenship into a *status* of equality.[102] This facilitates the European group-building process but lessens the relevance of national identities.

1. The Treaty's Mediation Efforts

The Treaty legislator attempted to address these conflicts by propagating the idea that European and national identities, rather than being mutually exclusive, are complementary. That is why Article 4(2) TEU mandates respect for national identity and Article 9(2) TEU builds Union citizenship on Member State citizenship. The Treaty legislator thus aims for multiple collective identities, with the national identities embedded in a common European identity.

Social psychology confirms the possibility of there being such multiple identities.[103] Empirical research has proved it in the European

[99] On the importance of writing (*Verurkundlichung*), see Frankenberg, 'The Return of the Contract: Problems and Pitfalls of European Constitutionalism', 6 *European Law Journal* (2000) 257, at 261 ff.

[100] European Commission, *Standard Eurobarometer 91, Spring 2019, First Results: Public Opinion in the European Union* (June 2019 survey) 16, https://europa.eu/eurobarometer/surveys/detail/2253 (last visited 14 August 2022). On the robustness of the data, see 2.5.A.

[101] European Commission, *Standard Eurobarometer 93, Summer 2020, Report: Public Opinion in the European Union* (Brussels 2020), https://ec.europa.eu/commfrontoffice/publicopinion/index.cfm/ResultDoc/download/DocumentKy/91061 (last visited 14 August 2022).

[102] CJEU, Case C-184/99, *Grzelczyk* (EU:C:2001:458) para. 31.

[103] Graumann, 'Soziale Identitäten', in R. Viehoff and R. T. Segers (eds), *Kultur Identität Europa. Über die Schwierigkeiten und Möglichkeiten einer Konstruktion* (1999) 59, at 67; Martiny and Kessler,

case,[104] particularly among younger persons.[105] There are also fewer differences among the latter between Eastern and Western Europe than among older people.[106] The younger generation is more likely to perceive the EU as a relevant part of its identity. Trust in EU institutions also supports the formation of a European identity.[107]

Nevertheless, there are concerns that the European identity threatens or damages national identity. Right-wing parties and political movements often fan such concerns.[108] Their electoral success shows that quite a few citizens share them. Some constitutional courts, particularly the Second Senate of the German Constitutional Court, are responsive to these concerns, provide their advocates with a public forum, substantiate them with doctrines of constitutional identity, and position themselves as their defenders. This may well serve to absorb fears, thereby eventually supporting the legitimacy of European politics.[109] Nevertheless, this approach strikes me as dangerous because it fuels nationalist narratives and results in problematic lines of jurisprudence.[110]

Moreover, policymakers do address the concern that the Union might endanger national identity. Already in 1992, the Treaty legislator imposed the duty on the Union to respect its Member States' identities. In 2007, in the Treaty of Lisbon, it substantiated this protection by linking the Member States' identities to their 'fundamental structures, political and constitutional' (Article 4(2) TEU). Thus, the Member States' fundamental principles play a central role.

Identity in the sense of Article 4(2) cl. 1 TEU covers understandings subsumed under both meanings of identity (see 3.2.B). The relative clause in Article 4(2) TEU demonstrates that the term 'national identity' first refers to the *substance* of

'Managing One's Social Identity. Successful and Unsuccessful Identity Management', 44 *European Journal of Social Psychology* (2014) 748.

[104] Fuss and Grosser, 'What Makes Young Europeans Feel European? Results from a Cross-Cultural Research Project', in I. P. Karolewski and V. Kaina (eds), *European Identity. Theoretical Perspectives and Empirical Insights* (2006) 209.

[105] Jugert, Šerek, and Stollberg, 'Contextual Moderators of the Link Between National and European Identity among European Youth', 22 *Journal of Youth Studies* (2019) 436.

[106] Ceka and Sojka, 'Loving It But Not Feeling It Yet? The State of European Identity after the Eastern Enlargement', 17 *European Union Politics* (2016) 482.

[107] Verhaegen, Hooghe, and Quintelier, 'The Effect of Political Trust and Trust in European Citizens on European Identity', 9 *European Political Science Review* (2017) 161; Stoeckel, 'Contact and Community. The Role of Social Interactions for a Political Identity', 37 *Political Psychology* (2016) 431.

[108] See Hentges, Nottbohm, and Platzer (n. 50); G. Levi and D. Preda (eds), *Euroscepticisms. Resistance and Opposition to the European Community/European Union* (2019).

[109] Voßkuhle, 'Die Zukunft der Verfassungsgerichtsbarkeit in Deutschland und Europa', 47 *Europäische Grundrechte-Zeitschrift* (2020) 165, at 170.

[110] See, e.g. the contributions by A. von Bogdandy, B. Çalı, S. Cassese, P. Cruz Villalón, D. Halberstam, B. Iancu, A. Jakab, M. A. Queralt Jimenez, H. Keller, S. Bates, K. Lenaerts, R. Miller, O. Pollicino, D. Sarmiento, A. Śledzińska-Simon, P. Sonnevend, M. Steinbeis, A. Vauchez, J. H. H. Weiler, and M. Wyrzykowski, in von Bogdandy *et al.*, 'German Legal Hegemony?', 43 *MPIL Research Paper* (2020).

identity. However, it also protects identification processes to the extent that they represent a prerequisite for the state.

The concept of 'national' in Article 4(2) TEU corroborates this interpretation. This concept is just as multifaceted as that of identity and broadly overlaps with it in its two main meanings.[111] One understanding of the nation revolves around commonalities such as language, history, destiny, ethnicity, and political institutions.[112] The other understanding focuses on the individuals' will to belong together, the proverbial 'plébiscite de tous les jours'.[113]

Article 4(2) TEU does not determine the individual Member States' national identity. By referring to the 'fundamental structures, political and constitutional, inclusive of regional and local self-government', it provides a framework for what Article 4(2) TEU protects, however. Not every constitutional provision qualifies as an expression of national identity under Article 4(2) cl. 1 TEU; only fundamental ones do so.[114] This corresponds to most constitutional courts' case law.[115]

Since Article 4(2) cl. 1 TEU protects national characteristics that shape the Member States' identity, such a characteristic can be specific to one country and need not be mentioned in Article 2 TEU.[116] Consider the prohibition of titles of nobility in Article 4(7) of the Greek Constitution, which is even protected against constitutional amendment. The parallel provision in Austrian law led to one of the first cases in which the CJEU invoked Article 4(2) TEU.[117] Given the many monarchies that still exist in European society, this principle is certainly not a common European one.

Nevertheless, there are limits on what the Union must respect under Article 4(2) cl. 1 TEU. They flow from Article 2 cl. 1 TEU as all Member States must uphold these principles without any reservation or exception. While European society is pluralistic, it is not radically pluralistic. Furthermore, the Treaty legislator tries to

[111] S. Dellavalle, *Una costituzione senza popolo? La Costituzione europea alla luce delle concezioni del popolo come 'potere costituente'* (2002) 94.

[112] F. Hanschmann, *Der Begriff der Homogenität in der Verfassungslehre und Europarechtswissenschaft. Zur These von der Notwendigkeit homogener Kollektive unter besonderer Berücksichtigung der Homogenitätskriterien 'Geschichte' und 'Sprache'* (2008) esp. at 149 ff.

[113] This is E. Renan's well-known, albeit ambivalent, metaphor: E. Renan, *Qu'est-ce qu'une nation?* (2020 [1882]) 51.

[114] CJEU, Case C-213/07, *Michaniki*, Opinion of AG Poiares Maduro (EU:C:2008:544) para. 33; E. Di Salvatore, *L'identità costituzionale dell'Unione europea e degli Stati membri. Il decentramento politico-istituzionale nel processo di integrazione* (2008) 35 ff.

[115] *Lisbon* (n. 61) paras 216 ff., 240; Ústavní soud (Czech Constitutional Court), Pl. ÚS 19/08, *Lisbon I*, paras 93, 94, 110; Ústavní soud, Pl. ÚS 29/09, *Lisbon II*, para. 112 ('material core'); Trybunał Konstytucyjny (Polish Constitutional Tribunal), K32/09, *Lisbon*, para. 2.1.

[116] CJEU, Case C-36/02, *Omega* (EU:C:2004:614) paras 37 f. with further references; Case C-244/06, *Dynamic Medien* (EU:C:2008:85) paras 44 ff.; Case C-438/14, *Bogendorff von Wolffersdorff* (EU:C:2016:401) para. 73.

[117] CJEU, Case C-208/09, *Sayn-Wittgenstein* (EU:C:2010:806) paras 83, 91.

cabin the Member States' courts: Article 4(2) TEU is a provision under Union law on which the CJEU has the final say (Articles 267 and 344 TFEU).[118]

These lines sketch the mediation between national identity and European integration that the Treaty legislator probably had in mind.[119] The CJEU determines the protection Article 4(2) cl. 1 TEU offers by considering what the constitutional court with jurisdiction deems its country's national identity. Article 24 of its Statute allows the CJEU to reach out to the Member State for the relevant national understanding. If the Court finds a violation of Article 4(2) TEU, it can either annul the EU provision or determine that its primacy is suspended for the affected Member State.

2. Principled Judicial Resistance

The attempt by the Treaty legislator—that is, by the united Member State governments and parliaments—to incorporate their courts' case law on identity into EU law has met resistance from some of these courts (see 4.4.B). The CJEU may have contributed to that resistance for it trivialized the protection of national identity in Article 4(2) TEU when it reduced it to just one factor in its proportionality test. This is unfortunate, but it does not run counter to the provision: the duty of respect in Article 4(2) TEU, unlike that in Article 1(1) cl. 2 of the Basic Law, does not provide absolute protection.[120]

Many constitutional courts find such relativization unacceptable. What is at stake is the core of their constitution, requirements that are mostly immune to balancing and certainly represent more than just one of many considerations. Above all, however, some courts are averse to the envisioned structure of mediation. They do not accept that the CJEU ultimately decides the conflict. Particularly, the Second Senate of the German Constitutional Court considers it paramount to have the final say.[121]

The domestic resistance is doctrinally grounded in the distinction between the national identity of Article 4(2) TEU and the Member States' constitutional identity. National courts posit the latter as an autonomous concept under their exclusive jurisdiction,[122] which gives them broad discretion to articulate and

[118] Rossi, '2, 4, 6 (TUE) ... l'interpretazione dell'"Identity Clause" alla luce dei valori fondamentali dell'Unione', in *Liber Amicorum Antonio Tizzano. De la Cour CECA à la Cour de l'Union. Le long parcours de la justice européenne* (2018) 858; *Gauweiler et al.*, Opinion of AG Cruz Villalón (n. 68).

[119] In detail, see von Bogdandy and Schill, 'Overcoming Absolute Primacy. Respect for National Identity under the Lisbon Treaty', 48 *Common Market Law Review* (2011) 1417.

[120] See, e.g. CJEU, Case C-673/16, *Coman et al.* (EU:C:2018:385) paras 42 ff.

[121] From the wealth of scholarship, see Kumm, 'Who Is the Final Arbiter of Constitutionality in Europe? Three Conceptions of the Relationship between the German Federal Constitutional Court and the European Court of Justice', 36 *Common Market Law Review* (1999) 351; Halberstam, 'Constitutional Heterarchy. The Centrality of Conflict in the European Union and the United States', in J. L. Dunoff and J. P. Trachtman (eds), *Ruling the World? Constitutionalism, International Law, and Global Governance* (2009) 326.

[122] Firmly, *OMT Decision* (n. 69) para. 29; more conciliatory, *Lisbon* (n. 61) paras 216 ff., 240.

impose their understanding of constitutional identity against European treaties, EU legal acts, and CJEU or European Court of Human Rights (ECtHR) decisions. The most active court in this respect has been the Second Senate of the German Constitutional Court.

Most of the resisting courts limit themselves to the general declaration that Union actions cannot violate the most fundamental national principles.[123] The Czech Constitutional Court is one of the few courts that have gone further. Referring to Article 1(1) and Article 9(2) of the Czech Constitution, it states that the 'foundations of state sovereignty . . . or the essential attributes of the democratic rule of law',[124] national and ethnic minorities, the principle of equality, and free competition among parties must be protected.[125]

No court goes into greater detail than the Second Senate of the German Constitutional Court. Its Lisbon judgment states that Germany's national identity is characterized by the limitations that constrain constitutional amendments under the 'eternity clause' in Article 79(3) of the Basic Law.[126] This comes as a surprise: a provision that was informed by the end-of-Weimar experience and seeks to prevent Germany from sliding into dictatorship now prohibits fulfilling the constitutional mandate to further the 'realization of a united Europe' (Preamble and Article 23(1) of the Basic Law). The extravagance of this judicial move becomes even more evident if we recall that, for decades, the party programme of the Christian Democratic Union (CDU) proclaimed the objective of a European federal state. The Second Senate's Lisbon judgment makes Konrad Adenauer's party almost look like an enemy of the Basic Law, like an anti-constitutional party.

Under these circumstances, one might expect the Second Senate to pursue a minimalist understanding of German constitutional identity.[127] Yet, the opposite is the case, with the Senate establishing a sweeping ambit of protection. In doing so, it seeks to ensure 'sufficient space [. . .] for the political formation of the economic, cultural and social living conditions'.[128] This covers all

> areas which shape the citizens' living conditions, in particular the private sphere of their own responsibility and of political and social security, protected by fundamental rights, as well as [. . .] political decisions that rely especially on cultural, historical and linguistic perceptions and which develop in public discourse in the party political and parliamentary sphere of public politics.[129]

[123] See, e.g. Conseil constitutionnel, Decision No. 2006-540 DC of 27 July 2006—'Copyright and related rights in the information Society', para 19.

[124] Ústavní soud (Czech Constitutional Court), Pl. ÚS 50/04; Pl. ÚS 66/04, para. 53.

[125] *Lisbon I* (n. 115) para. 208.

[126] *Lisbon* (n. 61) paras 216 ff., 239 f.

[127] Thus *Lisbon I* (n. 115) para. 109.

[128] *Lisbon* (n. 61) para. 249.

[129] Ibid.

In setting out concrete limits on EU action, the Second Senate has gone further than any other constitutional court.[130] The limits pertain to citizenship[131] as well as to

> decisions on substantive and formal criminal law (1), on the disposition of the monopoly on the use of force by the police within the state and by the military towards the exterior (2), fundamental fiscal decisions on public revenue and public expenditure, the latter being particularly motivated, inter alia, by social policy considerations (3), decisions on the shaping of living conditions in a social state (4) and decisions of particular cultural importance, for example on family law, the school and education system and on dealing with religious communities (5).[132]

Many authors have argued, persuasively, that the Court's understanding of constitutional identity is problematic,[133] and the criticism has not abated. Ten years later, Matthias Ruffert argued that the Lisbon decision disrupted integration more than the failure of the Defence Community, De Gaulle's policy of the 'empty chair', Eurosclerosis, and the failure of the Constitutional Treaty.[134]

Dimitri Spieker's comparison between different constitutional courts helps us better understand the Senate's path,[135] but he also shows how extreme it is. This insight is significant because the Senate tries to present its case law as part of the mainstream. Spieker compares the Belgian, German, French, Italian, Polish, Spanish, Czech, and Hungarian constitutional courts.[136] The Second Senate's citation practice suggests that these decisions are largely concordant.[137] Spieker controverts this image by comparing the courts' jurisprudence on identity, the type of legal act they review, and the level of scrutiny.

[130] See, e.g. Halberstam and Möllers, 'The German Constitutional Court Says "Ja zu Deutschland!"', 10 *German Law Journal* (2009) 1241, at 1249 ff.; Kottmann and Wohlfahrt, 'Der gespaltene Wächter? Demokratie, Verfassungsidentität und Integrationsverantwortung im Lissabon-Urteil', 69 *Zeitschrift für ausländisches öffentliches Recht und Völkerrecht* (2009) 443, at 460 f., 466; Schönberger, '*Lisbon* in Karlsruhe: *Maastricht*'s Epigones at Sea', 10 *German Law Journal* (2009) 1201, at 1209 f. For an affirmative stance, see Gärditz and Hillgruber, 'Volkssouveränität und Demokratie ernst genommen. Zum Lissabon-Urteil des BVerfG', 64 *JuristenZeitung* (2009) 872.

[131] *Lisbon* (n. 61) para. 249.

[132] Ibid., para. 252.

[133] On this problem, see Nettesheim, 'Ein Individualrecht auf Staatlichkeit? Die Lissabon-Entscheidung des BVerfG', 39 *Neue Juristische Wochenschrift* (2009) 2867, at 2868 f.; Tomuschat, 'Lisbon—Terminal of the European Integration Process? The Judgment of the German Constitutional Court of 30 June 2009', 70 *Zeitschrift für ausländisches öffentliches Recht und Völkerrecht* (2010) 251, at 272 f., 278 f.

[134] Ruffert, 'Eine Binnenperspektive auf die deutsche Europawissenschaft—zehn Jahre nach der großen Erschütterung', 68 *Jahrbuch des öffentlichen Rechts* (2020) 515, at 515 f.

[135] Spieker, 'Framing and Managing Constitutional Identity Conflicts. How to Stabilize the Modus Vivendi between the Court of Justice and National Constitutional Courts', 57 *Common Market Law Review* (2020) 361, at 387.

[136] On the following, see ibid. 365 ff. On individual lines of case law, see C. Calliess and G. van der Schyff (eds), *Constitutional Identity in a Europe of Multilevel Constitutionalism* (2020).

[137] *Identity Review I* (n. 63) paras 40 ff., esp. at 50.

As regards identity, it is noteworthy, in light of Article 2 TEU, that all courts except Hungary's[138] base their review solely on universal principles. This finding confirms European public law's basic structure: the fundamental principles of Article 2 TEU do, in fact, constitute the reference points across all legal orders (except Hungary). Regardless of how contentious an issue may be, European legal pluralism is not radical.

As for the reviewed legal acts, the main question is whether a constitutional court also reviews constitutional amendments that extend the scope of Union law. Only the Italian, the Czech,[139] and the German Constitutional Court go this far. Moreover, the Second Senate anchors the limitations it devises in Article 79(3) of the Basic Law, thereby entrenching its case law. Even a constitutional amendment cannot transfer such competences. Accordingly, only the original constituent power can, by adopting a new constitution, overcome the Second Senate's objections.[140]

The third dimension concerns the level of scrutiny. The Second Senate has developed a triad, with the *Solange* doctrine protecting German fundamental rights, the *ultra vires* review safeguarding German competences, and identity review defending Germany's identity. Only the Polish and Hungarian courts exercise a similarly exacting review. By contrast, the other courts limit themselves to fundamental rights, with certain extensions in Belgium and Spain.

In summary, the Second Senate's review is unique and, one is tempted to say, idiosyncratic. There is little on which to base the broad and uniquely detailed constitutional identity the Court develops. Notwithstanding the deficiencies of such an extreme doctrine of constitutional identity, the doctrine as such does, however, play a constructive role in European public law, expressing the latter's pluralism. It can provide checks and balances in European society and safeguard democracy as long as the courts cooperate (see 4.4.B).

Because of this development, Article 4(2) TEU has not become the key provision that mediates the national constitutional identity with Union law. Rather, the national and the European courts interweave their interpretations of fundamental principles.[141]

[138] Halmai, 'Abuse of Constitutional Identity' (n. 51).

[139] Roznai, 'Legisprudence Limitations on Constitutional Amendments? Reflections on The Czech Constitutional Court's Declaration of Unconstitutional Constitutional Act', 8 *ICL Journal* (2014) 29.

[140] Huber, 'Art. 146 GG', in M. Sachs (ed.), *Grundgesetz. Kommentar* (2018) paras 9, 18 ff. For suggestions on how to make this work, see Schilling, 'Eine neue Verfassung für Deutschland. Art. 146 GG und die Rolle des Bundesverfassungsgerichts', 53 *Der Staat* (2014) 95.

[141] A. Voßkuhle, *Die Idee der Europäischen Wertegemeinschaft* (2018) 30; Lenaerts, 'Die Werte der Europäischen Union in der Rechtsprechung des Gerichtshofs', 44 *Europäische Grundrechte-Zeitschrift* (2017) 639, at 640.

D. The Pluralism of Principles

Understanding European pluralism is key for understanding European principles and their interpretations. This pluralism already follows from the institutional dualism of the Union and the Council of Europe with the ECtHR. This duality originated as a historical contingency (see 2.2.A) but has since become a structure of European law (see 2.2.C). The Treaty legislator accorded it constitutional status with its decision to base the Union on human, rather than fundamental, rights (see 3.1.C).

The duality of the Union and the Council of Europe reflects European identity: on the one hand, European society's identity is centred in the Union. On the other hand, Dmitri Shostakovich, Emir Kusturica, and the Eurovision Song Contest are likely to play a role when European citizens conceive of themselves as European.[142] While the EU is at the heart of the European society described in Article 2 TEU, this society, unlike a nation, is not sharply delimited by the Union's external border and the attribution of citizenship. While scholarly thought that follows in the tradition of Carl Schmitt will regret such fuzziness, I, like Albrecht Koschorke or Joseph Weiler, consider it an achievement.[143]

Furthermore, the pluralism among Member States feeds European pluralism. Though all legal orders, including their constitutional principles, are committed to the values of Article 2 TEU, there are tremendous differences in their meaning and institutionalization. European understandings of principles must respond to this diversity.

There are republics and monarchies among the Member States; parliamentary and semi-presidential systems; strong and weak parliaments; strong and weak party structures; unitary and federal orders; strong, weak and non-existent constitutional courts; significant divergences in institutional guarantees of judicial independence, fundamental rights, and electoral systems; and, last but not least, Catholic, Protestant, secular, socialist, statist, anarcho-syndicalist, civic, Ottoman, and post-colonial constitutional traditions. European society surely does not feed on every aspect of these traditions, but it does rely on its pluralistic diversity and multiple modernities.[144] Today, European public law can never be a tool of unifying modernization.[145]

This also applies to theories of principles.[146] The principles of Article 2 TEU do play a fundamental role. But their meaning is much thinner than that of the parallel

[142] From the wealth of scholarship on the latter, see D. Vuletic, *Postwar Europe and the Eurovision Song Contest* (2018).

[143] See further below, 4.4.A; Koschorke (n. 25) 194 ff.; Weiler, 'Federalism without Constitutionalism. Europe's Sonderweg', in K. Nicolaïdis and R. Howse (eds), *The Federal Vision. Legitimacy and Levels of Governance in the United States and the European Union* (2001) 54.

[144] Eisenstadt, 'Multiple Modernities', 129 *Daedalus* (2000) 1.

[145] Zapf, 'Die Modernisierungstheorie und unterschiedliche Pfade gesellschaftlicher Entwicklung', 24 *Leviathan* (1996) 63.

[146] Schorkopf, 'Value Constitutionalism in the European Union' (n. 15).

principles under most domestic constitutions. European diversity is not folklore. The use of the term 'value' in Article 2 TEU suggests that we should understand its principles as particularly vague. Because of this vagueness, Union institutions lack the authority to develop the values into a detailed and mandatory blueprint for national constitutions.

National constitutional requirements regarding the EU must be interpreted with even greater restraint.[147] Germany exemplifies that need. Article 23(1) of the Basic Law only authorizes German membership in a Union that is 'committed to democratic, social and federal principles, to the rule of law and to the principle of subsidiarity and that guarantees a level of protection of basic rights essentially comparable to that afforded by this Basic Law'. If these principles demanded the same of the Union as they do of German state (*Länder*) bodies, the Union would be Germany's clone. The Basic Law would then mandate not a Europeanized Germany but a Germanized Europe (see 5.1.C).

European theories, doctrines, interpretations, and applications of principles must be sensitive to context. Operationalizing Article 2 TEU must distinguish between four constellations. In the first constellation, the principles of Article 2 TEU apply to Union bodies; here, they can be at their most exacting (see 3.3.B, 3.5). The second constellation concerns their operationalization vis-à-vis Member State institutions within the scope of Union law (see 3.3.C). While detailed standards are justified, they must respect the Member States' constitutional autonomy. General constitutional oversight of the Member States, exemplarily set out in Article 7 TEU (see 3.3.D, 3.6, 4.6.C, 5.4.B), represents the third constellation. Here, the requirements must be far more elementary. External action makes up the fourth constellation, for the Treaty legislator subordinates EU foreign policy to the values of the TEU (Articles 8(1), 21(2), and 32 TEU). It should be self-evident that the Article 2 TEU guidelines are even less exacting in this case. Thus, the Treaty does not require the EU to demand liberal democracy from China or the Vatican City State the same way it does from Poland or Hungary.

The pluralism of European society thus requires differentiated theories, doctrines, interpretations, and applications of principles that do justice to the various constellations. In this way, principles can grasp, frame, and deal with the explosive issue of identity.

[147] On the British opinion of the 1960s that the EEC must be subject to the House of Windsor for Great Britain to become a member, see W. Hallstein, *Die Europäische Gemeinschaft* (1973) 67.

3. The Rule of Law

A. Trust as a Vanishing Point

Like no other concept, Hallstein's community of law articulates the transformation of European public law in its first period (see 2.2.A, 2.3.A). This European *community* of law was considered a stepping stone towards the European rule of law. Thus, at the 1964 Kiel Conference of Teachers of Public Law, Badura's co-lecturer, Schmitt's estate executor Joseph H. Kaiser, ended his reflections with the appeal, 'It is the calling of our time to create a European rule of law state [*Rechtsstaat*].'[148]

Kaiser articulated a zeitgeist that animated many in the legal profession. A generation later, the Treaty of Amsterdam constitutionalized their life achievements. The English version of the Treaty, which speaks of the *rule of law*, almost conceals the significance of the step the Treaty legislator made in 1997. After all, the rule of law represents an established concept in international law, too.[149] But most of the other languages help underscore the magnitude of the decision. Instead of using concepts such as *prééminence du droit* or *Herrschaft des Rechts*, the Treaty legislator speaks of *État de droit* and *Rechtsstaatlichkeit*. Accordingly, the EU has achieved at least one core element of statehood, even though it is not a state (see 2.3.A). The transformation since 1964 has been profound, not least because hardly anyone contested the decision in 1997.

The European concept of the rule of law feeds on heterogeneous doctrinal and institutional phenomena. This pluralism is readily apparent in the diverse forms of judicial review of administrative action[150] and of constitutional adjudication[151] in

[148] Kaiser, 'Bewahrung und Veränderung demokratischer und rechtsstaatlicher Verfassungsstruktur in den internationalen Gemeinschaften', 23 *Veröffentlichungen der Vereinigung der Deutschen Staatsrechtslehrer* (1966) 1, at 28, 33. The awkwardness of the translation (European rule of law state) highlights the gulf between the Continental European and the Anglo-American legal tradition.

[149] Fitzmaurice, 'The General Principles of International Law Considered from the Standpoint of the Rule of Law (Volume 92)', in Hague Academy of International Law (ed.), *Collected Courses of the Hague Academy of International Law* (1957); Krieger and Nolte, 'The International Rule of Law—Rise or Decline?—Approaching Current Foundational Challenges', in H. Krieger, G. Nolte, and A. Zimmermann (eds), *The International Rule of Law. Rise or Decline?* (2019) 3.

[150] See contributions by J.-B. Auby, G. Biaggini, M. Bobek, A. von Bogdandy/P. M. Huber, M. Borabito, S. Cassese, M. Fromont, L. Heuschling, S. Hinghofer-Szalkay, I. B. Iniesta, H. Küpper, M. Loughlin, B. G. Mattarella, W. J. Novak, B. Schindler, J. H. H. Weiler, and E. Wiederin in A. von Bogdandy, P. M. Huber, and S. Cassese (eds), *The Max Planck Handbooks in European Public Law, Vol. I. The Administrative State* (2017); T. Ackermann, J. Barnes, A. Cassatella, S. Cassese, L. de Lucia, M. Eifert, A. Gaillet, M. Guttner/S. Waldmann, L. Hering, H. C. H. Hofmann, M. Kayser, H. Keller/C. Marti, B. Schindler, K.-P. Sommermann, B. Stepanek, S. Storr, S. Unger, C. Waldhoff, and F. Wollenschläger in A. von Bogdandy, S. Cassese, and P. M. Huber (eds), *Handbuch Ius Publicum Europaeum, Bd. IX. Verwaltungsgerichtsbarkeit in Europa: Gemeineuropäische Perspektiven und supranationaler Rechtsschutz* (2021).

[151] For greater detail, see the contributions by M. L. Amaral/R. A. Pereira, C. Behrendt, L. F. M. Besselink, G. Biaggini, R. Bifulco/D. Paris, A. von Bogdandy/C. Grabenwarter/P. M. Huber, A. Farahat, C. Grabenwarter, P. M. Huber, O. Jouanjan, P. E. Quint, J. L. Requejo Pagés, L. Sólyom, P. Tuleja, K. Tuori, and I. Ziemele/A. Spale/L. Jurcēna in A. von Bogdandy, P. M. Huber, and C. Grabenwarter (eds), *Max Planck Handbooks in European Public Law, Vol. III. Constitutional*

the various legal orders.[152] As a result, it is notoriously difficult to derive, from this principle, concrete requirements that fit all legal orders.[153] Member State governments accused of violating the rule of law often stress this point.[154]

However, European pluralism is not radical, and the rule of law in Article 2 TEU is not a contingency formula. In a concerted operationalization, the EU institutions have derived a set of requirements, which include the principles of lawfulness (legality), legal certainty, the prohibition of arbitrary decision-making, and access to independent and impartial courts. According to the institutions, the rule of law, interpreted in the light of the other principles of Article 2 TEU (see 3.1.C), also requires transparent, democratic, and pluralistic legislative procedures, the separation of powers as well as the protection of fundamental rights (see 4.6.C).

Of these many aspects, this paragraph will focus on what gives the rule of law primacy over the other principles of Article 2 TEU: the principle of legality. This principle ensures that norms can fulfil their social function at all.[155]

As suggested by the Hegelian tradition[156] and many other theories,[157] this function centres on social trust. To allow for constructive social interaction and communicative practice (see 1.2), societies create and stabilize expectations that indicate what is likely and socially accepted. Contrary to cognitive expectations, normative expectations are maintained even when they are disappointed. In this way, they facilitate and, indeed, enable social action, paving the way for social trust (see 2.5.A).

Normative expectations are constitutive of society. In today's highly differentiated societies, law plays a vital role in creating and stabilizing such expectations. This holds true for European society in particular as it does not amount to a nation

Adjudication: Institutions (2020); A. von Bogdandy/C. Krenn, A. von Bogdandy/C. Grabenwarter/P. M. Huber, M. Claes/B. de Witte, P. Cruz Villalón, M. de Visser, A. Farahat, C. Grabenwarter, C. Grewe, R. Grote, A. Jakab, C. Landfried, J. Martín y Pérez de Nanclares, D. Paris, and M. Vašek in A. von Bogdandy, P. M. Huber, and C. Grabenwarter (eds), *The Max Planck Handbooks in European Public Law, Vol. IV: Constitutional Adjudication: Common Themes and Challenges* (2023).

152 See the contributions of S. Biernat/D. Dąbek, P. Craig, P.-M. Efstratiou, P. Gonod, C. Grabenwarter, M. Holoubek, P. M. Huber, T. Jaag, W. Kahl, M. Kayser, G. Marcou, L. Marcusson, G. Melis/A. Meniconi, O. Mir, C. Möllers, G. Napolitano, V. Pereira da Silva/A. Salgado de Matos, D. de Pretis, M. Ruffert, K.-P. Sommermann, Z. Szente, and J. Ziller in A. von Bogdandy, S. Cassese, and P. M. Huber (eds), *Handbuch Ius Publicum Europaeum, Bd. V. Verwaltungsrecht in Europa* (2014).

153 European Commission for Democracy through Law (Venice Commission), Report on the rule of law, 86th Plenary Session (Venice, 25–26 March 2011) paras 4 f.; R. Grote, 'Rule of Law, Rechtstaat and "Etat de Droit"', in C. Starck (ed.), *Constitutionalism, Universalism and Democracy. A Comparative Analysis* (1999) 269.

154 J. Varga, 'Facts You Always Wanted to Know about Rule of Law But Never Dared to Ask', *Euronews* (22 November 2019); *Address by Prime Minister Viktor Orbán in the Debate on the So-Called Sargentini Report* (11 September 2018), http://www.miniszterelnok.hu/address-by-prime-minister-viktor-orban-in-the-debate-on-the-so-called-sargentini-report (last visited 14 August 2022).

155 Recital (6) of the Preamble of Regulation 2020/2092 (n. 22).

156 Hegel, *Elements of the Philosophy of Right* (n. 13) para. 268; Volkmann (n. 92) 490.

157 S. Romano, *Frammenti di un dizionario giuridico* (1953) 76, 81; N. Luhmann, *Das Recht der Gesellschaft* (1993) 150 ff.; J. Raz, *The Authority of Law. Essays on Law and Morality* (2nd edn, 2009) 222.

or a people and is less homogeneous. Therefore, there has always been great emphasis on the constitutive role of European law:[158] 'Nowhere is Europe more real than in the law.'[159]

The principle of the *rule of law* demands that *law rules*. A legal order is governed by the rule of law only if its norms guide actual conduct. Only then does the law fulfil its function of creating trust. Thus, the rule of law mandates that the standards of Article 2 TEU must be more than words on a piece of paper or slogans of political speech.

The rule of law requires that all public authority be exercised in accordance with the law. Therefore, all European legal orders recognize the doctrines that German law calls the primacy of parliamentary law (*Gesetzesvorrang*) and the requirement of a parliamentary (statutory) law for issues of particular importance (*Gesetzesvorbehalt*).[160] In Germany, these two doctrines are emblematic of the transformation of public law in the nineteenth century.[161] At the time, they constrained the administration, which was mostly under monarchical control, and allowed for incremental democratization. This entailed instituting the primacy of parliamentary law—that is, subjecting the executive power to parliament—and the

[158] Hallstein, 'Die EWG—eine Rechtsgemeinschaft (1962)', in T. Oppermann (ed.), *Europäische Reden* (1979) 341; see 2.2.B.

[159] Thus, the Comité de Réflexion sur le Préambule de la Constitution, *Redécouvrir le Préambule de la Constitution. Rapport du comité présidé par Simone Veil* (2008) 41; also Bermann, 'The Role of Law in the Functioning of Federal Systems', in Nicolaïdis and Howse (n. 143) 191; A. de Tocqueville, *Democracy in America* (1994 [1835]).

[160] See, e.g. Gonod, 'Frankreich. § 75', in von Bogdandy, Cassese, and Huber, *Handbuch Ius Publicum Europaeum, Bd. V* (n. 152) 159, at paras 81 ff.; de Pretis, 'Italien, § 78', in von Bogdandy, Cassese, and Huber, *Handbuch Ius Publicum Europaeum, Bd. V* (n. 152) 371, at paras 101 ff.; Dreier, 'Deutschland. § 1', in A. von Bogdandy, P. Cruz Villalón, and P. M. Huber (eds), *Handbuch Ius Publicum Europaeum, Bd. I. Grundlagen und Grundzüge staatlichen Verfassungsrechts* (2007) 3, at paras 121 ff.; Loughlin, 'Großbritannien. § 4', in A. von Bogdandy, P. Cruz Villalón, and P. M. Huber (eds), *Handbuch Ius Publicum Europaeum, Bd. I. Grundlagen und Grundzüge staatlichen Verfassungsrechts* (2007) 217, at para. 26; Dogliani and Pinelli, 'Italien. § 5', in A. von Bogdandy, A. Cassese, and P. M. Huber (eds), *Handbuch Ius Publicum Europaeum, Bd. I. Grundlagen und Grundzüge staatlichen Verfassungsrechts* (2007) 273, at para. 112; Besselink, 'Niederlande. § 6', in A. von Bogdandy, P. Cruz Villalón, and P. M. Huber (eds), *Handbuch Ius Publicum Europaeum, Bd. I. Grundlagen und Grundzüge staatlichen Verfassungsrechts* (2007) 327, at paras 82 ff.; Wiederin, 'Österreich. § 7', in A. von Bogdandy, P. Cruz Villalón, and P. M. Huber (eds), *Handbuch Ius Publicum Europaeum, Bd. I. Grundlagen und Grundzüge staatlichen Verfassungsrechts* (2007) 389, at paras 91 ff., 101; Tuleja, 'Polen. § 8', in A. von Bogdandy, P. Cruz Villalón, and P. M. Huber (eds), *Handbuch Ius Publicum Europaeum, Bd. I. Grundlagen und Grundzüge staatlichen Verfassungsrechts* (2007) 451, at paras 33, 77; Medina Guerrero, 'Spanien. § 11', in A. von Bogdandy, P. Cruz Villalón, and P. M. Huber (eds), *Handbuch Ius Publicum Europaeum, Bd. I. Grundlagen und Grundzüge staatlichen Verfassungsrechts* (2007) 625, at para. 61; Halmai, 'Ungarn. § 12', in A. von Bogdandy, P. Cruz Villalón, and P. M. Huber (eds), *Handbuch Ius Publicum Europaeum, Bd. I. Grundlagen und Grundzüge staatlichen Verfassungsrechts* (2007) 687, at para. 43; Nehmelman, 'Niederlande. § 32', in A. von Bogdandy, P. Cruz Villalón, and P. M. Huber (eds), *Handbuch Ius Publicum Europaeum, Bd. II. Offene Staatlichkeit—Wissenschaft vom Verfassungsrecht* (2008) 613, at para. 10; in summary, Zacharias, 'Terminologie und Begrifflichkeit, § 40', in A. von Bogdandy, S. Cassese, and P. M. Huber (eds), *Handbuch Ius Publicum Europaeum, Bd. II. Offene Staatlichkeit—Wissenschaft vom Verfassungsrecht* (2008) paras 27, 33.

[161] Siemek, 'Hegel als Philosoph des modernen Rechtsstaates', *Hegel-Jahrbuch* (2008) 169; Böckenförde, 'Entstehung und Wandel des Rechtsstaatsbegriffs (1969)', in E.-W. Böckenförde (ed.), *Recht, Staat, Freiheit. Studien zur Rechtsphilosophie, Staatstheorie und Verfassungsgeschichte* (2006) 143.

requirement of a statutory provision, especially for state interventions in personal liberty or property as well as for tax liabilities. The rule of law cabins and rationalizes public authority and is thus a progressive project (see 2.4.D).

All legal orders include, in some form, the doctrines of the primacy of parliamentary law and the requirement of statutory provision. Nevertheless, the European concept of the rule of law is anything but a copy of the German concept, as the comparison with the French republican understanding shows. Consider, for instance, the very purpose of judicial review. Put bluntly, in Germany, the *bourgeois* defends their individual rights, while in France, the *citoyen* defends the democratic legal order.[162]

Law thrives on breaches of the law. A breach of law does not endanger the law's social function. In functioning legal orders, unlawful action prompts social and institutional responses that confirm normative expectations and thereby contribute to their relevance and development. Without the CJEU's rulings, Union law would not be what it is today, and there would be no European society (see 4.3.B). Three aspects are especially relevant: the principle of legality (see 3.3.B); the principle of effectiveness (see 3.3.C); and the Member States' functionality (see 3.3.D).

B. Legality of Union Action

The rule of law in Article 2 TEU implies the principle of legality. The Union's principle of legality, in consonance with the European constitutional tradition, has a negative and a positive dimension.[163] Usually, we refer to them as the primacy of the higher law and the requirement of a statutory (mostly parliamentary) provision for important public measures (e.g. Article 52(1) CFR). We focus, here, on the first dimension as it illustrates best the EU's emancipation from the law of international organizations.

The principle of legality entails that each of the Union institutions' actions (including entering into international treaties) must comply with all primary law (Article 13(2) TEU).[164] This primacy establishes a strict internal hierarchy as the basic structure of the Union legal order: all law created by Union bodies is subordinate to primary law and must thus respect it. This applies without exception for

[162] L. Heuschling, *État de droit, Rechtsstaat, Rule of Law* (2002); J. Masing, *Die Mobilisierung des Bürgers für die Durchsetzung des Rechts. Europäische Impulse für eine Revision der Lehre vom subjektiv-öffentlichen Recht* (1997); C. Grewe and H. Ruiz Fabri, *Droits constitutionnels européens* (1995) 22 ff.

[163] von Bogdandy and Bast, 'The European Union's Vertical Order of Competences: The Current Law and Proposals for Its Reform', 39 *Common Market Law Review* (2002) 227; Bast, 'Art. 5 EUV [Prinzipien der Kompetenzordnung]', in E. Grabitz, M. Hilf, and M. Nettesheim (eds), *Das Recht der Europäischen Union* (2020) paras 10 ff.

[164] CJEU, Case 294/83, *Les Verts v. Parliament* (EU:C:1986:166) para. 23; Opinion 1/91, *EEA Agreement I* (EU:C:1991:490) para. 21; Opinion 2/15, *Free Trade Agreement with Singapore* (EU:C:2017:376) para. 235.

EU constitutional law enjoys absolute primacy. This corresponds to the primacy of a Member State constitution in most national legal orders.

That this primacy seems self-evident today reflects the depth of the transformation since it was by no means self-evident for the early Community.[165] In most international organizations, the primacy of the Founding Treaty over the acts of its institution is often precarious, as the United Nations shows.[166] The strict primacy of the EU Treaties is the result of the CJEU's jurisprudence. The Court decided early on that the Treaty amendment procedure (now Article 48 TEU) would constitute the only way to alter its provisions. This prevents other forms of impinging on normative expectations created by the EU Treaties, be it by the EU institutions or by the Member States.

Accordingly, the principle of legality protects the Union as well as the Member States. Only the Treaty legislator—that is, all the Member States in cooperation with Union bodies (Articles 5(1), 48, and 49 TEU)—may amend the Treaties.[167] Such discipline is, at best, embryonic in international organizations.[168]

Therefore, the Treaties' validity cannot be suspended by agreements among Member States,[169] and the EU institutions cannot derogate or set aside primary law.[170] Even decisions adopted unanimously by the Council are subject to primary law.[171] This is why Article 352 TFEU's designation as a competence to 'supplement the Treaty' is misleading.

Sometimes, the Member States' representatives, even when assembled in the Council, do not act as the EU body 'Council' but as a Conference of States. Metaphorically speaking, they thus 'change hats' and act outside Union law (i.e. under international law), which permits decisions that are not allowed under Union law. Such decisions made by the 'government representatives of the Member States convened in the Council' are not EU acts but rather international treaties or *memoranda of understanding*. They are often politically important and highly effective.[172]

[165] Carstens, 'Die kleine Revision des Vetrages über die Europäische Gemeinschaft für Kohle und Stahl', 21 *Zeitschrift für ausländisches öffentliches Recht und Völkerrecht* (1961) 1, at 1, 14.

[166] Nolte, 'Lawmaking through the UN Security Council. A Comment on Krika de Wet's Contribution', in R. Wolfrum and V. Röben (eds), *Developments of International Law in Treaty Making* (2005) 237, at 239 ff.

[167] CJEU, Opinion 1/94, *WTO* (EU:C:1994:384) para. 52; Opinion 2/94, *ECHR Accession I* (EU:C:1996:140) para. 30; Case C-370/12, *Pringle* (EU:C:2012:756) para. 33-36; Case C-572/15, *F. Hoffmann-La Roche* (EU:C:2016:739) para. 30.

[168] P. Reuter and P. Cahier, *Introduction au droit des traités* (rev. 3rd edn, 1995) paras 210 f.; H. G. Schermers and N. M. Blokker, *International Institutional Law* (2018) § 1163.

[169] CJEU, Joint Cases 90/63 and 91/63, *Commission v. Belgium and Luxembourg* (EU:C:1964:80) 634; Case 43/75, *Defrenne/SABENA* (EU:C:1976:56) para. 58; Joint Cases C-241/91 P and C-242/91 P, *RTE and ITP/Commission* (EU:C:1995:98) para. 86.

[170] CJEU, Joint Cases 31/86 and 35/86, *LAISA v. Council* (EU:C:1988:211) para. 12: Case 68/86, *United Kingdom v. Council* (EU:C:1988:85) para. 24; Case C-687/15, *Commission v. Council (WRC-15)* (EU:C:2017:803) para. 41.

[171] CJEU, Case 38/69, *Commission v. Italy* (EU:C:1970:11) paras 12 f.

[172] M. Goldmann, *Internationale öffentliche Gewalt. Handlungsformen internationaler Institutionen im Zeitalter der Globalisierung* (2015) 319 ff.

The CJEU regularly uses the primacy of Union law to oppose these attempts at bypassing Union law.[173] In a few cases, however, it has refrained from doing so. For example, it refused to review the so-called EU–Turkey Statement of 18 March 2016, which was issued by the members of the European Council together with their Turkish counterparts.[174] Many critics based their objections to this ruling on the EU's principle of legality,[175] stressing its importance for the normativity of EU law.

The principle of legality has a significant impact on the Member States' status and capacity to act. As actors who create and amend EU primary law, they have virtually total freedom to shape the Union, only through the demanding procedures of Articles 48 and 49 TEU. This supports the autonomy of the Union's constitutional order. As actors within the Union's institutions, in particular in the European Council and the Council, they have broad powers to shape the EU legal order but are strictly subject to primary law. This simultaneous exclusion and inclusion of the 'masters of the Treaties' resembles constitutional legality in the Member States, whose constitutions enjoy primacy over statutory law: while parliament represents the sovereign people, it is bound by the constitution.[176] The United Kingdom provides the only exception, but its constitution is not representative of European public law.

In Union law, as in the Member States' legal orders, positive legality exists alongside its negative dimension. Thus, the requirement of a statutory provision complements the primacy of the law. The EU is a public authority because it has the power to impose obligations. This power is subject to the principle of positive legality, which finds its most important concretization under Union law in the principle of conferral (Article 5(1) TEU). Consequently, the Union bodies' legal acts must always have a legal basis.[177] It can either result directly from a Treaty provision or from an act of secondary law that can be traced back to the Treaties. While negative legality merely limits public authority, the requirement of a competence adds another layer of constitutional discipline, requiring a specific ground of validity.

A competence represents formalized political power. That explains the intensity of conflicts about competences (see 3.2.C, 4.3.B) and the fact that positive legality became more pronounced the more the Union became more powerful. In response to challenges from national institutions, in particular some constitutional courts

[173] CJEU, Case 44/84, *Hurd v. Jones* (EU:C:1986:2) para. 39; *Pringle* (n. 167) para. 69.

[174] CJEU, Case T-192/16, *NF v. European Council* (EU:T:2017:128); Case T-193/16, *NG v. European Council* (EU:T:2017:129); Case T-257/16, *NM v. European Council* (EU:T:2017:130); CJEU, Joint Cases C-208/17 P–C-210/17 P, *NF and others v. European Council* (EU:C:2018:705).

[175] Bast, 'Scharade im kontrollfreien Raum: Hat die EU gar keinen Türkei-Deal geschlossen?', *Verfassungsblog* (3 March 2017); Carrera, den Hertog, and Stefan, 'It Wasn't Me! The Luxembourg Court Orders on the EU–Turkey Refugee Deal', 15 *CEPS Policy Insights* (2017).

[176] Luhmann, 'Verfassung als evolutionäre Errungenschaft', 9 *Rechtshistorisches Journal* (1990) 176, at 176 ff.

[177] Bast (n. 163) paras 15 ff.

(see 4.4.B), the Treaty legislator increasingly shaped the competences with a view to protecting the Member States' competences. The Lisbon Treaty acknowledges the Member States' constituent role (Article 1(1) TEU) and establishes prominent constraints, such as the principles of conferral, subsidiarity, and proportionality (Article 5 TEU).

The legality principle further protects the Member States by committing the European political process to demanding proceedings that ensure they have a voice. The CJEU's scrutiny of these proceedings is demanding.[178] In doing so, it ensures the polycentric and horizontal character of the political system as a system of mediation (see 3.5.B). All this helps foment trust in the EU institutions.

C. Effectiveness in National Law

Union law creates and stabilizes normative expectations, mostly through Member State institutions. To ensure this national mediation, the Court of Justice has developed what are perhaps the most famous doctrines of Community law: its autonomy, primacy, and *effet utile*. These doctrines are the seminal inventions of its first period. At the time, they were framed in functionalist, not constitutionalist, terms (see 2.4.A, 2.5.A, 2.6.A, 4.3.B). Today, these doctrines must be reconstructed in the light of Article 2 TEU, as manifestations of its rule-of-law principle.[179]

Nothing is more characteristic of Union law than its *effet utile*, its principle of effectiveness. Quantitative data illustrate this role: 'effectiveness' appears in 9,219 (German) documents on CJEU decisions, far more than any other key concept. The related term 'validity' appears 6,395 times, 'primacy' 3,820 times, and 'autonomy' 1,121 times, while 'the rule of law' is mentioned in 131 documents.[180] Effectiveness has shaped the relationship between the Union and the Member States more than any other principle. Indeed, it is the effectiveness of Community law that led to the emergence and democratization of European society.

The principle of effectiveness imposes the obligation on the Member States to realize the regulatory purpose of a Community provision. The general principle underlies such core doctrines as the direct effect of Treaty provisions,[181] decisions,[182] directives,[183] and international commitments,[184] as well as the requirements of effective enforcement,[185] interpreting national law in conformity with

[178] *United Kingdom v. Council* (n. 170) para. 24.
[179] Lenaerts, Gutiérrez Fons, and Adam, 'Exploring the Autonomy of the European Legal Order', 81 *Zeitschrift für ausländisches öffentliches Recht und Völkerrecht* (2021) 47.
[180] Hits on https://curia.europa.eu/juris/documents.jsf (last visited 14 August 2022).
[181] CJEU, Case 26/62, *Van Gend en Loos v. Administratie* der Belastingen (EU:C:1963:1) 24 f.
[182] CJEU, Case 9/70, *Grad v. Finanzamt Traunstein* (EU:C:1970:78) para. 5.
[183] CJEU, Case 8/81, *Becker* (EU:C:1982:7) paras 29 f.
[184] CJEU, Case 181/73, *Haegeman v. Belgian State* (EU:C:1974:41) paras 2 ff.
[185] CJEU, Joint Cases 205/82–215/82, *Deutsche Milchkontor GmbH* (EU:C:1983:233) para. 22.

Union law,[186] state liability,[187] and independent courts.[188] The autonomy of Union law and its primacy over Member State law[189] were also justified with the *effet utile* principle.

For the German concept of the *Rechtsstaat*, the rule of law primarily serves to limit government authority, much less to ensure its effectiveness: what was at stake in the nineteenth century was framing and controlling existing administrative authorities, which had mostly been established by the earlier processes of state formation (see 2.1). In the early 1960s, by contrast, there was no established authority of Community institutions. Since it was based in international law, the Community's effective authority did not provide the backdrop for the European rule of law; rather, the Community's effective authority depended on asserting the European rule of law. Such effectiveness distinguishes the EU Treaties from most international treaties, first and foremost from the United Nations Charter, which some conceive as the constitution of world society.[190]

Compared to international law, the Union's rule of law shines brightly. It is emancipatory because it turns nationals into subjects of a supranational legal order that provides greater freedom (see 2.4.D, 3.1.D). But the European rule of law would be even stronger if the rule of law were as strong in all Member States as it is in the Union. This is where its greatest deficiencies lie. The Union has recognized the problem and begun to address national deficiencies in the rule of law.

D. Strengthening Weak Statehood

The composite nature of European law makes the Union's rule of law dependent on the rule of law in the Member States. Until well into the second period of European public law, rule of law in the Member States was mainly an issue of fully implementing Union law.[191] Today, this challenge seems rather harmless. Today, authoritarian tendencies are front and centre (see 3.6, 4.6, 5.4), as are phenomena of state failure that originate in weak institutionality.[192]

[186] CJEU, Case C-684/16, *Max Planck Society for the Advancement of Science* (EU:C:2018:874) para. 59.

[187] CJEU, Joint Cases C-6/90 and C-9/90, *Francovich and Bonifaci v. Italy* (EU:C:1991:428) paras 33 ff.

[188] *Associação Sindical dos Juízes Portugueses* (n. 21) paras 36 ff.

[189] CJEU, Case 6/64, *Costa v. E.N.E.L.* (EU:C:1964:66) 1269; Case 92/78, *Simmenthal v. Commission* (EU:C:1978:106) para. 39.

[190] B. Fassbender, *The United Nations Charter as the Constitution of the International Community* (2009).

[191] See, on the one hand, H. Siedentopf and J. Ziller (eds), *L'Europe des administrations? La mise en oeuvre de la législation communautaire dans les Etats membres* (1988); on the other hand, Bobek, 'Europeanization of Public Law', in von Bogdandy, Huber, and Cassese, *Handbuch Ius Publicum Europaeum, Bd. IV* (n. 150) 631.

[192] The following reflections are based on Ioannidis and von Bogdandy, 'Systemic Deficiency in the Rule of Law: What It Is, What Has Been Done, What Can Be Done', 51 *Common Market Law Review* (2014) 59.

Occasional violations of the law do not weaken the rule of law (see 3.3.A). It is only weakened when violations become normal. This might occur once public institutions do not react to them properly, be it because of institutional weakness or corruption. Examples include companies that regularly circumvent tax, labour, or environmental law, misconduct of public officials that goes unpunished, and court cases that drag on for many years. Such phenomena undermine the rule of law because, at some point, a legal order ceases to fulfil its central function of supporting normative expectations. Trust is lost, giving rise to a *systemic deficiency* in the rule of law.

A systemic deficiency in the rule of law differs from a normal violation (see 3.6.B). When a normal violation of the law occurs, individuals maintain the disappointed normative expectation. By contrast, they are likely to modify their expectations when it comes to systemic deficiencies. They will then view the law and public institutions not out of a perspective of trust but with cynicism or disrespect. They stop expecting the legally required conduct to be the rule. Other mechanisms of stabilization (resorting to foreign legal orders, prepayment, kinship, Mafia-like organizations) will become more relevant. Talent and capital will emigrate. Democracy and all other principles of Article 2 TEU will be precarious at best, which explains the rule of law's primacy (see 3.4.A).

A systemic deficiency in the rule of law exists when the law is not able to stabilize normative expectations in vital areas of society. Social-science indicators help determine when this is the case. The World Bank generates such data with its Worldwide Governance Indicators (WGI).[193] They include the control of corruption, regulatory quality, the rule of law, and government effectiveness. The World Justice Project has a similar thrust. It maintains a Rule of Law Index that monitors constraints on government power, the absence of corruption, order and security, fundamental rights, open government, regulatory enforcement, and civil and criminal justice.[194]

These indicators provide many important insights. First, the rule of law is not simply a question of financial resources: there are middle-income states that perform much better than EU Member States with significantly higher incomes. According to World Bank data, states such as Costa Rica, Uruguay, and Malaysia observe the rule of law more faithfully than Bulgaria, Greece, Italy, or Romania.[195] Second, there is an immense discrepancy between EU Member States: according to the World Bank, Denmark's government effectiveness is in the 99.04th percentile, while Romania's is in the 40.38th percentile. (A percentile rank of 99.04 means that

[193] See World Bank, *Control of Corruption*, http://info.worldbank.org/governance/wgi/pdf/cc.pdf (last visited 14 August 2022).

[194] See World Justice Project, http://worldjusticeproject.org/what-rule-law (last visited 14 August 2022).

[195] The index is available at World Bank, *Worldwide Governance Indicators*, http://info.worldbank.org/governance/wgi/index.aspx#home (last visited 14 August 2022).

99.04 per cent of the countries considered in the statistical population rank below the country in question.) When it comes to the rule-of-law criterion, Finland holds first place worldwide, while Bulgaria only occupies a middle place among the more than 200 states and territories.[196]

It bears emphasizing that no EU Member State is a failed or even a weak state in global comparison.[197] However, the rule of law of Article 2 TEU demands more from EU Member States than maintaining standards that distinguish them from the Democratic Republic of Congo. Bulgaria or Romania are not weak states in the sense of international law. They are, however, weak members in the sense of Union law.[198]

Such weaknesses impinge on individual rights, such as the rights to good administration (Article 41 CFR), an effective remedy, and an impartial tribunal (Article 47 CFR). One might say that they impinge on the European right to have European rights.[199] Perhaps the most fundamental right of Union law is to truly live under EU law; it is violated by systemic deficiencies in the rule of law.[200] The right to rights confirms the logical primacy of the rule of law over the other principles. In consequence, weak statehood is a European concern.

Thanks to the euro crisis, Greece has received much attention in this regard.[201] On 26 February 2012, the *New York Times* published a report entitled 'The Failing State of Greece'.[202] It describes incidents where the police and the judiciary seemed unable to prevent, or at least prosecute, the destruction of public and private property, looting, and arson. Less violent but common phenomena, such as widespread corruption or the extraordinary length of judicial proceedings, also became a European issue. The inefficiency of the Greek tax authorities was considered one reason for the financial crisis in Greece that brought the EU to the brink of disaster in the early 2010s.[203] Although Greece was not at any point a weak, or even failed,

196 World Bank, *Worldwide Governance Indicators*, status of 2019, http://info.worldbank.org/governance/wgi/Home/Reports (last visited 14 August 2022).

197 See Fragile States Index, *Measuring Fragility: Risk and Vulnerability in 179 Countries*, Fund for Peace, https://fragilestatesindex.org (last visited 14 August 2022); Brookings Institution, *Index of State Weakness in the Developing World* (26 February 2008), https://www.brookings.edu/research/index-of-state-weakness-in-the-developing-world (last visited 14 August 2022); Center for Systemic Peace and Center for Global Policy at Maryland University State, *State Fragility Index* (2018), http://www.systemicpeace.org/inscr/SFImatrix2018c.pdf (last visited 14 August 2022).

198 Ioannidis, 'Weak Members and the Enforcement of EU Law', in A. Jakab and D. Kochenov (eds), *The Enforcement of EU Law and Values: Ensuring Member States' Compliance* (2017) 476, at 480 ff.

199 H. Arendt, *The Origins of Totalitarianism* (1951) 294. On the fundamental European right to have European rights, see Russo, 'La cittadinanza "sostanziale" dell'UE alla luce della proposta del gruppo di Heidelberg: Verso una "reverse Solange"?', 8 *federalismi.it.* (2014) 1, at 7 ff.

200 On this, see *LM* (n. 17) paras 36 f., 48 ff (dealing with the parallel constellation of authoritarian tendencies).

201 K. Featherstone and D. Papadimitriou, *The Limits of Europeanization: Reform Capacity and Policy Conflict in Greece* (2008) 5.

202 Donadio, 'The Failing State of Greece', *New York Times* (26 February 2012) 8, Section SR.

203 Combatting tax evasion has since become one of the EU's priorities. See European Council Conclusions of 23 May 2013 (EUCO 75/1/13 REV 1).

state by international standards, many people—not least many Greeks—wonder whether Greece is a kind of 'weak' state when measured by European standards.[204]

Reports of the EU Task Force for Greece, which was supposed to help with the EU and International Monetary Fund (IMF) adjustment programmes and support Greek reform efforts, confirm such doubts.[205] While the reforms, which were agreed upon with European and international partners and adopted by the Greek parliament, have brought improvements, progress remains slow.[206] According to the World Bank, Greece still only scores in the 60.58th percentile for the rule-of-law criterion and only in the 56.25th percentile for the anti-corruption criterion in 2019.[207]

In addition, Greece is ranked 146th for the enforcement of contracts in the World Bank's *Doing Business* ranking.[208] Data from the Council of Europe also shows the weaknesses of the Greek judiciary when it comes to Articles 6 and 13 of the European Convention on Human Rights (ECHR). For example, the ECtHR determined that Greece is incapable of providing timely and effective judicial protection.[209] It stressed the 'chronic and persistent nature' of the problem and pointed out that the situation in Greece 'could in practice be regarded as a denial of justice'.[210] Crucially, the problem persists.[211]

Italy faces similar problems.[212] According to the World Bank's WGI, many Italian institutions perform well below the European average where the rule of law is concerned, be it with regard to government effectiveness, the control of corruption, or the length of judicial proceedings: In 2019, Italy was only barely ahead of Greece in terms of the rule of law and fighting corruption.[213] The problems with

[204] Featherstone, 'The JCMS Annual Lecture: The Greek Sovereign Debt Crisis and EMU: A Failing State in a Skewed Regime', 49 *Journal of Common Market Studies* (2011) 193; Malkoutzis, 'Is Greece a Failed State?', *Foreign Policy* (2 March 2012).

[205] Task Force for Greece, First Quarterly Report, SI(2011) 399/3, 14.

[206] See European Commission, *EU Financial Assistance*, http://ec.europa.eu/economy_finance/assistance_eu_ms/greek_loan_facility/index_en.htm (last visited 14 August 2022).

[207] World Bank, *World Governance Indicators* (n. 196).

[208] World Bank, *Doing Business*, https://www.doingbusiness.org/en/data/exploretopics/enforcing-contracts?data%2520PointCode=DB_ec_time (last visited 14 August 2022).

[209] ECtHR, *Vassilios Athanasiou and others v. Greece*, Appl. no. 50973/08, Judgment of 21 December 2010; see also the pilot judgments in *Michelioudakis v. Greece*, Appl. no. 54447/10, Judgment of 3 April 2012; *Glykantzi v. Greece*, Appl. no. 40150/09, Judgment of 30 October 2012.

[210] ECtHR, *Vassilios Athanasiou and others v. Greece* (n. 209) paras 44, 52; M. Mitsopoulos and T. Pelagidis, *Understanding the Crisis in Greece. From to Boom to Bust* (2011) 103 f.

[211] European Commission, Commission Staff Working Document, 2020 Rule of Law Report, Country Chapter on the rule of law situation in Greece, accompanying the document 'Communication from the Commission to the European Parliament, the Council, the European Economic and Social Committee and the Committee of the Regions 2020 Rule of Law Report', Brussels, 30 September 2020, SWD(2020) 307 final, 4.

[212] On the Italian reform discussion, see S. Cassese, *L'Italia: Una società senza stato?* (2011) 82–94, 110; M. Clarich, 'Riforme amministrative e sviluppo economico', *Rivista trimestrale di diritto pubblico* (2020) 159; L. Casini, 'Politica e amministrazione: "The Italian Style"', *Rivista trimestrale di diritto pubblico* (2019) 13.

[213] World Bank, *World Governance Indicators* (n. 196); M. Delsignore and M. Ramajoli, 'La prevenzione della corruzione e l'illusione di un'amministrazione senza macchia', *Rivista trimestrale di diritto pubblico* (2019) 61.

lengthy judicial proceedings are well known.[214] Italy is in 122nd place in the World Bank's *Doing Business* ranking for the enforcement of contracts,[215] and the EU Justice Barometer confirms this data.[216]

Bulgaria and Romania, both EU Member States since 2007, have even graver weaknesses. According to the World Bank's rule-of-law indicator, Bulgaria and Romania lag far behind all other newly acceded EU Member States.[217] Both countries score poorly when it comes to fighting corruption, regulatory quality, and government effectiveness. Thus, the mechanisms with which the EU prepares candidate countries for membership have evidently not been sufficient to achieve the standards of Article 2 TEU (see 2.6.D). Data from the Council of Europe confirms the Bulgarian and Romanian problems.[218]

The problems with the rule of law in these states are well known. But for a long time, they were hardly discussed and largely tolerated. Perhaps the assumption—based either on a Hegelian philosophy of history or on modernization theory—was that once the states became part of European society, they would transform in light of the European mainstream. This conviction has evaporated. Transforming such Member States towards a greater rule of law has become an object of European politics.[219] In 2016, the Commission set up its own policy unit for the rule of law, and there is a separate Directorate-General for Structural Reform Support (DG REFORM). In the early 2020s, this transformation received an additional boost from two new instruments, each of which has transformative potential in its own right: the European Public Prosecutor's Office and the rule-of-law conditionality for EU funding.[220]

Important examples for such transformative European policies include those on the Greek judiciary and administration.[221] The conditions that accompanied all three bailout packages for Greece (2010, 2012, and 2015) seem to have made a difference after all. Most of these requirements concern the budget and economic

[214] European Commission, Commission Staff Working Document, 2020 Rule of Law Report Country Chapter on the rule of law situation in Italy, Accompanying the document 'Communication from the Commission to the European Parliament, the Council, the European Economic and Social Committee and the Committee of the Regions 2020 Rule of Law Report', Brussels, 30 September 2020, SWD(2020) 311 final, 7.

[215] World Bank, *Doing Business* (n. 208).

[216] European Commission, The 2020 EU Justice Scoreboard, Communication from the Commission to the European Parliament, the Council, the European Central Bank, the European Economic and Social Committee and the Committee of the Regions, COM(2020) 306 final, 8 ff.

[217] World Bank, *World Governance Indicators* (n. 196).

[218] Council of Europe (Committee of Ministers), Supervision of the Execution of Judgments and Decisions of the European Court of Human Rights 2020, 14th Annual Report of the Committee of Ministers (2021) 58–59.

[219] Crabit and Perego, 'L'État de droit: Une politique de l'Union européenne', 20 *Revue du droit de l'Union européenne* (2019) 7.

[220] Council Regulation 2017/1939 implementing enhanced cooperation on the establishment of the European Public Prosecutor's Office, OJ 2017 L 283/1; Regulation 2020/2092 (n. 22).

[221] Dimitrakopoulos and Passas, 'Reforming Greece's Tax Administration during the Financial Crisis: The Paradox of Power Asymmetry', 25 *South European Society and Politics* (2020) 27.

reforms, but some try to help strengthen the state, especially the administration and the judiciary.[222] Among other things, Greece substantially reformed its judiciary; it set up the electronic registration and electronic tracking of proceedings in all courts, the organization of its courts, and the enforcement of court decisions. Many also believe that the Greek authorities have managed to vaccinate the population against COVID-19 more successfully than their German counterparts in 2021, the year this book was written.

Successfully addressing systemic deficiencies is a protracted transformative process.[223] It might amount to transformative constitutionalism (see 3.6). Yet, this requires that constitutional principles, not just the criteria of effectiveness, guide the strengthening of the judiciary and the administration (see 3.1.C). Accordingly, European policies on the rule of law must decide whether they are primarily concerned with the smooth functioning of the internal market or, conversely, with the democratic rule of law. In that respect, the deficiencies of the transformation policies of the 1990s are instructive (see 2.6.D).

Jürgen Habermas famously portrayed modernity as an unfinished project.[224] This portrayal aptly describes the rule of law in European society. Since the rule of law is essential to modern statehood (see 3.1.C, 3.3.A), one might state that some Member State societies have not yet completed their transformation into statehood (see 2.1.A). Some national societies might accomplish their state formation only as part of European society. The same applies to democracy.

4. The Arduous Path to European Democracy

A. The Debates of the First Period

The path to European democracy is even more arduous than the path to the European rule of law. After all, it was largely uncontentious already in the 1950s that core requirements of the rule of law apply *directly* to the actions of supranational bodies (see 3.3.A).[225] The same holds true for fundamental rights, which,

[222] Ioannidis, 'The Judiciary', in K. Featherstone and D. A. Sotiropoulos (eds), *The Oxford Handbook of Modern Greek Politics* (2020) 117.

[223] Weinzierl, 'Die EU-Task-Force für Griechenland: Internationale Beratung am Beispiel der griechischen Steuerverwaltung', in U.-D. Klemm and W. Schultheiß (eds), *Die Krise in Griechenland. Ursprünge, Verlauf, Folgen* (2015) 448, at 458.

[224] Habermas, 'Modernity: An Unfinished Project', in C. J. Calhoun *et al.* (eds), *Contemporary Sociological Theory* (2007) 444.

[225] For the first ruling in this regard, see CJEU, Case 7/56, *Algera and others v. Assemblée commune* (EU:C:1957:7) para. 118; H. Lecheler, *Der Europäische Gerichtshof und die allgemeinen Rechtsgrundsätze* (1971).

thanks to the CJEU, have directly bound the Community institutions since the late 1960s.[226]

The path to the democratic principle is considerably longer. For a long time, the question of the Community's democratic legitimacy was resolved by referring to its democratic Member States, meaning that its legitimacy was *indirect*. The prevalent argument until the 1990s held that, in legal terms, the Community did not require democratic legitimation. Of course, the issue of European democracy was present from the beginning, but only as a political idea.[227]

Of course, European federalists demanded a powerful parliament to provide the Community with democratic legitimation.[228] But the coalition for a stronger European parliament always reached beyond the federalists. One excellent example is the 1972 report of the Groupe Vedel, which was composed of the who's who of European public law.[229] The report concluded that parliamentarizing the Community is a necessary but by no means sufficient condition for the democratic legitimacy of impactful European policies.

If we look at European democracy today, we see much of what the Vedel report recommended. But its realization proved slow as many remained sceptical about the possibility of European democracy. The path thereto is paved with compromises.

Consider the 'Act concerning the election of the representatives of the Assembly by direct universal suffrage' of 20 September 1976. It represented a democratic breakthrough because it instituted direct elections to the European Parliament, as suggested by the Vedel Report. At the same time, it exemplifies a typical compromise between the two views, for the term 'democracy' is nowhere to be found in the Direct Election Act. Moreover, the Act called the institution an 'Assembly', not a 'Parliament'.[230] It is no surprise, then, that the judiciary hesitated to invoke the principle of democracy.[231]

[226] I. Pernice, *Grundrechtsgehalte im Europäischen Gemeinschaftsrecht. Ein Beitrag zum gemeinschaftsimmanenten Grundrechtsschutz durch den Europäischen Gerichtshof* (1979); Weiler, 'Eurocracy and Distrust. Some Questions Concerning the Role of the European Court of Justice in the Protection of Fundamental Human Rights within the Legal Order of the European Communities', 61 *Washington Law Review* (1986) 1103; Gaja, 'Aspetti problematici della tutela dei diritti fondamentali nell'ordinamento comunitario', *Rivista di diritto internazionale* (1988) 574.

[227] Randelzhofer, 'Zum behaupteten Demokratiedefizit der Europäischen Gemeinschaft', in P. Hommelhoff and P. Kirchhof (eds), *Der Staatenverbund der Europäischen Union. Beiträge und Diskussionen des Symposions am 21./22. Januar 1994 in Heidelberg* (1994) 39, at 40.

[228] A. Spinelli, *Rapporto sull'Europa* (1965).

[229] Report of the Working Party examining the problem of the enlargement of the powers of the European Parliament (Report Vedel), Bull. EC suppl. 4-72, 7; on this, see Frowein, 'Erinnerungen an die "Groupe Vedel"', in U. Becker *et al.* (eds), *Verfassung und Verwaltung in Europa. Festschrift für Jürgen Schwarze zum 70. Geburtstag* (2014) 57.

[230] Act concerning the election of the representatives of the Assembly by direct universal suffrage of 20 September 1976, OJ 1976 L 278/5.

[231] CJEU, Case 138/79, *Roquette v. Council* (EU:C:1980:249) para. 33; Case C-300/89, *Commission v. Council* (EU:C:1991:244) para. 20; on this development, see Lenaerts, 'The Principle of Democracy in the Case Law of the European Court of Justice', 62 *International and Comparative Law Quarterly* (2013) 271.

While important forces want to provide the Union with its own democratic institutions, others have considerable reservations. One states that democracy requires collective identity (see 3.2). No less difficult questions concern the democratic subject, the possibility of representation without a people, and without electoral equality, and, ultimately, the very meaning of democracy.

Almost no one personifies these doubts as well as Joseph Weiler in his canonical essay 'The Transformation of Europe' of 1991.[232] There are many factors that contributed to the influence of this text: its publication in one of the world's most renowned journals (the *Yale Law Journal*), its appearance precisely during the second threshold phase of public European law, its author's reputation, its succinctness, and its reluctance to offer concrete suggestions. Most importantly, however, the essay depicts a pro-European author rejecting the standard answer of pro-European forces to the democratic question.

Weiler recapitulates the standard diagnosis of democratic deficiency: the Treaties grant too many powers to the executive branch, over which the national parliaments exercise too little control. The transition, in the late 1980s, to majority decision-making in the Council (see 2.5.A) exacerbated the problem. But Weiler then rejects the standard pro-European solution, which consists of strengthening the European Parliament. For him, this represents an errant path.

Strengthening the European Parliament is inadequate because essential democratic requirements, such as 'closeness, responsiveness, representativeness, and accountability' as well as 'belonging', are lacking, says Weiler.[233] Societal meaning, belonging, and identity remain national phenomena.[234] His position thus belongs to the camp that demands a strong collective identity for democracy to function (see 3.2.B). While Weiler is not a Hegelian thinker, let alone a Schmittian one, one can read his stance as representative of communitarianism (see 1.4).[235]

Last but not least, Weiler warns of the dark side that would accompany the Union's successful democratization: it could lead to a European federal state. For Weiler, this development would squander European integration's epochal achievement: cabining the nation state's destructive potential while maintaining its civilizational gains of democratic nationality.

Weiler's alternative is to dispense with the idea of a democratic Union. For him, the Union finds its legitimacy in the fact that it enables democratic life in the Member States but tames the dark sides of the nation state.

[232] Weiler, 'The Transformation of Europe' (n. 85). See also the contributions in M. Poiares Maduro and M. Wind (eds), *The Transformation of Europe. Twenty-Five Years On* (2017).

[233] Weiler, 'The Transformation of Europe' (n. 85) 2470 f.

[234] J. H. H. Weiler, *The Constitution of Europe. 'Do the New Clothes Have an Emperor?' and Other Essays on European Integration* (1999) 249–251, 340–342; Weiler, 'Bread and Circus. The State of European Union', 4 *Columbia Journal of European Law* (1998) 223, at 225.

[235] Weiler, 'Not on Bread Alone Doth Man Liveth (Deut. 8:3; Mat 4:4): Some Iconoclastic Views on Populism, Democracy, the Rule of Law and the Polish Circumstance', in A. von Bogdandy *et al.* (eds), *Defending Checks and Balances in EU Member States* (2020) 3.

Weiler convinced many academics but not the Treaty legislator of either the Maastricht, Amsterdam, Nice, or Lisbon Treaties. According to all their preambles, these Treaties always strive to strengthen democracy in the supranational bodies and to do so through further parliamentarization in particular. They ennobled the Assembly of the European Community by turning it into a parliament with a role in most policy fields. Moreover, they introduced a Union citizenship. But this did not suffice to convince all sceptics. On the contrary, the Maastricht Treaty gave rise to a new debate in which the democratic principle took on a new role: defending the nation state.

B. The Maastricht Judgment of the Second Senate

With its seminal Maastricht judgment, the Second Senate of the German Constitutional Court made the first major judicial contribution to this debate.[236] Although the judgment does not strike down the Treaty, it lays the foundation for judicial resistance to European institutions. Building on my presentation in section 3.2.C, I analyse its key argument, the democratic principle, here.

The Second Senate issued the Maastricht judgment on 12 October 1993, at the heart of the second threshold phase of European public law (see 2.5.A). The Iron Curtain had just fallen. Furthermore, the negotiation and ratification of the Maastricht Treaty had politicized European integration, as highlighted by the failure of the first Danish referendum and the very narrow outcome of the French one. The proceedings before the Karlsruhe Court were part of the pan-European controversy about the sense or nonsense of 'ever closer union'.[237]

In Germany, the controversy was particularly significant because it affected a recently reunified nation that had regained its full sovereignty.[238] With reunification, globalization, and the disappearance of the Soviet threat, ever closer European union might have exhausted its appeal for Germany. Global integration, as negotiated in the Uruguay Round of the General Agreement on Tariffs and Trade (GATT) with a view to establishing a World Trade Organization (WTO), might have offered an alternative future. The United Kingdom decided to pursue this path 25 years later. But German policymakers ultimately opted for the European path,

[236] *Maastricht* (n. 60). On its impact, see Baquero Cruz, 'The Legacy of the Maastricht-Urteil and the Pluralist Movement', 14 *European Law Journal* (2008) 389. The materials of the proceedings are presented comprehensively in I. Winkelmann (ed.), *Das Maastricht-Urteil des Bundesverfassungsgerichts vom 12. Oktober 1993. Dokumentation des Verfahrens mit Einführung* (1994).

[237] On the pan-European discussion, see Franklin, Marsh, and McLaren, 'Uncorking the Bottle. Popular Opposition to European Unification in the Wake of Maastricht', 32 *Journal of Common Market Studies* (1994) 455.

[238] B. Olivi, *L'Europa difficile. Storia politica dell'integrazione europea 1948–2000* (2000) 338 f., 341 f., 36 ff.

and they did so with an overwhelming majority: 543 members of the *Bundestag* voted for the Maastricht Treaty, while only 17 were against it.

Manfred Brunner, a politician of the Free Democratic Party (FDP) and former head of cabinet of the German EC Commissioner Bangemann, and Claudia Roth, subsequently the federal chairperson of the *Bündnis 90/Die Grünen* party and vice-president of the German *Bundestag*, were dissatisfied with this outcome. They filed a constitutional complaint. In a tactical masterstroke, the Second Senate waited until it had the final say, that is, until all referendums had taken place, all parliaments had decided, all other courts had spoken, and the European public focused on the Karlsruhe Court. Some appeared embarrassed by the limelight: Federal President Richard von Weizsäcker sent the German ratification to the Italian government, the depositary, right after the Court handed down the judgment; one day after the ruling, on 13 October 1993, the Italian government announced receipt of the ratification.

The decision packed a punch, justifying the extreme tension with which it had been anticipated. The Second Senate rejected the constitutional complaints against the Act of 28 December 1992 ratifying the TEU and the amendment of the Basic Law of 21 December 1992 that permitted the ratification. In so doing, the Senate removed the last obstacle to a quantum leap in European public law. But at the same time, it positioned itself—far more than all other courts (see 3.2.C)—as a veto player, imposing limits on German and EU institutions that it would specify in the Lisbon judgment. Ultimately, in one of the biggest power grabs in the history of constitutional adjudication, the Senate claimed the final say on the further development of Europe. It justified its approach with the principle of democracy.

The judgment prompted many reactions, ranging from delight[239] to vehement rejection.[240] Weiler, too, was extremely critical of it, although the judgment's premises resemble his views on European democracy.[241] No other national ruling had triggered a similar reception across Europe. Ultimately, the decision of the Karlsruhe Court became an event in which European society produced itself (see 1.2, 1.4, 3.2.B).

[239] Huber, 'Das Kooperationsverhältnis zwischen BVerfG und EuGH in Grundrechtsfragen. Die Bananenmarktordnung und das Grundgesetz', *Europäische Zeitschrift für Wirtschaftsrecht* (1997) 517, at 518 ff.; F. W. Scharpf, *Regieren in Europa. Effektiv und demokratisch?* (1999) 19 f.; T. C. Hartley, *The Foundations of European Community Law* (1998) 240; H. Rasmussen, *The European Court of Justice* (1998) 272 ff.

[240] For a compilation, see H.-P. Folz, *Demokratie und Integration. Der Konflikt zwischen Bundesverfassungsgericht und Europäischem Gerichtshof über die Kontrolle der Gemeinschaftskompetenzen* (1999) 4; Koopmans, 'Rechter, D-mark en democratie. Het Bundesverfassungsgericht en de Europese Unie', 69 *Nederlands Juristenblad* (1994) 245; MacCormick, 'The Maastricht-Urteil. Sovereignty Now', 1 *European Law Journal* (1995) 259; A. López Castillo, *Constitución e integración. El fundamento constitucional de la integración supranacional europea en España y en la R.F.A.* (1996) 193 ff., 354 ff.; Mancini, 'Europa. Gründe für einen Gesamtstaat', 81 *Kritische Vierteljahresschrift für Gesetzgebung und Rechtswissenschaft* (1998) 386, at 393 f.

[241] Weiler, 'The State "über alles". Demos, Telos and the German Maastricht Decision', in O. Due, M. Lutter, and J. Schwarze (eds), *Festschrift für Ulrich Everling, Bd. 2* (1995) 1651, at 1654 f.

The Second Senate's holdings are deeply ambivalent. On the one hand, the judgment sketches a dualistic model of Union acts' democratic legitimation, one in which the national and the genuinely European strands of legitimation complement each other. On the other hand, the ruling suggests that democracy requires a people, a nation.[242] Because of this ambivalence, analysing the ruling more closely helps understand European democracy.

Since the German Constitutional Court only has jurisdiction in matters implicating the Basic Law, the judgment must rely on one of the latter's provisions. The Second Senate takes Article 38 as the starting point (at 417)[243], which, among other things, confers a right to vote for the federal parliament. The Senate considers other rights' asserted violations unsubstantiated and inadmissible (at 411). Thus, it identified the democratic principle as the Union's central problem. This take has proved tremendously successful for the question of how to deal with the principle of democracy became key to European society's constitutional future. We may wonder how the European constitutional settlement would have evolved had the Italian or Spanish Constitutional Court granted the principle of solidarity a similar role.[244]

The Second Senate based its argument on Article 38 of the Basic Law even though this provision does not mention the EU at all. Rather, it ensures the right to vote in elections to the German *Bundestag*. The Senate centred on this provision because its violation can be claimed by means of a constitutional complaint, which is not the case for violations of the democratic principle (Article 20(1 and 2) of the Basic Law). Taking a tremendous leap, the Senate inferred from the right to vote a right to a parliament with significant powers (at 409 f., 417). On this narrow basis, it positioned itself as a key European decision-maker—a massive expansion of its jurisdiction that met with massive criticism.[245]

The Senate then defined democracy's inviolable core. For this purpose, it paraphrased Article 20(2) cl. 1 of the Basic Law, whereby '[a]ll state authority is derived from the people'. It argued that it is an 'inviolable element of the principle of democracy that the performance of state functions and the exercise of state authority derive from the people of the State and that they must, in principle, be justified to that people'. Note the small but important addition: while Article 20 of the Basic

[242] Bryde, 'Die bundesrepublikanische Volksdemokratie als Irrweg der Demokratietheorie', 5 *Staatswissenschaften und Staatspraxis* (1994) 305. An English translation might be: 'The Federal People's Democracy as an errant path of democratic theory'.

[243] The text passages and pages in this chapter are quoted from the English translation in Wegen and Kuner, 'Text of Decision: Judicial and Similar Proceedings: Germany: Federal Constitutional Court Decision Concerning the Maastricht Treaty', 33 *International Legal Materials* (1995) 395.

[244] On the counterfactual method in law, see I. Venzke, 'What If? Counterfactual (Hi)Stories of International Law', 8 *Asian Journal of International Law* (2018) 403.

[245] Winkelmann (n. 236) 61 ff.; C. Tomuschat, 'Die Europäische Union unter Aufsicht des Bundesverfassungsgerichts', *Europäische Grundrechte-Zeitschrift* (1993) 489.

Law speaks of the people, the Senate refers to the 'people of the State' (*Staatsvolk*, at 418), giving the concept a statist bias.

This definition of democracy is formal because it focuses on derivability and accountability. The Court's third step then qualified this attribution by demanding a 'sufficient proportion of democratic justification', thereby introducing a substantive criterion. To justify this step, it cites Ernst-Wolfgang Böckenförde, one of the justices involved in the decision, and his theory of the 'legitimation chain'. This doctrine represents one of his major contributions to the Federal Republic's thought as well as an important adaptation of Schmitt's writings (see 1.4).[246]

In doing so, the Senate made the far-reaching decision to conceptualize the Community (today's Union) as an institution of administrative law. It should be stressed that the doctrine of the legitimation chain has served to democratize the German administration (see 2.4). The Second Senate's *ultra vires* review also builds on a doctrine of administrative law, in this case of English administrative law.[247] The same is true of its later doctrine of the 'drop in influence' (*Einflussknick*).[248] However, the Union cannot be reduced to an administration. Today, it is a transnational polity that includes its own parliament and citizenship. I presented the shortcomings of this approach when discussing Ipsen's executive understanding of the Community (see 2.4.C).

On this conceptual basis, the Senate demanded that the German people's legitimation of, and their influence on, supranational union's political process be secured. The German principle of democracy requires German control. Two requirements stand out: the German Act of Approval of the Maastricht Treaty may not transfer the competence to allocate competences (*Kompetenz-Kompetenz*) to the Union, and the Council must remain a central decision-making body.

Critics maintain that it was wrong to focus on a collective (namely, the 'people') since the true democratic question is how to create opportunities for individual citizens to participate in government.[249] While I see the point of this criticism, a reconstruction in the light of the EU Treaties must acknowledge that the Treaty legislator also attributes a significant role to the people or, more precisely, to the peoples of the Member States. They are essential to European democracy (see 3.5.A).

The Second Senate's novel description of the Union as a 'multi-level cooperation of states' (*Staatenverbund*, also translated as 'alliance of States', 'community of States', 'inter-governmental community') has prompted further criticism because it

[246] Böckenförde, 'Demokratie als Verfassungsprinzip', in Kirchhof and Isensee (n. 71) 429, at paras 11 ff.

[247] M. Shapiro, *Courts. A Comparative and Political Analysis* (1981) 116.

[248] *OMT Programme* (n. 64) para. 131. For an article that lays the groundwork for the Court's reasoning, see Huber, 'Das europäisierte Grundgesetz', *Deutsches Verwaltungsblatt* (2009) 574, at 576.

[249] Bryde (n. 242) 308 f., 324; Habermas, *Between Facts and Norms* (n. 10) 110 f.; Zuleeg, 'What Holds a Nation Together? Cohesion and Democracy in the United States of America and in the European Union', 45 *American Journal of Comparative Law* (1997) 505, at 523 f., at the time the German judge at the CJEU.

minimizes the Union's role as an independent authority or polity. Indeed, it almost makes the Union disappear, thus facilitating the Senate's general state-centred approach.[250] The Court's subsequent decisions continued down this road (see 3.2.C),[251] as did the rulings on the doctrine of the 'drop in influence'.[252] This path created an ever stronger contrast to the Treaty legislator's understanding (see 3.5).

Contrary to the Second Senate's later rulings, the Maastricht judgment ultimately comprises two different conceptions of democracy; perhaps this was the price for handing down a unanimous decision. The two conceptions mirror two of the three major conceptions for dealing with the democratic question in European integration. In a nutshell, we may speak of a federal state, a third-way, and a nation-centred camp.

The federal state camp pushes for a European Parliament which, like the Belgian Chamber of Deputies, the German *Bundestag*, or the Austrian National Council, bears the principal democratic burden.[253] Here, political will and institutional engineering provide an answer to the question of the EU's democratic legitimation. To little surprise, the Second Senate's judgment does not include any voices from this camp. By contrast, the ECtHR does argue along these lines in its decision in *Matthews v. United Kingdom*. This ruling, which reads like an implicit criticism of the German Constitutional Court's Maastricht judgment, conceives of the European Parliament as the Union's central democratic body.[254]

Unlike the federal state view, the third-way view advocates a dualist structure of justification, as proposed by the Vedel Report in 1972 (see 3.4.A). In my reading of the judgment, the Second Senate's assessment of the European Parliament on pages 419–421 is compatible with this view. Here, it emphasizes the 'necessity' of the European Parliament. Moreover, the Senate states (as early as 1993) that it provides democratic legitimation. It also holds that the Parliament's legitimizing role would grow stronger if certain 'pre-legal requirements', such as a European public opinion in a European communication space, were met—i.e. if there were a European society. Unlike later decisions of the Second Senate, the judgment never calls into question the European Parliament's parliamentary quality and its democratic role.

[250] For close analysis, see von Bogdandy, 'Das Leitbild der dualistischen Legitimation für die europäische Verfassungsentwicklung: Gängige Missverständnisse des Maastricht-Urteils und deren Gründe (BVerfGE89,155 ff.)', 83 *Kritische Vierteljahresschrift für Gesetzgebung und Rechtswissenschaft (KritV)* (2000) 284.

[251] On the case law regarding the Euro's rescue, see Farahat (n. 92) 181 ff.

[252] But see Voßkuhle, 'Über die Demokratie in Europa', 62 *Aus Politik und Zeitgeschichte* (2012) 3.

[253] Schulz, 'Parlamente in Not?', in C. Franzius, F. C. Mayer, and J. Neyer (eds), *Modelle des Parlamentarismus im 21. Jahrhundert. Neue Ordnungen Von Recht und Politik* (2015) 35, at 42 f.; U. Guérot, *Warum Europa eine Republik werden muss! Eine politische Utopie* (2016) 81 ff.; G. Verhofstadt, *Europe's Last Chance. Why the European States Must Form a More Perfect Union* (2017) 229 ff.

[254] ECtHR, *Matthews v. United Kingdom*, Appl. no. 24833/94, Judgment of 18 February 1999, para. 52; Ress, 'Das Europäische Parlament als Gesetzgeber. Der Blickpunkt der Europäischen Menschenrechtskonvention', 2 *Zeitschrift für Europarechtliche Studien* (1999) 219, at 226. At the time, Ress was the German justice at the ECtHR.

Of course, the Senate states that the national parliaments impart democratic legitimation 'in the first instance'. This could be a factual assessment of how democratic legitimation operated in 1992, but it could just as well represent the legal entrenchment of national parliaments' status. The first interpretation seems more convincing as the second lacks a legal basis. Moreover, the first is largely consensual: hardly anybody would dispute that, in 1992, the Union's democratic legitimation originated in the national parliaments. After all, the latter ratified the Treaties and legitimized the government representatives in the Council.

What the Senate did, then, was to diagnose the gradual realization of a dual structure of legitimation. Accordingly, it declared that the necessity of democratic legitimation through the European Parliament grows 'in view of the degree to which the nations of Europe are growing together'.

But the third understanding of how to provide for European democracy is present in the judgment as well. And indeed, many read it as a manifestation of this nation state-centred view. Shortly after the aforementioned passage, the justices' argumentative logic changes. Now, suddenly, the Member State peoples alone provide legitimation, and the legitimation by way of the European Parliament disappears. The focus now lies exclusively on the *state demos* as the decisive subject of democracy.

C. Homogeneity and Heller's Europe

Many read the Maastricht judgment as a manifestation of the nation-state-centred view because it alludes to the charged concept of homogeneity (see 1.4, 3.2.B). Thus, the Senate postulated that

> The States require sufficient areas of significant responsibility of their own, areas in which the people of the State concerned may develop and express itself within a process of forming political will which it legitimates and controls, in order to give legal expression to those matters which concern that people on a relatively homogenous basis spiritually, socially, and politically (see H. Heller, Politische Demokratie und soziale Homogenität, Gesammelte Schriften, Vol. 2, 1971, p. 421 <427 ff.>).[255]

Does the Senate hereby elevate the nation state to the vanishing point of the principle of democracy?[256] The Senate's chief concern in this part of the judgment was not the European but the German democratic process. It does not claim that

[255] *Maastricht* (n. 60).

[256] See Mancini (n. 240) 393 f.; Weiler, 'The State "über alles" (n. 241) 1654 f.; Schwarze, 'Europapolitik unter deutschem Verfassungsrichtervorbehalt', 48 *Neue Justiz* (1994) 1.

'relative homogeneity', a nation or state, are indispensable prerequisites for any democratic process. The only thing to suggest that the Senate is making a bigger point is that the quote cited above represents the only theoretical reference, which might imply that the Senate derives its overall understanding of democracy from this source. This would be innocuous if it did, in fact, go back to Hermann Heller, an upstanding democrat. However, Heller quoted Carl Schmitt's *The Concept of the Political*. Therefore, some have argued that the Second Senate's understanding of democracy is basically Schmittian.[257] If this were correct, the Court would believe that attempts at a proper European democracy were destined to fail and were, accordingly, highly dangerous (see 2.3.C).

I have already presented my objection to this approach (see 3.2.C). Now, I will show why the excerpt from Heller, as quoted by the Second Senate, is grist to the mill of this book's overall argument.

Heller's work analysed the prerequisites of democracy under the circumstances of the Weimar Republic's class conflicts. Like many theorists of the Hegelian tradition,[258] Heller surely considered a collective identity essential for a functioning democracy (see 3.2.B). But he dismissed traditional factors that help determine identity—such as a shared language, history, and culture—as phenomena of the past, and he did so in the extreme past tense, the pluperfect (past perfect): 'In modern Europe [...], a shared language, a shared culture and political history had been the most important factors of socio-psychological alignment.'[259] As a Jew, Heller made no mention of Christianity, which was so important to the Catholic Böckenförde.[260] According to Heller, what was at stake in the Weimar Republic was something else entirely.

For Heller, the viability of the democratic republic hung by a single thread: the ruling classes had to make members of the working class believe that they could improve their lot through the procedures and under the principles of the Weimar Constitution. Later research has confirmed this nexus between democratic stability and the people's material condition.[261] In other words, Heller deemed a people or nation's homogeneity much less significant. Indeed, he postulated a European federal state as a political option. As early as 1928 (i.e. before the catastrophe of the Second World War), he wrote that

> in post-war [that is, First World War] Europe, the idea of the sovereign nation state has lost much of its persuasiveness among all classes. The question that has

[257] Dubber, 'The German Jury and the Metaphysical *Volk*. From Romantic Idealism to Nazi Ideology', 43 *American Journal of Comparative Law* (1995) 227, at 259 ff.

[258] Heller, 'Hegel und die deutsche Politik', 13 *Zeitschrift für Politik* (1924) 132.

[259] Heller, 'Politische Demokratie und soziale Homogenität', in M. Drath and C. Müller (eds), *Gesammelte Schriften, Bd. 2* (1971 [1928]) 421, at 429.

[260] But see J. H. H. Weiler, *Ein christliches Europa. Erkundungsgänge* (2004).

[261] D. Acemoglu and J. A. Robinson, *Why Nations Fail. The Origins of Power, Prosperity and Poverty* (2013); Acemoglu *et al.*, 'Democracy Does Cause Growth', 127 *Journal of Political Economy* (2019) 47.

> become highly problematic for the ruling class itself is whether today's nation state serves the nation's self-preservation better than a European federal state. Very soon, therefore, the national idea will prove insufficient to legitimize the democratic formation of unity' (at 433).

Consider the irony of this quote. Even before the catastrophe of the Second World War, Hermann Heller, the Second Senate's most important authority on democracy, considered a European federal state a plausible option for dealing with societal conflicts, thereby safeguarding democracy.[262] In Heller's view, such a federal state will give rise to a collective identity if it establishes, through democratic means, the *social* rule of law.[263] This view is quite close to what the Treaty legislator established first in the Treaty of Amsterdam of 1997 and then, even more clearly, in the Treaty of Lisbon of 2007: following the experience of fascism, national socialism, Iberian and Greek authoritarianism, and Soviet communism, Heller's vision is largely enshrined in Article 2 TEU's 12 principles.

5. A Democracy of Many Mediations

The first paradigmatic position of the second threshold phase considers European democracy the salvation of national democracy, as envisioned by Hermann Heller. The second, which is exemplified by Weiler and the Second Senate, articulates strong doubts about the possibility of supranational democracy. In the following years, European society debated this issue extensively in the media, political parties, and academic circles.[264] In 2007, the Treaty legislator then presented a mediation between many of the positions. Articles 2 and 9–12 TEU represent its core. It is only fitting that it is a democracy of mediations. Thus, the Treaty legislator opted for a complex system of government that lacks precisely what authoritarian thought often touts as democracy's core promise: immediacy.[265]

The Treaty legislator determined that the Union operates as a representative democracy (Article 10(1) TEU). That political decision requires reconstructing the concept of democracy. Such reconstruction must tread a path between utopia and

[262] On the context of the debates during the Weimar period, see Osiander, 'Missionare oder Analytiker? Versuch einer Neubewertung der "idealistischen" Schule in der Lehre von den internationalen Beziehungen', in J. Steffek and L. Holthaus (eds), *Jenseits der Anarchie. Weltordnungsentwürfe im frühen 20. Jahrhundert* (2014) 25.

[263] Heller, 'Rechtsstaat or Dictatorship?' (n. 46) 131, 141.

[264] Kohler-Koch and Rittberger, 'Charting Crowded Territory. Debating the Democratic Legitimacy of the European Union', in B. Kohler-Koch and B. Rittberger (eds), *Debating the Democratic Legitimacy of the European Union* (2007) 1; for the representative turn which I follow, see S. Kröger and D. Friedrich, 'Introduction: The Representative Turn in EU Studies', 20 *Journal of European Public Policy* (2013) 155; S. Näsström, 'Where Is the Representative Turn Going?', 10 *European Journal of Political Theory* (2011) 501.

[265] G. Frankenberg, *Autoritarismus. Verfassungstheoretische Perspektiven* (2020) 255 ff.

apology (see 1.4).[266] Comparative legal analysis is essential because the democratic principle of Article 2 TEU must respond to the Member States' common constitutional traditions (see 3.2.D, 5.2.C).

I begin by discussing how representative institutions can function without a European *demos* (see 3.5.A). Then, I show how elections without electoral equality can result in a representative parliament, why the Councils are representative, and why the frequently maligned trilogues represent a democratic achievement (see 3.5.B). Finally, I discuss how to further the democratic transformation (see 3.5.C).

A. In Whose Name?

Etymologically, democracy means the rule of the people. However, there is no European people, either in the European Treaties or in the minds of most European citizens (see 1.2, 3.2.A, 3.2.C).[267] Nevertheless, the Treaty legislator defines the Union as a democracy. Therefore, it might find itself on a treacherous path, building pseudo-democratic institutions for a society that is only nominally democratic.

Another interpretation strikes me as more plausible. On this view, the Treaty legislator succeeded in what Peter Badura identified as the key to a democratic future already in 1964 (see 3.1.A): freeing democracy (including its theory) from the framework of the nation state.[268] To do so, the Treaty legislator did not demolish the existing edifice of democratic institutions, theories, and mindsets. Rather, it created openings in this edifice, thus allowing for an expansion capable of housing 27 national democracies under a new roof. This roof, which covers almost an entire continent, creates a new dimension of democracy, namely, a democratic European society, as Article 2 TEU puts it.

To build a European democracy, the Treaty legislator relied on what already existed. Instead of postulating a European people, the Treaty speaks of the 'peoples of Europe' (Article 1(2) TEU). At the same time, it transforms these peoples, for Article 3(1) TEU speaks of the peoples of the Union ('its peoples'). Accordingly, each people belongs not only to its Member State but also to the Union.

The EU Treaty assigns the peoples of the Member States a central role in European democracy. It certainly values national democracy. After all, the peoples legitimize the Union as democratic subjects by ratifying the Treaties,

[266] F. W. Scharpf, *Demokratietheorie zwischen Utopie und Anpassung* (1970); D. Innerarity, *Democracy in Europe. A Political Philosophy of the EU* (2018) 61 ff..

[267] A European *demos* is nonetheless postulated by A. Augustin, *Das Volk der Europäischen Union. Zu Inhalt und Kritik eines normativen Begriffs* (2000), and by Advocate General Eleanor Sharpston, CJEU, Joined cases C-715/17, C-718/17 and C-719/17, *European Commission v. Poland and others*, Opinion of AG Sharpston (EU:C:2019:917) para. 253 (reacting to the Brexit vote).

[268] Badura (n. 2) 38; Nettesheim, 'Demokratisierung der Europäischen Union und Europäisierung der Demokratietheorie', in H. Bauer, P. M. Huber, and K.-P. Sommermann (eds), *Demokratie in Europa* (2005) 143.

accessions, and financial resources (Articles 48–49 TEU, Article 311 TFEU) and by participating, through their governments, in the European Council and the Council (Article 10(2) sub-para. 2). The strong role of the national parliaments and the Councils is vital to securing democracy in the EU: it counters a concern already articulated by Kant, namely, that a centralized Continental government could prove particularly despotic.[269]

The concept of the people continues to play a major role, but the plot is new. Consider that the Treaty legislator employs this term in the plural and not, as do most constitutions, in the singular. This shift is reflected in the proposal to conceive of the Union as a *demoicracy*. The Union represents the rule of 27 peoples rather than only one.[270]

Understanding democracy as a *demoicracy* does not fail the idea of democracy, as comparative analysis shows. The constitutional thought of the continental democracies in the United States and India contain similarly plural understandings of the 'people'.[271] One of the core points of the Bolivian constitution of 2009, which seeks to bring democracy to a diverse country, is to constitute a plurinational state. Thus, the nation state has never been the only edifice to house democracy.

Conceiving of the Union as a democracy of peoples, as a demoicracy, is only the first step to understanding the political choices set out in Article 10 TEU. It alone does not explain the EU Treaty's democratic structures. To stay with the metaphor of the house, demoicracy captures only the lateral openings, not the additional common floor.

The Treaty legislator bases the Union's democratic legitimation not only on its peoples but also on Union citizenship. This is in the tradition of democratic thought, as represented by Bryde's critique of the Maastricht judgment (see 3.4.B). It has deep roots even in Germany: in one of his most famous essays, Peter Häberle conceptualizes German democracy precisely as a 'citizens' democracy', not as a 'people's democracy'.[272]

This fits in with the EU Treaty, whose Title II, the 'Provisions on Democratic Principles', begins with Union citizenship in Article 9 TEU. Transnational citizenship as the democratic basis of public authority thus constitutes a further breakthrough. Article 10 TEU commits the Union to representative democracy and determines that 'citizens are directly represented [. . .] in the European Parliament'.

[269] I. Kant, *Perpetual Peace. A Philosophical Essay* (1903 [1795]).

[270] Nicolaïdis, 'The New Constitution as European "Demoi-cracy"?', 7 *Critical Review of International Social and Political Philosophy* (2004) 76; Cheneval and Schimmelfennig, 'The Case for Demoicracy in the European Union', 51 *Journal of Common Market Studies* (2013) 334.

[271] Dann and Thiruvengadam, 'Comparing Constitutional Democracy in the European Union and India: An Introduction', in P. Dann and A. K. Thiruvengadam (eds), *Democratic Constitutionalism in India and the European Union. Comparing the Law of Democracy in Continental Polities* (2021) 1, at 2. On the United States, see 3.2.A.

[272] Häberle, 'Die offene Gesellschaft der Verfassungsinterpreten', 30 *JuristenZeitung* (1975) 297, at 302.

The Treaty legislator grounded the democratic legitimacy of the Union's institutions in the peoples of the Member States *and* the citizens of the Union.[273] Article 10(2) TEU establishes two strands of democratic representation (one embodied by the European Council and the Council and the other by the European Parliament), which Union citizens elect directly. We can designate this as dual legitimation.[274]

Dual democratic legitimation goes beyond authority 'in the name of the people' (see 4.5.A). Following the idea of union expressed in Article 1(2) TEU (see 2.2.D), the EU derives its democratic justification from the interplay between different institutions of different legal orders. The democratic legitimation of the Union's institutions is complex. This pluralistic structure is not marred by the insight that, ultimately, the same individuals vote both as nationals and as citizens of the Union.[275] The European democratic mediations occur in different institutions and procedures, reflecting the multiple roles and identities of the represented individuals.[276]

Of the two democratic strands, the one that brings together the 27 national systems is thicker; consider the national ratification of the Treaties and the European Council's key role. In this respect, the Treaty legislator's assessment coincides with that of the Second Senate in the Maastricht judgment (see 3.4.B). Giving the Member States such a central role in European democracy requires the Union to oversee the Member States' own democratic credentials. Thus, the Union's interest in its Member States' democratic conditions is both elementary and justified (see 3.6, 4.6, 5.4). The CJEU has frequently attended to this question, often in extremely delicate matters; Brexit and the disputes between the Spanish central state and the Catalan separatists are two salient examples.[277] In fact, protecting democracy in some Member States has become perhaps the most challenging task facing the Union.[278]

As important as the national strand is, it is not sufficient. Only a few voices, such as the party *Alternative für Deutschland* (Alternative for Germany), advocate a Union constituted solely of the Councils, that is, a Union without the European

[273] Oeter, 'Federalism and Democracy', in A. von Bogdandy and J. Bast (eds), *Principles of European Constitutional Law* (2007) 55, at 66.

[274] Probably the first to do so was W. Kluth, *Die demokratische Legitimation der Europäischen Union. Eine Analyse der These vom Demokratiedefizit der Europäischen Union aus gemeineuropäischer Verfassungsperspektive* (1995) 67 ff.

[275] Pernice, 'Europäisches und nationales Verfassungsrecht', 60 *Veröffentlichungen der Vereinigung der Deutschen Staatsrechtslehrer* (2001) 148, at 176; J. von Achenbach, *Demokratische Gesetzgebung in der Europäischen Union. Theorie und Praxis der dualen Legitimationsstruktur europäischer Hoheitsgewalt* (2014) 463.

[276] Habermas, 'The Crisis of the European Union in the Light of a Constitutionalization of International Law', 23 *European Journal of International Law* (2012) 335, at 342 ff.

[277] *Wightman et al.* (n. 8) para. 66; Case C-502/19, *Junqueras Vies* (EU:C:2019:1115) para. 63.

[278] See the contributions of B. Bakó, S. Biernat, A. von Bogdandy, P. Bogdanowicz, M. Bonelli, I. Canor, C. Dupré, A. Frackowiak-Adamska, P. Filipek, J. Kirchmayr, J. Łacny, A. Nowak-Far, J. Polakiewicz, G. Rugge, W. Sadowski, M. Schmidt, W. Schroeder, P. Sonnevend, D. Spieker, M. Taborowski, J. Weiler, and M. Wiacek in von Bogdandy *et al.* (n. 235).

Parliament.[279] The Treaty legislator, by contrast, assigned the Parliament a constitutive role, placing it at the apex of the Union's institutions. Both Articles 10 and 13 TEU list it even before the European Council.

The Union's representative institutions represent the peoples and the citizens of the Union. Do they therefore represent a democratic 'we'? This question is as important as that of a European people. While many authors do not require the existence of a people for a democracy, they do demand a collective identity in the sense of a 'we' (see 3.2.B) because they postulate collective self-determination as democracy's ultimate aim.[280]

Although European policy aims to create a collective European identity (see 3.2.A), there is no indication that the Treaty legislator conditioned European democracy on a European 'we'. This assessment is realistic: while there are self-reflexive processes in European society (see 1.2, 3.2.B), hardly anyone claims that there is a European 'we' of collective self-determination. The 'We, the People' of the American Constitution may be on Europeans' mind (see the Preamble of the Treaty establishing the European Political Community), but it does not feature in the text of the European Treaties, which begin with His Majesty the King of the Belgians, followed by Her Majesty the Queen of Denmark.

Conceptualizing democracy as collective self-determination implies declaring the Union incapable of democracy. This view does exist in European society, fuelling its self-critical attitude. To be sure, it represents an honourable theoretical idea.[281] But it is not useful for interpreting Articles 2 and 10 TEU since it fails to elaborate the political decision underlying these provisions. Thus, a legal scholar with reconstructive endeavours (see 1.4, 5.4) requires other theories.

By opting against the conception of democracy as self-determination, the Treaty legislator did not betray democracy. There are numerous respectable theories that present democracy not as collective self-determination but as the process of a pluralistic society.[282] Union citizens who perceive the Union as a democracy implicitly share this view (see 3.5.C).

The Treaty legislator's decision not to conceptualize democracy as self-determination did not enshrine a minimalist concept.[283] Article 2 TEU demands that Union acts comply with the principles of pluralism, non-discrimination, tolerance, justice, solidarity and equality between women and men, respect for human

279 Klausmann, 'Nur Populismus? AfD will das Europäische Parlament "abschaffen"', *Polis Blog* (23 May 2019).

280 C. Möllers, *Gewaltengliederung. Legitimation und Dogmatik im nationalen und internationalen Rechtsvergleich* (2005) 28 ff.

281 Habermas, *Between Facts and Norms* (n. 10) 90.

282 H. Preuß, *Gemeinde, Staat, Reich als Gebietskörperschaften. Versuch einer deutschen Staatskonstruktion auf Grundlage der Genossenschaftstheorie* (1889); H. J. Laski, *The Foundations of Sovereignty* (1921) 251; Voßkuhle, 'Hugo Preuss als Vordenker einer Verfassungstheorie des Pluralismus', 50 *Der Staat* (2011) 251.

283 On minimalist approaches, see J. Habermas, *Legitimation Crisis* (1992 [1973]) 123 ff.

dignity, freedom, democracy, equality, the rule of law, and respect for human rights, including the rights of persons belonging to minorities. This is a rich and demanding understanding, one that befits the complexities of European society.

The Treaty legislator does not answer the question of who constitutes the democratic subject. But it is clear about the fact that the Union's institutions, while not representing a European people, do represent almost 450 million individuals who are simultaneously nationals, Union citizens, and members of European society.

B. Democratic Representation

Pursuant to Article 10(2) TEU, the European Parliament, the European Council, and the Council provide democratic representation.[284] The question is whether this statement betrays the Member States' constitutional traditions. After all, the Treaty legislator opted for unequal elections to the European Parliament and staffs the Councils with members of the national executives. Moreover, the institutions' political life strikes some observers as devoid of democratic substance.

I take a different view. It rests on a complex conception of democracy that encompasses many mediations and transcends Schmitt, Leibholz, and the partisanship that characterizes the Westminster model. In choosing among the great legal theorists of democracy, I opt for Schmitt's nemesis, Hans Kelsen, for whom compromise lies as the heart of democracy.[285]

To avoid the impression of an apology, let me emphasize that this section focuses on the classificatory dimension of democracy. Thus, I discuss whether to classify the Union as a democratic or an undemocratic system of government. I do not claim that it is the best of all possible democratic systems of government or that it cannot improve its democratic credentials. There are many possibilities for improvement (see 3.5.C).

1. Unequal Voting Rights

Those who doubt the European Parliament's representative nature speak with the authoritative voice of the German Constitutional Court's Second Senate. In its Lisbon judgment, the Senate held that the Treaty legislator committed a conceptual error when it decided to call this institution a parliament.[286] I have already refuted one doctrine underlying this view, namely, that a true European parliament would

[284] On democratic representation by the European Commission, see G. Rugge, *Trilogues: The Democratic Secret of European Legislation* (2021) ch. VI.2.d.

[285] Kelsen, 'On the Essence and Value of Democracy (1929)', in A. J. Jacobson and B. Schlink (eds), *Weimar: A Jurisprudence of Crisis* (2000) 102; van Ooyen, 'Verfassungsrealismus als sozial-liberal-demokratisches Projekt: Lassalle – Kelsen – Fraenkel – Loewenstein', in R. C. van Ooyen (ed.), *Verfassungsrealismus. Das Staatsverständnis von Karl Loewenstein* (2007) 103.

[286] *Lisbon* (n. 61) paras 276 ff.

require one European people (see 3.5.A). However, the Senate's disqualification of the European Parliament also rests on the fact that not every vote in its election carries the same weight.

Pursuant to Article 14(3) TEU, the members of the European Parliament are elected by universal, but not by equal, suffrage. The inequality first results from the fact that the Member State laws regulating the elections differ from one another (as they do in the United States). The problem is well known, which is why Article 223(1) TFEU mandates adopting a uniform law.[287]

Above all, however, arguments to disqualify the European Parliament can point to Article 14(2) TEU, whereby representation in the European Parliament is 'degressively proportional'. Degressive proportionality means that the populous Member States have proportionally fewer representatives than the less populous ones. On average, one seat in the European Parliament represents about 630,000 citizens. But the numbers differ greatly between the different Member States. For example, each of the 96 German seats represents about 860,000 inhabitants, while each of the six Maltese seats represents about 77,000 inhabitants. The value of a German compared to a Maltese vote is reminiscent of the value of a vote from the third estate compared to one from the first estate under the undemocratic Prussian three-class electoral system of the late nineteenth century.

The current electoral system for the European Parliament is certainly no model of democratic parliamentarism; there is much room for improvement.[288] But the Treaty legislator did not opt for a pre-democratic model of representation by estates[289] or for Maltese class rule over the Germans. The German Constitutional Court's Second Senate failed to recognize that the requirement of electoral equality emerged to counteract privileging social classes.[290] However, the over-representation of the populations of small Member States does not privilege a class. Rather, it reflects pluralism and the protection of minorities, both of which are enshrined in Article 2 TEU.[291] They justify the over-representation of, say, the Danish and Sorbian minorities under the German Constitution,[292] as they do in

[287] On the reasons, see S. Alonso de León, 'Four Decades of the European Electoral Act: A Look Back and a Look Ahead to an Unfulfilled Ambition', 42 *European Law Review* (2017) 353.

[288] Arndt, 'Ausrechnen statt aushandeln: Rationalitätsgewinne durch ein formalisiertes Modell für die Bestimmung der Zusammensetzung des Europäischen Parlaments', 68 *Zeitschrift für ausländisches öffentliches Recht und Völkerrecht* (2008) 247.

[289] For an example, see Hegel, *Elements of the Philosophy of Right* (n. 13) para. 301.

[290] Morlok, 'Art. 38 GG', in H. Dreier (ed.), *Grundgesetz Kommentar, Bd. 2* (2015) 1053, at paras 57, 99.

[291] Habermas, 'Zur Prinzipienkonkurrenz von Bürgergleichheit und Staatengleichheit im supranationalen Gemeinwesen. Eine Notiz aus Anlass der Frage nach der Legitimität der ungleichen Repräsentation der Bürger im Europäischen Parlament', 53 *Der Staat* (2014) 167; Lord and Pollak, 'Unequal But democratic? Equality According to Karlsruhe', 20 *Journal of European Public Policy* (2013) 190.

[292] § 6 para. 3 cl. 2 of the Federal Electoral Act; § 3 para. 1 cl. 2 of the Electoral Act of Schleswig-Holstein; § 3 para. 1 cl. 2 of the Electoral Act of Brandenburg; for a comparative analysis, see Pennicino, 'Elections', in R. Grote *et al.* (eds), *Max Planck Encyclopedia of Comparative Constitutional Law* (2017) para. 17.

other democratic federations. There are good democratic reasons against absolutizing the equality of a vote's impact. The European settlement in Article 14(2) TEU is democratic in substance and not just because it received all national parliaments' blessing.

2. An Executive Aberration of Democratic Thought?

The democratic legitimation of European politics has a second strand. It begins with national elections and passes through the European Council and the Council. The representatives in these two bodies are part of the national executives. They are not, then, appointees of the Member States' parliaments, as has been the case with the Austrian Federal Council and, until 1913, the US Senate (Article 35 of the Austrian Federal Constitutional Act, Article I s 3 of the US Constitution, amended by the 17th amendment). Since the European Council and the Council comprise members of the Member State governments, they resemble the German *Bundesrat*. There is, however, one essential difference: while Article 10(2) TEU declares the European Council and the Council bodies that provide for democratic representation, the Basic Law includes no such declaration.

Because the two councils are composed of representatives from the national *executive* branch, Article 10(2) TEU might, again, betray the national democratic traditions. This impression rests on the idea that representative institutions are fundamentally distinct from executive bodies. It is particularly present in constitutional traditions where parliaments had to struggle against the monarchical control of government.[293] However, this battle has been fought and won. In all Member States, especially in the European monarchies, the governments require parliamentary confirmation and support. This strengthened the national governments, which became capable of forming a true power centre, one that could realize democratic rule.[294]

The latter aspect explains the emergence and strengthening of the European Council, revealing a deep transformation in the European system of government.[295] In the first decades of integration, the Community method, whereby the Commission orientates and advances European politics, constituted the paradigm. But that paradigm never worked. To the chagrin of many an Euro-federalist, the European Council filled the void, starting in the 1970s.[296] In the second period, the European Council then went further and further in assuming the role that the Member State constitutions ascribe to the office holders of which it is

[293] C. Schönberger, *Das Parlament im Anstaltsstaat. Zur Theorie parlamentarischer Repräsentation in der Staatsrechtslehre des Kaiserreichs (1871–1918)* (1997) 13 ff.

[294] Comparatively, see A. von Bogdandy, *Gubernative Rechtsetzung. Eine Neubestimmung der Rechtsetzung und des Regierungssystems unter dem Grundgesetz in der Perspektive gemeineuropäischer Dogmatik* (2000) 39 ff., 107 ff.

[295] J. Werts, *The European Council* (2008) 184 f.

[296] Pescatore, 'Some Critical Remarks on the Single European Act', *Common Market Law Review* (1987) 9, at 11 ff.

composed: political leaders. Many constitutions—and many citizens—conceive of the executive as a centre of power that ought to determine the general direction in difficult policy fields, ensure that decisions are made, and even make critical decisions itself. This development has sound democratic credentials for there is no democracy absent political agency in exercising public authority.[297]

Today, the European Council, more than any other institution, ensures the Union's agency—as a provider of guidelines; as a shaper, mediator, and crisis manager; and as a public communicator.[298] Here, then, is one of the most surprising turns of the European transformation: an institution that initially appeared to evince the EU's intergovernmental atrophy arguably became its most powerful engine for ever-closer union.[299] Accordingly, the media is correct to present the European Council as the quintessence of the European machine for forging compromise.

Compromises are valuable; but not always (see 1.1) for they can also compromise democracy. We find the constitutional standards for evaluating a compromise in Article 2 TEU. This raises questions when it comes to the European Council, for the separation of powers constitutes an expression of the rule of law.

Some considered the European Council's influence on Regulation 2020/2092 (see 2.6.C, 3.1.B, 3.6.C) on a general regime of conditionality for the protection of the Union budget a transgression of its powers.[300] However, we ought not to criticize the European Council for playing a leading role in that supremely important legislative process. The issue at hand concerns the Member States' essential interests and has encountered serious opposition from Poland and Hungary (see 3.6.A). It corresponds to the European system of government for the European Council to perform a core role. Article 15(1) cl. 1 TEU provides that the European Council establishes the 'general political directions and priorities' of the Union's development and 'provides the necessary impetus'.[301]

In that role, however, the European Council might override the legislative procedures established by the Treaty legislator to provide for democratic legitimacy.[302] Article 15(1) cl. 2 TEU expressly excludes the European Council from exercising legislative functions, thus protecting the role of the Parliament and the Council, the two co-legislators. If European Council conclusions determined in

[297] S. Cassese, *Il buon governo. L'età dei doveri* (2020) 6–11.

[298] L. van Middelaar, *Alarums & Excursions. Improvising Politics on the European Stage* (2019) 178 ff.

[299] For a history written entirely from this perspective, see L. van Middelaar, *The Passage to Europe. How a Continent Became a Union* (2014).

[300] Regulation 2020/2092 (n. 22).

[301] See, e.g. the guidelines established by the European Council in the context of dealing with the Covid pandemic's financial repercussions. European Council Conclusions of 21 July 2020 (EUCO 10/20) 15 f.

[302] See the contrasting views in Editorial Comments, 'Compromising (on) the General Conditionality Mechanism and the Rule of Law', *Common Market Law Review* (2021) 267 (infringement); de Witte, 'The European Union's COVID-19 Recovery Plan: The Legal Engineering of an Economic Policy Shift', *Common Market Law Review* (2021) 635, at 667 ff., 681 (no infringement).

detail what the European legislature should enact, they would violate their democratic functions. In the case of Regulation 2020/2092, the European Council conclusions were detailed and even contained requirements for its application.[303] The European Council may not undo the pluralism enshrined in the European system of government.

If specific acts of the European Council may reasonably cause concern, its general role under Article 15(1) TEU does not as it corresponds to the role of most of its members in their domestic systems of government. Indeed, it is consonant with a process often called presidentialization.[304] This does not mean that the head of government is directly elected; rather, it draws attention to the fact that they have been gaining power and authority at the expense of other institutions. This has less to do with the sheer will of charismatic personalities or authoritarian tendencies than with increasing complexity, globalization, the medialization of politics, the dynamics of election campaigns, the weakness of traditional party structures, and—last but not least—the very existence of the European Council.

Presidentialization allows for democratic agency, which, in turn, provides democratic justification. It also provides for democratic accountability, as the former socialist regimes of Central and Eastern Europe show. As a result of their democratic transformations, the government gained in stature compared to the ruling party.[305] One reason why the situation in Poland after 2015 was deficient was that the country's most powerful politician, Jarosław Kaczyński, was not part of the government (until the autumn of 2020) but determined the country's fate as a party leader. As such, he never had to justify himself in the European Council, where he would have faced his peers.

A comparison with the German Federal Council, the *Bundesrat*, sheds further light on the two Councils' democratic role. Contrary to Article 10(2) sub-para. 2 TEU, the German Basic Law does not declare the *Bundesrat* a body of democratic representation, and mainstream German constitutional theory denies such a role.[306] The prevalent argument is that the German people, represented solely by the *Bundestag*, bears the entire burden of democratic legitimation. The Federal Republic is, after all, a *unitary* federal state.[307] Yet, that is not the case with the pluralist EU, which values its 27 peoples. To conceive of the pluralistic Union's executive

[303] European Council Conclusions of 11 December 2020 (EUCO 22/20) 1–4.

[304] Poguntke, 'Die Präsidentialisierung des politischen Prozesses: Welche Rolle bleibt den politischen Parteien?', in J. Krüper, H. Merten, and T. Poguntke (eds), *Parteienwissenschaften* (2015) 261.

[305] Goetz and Wollmann, 'Governmentalizing Central Executives in Post-Communist Europe: A Four-Country Comparison', 8 *Journal of European Public Policy* (2001) 864.

[306] On the discussion, see A. Hanebeck, *Der demokratische Bundesstaat des Grundgesetzes* (2004) 199–205, 279–282, 312–313.

[307] K. Hesse, *Der unitarische Bundesstaat* (1962); H. Hestermeyer, *Eigenständigkeit und Homogenität in föderalen Systemen. Eine vergleichende Studie der föderalen Ordnungen der Bundesrepublik Deutschland, der Vereinigten Staaten und der Europäischen Union* (2019) 115 ff.

federalism as democratic does not, then, betray the democratic principle; it advances it.[308]

3. Weiler's Doubts

The Treaty legislator conceives of the Parliament and the Councils as democratic institutions. However, legislative will cannot create a living democracy on its own. It is beyond question that true democracy requires more than that, and many doubt that the EU has what it takes.

If some doubt that European democracy is alive, no one can doubt that European politics are lively. After all, the Union institutions are buzzing with activity. Moreover, the European political process has been politicized, which means that it is subject to contestation and of public interest (see 2.2.B, 2.5.A). However, many dispute that the TEU's institutions allow for a democratic process. Joseph Weiler's doubts, voiced continuously over the past 30 years, are exemplary.[309] Confronting his doubts helps clarify further structures of European democracy.

Weiler emphasizes the first-person plural. For him, democracy means that *we* decide by means of elections. The conception of democracy that underlies the 'we' requires a strong collective identity. In Weiler's view, the meaning of elections ultimately lies in *us* deciding between different candidates for the office of head of government. Thus, elections determine *our* will and *our* destiny. *Nota bene*: Weiler does not advocate democratizing the Union along these lines, as that would imply a European federal state and a European people, both of which he rejects (see 3.4.A). Weiler's understanding of democracy only serves to criticize the Union. It reveals neither the path towards a more democratic Union nor how to interpret Articles 2 or 10 TEU.

In contrast to Weiler, I am convinced that the Treaty legislator's decision in favour of a European democracy without a collective identity and Westminster-like structures is theoretically plausible, conforms with the Member States' constitutional traditions, and enjoys democratic legitimacy (see 3.2.B, 3.5.A). The same applies to elections that do not decide who shall become the head of government.

The Treaty legislator decided in favour of a democracy of many mediations, of compromise, concordance, consensus, and negotiation.[310] Just consider the composition and voting modes in the two Councils and in the European Parliament, the composition of the Commission, and the interdependence of these

[308] On executive federalism, see Dann, 'The Political Institutions', in von Bogdandy and Bast (n. 42) 243 ff.

[309] See 3.4.A; Weiler, 'The Transformation of Europe' (n. 85); Weiler, 'Deciphering the Political and Legal DNA of European Integration. An Exploratory Essay', in J. Dickson and P. Eleftheriadis (eds), *Philosophical Foundations of European Union Law* (2012) 137; Weiler, 'The Crumbling of European Democracy', in M. A. Graber, S. Levinson, and M. Tushnet (eds), *Constitutional Democracy in Crisis?* (2018) 629.

[310] Dann (n. 308); Oeter (n. 273); on the individual approaches, agreements, and differences, see M. G. Schmidt, *Demokratietheorien. Eine Einführung* (2019) 319–328.

institutions. The logic of Articles 15(4), 16(4), and 17(7) TEU forces European politics to consider the interests of many political camps. European democracy understands and uses the legitimizing power of consensus.[311] The idea of competing *Spitzenkandidaten* (lead candidates), whereby the candidate of the largest group in the European Parliament should preside over the Commission, can go with a democracy of compromise, concordance, consensus, and negotiation.[312]

For Weiler, the Treaty legislator's decision in favour of a democracy of many mediations fails the idea of democracy. This position could be substantiated if Member State elections usually determined the head of government and decided between right-wing and left-wing politics, but that is hardly the case. In most Member States, electoral law has come to reflect societal pluralism. Thus, the electoral decision is only one stage of an often long and unpredictable path to a government and a programme.[313] Seeking compromise, consensus, concordance, and negotiation characterizes many Member States' politics today. While nobody disputes the ensuing problems,[314] neither does anyone call into question the democratic nature of the Member States. If a government were only democratic if elections directly decided who shall become the head of government, proceedings under Article 7 TEU would be required against many Member States.

In a similar fashion, some critics claim that decision-making in the EU is undemocratic because it is so complex that hardly anyone understands it.[315] I do not share this opinion. The public perceives Brussels as the site of arduous struggles for compromise. Indeed, as a rule, the Councils decide all important issues by consensus. Only rarely, as a last resort, do they pass legislation by majority vote against opposing Member States. And even that happens according to a complex formula that requires broad coalitions. Therefore, the Union is a consensus system in the shadow of qualified-majority voting. This is sensible, harnesses the intuitive legitimacy of consensus, and is also well known as the media and politicians mostly use this vocabulary to present European outcomes.

Weiler also calls the elections to the European Parliament into question by pointing out low voter turnout. In his view, this confirms that European elections are insufficiently meaningful.[316] It is true that voter turnout fell from 63 per cent

[311] Reh, 'European Integration as Compromise: Recognition, Concession and the Limits of Cooperation', 47 *Government and Opposition* (2012) 414.

[312] For a recent assessment, see Lupo, 'La forma di governo dell'Unione, dopo le elezioni europee del maggio 2019', in P. Caretti *et al.* (eds), *Liber Amicorum per Pasquale Costanzo. Diritto costituzionale in tranformazione, Vol. VI. Diritto costituzionale eurounitario e comparazione costituzionale* (2020) 25; Reestman and Besselink, 'Editorial. Spitzenkandidaten and the European Union's System of Government', 15 *European Constitutional Law Review* (2019) 609.

[313] A. Lijphart, *Patterns of Democracy. Government Forms and Performance in Thirty-Six Countries* (2012) 130–157; but see also Renwick and Weichsel, 'Im Interesse der Macht: Ungarns neues Wahlsystem', 62 *Osteuropa* (2012) 3.

[314] On the similarity of the problems afflicting the Federal Republic and the EU, see F. Meinel, *Vertrauensfrage. Zur Krise des heutigen Parlamentarismus* (2019) 25.

[315] C. Möllers, *Die Europäische Union als demokratische Föderation* (2019) 24.

[316] Weiler, 'The Crumbling of European Democracy' (n. 309) 630.

in 1979 to 51 per cent in 2019, having reached its lowest point with 43 per cent in 2014. However, such turnout rates hardly support Weiler's argument. Elections in German states generally have similarly low turnout rates, yet no one doubts the legitimacy of *Länder* parliaments and governments. Even in the motherland of modern democracy, the United States of America, the elections with the highest participation, the presidential elections, have seen voter turnout of only 55 per cent (in 2016) and 66 per cent (in 2020), with the latter representing the best turnout in decades. Moreover, only 38 per cent and 49 per cent of the electorate participated in the midterm elections of 2012 and 2018, respectively.

For Weiler, European elections also lack European meaning.[317] Indeed, many voters seem to make up their mind on how to vote based on domestic politics, paying little attention to European election programmes. To me, this seems sensible. The European election enables voters to guide their government's policies in the two councils. Moreover, they have reason to assume that the representatives of a party in the European Parliament pursue similar policies as in the national context. These positions are thus introduced in the many mediations of the European political process and help determine how Union citizens are governed. Of course, what is at stake is usually not a grand or sweeping right–left decision. The elections to the European Parliament are just one of many instances of mediation and need to be seen as such.

Finally, Weiler addresses what he perceives as a lack of political accountability in the Union, as no one can 'throw the scoundrels out'.[318] But a closer look shows otherwise. Every member of parliament must stand for re-election. The Commission has a limited term of office and can be censured under Article 234 TFEU, a mechanism that resembles the impeachment proceedings against the US President under Article I s 3 of the US Constitution but has a broader scope. The councils are likewise accountable as they are tied to the national democratic systems, in which the government's European policies often play a decisive role.[319]

The European system of government has many mechanisms of democratic accountability. It is true that, being a democracy of compromise, it does not seek to bring about political catharsis. The US elections of 3 November 2020 provide one example for the latter. A majority of Americans probably consider them a catharsis, a liberation, and a choice of direction for the American people. But quite a few other Americans believe that there was election fraud and that the new government is illegitimate. Some are ready to resist by force.[320]

[317] Weiler, *The Constitution of Europe* (n. 234) 350.

[318] Weiler, 'Europe in Crisis—On "Political Messianism", "Legitimacy" and the "Rule of Law"', *Singapore Journal of Legal Studies* (2012) 248, at 252.

[319] On this nexus, see Pinelli, 'Il doppio cappello dei governi fra Stati e Unione europea', *Rivista trimestrale di diritto pubblico* (2016) 639.

[320] Bright Line Watch, *A Democratic Stress Test—The 2020 Election and Its Aftermath. Bright Line Watch November 2020 Surveys*, http://brightlinewatch.org/a-democratic-stress-test-the-2020-election-and-its-aftermathbright-line-watch-november-2020-survey (last visited 30 August 2022).

The true difference between American and European society does not lie in their respective heterogeneity but in the logic of how it is addressed. To bring matters to a head, the current political system in the United States is defined by its *partisanship*, by the Schmittian scheme of friend and foe (see 2.3.C), while the European system is defined by its many mediations.[321] On the other side of the Atlantic, compromise appears like a betrayal of the cause; on this side, it is regarded as a political virtue.

4. The Democratic Value of Trilogues

According to a defining doctrine of European public law, laws (*lois*, *Gesetze*) constitute the centre of the legal order because legislation fuses the many individual wills into the *volonté générale*.[322] Hardly any other principle shapes the law of democracy like Article 6 of the French Declaration of the Rights of Man and of the Citizen of 1789: 'the law (*la loi*) is the expression of the general will. Every citizen has a right to participate personally, or through his representative, in its formation.'

Therefore, the laborious, and still incomplete, path towards European laws and legislation highlights European society's path towards its democracy.[323] Already the ECSC Treaty of 1951, followed by the EEC Treaty of 1957, authorized the enactment of general and abstract rules, albeit not in the form of statutes (*lois*) but only as regulations and directives. In Member States, regulations and directives are, as laws, general and abstract norms, but they express only the will of the executive branch. For that reason, they lack the dignity and legitimacy of a statute, which can only originate in parliament.

The Treaty legislator introduced the concept of the legislature only in 1997, but in an entirely subordinate position and, ironically, in relation to the Council's law-making role—not, as one would expect, Parliament's. In 2004, European politics attempted a great leap forward with the Constitutional Treaty. Under this Treaty, the Union legislature was supposed to enact Union statutes (*lois*, *Gesetze*) by means of a legislative procedure. As is well known, the leap failed.

The Treaty legislator's reaction to this failure is characteristic of the tortuous, but eventually successful, emergence of the democratic European society. With the blessing of all national parliaments, the Union today has a *legislative function* (Article 14 TEU; the German version speaks of a 'legislature'), which adopts

[321] Greenwood and Roederer-Rynning, 'Taming Trilogues: The EU's Law-Making Process in a Comparative Perspective', in O. Costa (ed.), *The European Parliament in Times of EU Crisis. Dynamics and Transformations* (2019) 121; Martin, 'Conditions for Successful Negotiation: Lessons from Europe', in J. Mansbridge and C. J. Martin (eds), *Political Negotiation. A Handbook* (2016) 199.

[322] A. Ross, *Theorie der Rechtsquellen. Ein Beitrag zur Theorie des positiven Rechts auf Grundlage dogmenhistorischer Untersuchungen* (1929) 34 f.; R. Carré de Malberg, *La loi, expression de la volonté générale. Étude sur le concept de la loi dans la Constitution de 1875* (1931); M. Stolleis, *Im Namen des Gesetzes* (2004) 14.

[323] Bast, 'Europäische Gesetzgebung—Fünf Stationen in der Verfassungsentwicklung der EU', in Franzius, Mayer, and Neyer (n. 253) 171.

legislative acts (Article 12 TEU) in the ordinary *legislative procedure* (Article 289 TFEU). The Treaty legislator also accorded legislation the same position it occupies in the Member States' constitutional traditions. Thus, it is always named first, reflecting its paramount public function (Articles 14 and 16 TEU).[324] However, the Lisbon Treaty does not refer to the Union's legislative acts as statutes (*lois*, *Gesetze*); instead, it continues to use the terms 'regulation' and 'directive'. The incomplete terminological transformation is representative of the general incompleteness of the Union's democratic transformation.

Trilogues represent a core part of the European legislative process. For that reason, scholars call into question the process's democratic credentials.[325] But I shall argue that the trilogue structures do not betray European democracy. On the contrary, they represent a significant democratic innovation.

The Union's legislative procedure is complex, as is commensurate with the concept of dual legitimation. A legislative act requires 'joint adoption by the European Parliament and the Council [...] on a proposal from the Commission' (Article 289(1) TFEU). This accommodates a Hegelian approach, which relies on mediation. The Hegelian tradition focuses on the cooperation of powers, not their separation.[326]

The Treaty sets up a legislative procedure that requires a lot of mediation between the institutions. To this end, it creates the Conciliation Committee as a forum for consolidating the different interests, preferences, and positions into a general European will. The committee consists of 'the members of the Council [...] and an equal number of members representing the European Parliament' and has 'the task of reaching agreement [...] by a qualified majority of the members of the Council ... and by a majority of the members representing the European Parliament within six weeks of its being convened' (Article 294(10) TFEU). Given, on average, 120 legislative acts per year, we would expect this forum—this agora, this marketplace of European democracy—to be full, bustling, noisy. But it is empty, sleepy, quiet.

In 2019 and 2020, the Conciliation Committee did not meet once. Matters are similar in Germany. The committee for the joint consideration of bills under Article 77(2) of the German Basic Law, which is supposed to mediate between the *Bundestag* and the *Bundesrat*, has concluded only six mediation procedures in the last legislative period, that is, in the span of four years. This allows us better to comprehend a significant innovation of European democracy.

[324] Approaches that focus on events have difficulties seeing this phenomenon. See, e.g. van Middelaar, *The Passage to Europe* (n. 299).

[325] Curtin and Leino, 'In Search of Transparency for EU Law-Making: Trilogues on the Cusp of Dawn', 54 *Common Market Law Review* (2017) 1673; von Achenbach, 'Verfassungswandel durch Selbstorganisation: Triloge im europäischen Gesetzgebungsverfahren', 55 *Der Staat* (2016) 1.

[326] Hegel, *Elements of the Philosophy of Right* (n. 13) paras 272, 300.

The declining importance of the German mediation committee is a consequence of the fragmented party-political landscape.[327] According to Leibholz's conception of democracy, societal mediations mainly happen within the governing party (see 1.3). This model no longer serves the Federal Republic as its party system has fragmented. While fragmentation has certainly not put an end to the party state, it has transformed German politics. Today, more than in the past, political mediations involve several parties, often including the opposition.[328] The parties negotiate directly, which explains the mediation committee's irrelevance.

With 190 parties in the European Parliament and no truly European parties, EU legislation cannot be negotiated like German legislation. For that reason, the Union has developed another and, indeed, more democratic way: the trilogue.[329] Though frequently called into doubt, it has a legitimating legal basis, for Article 295 TFEU allows this interinstitutional cooperation. It has existed for quite some time, namely, since the mid-1970s. Trilogues are committees that bring together representatives of the Council, Parliament, and Commission. They are much smaller than the Conciliation Committee. The Presidency of the Council participates, assisted by the General Secretariat. The European Parliament sends the concerned rapporteur, who is accompanied by the shadow rapporteurs of the other political groups. The Commission is present with its top administrative staff. As a rule, the meetings involve fewer than 30 people. This is essential because the smaller number of participants enables dialogic encounter and substantive negotiation. In this way, the trilogue differs from the much larger Conciliation Committee, which brings together more than twice the number of people. The fact that the meetings are not open to the public and that there are no minutes also facilitates dialogue and negotiations. However, the meetings are by no means secret. Thus, the public is kept informed, and the shadow rapporteurs, who are often critical, can report on the proceedings to the public.[330]

A trilogue is not an institution as it cannot decide anything. But the participants can establish a consensus. Such consensus is highly influential because all subsequent steps in the legislative procedure usually represent a mere formality. The legislative project, in its consented form, is transmitted to the Council and the Parliament, which almost always enacts it, without debate, as the European general will.

[327] Meinel (n. 314) 35 f.

[328] Schmidt, *Demokratietheorien* (n. 310) 319. For criticism of all-party governments, see Böckenförde, 'Sozialer Bundesstaat und parlamentarische Demokratie', in J. Jekewitz, M. Melzer, and W. Zeh (eds), *Politik als gelebte Verfassung: Aktuelle Probleme des modernen Verfassungsstaates* (1980) 182, at 191 f.

[329] The following remarks are based on the dissertation of Rugge, *Trilogues: The Democratic Secret of European Legalisation* (n. 284).

[330] On the problems with the representatives of Eurosceptic parties, see Ripoll Servant and Panning, 'Eurosceptics in Trilogue Settings: Interest Formation and Contestation in the European Parliament', 42 *West European Politics* (2019) 755.

The high success rate shows that there is enormous pressure on all participants to succeed. It also proves that they have a strong mandate. Thus, all participants can assume that the Parliament and the Council will enact any outcome within the mandate. The mandate, in turn, requires a great deal of internal negotiation beforehand. The institutions will only commence a trilogue when both sides can point to a strong mandate. Thus, there has been no trilogue so far on the Commission's 2016 proposal for a reform of European refugee law because the Council has not been able to formulate a viable negotiating mandate; the positions within it are too heterogeneous and hardened.

The European Parliament develops its negotiating mandate in what is called a double filtering system. According to the latter, both a majority within the negotiator's political group and the majority of the committee members responsible must support it.[331] This system of will formation aims for broad majorities, similar to the procedure in the Council. Importantly, the political groups and the committee not only serve to formalize agreements reached elsewhere but are also often the actual place of mediation. Therefore, the members of the European Parliament often provide better democratic representation than their national counterparts as the latter frequently have to support their government line.[332] For me, one of the strengths of European democracy is that it allows for such pluralism and does not subordinate the various conflicts to one overarching line of conflict.[333]

Moreover, because the Union is not a parliamentary system of government, its institutional logic prompts the parliamentary delegation to propose a political alternative to the Commission and the Council, thus increasing public awareness of the parliamentarians' political profile. This can address an important deficiency of the European political process, namely, the technocratic argument that there is no alternative to a specific policy suggestion.[334] The logic of European parliamentarism is to bring forth alternatives that might have an impact on a certain policy.

Trilogues draw a great deal of criticism.[335] After all, they involve parliamentarians who are unknown to most citizens and appointed as rapporteurs in obscure procedures developing a text with the Council Presidency in a non-transparent process of wheeling and dealing that takes place far from the public eye. Moreover, this text then almost automatically becomes the European *volonté générale*.

[331] Rugge, *Trilogues: The Democratic Secret of European Legalisation* (n. 284) 50.

[332] Mair and Thomassen, 'Political Representation and Government in the European Union', 17 *Journal of European Public Policy* (2010) 20, at 23 ff.

[333] But see Möllers, *Die Europäische Union als demokratische Föderation* (n. 315) 18 (considering this a weakness, not a strength).

[334] Dehousse, 'Constitutional Reform in the European Community. Are There Alternatives to the Majoritarian Avenue?', 18 *West European Politics* (1995) 118, at 122, 124 f.; van Middelaar, *The Passage to Europe* (n. 299) 240.

[335] Curtin and Leino (n. 325) 1712; von Achenbach, 'Verfassungswandel durch Selbstorganisation' (n. 325) 39.

However, Giacomo Rugge has shown that trilogue proceedings constitute the functional equivalent of strong parties and even have several democratic advantages.[336]

According to the traditional model of parliamentarism, parliament determines the general will after a debate in public session that brings forth the best solution. The practice of twentieth-century parliamentary democracies falls short of this model, as Schmitt pointed out to delegitimize liberal parliamentarism.[337] Gerhard Leibholz turns Schmitt's critique into something constructive (see 1.3), recoding the haggling of party politics as the centre of democratic politics.[338] This recoding helped understand the Federal Republic as a democratic polity. Similar recodings occurred in other European states as well.[339]

However, Leibholz's mediation happens outside the institutions and is hardly cabined by procedural law. Political parties are private associations. The provisions of the German Political Parties Act do not address their decision-making process on legislative proposals. In consequence, there is no duty to inform the public, access to the mediation is not regulated, and the opposition is mostly excluded unless its participation is required, which prevents it from monitoring the government. For these reasons, there are few checks on the exercise of raw intra-party power.

Trilogues are more democratic than that. Both the access to them and their procedure are regulated, including in the Joint Declaration on Practical Arrangements for the Codecision Procedure, the Rules of Procedure of the European Parliament, and the Parliament's Code of Conduct for Negotiating in the Context of the Ordinary Legislative Procedure. Critics point out that the public does not have access to a trilogue and that the lead negotiators need not publicly justify how they conduct the negotiations. However, they do have to inform the parliament,[340] and they are monitored by the shadow rapporteurs of the competing parties. In other words, the opposition is always involved. As Rugge demonstrates, the European system of government accomplishes the feat of institutionalizing a democratically framed space of informality that allows for actual mediation. It is difficult to dispute the democratic nature of this process, in particular if one compares it to Germany.

This is especially true when considering trilogues in their constitutional context rather than in isolation. A trilogue is only one step on a long path of democratic mediations. The first step involves the negotiation and national ratifications of the

[336] Rugge, *Trilogues: The Democratic Secret of European Legalisation* (n. 284) chs V and VI.

[337] C. Schmitt, *Die geistesgeschichtliche Lage des heutigen Parlamentarismus* (1926). On this conception, see von Bogdandy, 'Parlamentarismus in Europa. Eine Verfalls- oder Erfolgsgeschichte?', 130 *Archiv des öffentlichen Rechts* (2005) 445.

[338] G. Leibholz, *Der Strukturwandel der modernen Demokratie. Vortrag, gehalten in der Juristischen Studiengesellschaft in Karlsruhe am 30. April 1952* (1952). On Leibholz's role A.-B. Kaiser (ed.), *Der Parteienstaat. Zum Staatsverständnis von Gerhard Leibholz* (2013).

[339] Schmidt, *Demokratietheorien* (n. 310) 439–452; P. Scoppola, *La repubblica dei partiti. Evoluzione e crisi di un sistema politico (1945–1996)* (1997).

[340] Brandsma, 'Transparency of EU Informal Trilogues through Public Feedback in the European Parliament: Promise Unfulfilled', 26 *Journal of European Public Policy* (2019) 1464.

EU competences and Treaty objectives. The second step consists of the European Council's mediations in the shape of its 'impulses', 'objectives', and 'priorities' for European legislation. Agreeing on the annual roadmap of European legislation negotiated by the Parliament, the Council, and the Commission represents a third step.[341] On that basis, the Commission makes proposals that Council and Parliament process internally, mediating between different interests, preferences, and positions before articulating a mandate that makes a trilogue possible. Only then can a trilogue consolidate the various interests, preferences, and positions into the general will of European society.

Such mediations would appear undemocratic if the general will reflected a compact majority. But in a pluralistic society, compact majorities of this kind hardly ever exist. Today, a majority is usually something much more fluid and diverse, that is, a compromise.[342] We should not disqualify this compromise by designating it as the lowest common denominator. If it meets the principles of Article 2 TEU, we should celebrate it as a sign of European democracy.

C. Further Democratic Transformation

Thus far, I have focused on the classificatory dimension of the concept of democracy, discussing whether the Union is a democratic system of government. But democracy has not only a classificatory but also a comparative dimension. It can be more and less democratic.[343] Indeed, democracies can, and should, become more democratic (see 1.4, 2.6.A, 3.1.A). In the Union, this is an outright obligation: the Treaty legislator mandates its institutions to advance European democracy (Article 13(1) TEU). This requires us to discuss further structural transformations.[344]

According to *Eurobarometer 2019*, 55 per cent of respondents are satisfied with the EU's democracy.[345] This is remarkable, given the criticism that influential academics, courts, and some political parties direct against it (see 3.4.B–5.B). At the same time, it is not satisfactory. In comparison, the 55 per cent for the EU's institutions rank in the lower midfield, while frontrunners like Denmark's democracy have a satisfaction rate of 95 per cent, Ireland's democracy achieves 80 per cent, and Germany's 74 per cent. At the same time, satisfaction with French democracy, at 53

[341] Interinstitutional Agreement between the European Parliament, the Council of the European Union and the European Commission on Better Law-Making, OJ 2016 L 123/1.

[342] P. Rosanvallon, *La légitimité démocratique. Impartialité, réflexivité, proximité* (2008) 10–12.

[343] H.-J. Lauth, *Demokratie und Demokratiemessung. Eine konzeptionelle Grundlegung für den interkulturellen Vergleich* (2004). See, concretely, the democracy index, Freedom House, *Freedom in the World*, https://freedomhouse.org/report/freedom-world (last visited 30 August 2022); Varieties of Democracy (V-Dem), https://www.v-dem.net (last visited 30 August 2022); Bertelsmann Transformation Index, https://bti-project.org/de/?&cb=00000 (last visited 30 August 2022).

[344] S. Goulard and M. Monti, *La democrazia in Europa. Guardare lontano* (2012); A. Vauchez, *Démocratiser l'Europe* (2014); Möllers, *Die Europäische Union als demokratische Föderation* (n. 315).

[345] European Commission, *Standard Eurobarometer 91* (n. 100).

per cent, Greek democracy, at 35 per cent, and Croatian democracy, at only 33 per cent, is worse than with the EU. The various components of European democracy are not only diverse but also very differently appreciated.[346]

The Union should become more democratic. In many respects, this objective seems vague but, in others, it does not. For example, almost no one advocates modelling the Union on the US, UK, or Swiss type of government, not to speak of China or Russia. European society is forging its own democratic path.

The Treaty legislator's mandate to advance European democracy gains substance if we read it in the light of all provisions in the EU Treaty's three introductory titles. They convey the idea of a representative and just democracy that reflects the 12 principles of Article 2 TEU and truly advances the objectives of Article 3 TEU. No one will doubt that social life and political structures and processes, as well as the law (including provisions in the Treaties) do not fully live up to this idea. Accordingly, change, even transformation, is necessary.

However, the mandate of Article 13(1) TEU does not authorize constitutional amendments, neither does it allow the institutions to disregard specific Treaty provisions (see 3.3.B). The principle of the rule of law, Articles 4 and 48 TEU, clearly attest to this.[347] The Treaty provisions are the fruit of democratic compromises and express European pluralism. Moreover, the Treaty legislator keeps the EU institutions on a short leash on important issues, which is why many Treaties provisions are rather precise and detailed.[348]

Against this backdrop, I will address three issues. The first attends to the principle of democracy in the Union's institutions. The second aims to reconstruct, in the light of Article 2 TEU, the primary law concerning specific EU policies. The third deals with the transformative thrust of Article 2 TEU for Member States that suffer from systemic deficiencies (see 3.6).

There is certainly more to say about the means for strengthening European democratic legitimacy. Like Heller, and as confirmed by Eurobarometer, I suspect that one of the most important questions is whether most citizens feel that their concrete situation is secure and will improve. Output is decisive for legitimacy,[349] which explains the prominent role of policy objectives at the very beginning of the EU Treaty (Article 3 TEU).

When it comes to the democratic nature of the Union institutions' operation, it bears mentioning that the European Parliament's gradual strengthening has vitally transformed the EU's system of government. But even after the Amsterdam Treaty of 1997, one could still doubt whether the Treaty legislator had committed

[346] Ibid. 141.

[347] *ECHR Accession I* (n. 167) paras 10 ff; Case C-376/98, *Germany v. Parliament and Council* (EU:C:2000:544) paras 76 ff.; Case C-358/14, *Poland v. Parliament and Council* (EU:C:2016:323) paras 31 ff.

[348] J.-C. Piris, *The Constitution for Europe. A Legal Analysis* (2006) 59.

[349] On the democratic dignity of output, see Scharpf, *Regieren in Europa* (n. 239).

to a constitutional model of parliamentary law-making. While the Amsterdam Treaty conferred many competences on the Parliament, it reserved legislation to the Council in many areas. There was no provision declaring co-legislation by the Council and Parliament the rule. For that reason, many rejected a rule of interpretation whereby law-making should, in doubt, be based on a competence that included parliamentary participation.[350]

Only in 2007 did the Lisbon Treaty introduce such a principle (Article 10 TEU). It suggests giving preference, when in doubt, to the competence that provides for parliamentary participation.[351] The presumption of parliamentary involvement goes even further, however, since Article 10(1) TEU is not limited to legislation but covers the entire 'functioning' of the Union. Thus, it supports interpretations that strengthen the Parliament's powers of supervision. The European foreign and security policy provides relevant examples.[352]

Article 10(1) TEU offers a legal standard for democratic criticism. The regulation of how funds are raised and allocated to overcome the consequences of the COVID-19 pandemic is one example. Having the Council alone decide on this matter fails that standard. The election of judges to the CJEU (see 4.5.B) is similarly deficient.[353]

European democracy amounts to more than representation. Pursuant to Article 11 TEU, the Union's governmental bodies should work in an open, participatory, dialogic, and transparent manner in order to enhance European democracy. This is not a secondary concern for it is also stated in the very first provision of the Treaty. Under Article 1 TEU, the Union should make its decisions 'as openly as possible and as closely as possible to the citizen'. This certainly invites cynical comments since many EU consultations seem to be more concerned with advertising than with dialogue. But it is possible to make the principle operational: the EU law on transparency shows how secretive bureaucracies can be transformed into more democratic administrations.[354]

Some Union policies also provide a field for democratic transformations because their legal regime stands in tension with the constitutional core. Consider

[350] *Commission v. Council* (n. 231) paras 20 f.; differently already at the time, *Commission v. Council*, Opinion of AG Tesauro (EU:C:1991:115) I-2892 f; see also Joint Cases T-222/99, T-327/99 and T-329/99, *Martinez and others v. Parliament* (EU:T:2001:242) paras 196, 200.

[351] *Commission v. Council* (n. 231) para. 20; on the limits, see Case C-130/10, *Parliament v. Council*, (EU:C:2012:472) para. 79.

[352] CJEU, Case C-263/14, *Parliament v. Council* (EU:C:2016:2436) paras 70 f. On the multi-faceted case law, see Moser and Rittberger, 'The CJEU and EU (De)constitutionalization—Unpacking Jurisprudential Strategies', 9 *Max Planck Institute for Comparative Public Law & International Law Research Paper Series* (2021) 1, at 15 ff.

[353] Nettesheim, '"Next Generation EU": Die Transformation der EU-Finanzverfassung', 145 *Archiv des öffentlichen Rechts* (2020) 381, at 434.

[354] CJEU, Case C-39/05 P, *Sweden and Turco v. Council* (EU:C:2008:374); Case C-280/11, *Council v. Access Info Europe* (EU:C:2013:671); Case C-57/16 P, *ClientEarth v. Commission* (EU:C:2018:660); Case T-540/15, *De Capitani v. Parliament* (EU:T:2018:167); Rugge, 'Trilogues and Access to Documents: De Capitani v. Parliament', 56 *Common Market Law Review* (2019) 237.

the principles of Article 2 TEU, on the one hand, and constitutional provisions on economic and monetary policy, on the other. Most of that tension flows from the demise of many theoretical and ideological assumptions on which the economic and monetary union is based.[355] A corresponding transformation has by now been set into motion.[356] The EU's measures in response to the COVID-19 pandemic could propel this transformation by significantly advancing European solidarity.[357]

Such transformations require doctrinal reconstructions that imbue the Union's economic and monetary constitution with the principles of Article 2 TEU. Article 3(3) TEU, Article 119 TFEU, and the provisions concretizing them should be interpreted in the light of Articles 2 and 3(1) TEU. The economic and monetary constitution can thus become more responsive to European democracy.

The role of the European constitutional core in guiding the interpretation of economic and monetary union suggests that what is arguably the most transformative of all steps ever taken by the Union's institutions is lawful: Mario Draghi's 'whatever-it-takes' declaration. It not only complies with the Treaties[358] but also reflects the legal logic to which European society owes its existence.

The full quote reads: '*Within our mandate*, the ECB is ready to do whatever it takes to preserve the euro.'[359] The mandate originates in Articles 127(1) and 282(2) TFEU, interpreted teleologically.[360] Article 127(1) TFEU refers to Article 3 in its entirety, that is, including Article 3(1) TEU. Moreover, Article 13(1) TEU, as well as Article 127 TEU, impose a duty on the ECB to promote the fundamental principles. On that basis, it becomes relevant that a disintegrating monetary union could have prompted a dynamic similar to that occasioned by the German monetary meltdown of the early 1930s.[361]

Such reconstruction of the economic and monetary constitutional provisions requires abandoning the sort of constitutional thinking that interprets EU primary

[355] Dobre, 'Constitución económica: Una propuesta al debate conceptual', 3 *Revista de Derecho Público: Teoría y Método* (2021) 157; A. Sandulli, *Il ruolo del diritto in Europa. L'integrazione europea dalla prospettiva del diritto amministrativo* (2018) 59 ff.

[356] Ioannidis, 'Europe's New Transformations. How the EU Economic Constitution Changed during the Eurozone Crisis', 53 *Common Market Law Review* (2016) 1237; Ioannidis, 'Between Responsibility and Solidarity. COVID-19 and the Future of the European Economic Order', 4 *Zeitschrift für ausländisches öffentliches Recht und Völkerrecht* (2020) 773.

[357] The first step was Council Regulation 2020/672 on the establishment of a European instrument for temporary support to mitigate unemployment risks in an emergency (SURE) following the COVID-19 outbreak, OJ 2020 L 159/1; European Council Conclusions of 21 July 2020 (n. 301); Habermas, '30 Jahre danach: Die zweite Chance', 9 *Blätter für deutsche und internationale Politik* (2020) 41.

[358] For this view, see the arguments in *OMT Programme* (n. 64) paras 16 ff. See also the reconstruction in Ruffert, 'The European Debt Crisis and European Union Law', 48 *Common Market Law Review* (2011) 1777.

[359] European Central Bank, *Speech by Mario Draghi, President of the European Central Bankat at the Global Investment Conference in London, 26 July 2012*, https://www.ecb.europa.eu/press/key/date/2012/html/sp120726.en.html (last visited 30 August 2022), emphasis added.

[360] In detail, CJEU, Case C-62/14, *Gauweiler* (EU:C:2015:400), paras 32 ff.

[361] Goldmann, 'The Great Recurrence. Karl Polanyi and the Crises of the European Union', 23 *European Law Journal* (2017) 272.

law primarily as a liberal market constitution with a monetarist orientation.[362] This process is well under way. One example, which leads to Chapter 4, is provided by the CJEU's case law on market freedoms. In the past, the freedoms mainly served economic integration; today, they also defend democratic essentials in the Member States.[363]

6. Transformative Constitutionalism

A. Difficult, But Necessary

Section 3.3.C, which dealt with systemically deficient Member States, focused on institutional weaknesses. Now, deficiencies for authoritarian tendencies are at issue. These two types overlap, such as in matters of corruption. Nevertheless, it makes sense to distinguish a special field of European constitutional oversight[364] that counteracts authoritarian tendencies. It raises monumental legal questions.

In 2007, the Treaty legislator renamed and repositioned the EU Treaty's fundamental principles as European values. In doing so, it postulated them not only as legal norms but also as broadly shared and entrenched ethical (or moral) principles that not only underlie the European legal order but also 'prevail' in European society (see 3.1.B). This move probably sought to grant Union law a new source of legitimacy and stability. But today, stipulating a union of values is proving to be as risky as stipulating a union of money. The European discourse on values has mutated from one of self-congratulation into one of crisis and alarm.[365]

This is because of measures some national governments use to weaken domestic checks and balances.[366] While most observers and institutions talk of threats to the rule of law, human rights and democracy are equally at risk (see 3.1.C). Political scientists consider such measures symptomatic of defective democracies.[367]

Article 49 TEU requires that a state acceding to the Union 'respects the values referred to in Article 2 and is committed to promoting them'. That establishes a

[362] Mestmäcker, 'Zur Wirtschaftsverfassung in der Europäischen Union', in R. H. Hasse, J. Molsberger, and C. Watrin (eds), *Ordnung in Freiheit. Festgabe für Hans Willgerodt zum 70. Geburtstag* (1994) 263; Müller-Graff, '§ 1 Europäisches Wirtschaftsordnungsrecht: Das System', in P.-C. Müller-Graff (ed.), *Enzyklopädie Europarecht, Bd. 4. Europäisches Binnenmarkt- und Wirtschaftsordnungsrecht* (2021) paras 25 ff.

[363] CJEU, Case 78/18, *Commission v. Hungary (Transparency of Associations)* (EU:C:2020:476); see 4.6.A.

[364] On the concept, see M. Schmidt, *Verfassungsaufsicht in der Europäischen Union. Eine akteurszentrierte Analyse der Rechtsstaatlichkeitskrise der Europäischen Union* (2021).

[365] Voßkuhle, *Die Idee der Europäischen Wertegemeinschaft*, (n. 141) 16 ff.

[366] The following reflections are informed by the contributions of B. Bakó, S. Biernat, A. von Bogdandy, P. Bogdanowicz, M. Bonelli, I. Canor, C. Dupré, A. Frackowiak-Adamska, P. Filipek, J. Kirchmayr, J. Łacny, A. Nowak-Far, J. Polakiewicz, G. Rugge, W. Sadowski, M. Schmidt, W. Schroeder, P. Sonnevend, D. Spieker, M. Taborowski, J. Weiler, and M. Wiacek, in von Bogdandy *et al.* (eds) (n. 278).

[367] Merkel *et al.*, 'Defekte Demokratie', in W. Merkel *et al.* (eds), *Defekte Demokratie* (2003) 65.

presumption that all Member States adhere to the values at any time after accession. The presumption feeds the self-understanding of European society as a union of liberal democracies, legitimizes decision-making in the EU, justifies the mutual recognition of decisions, and establishes mutual trust in the lawfulness of all public institutions. As long as this presumption holds, violations of Union law do not challenge the European legal order (see 3.3.A).

Today, various Member States put a strain on the presumption. The European Commission for Democracy through Law of the Council of Europe (Venice Commission, see 2.6.D) documents problems in eight reports on Hungary (rule of law, fundamental rights, freedom of the media), six on Poland (judiciary, separation of powers), and five each on Bulgaria (corruption, rule of law), Malta (separation of powers, human rights), and Romania (corruption, judiciary)—all in the past five years alone.[368] Hungary is of even more concern.[369]

What mobilized the EU institutions' constitutional oversight, however, was the PiS government's weakening and capture of the Polish judiciary.[370] As one of its first actions in 2015, the new majority first proceeded to debilitate the Constitutional Tribunal and then appointed pro-government justices; today, the Court seems captured, an instrument of the government.[371] The majority then honed in on the National Judicial Council, retired 150 out of 700 Court presidents and vice-presidents as well as almost 40 per cent of the Supreme Court judges, and increased the number of Supreme Court judgeships. It established a new disciplinary chamber with pro-government judges that can sanction all other judges. With the help of this chamber, the Polish government tries to prevent preliminary references to the CJEU concerning the lawfulness of its measures, thus depriving the Polish judiciary of the Luxembourg Court's support. The disciplinary measures against Igor Tuleya, a figurehead of those judges critical of the government, are emblematic in this regard.[372] The Polish Minister of Justice called on the Polish Constitutional Court to declare Article 267 TFEU unconstitutional insofar as

[368] Available at https://www.venice.coe.int/WebForms/documents/by_opinion.aspx?v=countries (last visited 30 August 2022).

[369] EP Resolution on a proposal calling on the Council to determine, pursuant to Article 7(1) of the Treaty on European Union, the existence of a clear risk of a serious breach by Hungary of the values on which the Union is founded (2017/2131(INL)).

[370] European Commission, Proposal for a Council Decision on the determination of a clear risk of a serious breach by the Republic of Poland of the rule of law, COM(2017) 835 final; Report of the Polish Judges' Association 'Iustitia', J. Kościerzyński (ed.), *Justice under Pressure—Repressions as a Means of Attempting to Take Control over the Judiciary and the Prosecution in Poland. Years 2015–2019* (2020); W. Sadurski, *Poland's Constitutional Breakdown* (2019) 1–34.

[371] Łętowska, 'A Tragic Constitutional Court Judgment on Abortion' *Verfassungsblog* (12 November 2020).

[372] Werner, 'Kampf um die Unabhängigkeit der Gerichte in Europa: Interview mit Beata Morawiec und Igor Tuleya', 99 *Deutsche Richterzeitung* (2021) 142; European Commission, Rule of Law Report 2020, Country Chapter on the Situation of the Rule of Law in Poland, SWD(2020) 320 final, 7.

CJEU decisions concern the judiciary's internal organization.[373] The government also took ruthless action against a second bastion of the checks and balances that substantiate the democratic rule of law: the free press (see 5.4.A).

The Member States' observance of the European principles is a legal presumption, not a legal fiction. The difference between a presumption and a fiction is that the former is rebuttable, whereas the latter is irrebuttable and, in common parlance, often devoid of a factual basis. If Member States' observance of the principles appears fictitious, the current identity of European society is in danger (see 2.6.D).

Ultimately, the question is whether European society *embraces* or *fights* deficient democracies. Both choices entail transformation. If the European institutions do nothing, deficient democracies will participate in shaping the principles of Article 2 TEU, as follows from the principle of the Member States' equality (Article 4(2) TEU) and the role of the common traditions. To avoid this, European public law must develop mechanisms of constitutional oversight and support democratic transformations in these Member States.

But does EU constitutional oversight make any sense? In one of the most famous dicta of federal German constitutional theory, Böckenförde (see 1.4) argued that a liberal legal order could not guarantee its prerequisites.[374] Böckenförde probably assumed that only Christian faith could offer this guarantee. If that is hardly convincing today,[375] it seems plausible to ascribe a foundational role to the citizens' civic mindset (see 3.2.B). Article 2 TEU breathes this understanding when it founds the Union in values, that is, widespread ethical convictions (see 3.1.B). Moreover, the Hegelian tradition supports the assumption that public policy can promote such a mindset: Hegel speaks of civic ethics as 'the result of the institutions existing in the state'.[376] Böckenförde, who was neither a fatalist nor against civic education, does not dispute this conclusion.

Thus, a policy of entrenching democratic principles and fostering corresponding societal structures can work. At the same time, it is clear that such policies are difficult and time-consuming. Hegel is particularly sceptical of externally imposed constitutional policies; his prime example is the failed Napoleonic modernization in Spain. The difficulties of constitutional transformations that Hegel identified are widely documented today. Nevertheless, promoting democracy became an important policy field in the second half of the twentieth century.[377]

373 Pending as Case K 7/18. See Biernat and Kawczyńska, 'Though This Be Madness, Yet There's Method in't: Pitting the Polish Constitutional Tribunal against the Luxembourg Court', *Verfassungsblog* (26 October 2019).

374 Böckenförde, 'Die Entstehung des Staates als Vorgang der Säkularisation', *Säkularisation und Utopie. Ebracher Studien. Ernst Forsthoff zum 65. Geburtstag* (1967) 75, at 94; on this Müller, 'What the Dictum Really Meant—And What It Could Mean for Us', 25 *Constellations* (2018) 196; Habermas, 'Vorpolitische Grundlagen des demokratischen Rechtsstaats?', in J. Habermas and J. Ratzinger (eds), *Dialektik der Säkularisierung. Über Vernunft und Religion* (2005) 15.

375 Volkmann (n. 92) 502 ff.

376 Hegel, *Elements of the Philosophy of Right* (n. 13) para. 268.

377 Ibid. para. 274 Addition.

A key figure in creating this policy field was Karl Loewenstein, a constitutional scholar from Munich. In 1943, as a refugee in the United States, he coined the term 'militant democracy'.[378] After Germany's defeat, he participated in the US policy of democratization. This included democratic education, which is why Löwenstein advocated that Schmitt be arrested and banned from writing.[379] After all, legal scholarship affects a society's political consciousness (see also 1.4, 5.1.A on further proceedings against Schmitt).

Allied policy in Germany refuted Hegel's categorical scepticism of exogenous constitutional policies. American democratization proved successful in Germany, and Löwenstein's ideas became the building blocks of modern constitutionalism. Promoting democracy developed into an important transnational policy field that has achieved many successes, many failures notwithstanding. In conclusion, external pressure can help democratic transitions, and it is frequently indispensable to a transformation's success (see 2.6.C, 2.6.D). The European Treaties thus carry on Löwenstein's legacy.[380]

Any European policy on Poland needs to take into account that the Polish governing majority has entrenched itself in many institutions since 2015 and that it again won the parliamentary elections in 2019 as well as the presidential elections in 2020. There is much to suggest that the democratic transformation of Polish society, initiated in the Lenin (Gdańsk) Shipyard in the early 1980s, has come to a standstill (see 2.6.D). What is required, then, is not a quick fix but a long-term transformation of social structures (see 2.6.B).

Any such transformation will encounter many difficulties. Polish institutions vehemently dispute the lawfulness and legitimacy of EU measures and have mobilized the Polish Constitutional Tribunal for a counterattack.[381] In 2017, the Polish ambassador in Berlin announced that Poland upholds all European values: 'The problem is one of interpretation. Brussels is too ideologically biased—biased in favour of a left-liberal ideology.'[382] But voices that do not belong to the Polish government camp also consider a European answer problematic.[383] Weiler sees a problem of legitimacy because the Union does not abide by the values it demands from its

[378] Loewenstein, 'Militant Democracy and Fundamental Rights, I', 31 *American Political Science Review* (1937) 417; K. Loewenstein, *Verfassungslehre* (1959) 449 ff.

[379] R. Mehring, *Carl Schmitt. Aufstieg und Fall* (2009) 442.

[380] F. Schorkopf, *Die Maßnahmen der XIV EU-Mitgliedstaaten gegen Österreich* (2002) 119 ff.; Müller, 'The EU as a Militant Democracy, or: Are There Limits to Constitutional Mutants within EU Member States?', 165 *Revista de Estudios Políticos* (2014) 141; M. Klamt, *Die Europäische Union als streitbare Demokratie. Rechtsvergleichende und europarechtliche Dimensionen einer Idee* (2012).

[381] See Steinbeis, 'The Deed, Not the Doer', *Verfassungsblog* (3 February 2018). On the mobilization of the Constitutional Court, see 5.4.A.

[382] Quoted from Voßkuhle, *Die Idee der Europäischen Wertegemeinschaft* (n. 141) 17.

[383] Schorkopf, 'Wertesicherung in der Europäischen Union. Prävention, Quarantäne und Aufsicht als Bausteine eines Rechts der Verfassungskrise?', 51 *Europarecht* (2016) 147, at 159.

members.[384] Even the European Parliament criticized the Commission's approach as one-sided.[385]

The defence of constitutional principles must be lawful.[386] But inaction in the name of avoiding illegality is not an option for the EU[387] because its institutions must 'promote' its values (Articles 3(1) and 13(1) TEU). Given the evidence of Polish value violations, European silence would indicate that European society is not what it professes to be. It could imply that the Polish measures do, in fact, conform with European values. In that event, the current European self-understanding would come under severe pressure, and European society would run the risk of an identity crisis.

It is not just for the sake of European identity that action is warranted. As the Charter of Fundamental Rights professes, the Union 'places the individual at the heart of its activities'. The Union has a mandate to protect. This includes the protection of Polish citizens against their own state authority, even when the threshold of state terrorism has not yet been reached.[388] Union citizens have a right to effective European rights (see 3.3.D). Most Poles—to wit, 84 per cent—consider themselves part of European society,[389] and many are fighting for their country's liberal constitutionalism. It is time for European citizenship to prove its worth.

The principle of mutual trust also requires constitutional oversight. Trust is an essential resource in societies (see 3.3.A). The need for trust characterizes the second period of European public law (see 2.5.A). Without mutual trust, the current integration of European society is untenable.[390] The CJEU has established the principle that all Member States must trust each other to respect Union law, especially its fundamental rights.[391] But the required trust is not blind as it is accompanied by instruments designed to foster and stabilize trust, including that of constitutional oversight.

European constitutional oversight is, in principle, legal and legitimate under Union law. However, it must respect both the principle of the protection of national identity and European pluralism (see 3.2.C). Article 2 TEU must not become a homogeneity clause for the Member States similar to Article 28 of the Basic Law or

[384] Weiler, 'Epilogue: Living in a Glass House: Europe, Democracy and the Rule of Law', in C. Closa and D. Kochenov (eds), *Reinforcing Rule of Law Oversight in the European Union* (2016) 313, at 326.

[385] Recital (K) of EP Resolution on the need for a comprehensive EU mechanism for the protection of democracy, the rule of law and fundamental rights (2018/2886(RSP)).

[386] Böckenförde, 'Der verdrängte Ausnahmezustand', *Neue Juristische Wochenschrift* (1978) 1881, at 1883; P. Cruz Villalón, *Estados excepcionales y suspensión de garantías* (1984).

[387] Hillion, 'Overseeing the Rule of Law in the EU: Legal Mandate and Means', in Closa and Kochenov (n. 384) 59, at 60–64.

[388] Franzius, 'Der Kampf um Demokratie in Polen und Ungarn—Wie kann und soll die Europäische Union reagieren?', 71 *Die öffentliche Verwaltung* (2018) 381, at 384.

[389] European Commission, *Standard Eurobarometer 91* (n. 100) 17.

[390] CJEU, Joint Cases C-411/10 and C-493/10, *N.S. et al.* (EU:C:2011:865) para. 83; Case C-578/16 PPU, *C.K. et al.* (EU:C:2017:127) para. 95.

[391] Thus *ECHR Accession II* (n. 8) para. 191; Lenaerts, 'La vie après l'avis. Exploring the Principle of Mutual (Yet Not Blind) Trust', 54 *Common Market Law Review* (2017) 805.

Article IV s 4 and Articles XIII to XV of the US Constitution.[392] It cannot impose detailed requirements on the Member States or push them towards what the EU institutions consider best practice (see 3.2.D). There is no mandate to develop the principles of Article 2 TEU into a pan-European blueprint of Member State constitutional law; constitutional homogenization is off the table.

Restrained constitutional oversight will also garner support in European society more easily. Support is essential, for the attempt to force the hand of a Member State's elected government easily leads to serious conflicts. Recall the escalation that accompanied the Spanish central state's exercise of constitutional oversight against the Catalan government majority in 2017.[393] European measures face even more difficulties because they can rely neither on a national 'we' nor on armed federal execution, which supported the Spanish state's action against the Catalan government. In consequence, it is all the more important that as many institutions and societal forces as possible rally behind European constitutional oversight. To this end, such oversight must centre on systemic deficiencies.

B. Putting a Focus on Systemic Deficiencies

Reasoning from democracy, the German Constitutional Court prohibited the *Land* of Schleswig-Holstein from slightly expanding the powers of staff councils in its public authorities, which would have made them resemble staff councils in private companies. A minister, the justices argued, must have more authority to organize his or her administration than a Chief Executive Officer of his or her company.[394] By contrast, the Union's constitutional oversight may only address far graver problems, often termed as *systemic deficiencies*.[395] Systemic deficiency and related expressions (*structural*, *general*, or *systemic threats*, *deficiencies*, *problems*, *defects*, or *weaknesses*) refer to a situation that challenges the constitutional core (see 3.1.C). What follows is a doctrinal construction of that concept.

Article 7 TEU is the constitutional linchpin of this conceptualization. It clearly empowers the Union to demand of Member States that they comply with the principles of Article 2 TEU. Member States cannot deny such demands by relying on their national identity (Article 4(2) TEU). When it comes to violations of Article 2 TEU, there is no possible justification, no *domaine reserve*, no proviso of sovereignty for the Member States.[396] All exercise of public authority in European

[392] From a comparative perspective, see F. Palermo and K. Kössler, *Comparative Federalism. Constitutional Arrangements and Case Law* (2017) 321 ff.

[393] Morales, 'Federal Execution, Article 155 of the Spanish Constitution and the Crisis in Catalonia', 73 *Zeitschrift für öffentliches Recht* (2018) 791.

[394] BVerfGE 93, 37, 66, *Mitbestimmung Schleswig-Holstein*.

[395] Ioannidis and von Bogdandy (n. 192) 59, at 66 ff. For comprehensive discussion, see Schmidt, *Demokratietheorien* (n. 310).

[396] Communication from the Commission to the Council and the European Parliament on Article 7 of the Treaty on European Union: Respect for and promotion of the values on which the Union is based,

society must abide by the fundamental principles of Union law. Article 7 TEU is not limited to national measures implementing Union law because Article 51(1) cl. 1 CFR does not apply here; in other words, the Union's constitutional oversight of the Member States is limited in depth but not in scope. Therefore, a national measure can be a systemic deficiency under EU law regardless of the policy field it regulates.

Article 7 TEU makes clear that a systemic deficiency takes more than any breach of Union law. Its activation requires the 'clear risk of a serious breach' of the values of Article 2 TEU, while sanctions require a 'serious and persistent breach'. These thresholds protect Member States' constitutional autonomy, acknowledge their primary responsibility for the values of Article 2 TEU, and respond to the principle of subsidiarity (Article 5(3) TEU). This logic shapes the concept of systemic deficiency and the legal regime of any instrument of constitutional oversight.

The term 'systemic' helps operationalize this logic. It excludes normal violations of the law from the scope of constitutional oversight. A normal violation is characterized by the fact that public institutions can process it as a matter of routine, that the law continues to be authoritative.[397] All situations described as *systemic*, *structural*, or *generally deficient* have in common that they go beyond such cases. They must be critical in the sense of posing a threat to law's authority, to the legal system as such. Examples include state terrorism, coups d'état, and armed uprisings but also the dismantling of checks and balances, as in the Hungarian and the Polish case.

In its original biological and medical usage, the term 'systemic' concerns *the entire organism*. Its antonyms are *isolated*, *occasional*, *local*, or *random*. In legal usage, *systemic* deficiencies are violations that occur regularly, are widespread or deeply rooted, or represent the highest authorities' policy. Phenomena of this kind are no longer exceptions; rather, they are characteristic of a system.[398] Indeed, the CJEU uses *systemic* and *general* as synonyms.[399]

Accordingly, the EU Commission excludes isolated violations of fundamental rights or miscarriages of justice from the scope of the rule-of-law framework.[400] However, an individual phenomenon (e.g. a breach of a taboo, such as a single case of torture or a political murder) can indicate a systemic deficiency. This holds especially true if there is no adequate institutional response to the breach, suggesting

COM(2003) 0606 final, 5; European Convention, Note from the Praesidium: Draft of Articles 1 to 16 of the Constitutional Treaty, CONV 528/03, 1.

[397] Ioannidis and von Bogdandy (n. 192) 71 ff.

[398] See the entries for 'systemic' in the *Merriam-Webster Dictionary* and Wikipedia and for 'systemisch' in the *Duden* and Wiktionary.

[399] *LM* (n. 17) paras 34, 61, 68; Case C-404/15, *Aranyosi and Căldăraru* (EU:C:2016:198) paras 89, 93, 104.

[400] European Commission, Communication to the European Parliament and the Council: A New EU Framework to Strengthen the Rule of Law, COM(2014) 158 final, 7.

a systemic failure. There were signs of this in Malta after the 2017 murder of journalist Daphne Caruana Galizia and in Slovakia after the 2018 murders of journalist Ján Kuciak and his partner Martina Kušnírová (see 5.4.A).

Externalities in other systems likewise suggest that a *systemic deficiency* exists. European banking regulation law understands *systemic risks* as 'risks of disruption to financial services [...] that have the potential to have serious negative consequences for the internal market and the real economy.'[401] Systemic deficiencies in Member States create externalities by affecting the self-understanding of European society, the legitimacy of decision-making in the EU, and the possibility of the mutual recognition of decisions. European constitutional oversight exists to combat such problems. Since the deficiencies are often entrenched within society, the European response may lead to transformative constitutionalism (see 2.6.D).

C. Instruments

The Union's instruments lie at the core of constitutional oversight. Doctrinally, this follows from the key position of Article 2 TEU (see 3.1.C). But there are also pragmatic reasons. If the Union exercises the oversight, the other Member States can stay out of view and the conflict does not become one between Member States. This is significant because the relationship between the Member States is the most explosive one, given memories of centuries of antagonism.[402]

While the Union has never hesitated to exercise constitutional oversight over candidate countries, it has long shied away from such oversight over Member States. In 2013, in perhaps his most famous statement, President of the Commission Barroso called the use of Article 7 TEU a 'nuclear option', thus branding the instrument practically illegitimate.[403] The Union subsequently left systemic deficiencies in its Member States to the Council of Europe, thus avoiding difficult and perhaps paralysing conflicts in its institutions.[404] The CJEU also evaded the problem at first. For instance, it analysed Orbán's capture of the Hungarian judiciary, which involved forcibly retiring older judges, under Directive 2000/78 concerning

[401] Recital (27) of Regulation 1092/2010 on European Union macro-prudential oversight of the financial system and establishing a European Systemic Risk Board, OJ 2010 L 331/1; J. Kleinow, *Systemrelevante Finanzistitute. Systemrisiko und Regulierung im europäischen Kontext* (2016) 19 f.

[402] Müller, 'Should the EU Protect Democracy and the Rule of Law inside Member States?', 21 *European Law Journal* (2015) 141, at 145.

[403] M. Barroso in European Commission, *State of the Union Address 2013* (11 September 2013), http://europa.eu/rapid/press-release_SPEECH-13-684_en.htm (last visited 30 August 2022); Legality of the Threat or Use of Nuclear Weapons, Advisory Opinion, Ist C.J. Reports 1996, 226–267.

[404] Tuori, 'From Copenhagen to Venice', in Closa and Kochenov (n. 384) 225, at 237.

antidiscrimination.[405] This avoided any discussion of the constitutional core and of what was actually at stake.

But now, the picture has changed. Both the Commission and the Parliament have brought proceedings against systemically deficient Member States under Article 7 TEU. In 2020, the European legislature enacted the general regime of conditionality for the protection of the Union budget, whereby violations of the rule of law can lead to severe financial losses.[406] Since some of the deficiencies involve systemic corruption, the advent of the European Public Prosecutor's Office represents another step.[407] In addition, the Commission has set up monitoring instruments, such as the European Commission's rule-of-law framework, its *Justice Scoreboard*,[408] and its reports within the framework of the European Semester.[409] Furthermore, the Council set up an institutionalized dialogue on the rule of law.[410] The European Parliament can also sanction such orientations.[411] Moreover, the European party families can put pressure on their members.[412]

Are these instruments of constitutional oversight permissible, or does Article 7 TEU provide the only lawful instruments to enforce Article 2 TEU vis-à-vis the Member States? The Polish and Hungarian governments argued the latter in their lawsuit against Regulation (EU) No. 2020/2092. If they are right, European constitutional oversight is underwhelming.

However, the Polish and Hungarian argument founders on one of the oldest tenets of Community law: that the Treaty establishes a specific procedure to combat a particular problem does not prohibit the development of further instruments.[413] Based on this logic, the *Van Gend en Loos* decision[414] established the preliminary ruling procedure as an instrument for enforcing Community law and overseeing

[405] *Commission v. Hungary (Transparency of Associations)* (n. 363) paras 24 ff. On the failure of this approach, see Halmai, 'The Early Retirement Age of the Hungarian Judges', in F. Nicola and B. Davies (eds), *EU Law Stories: Contextual and Critical Histories of European Jurisprudence* (2017) 471.

[406] Regulation 2020/2092 (n. 22). On this, see Łacny, 'The Rule of Law Conditionality Under Regulation No 2092/2020—Is It All About the Money?', 13 *The Hague Journal on the Rule of Law* (2021) 1.

[407] Council Regulation 2017/1939 (n. 220).

[408] See Communication from the Commission to the European Parliament, the Council, the European Central Bank, the European Economic and Social Committee and the Committee of the Regions, the 2018 EU Justice Scoreboard, COM(2018) 364 final, 4 ff.

[409] Commission Staff Working Document, Country Report Poland 2018 accompanying the document Communication from the Commission to the European Parliament, the Council, the European Central Bank and the Eurogroup: 2018 European Semester: Assessment of progress on structural reforms, prevention and correction of macroeconomic imbalances, and results of in-depth reviews under Regulation (EU) No. 1176/2011, SWD(2018) 219 final, 3, 29.

[410] Conclusions of the Council of the European Union and the Member States Meeting within the Council on Ensuring Respect for Rule of Law, Doc. No. 16134/14, 12 December 2014.

[411] Regulation 1141/2014 of the European Parliament and of the Council on the statute and funding of European political parties and European political foundations, OJ 2014 L 317/1.

[412] Thus, Art. 9 of the EPP Statutes (n. 411) permits exclusions but does not define the grounds for exclusion.

[413] J. Bast, *Grundbegriffe der Handlungsform in der EU* (2006) 60 ff.

[414] *Van Gend en Loos* (n. 181) para. 26.

the Member States, in addition to the infringement procedure, which the Treaty legislator had tailored to this objective (see 4.3.B). The same logic also helped the Court develop the doctrine of Member State liability.[415]

Thus, Article 7 TEU does not prohibit further instruments. It does, however, impose limits on them. The extremely intricate procedures in Article 7 TEU suggest that this provision represents the most intensive form of constitutional oversight.[416] Hence, the Union probably lacks the competence for more severe instruments, such as expelling the Member State[417] or deposing its government, which is what the Spanish government did in 2017 with the rebellious Catalan government.

The Union's constitutional oversight does not exist in isolation. Member State institutions can defend and promote European principles, too. Member States can refuse to cooperate with a deficient Member State, thereby exerting pressure on it. Non-cooperation under the European arrest warrant provides an important example.[418] To be successful, coordination is important.[419]

Furthermore, Member States might consider whether to use foreign-policy instruments to exert pressure on deficient states. Examples include reprisals, suspension, or termination under the Vienna Convention on the Law of Treaties and, for the most serious violations, humanitarian interventions.[420] However, EU law imposes strict limits on such action. The action of the 14 EU Member States against Austria in 2000, which sought to prevent a right-wing party from participating in government, was widely considered to be in violation of Union law.[421]

The Council of Europe also has relevant instruments at its disposal, in particular if used in cooperation with the EU (see 4.4.C). Opinions of the Venice Commission of the Council of Europe (see 2.6.D) are a fast and impactful instrument to identify constitutional deficiencies. Moreover, there are the resolutions and recommendations of the Parliamentary Assembly, the Committee of Ministers, and the Commissioner for Human Rights of the Council of Europe.

Consequently, Europe has instruments for constitutional oversight that can address systemic deficiencies and push for transformations. We will now investigate

[415] *Francovich* (n. 188) paras 33 ff.

[416] In this sense, see *LM* (n. 17) paras 70–73.

[417] But see Stein, 'Die rechtlichen Reaktionsmöglichkeiten der Europäischen Union bei schwerwiegender und anhaltender Verletzung der demokratischen und rechtsstaatlichen Grundsätze in einem Mitgliedstaat', in V. Götz *et al.* (eds), *Liber amicorum Günther Jaenicke—Zum 85. Geburtstag* (1998) 871, at 873, 890; Blagoev, 'Expulsion of a Member State from the EU after Lisbon: Political Threat or Legal Reality?', 16 *Tilburg Law Review* (2011) 191.

[418] See *LM* (n. 17).

[419] This is now recognized by the German Constitutional Court. Order of 1 December 2020, 2 BvR 1845/18, *European Arrest Warrant II*. The Court has thus abandoned its approach in *Identity Review I* (n. 63). In detail, see 4.4.A.

[420] On this much-disputed doctrine, see International Law Association, *Final Report on Aggression and the Use of Force* (2018) 20 ff.

[421] On this, see M. Ahtisaari, J. A. Frowein, and M. Oreja, Report adopted in Paris on 8 September 2000 ('The Wise Men Report') para. 116; Lachmayer, 'Questioning the Basic Values—Austria and Jörg Haider', in Jakab and Kochenov (n. 198) 436.

one instrument in greater detail: court judgments. At first blush, court-driven reactions appear negligible. Alexander Hamilton famously described the judiciary as the weakest branch.[422] Accordingly, the CJEU took a back seat for several years. But on 27 February 2018, it issued the judgment *Associação Sindical dos Juízes Portugueses v. Tribunal de Contas*,[423] adding a completely new dimension to EU law.

On the face of it, the judgment does not concern systemic deficiencies in Central Europe. It addresses the complaint of a Portuguese judges' union against salary cuts due to austerity measures. No one accused the Portuguese government of systemic deficiencies or authoritarian tendencies. But in its decision, the CJEU charted a path for litigating the values of Article 2 TEU. Numerous statements from members of the bench make clear that the Court took this step to face up to the Polish government's dismantling of checks and balances.[424] Activating the judiciary in this way builds on one of the most significant institutional transformations in European public law over the past 50 years: the strengthening of constitutional adjudication.

[422] A. Hamilton, 'Federalist No. 78', *The Federalist Papers* (1788).

[423] *Associação Sindical dos Juízes Portugueses* (n. 21).

[424] See, e.g. Lenaerts, 'Upholding the Rule of Law through Judicial Dialogue', 38 *Yearbook of European Law* (2019) 3; Rossi, 'La valeur juridique des valeurs. L'article 2 TUE: Relations avec d'autres dispositions de droit primaire de l'UE et remèdes juridictionnels', 3 *Revue trimestrielle de droit européen* (2020) 639; von Danwitz, 'Values and the Rule of Law: Foundations of the European Union—An Inside Perspective from the ECJ', 4 *Revue du droit de l'union européenne* (2018) 263; Levits, 'Die Europäische Union als Wertegemeinschaft. Art 2 iVm Art 7 des Vertrages über die Europäische Union als Grundlage und Begrenzung des Staatsordnungsmodells des demokratischen Verfassungsstaates der Mitgliedstaaten', in T. Jaeger (ed.), *Europa 4.0? Die EU im Angesicht politischer und technologischer Herausforderungen* (2018) 239; Safjan, 'The Rule of Law and the Future of Europe', *Il Diritto dell'Unione Europea* (2019) 425.

4
Courts

1. A New Actor

Chapter 2 of this book reconstructed the transformation of European public law from the perspective of its fundamental concepts, Chapter 3 from that of its fundamental principles. Now, a Hegelian approach demands that we go beyond concepts and principles. These are but a stepping stone for more concrete insights, particularly on societal institutions and their operations (see 1.4). Public law scholarship can contribute to this endeavour by reconstructing the institutions that a legal order endows with public authority.

In studying European integration, it seems natural to focus on executive institutions. The Treaty legislator of the first threshold phase (*Sattelzeit*) laid the foundation for the new European public law by establishing the High Authority of the European Coal and Steel Community (ECSC), a thoroughly executive body. To this day, many think of European public law's institutions as a mere expansion of the executive branch. This includes the two Councils (the Council of the Heads of State and Government as well as the Council of Ministers, where national executives double as European Union (EU) actors), the Commission, the European Central Bank (ECB), the manifold agencies, and, of course, the Member State governments with their vast bureaucratic apparatus. The individuals who come to mind include men like Schuman, Hallstein, Giscard, Schmidt, Delors, and Draghi, and later also women like Thatcher, Merkel, von der Leyen, and Lagarde, as well as the many thousands of civil servants who turn Europe into a busily humming machine. Many conceptualize the governmental system of European society as transnational executive federalism[1] and multilevel administrative cooperation (see 2.4). In short, the executive branch has been thoroughly Europeanized.

Yet, the transformation of parliaments is hardly less remarkable than that of governments and administrations. In addition to national assemblies, there have been two transnational ones since the 1950s: the Parliamentary Assembly of the Council of Europe and the Parliamentary Assembly of the ECSC, which became a fully fledged parliament during the second period of public law (see 3.5.B). The national parliaments changed, too: they evolved into *Member State* parliaments, established

[1] Oeter, 'Federalism and Democracy', in A. von Bogdandy and J. Bast (eds), *Principles of European Constitutional Law* (2007) 55; J. Habermas, *The Crisis of the European Union: A Response* (2012) 12 ff.

The Emergence of European Society through Public Law. First Edition. Armin von Bogdandy, Oxford University Press.
 DOI: 10.1093/oso/9780198909347.003.0004

networks among themselves, and started controlling European politics.[2] By now, influential national parliamentarians have often spent some time in the European Parliament, where they are socialized as EU citizens' representatives. Long gone are the times when a European Parliament (EP) mandate signified the inauspicious end of a political career.[3]

The institutional transformation of European public law can be reconstructed from an executive as well as from a parliamentary perspective. Here, however, I will adopt the institutional perspective of the judiciary, especially of constitutional adjudication. This might seem inconsistent as constitutional adjudication does not feature in Hegel's philosophy of law. However, I argue that constitutional adjudication exemplifies the sort of institution that, according to Hegel, 'uphold[s] and develop[s] earlier decisions'.[4] For constitutional adjudication after the Second World War, 'earlier decisions' refer to the post-war constitutions' decision to establish democratic rule of law. That is what the courts must 'uphold and develop' through their judgments.[5]

A sceptic might object that Hegel is a bad reference for a study that emphasizes judicial independence (see 5.4.A). After all, Hegel reconstructs the courts as part of the executive, not as a third independent branch. Indeed, he considers the separation of powers a misguided idea of the Enlightenment and advocates not the separation but a structuring of institutions, one that furthers their potential in a common enterprise (*Gewaltengliederung* rather than *Gewaltenteilung*).[6] However, reconstructing the courts as part of the executive branch does not imply they should be subordinated to the government's whim.[7] A dependent or partial institution fails the concept of a court under any meaningful theory (see 4.1.C).

[2] P. Dann, *Parlamente im Exekutivföderalismus. Eine Studie zum Verhältnis von föderaler Ordnung und parlamentarischer Demokratie in der Europäischen Union* (2004) esp. at 163 ff., 279 ff., summarized in English, Dann, 'European Parliament and Executive Federalism: Approaching a Parliament in a Semi-Parliamentary Democracy', 9 *European Law Journal* (2003) 549; for the particularly critical area of the euro crisis, see S. Ragone (ed.), *Managing the Euro Crisis. National EU Policy Coordination in Debtor Countries* (2017).

[3] Rütters, '"Verbleib" von in Deutschland gewählten Europa-Abgeordneten', 44 *Zeitschrift für Parlamentsfragen (ZParl)* (2013) 783.

[4] G. W. F. Hegel, *Elements of the Philosophy of Right* (1991 [1821]) para. 287 (translation altered). The cited translation reads, 'The execution and application of the sovereign's decisions, and in general the continued implementation and upholding of earlier decisions, existing laws, institutions, and arrangements to promote common ends, etc., are distinct from the decisions themselves.'

[5] On regressive tendencies, see Tanasescu, 'Can Constitutional Courts Become Populist?', in M. Belov (ed.), *The Role of Courts in Contemporary Legal Orders* (2019) 305; Szente, 'Subverting Judicial Independence in the New Authoritarian Regimes: Comparing Polish and Hungarian Judicial Reforms', in M. Belov (ed.), *The Role of Courts in Contemporary Legal Orders* (2019) 341. See below 4.6 and 5.4.

[6] Hegel, *Elements of the Philosophy of Right* (n. 4) para. 300.

[7] Hans Kelsen, the holy saint of constitutional adjudication, is similarly dismissive of the traditional separation of powers doctrine; see Hwang, 'Rechtsandwendung in der pluralistischen Demokratie: Hans Kelsens Verständnis der Verfassungsgerichtsbarkeit unter besonderer Berücksichtigung seiner Demokratietheorie', 46 *Der Staat* (2007) 442; similarly Luhmann, 'Funktionen der Rechtsprechung im politischen System', *Politische Planung: Aufsätze zur Soziologie von Politik und Verwaltung* (1971) 46.

Hegel's approach illuminates the role of courts, in particular constitutional courts, better than the mechanistic doctrine of the separation of powers.[8] Because the latter focuses on checks and balances, it fails to grasp the judiciary's transformative role. By contrast, a Hegelian approach suggests also taking into account 'the development of earlier decisions'.[9] Consequently, it jibes with a study on how courts have propelled societal transformation in light of the constitutional decision for a democratic rule of law.

This part will sketch the processes through which democratic societies granted courts great authority, including broad law-making authority (see 4.1). It will then address these courts' Europeanization (see 4.2) before focusing on the role of the Court of Justice of the European Union (CJEU) and the European Court of Human Rights (ECtHR) in the emergence and democratization of European society (see 4.3). As numerous courts play a role in European society, this part focuses on their common but differentiated responsibilities (see 4.4). Then, our analysis turns to the mandate for structural transformation (see 4.5) and concludes by tackling its most difficult case: transformative constitutionalism (see 4.6).

A. An Unexpected Development

The courts' role in European society rests on their power in many national societies. Today, the judiciary (in particular, apex courts) by no means settle only individual disputes, neither do they act solely as Kelsen's 'negative legislator'.[10] Almost everywhere, the apex courts shape important issues and, in doing so, propel transformations that are rarely constitutionally predetermined. Giuliano Amato once told me that he has more power to shape Italian society as one of the 15 Italian constitutional justices than he did in his previous role as Italian prime minister. Michael Stolleis has even characterized the two senates of the Federal Constitutional Court as the 'heart chambers of the Republic'.[11]

Such power evinces structural transformation. In the European public law of old, courts played a small role at best. For Hegel, the 'spirit of the people' and political institutions, not the courts, guarantee the constitution.[12] Carl Schmitt's *Jus*

[8] A. von Bogdandy, *Gubernative Rechtsetzung. Eine Neubestimmung der Rechtsetzung und des Regierungssystems unter dem Grundgesetz in der Perspektive gemeineuropäischer Dogmatik* (2000) 147 ff, 422 ff.; C. Möllers, *Three Branches: A Comparative Model of Separation of Powers* (2015) 51 ff.

[9] Hegel, *Elements of the Philosophy of Right* (n. 4) para. 287.

[10] Cruz Villalón, 'The Evolution of Constitutional Adjudication in Europe', in A. von Bogdandy, P. M. Huber, and C. Grabenwarter (eds), *The Max Planck Handbooks in European Public Law, Vol. IV. Constitutional Adjudication: Common Themes and Challenges* (2023), 1–50; C. Schmitt, *Der Hüter der Verfassung* (1932), partially translated in L. Vinx, *The Guardian of the Constitution: Hans Kelsen and Carl Schmitt on the Limits of Constitutional Law* (2015).

[11] M. Stolleis (ed.), *Herzkammern der Republik. Die Deutschen und das Bundesverfassungsgericht* (2011).

[12] Hegel, 'The Philosophy of Mind (1830)', in W. Wallace (ed.), *Hegel's Philosophy of Mind* (1894) 3, at para. 540.

Publicum Europaeum cites a single judgment, his *Constitutional Theory* a mere handful. For a long time, the British courts hardly took part in public law.[13] The iconic public law court of the nineteenth century, the French *Conseil d'État*, served to control the subordinate administration but not the government. Finally, the German administrative courts, established in the nineteenth century, were also tame.[14] The most famous judgment of the most famous administrative court, the *Kreuzberg* judgment of the Prussian Higher Administrative Court, declared unlawful a police order that impeded a construction project.[15]

The courts' narrow role in constitutional law constituted the European standard until well into the twentieth century.[16] Judicial review of legislation against standards such as those entrenched in Article 2 of the Treaty on European Union (TEU) was at best an *optional* component of democratic constitutions. Many rather considered it a democratic imperative to immunize legislation (i.e. parliamentary statutes) against judicial review.[17]

By the time of the Second World War, only a few European states (namely, Norway, Austria, and Switzerland) had truly instituted constitutional adjudication, while Czechoslovakia, the Second Spanish Republic, and the Weimar Republic had taken the first steps in that direction. Even after the Second World War, constitutional adjudication advanced only slowly. The German Basic Law established a constitutional court without much fuss as a result of the national socialists' crimes and the Allies' instructions. But in post-fascist Italy, constitutional adjudication was highly contentious. In the Constituent Assembly, former Prime Minister Francesco Saverio Nitti lambasted the envisaged constitutional court as an 'absurd novelty' that 'does not exist in any country in the world', an 'unnecessary and harmful' institution for a 'serious state'.[18]

[13] Murkens, 'Verfassungsgerichtsbarkeit im Vereinigten Königreich. § 108', in A. von Bogdandy, C. Grabenwarter, and P. M. Huber (eds), *Handbuch Ius Publicum Europaeum, Bd. VI. Verfassungsgerichtsbarkeit in Europa: Institutionen* (2016) 795.

[14] B. Schaffarzik and K.-P. Sommermann (eds), *Handbuch der Geschichte der Verwaltungsgerichtsbarkeit in Deutschland und Europa* (2019).

[15] Decision of the Prussian Higher Administrative Court of 14 June 1882, PrOVGE 9, 353.

[16] On the paradigmatic function of German, English, and French public law, see Cassese, 'The Administrative State in Europe', in A. von Bogdandy, P. M. Huber, and S. Cassese (eds), *The Max Planck Handbooks in European Public Law, Vol. I. The Administrative State* (2017) 57, at 57, 60 ff.; Fromont, 'A Typology of Administrative Law in Europe', in A. von Bogdandy, P. M. Huber, and S. Cassese (eds), *The Max Planck Handbooks in European Public Law, Vol. I. The Administrative State* (2017) 579, at 585 ff.

[17] Exerting great influence, see É. Lambert, *Le gouvernement des juges et la lutte contre la législation sociale aux États-Unis. L'expérience américaine du contrôle judiciaire de la constitutionnalité des lois* (1921).

[18] See Bifulco and Paris, 'The Italian Constitutional Court', in A. von Bogdandy, C. Grabenwarter, and P. M. Huber (eds), *The Max Planck Handbooks in European Public Law, Vol. III. Constitutional Adjudication: Institutions* (2020) 447, at 450 f.; Kosař and Vyhnánek, 'The Constitutional Court of Czechia', in A. von Bogdandy, C. Grabenwarter, and P. M. Huber (eds), *The Max Planck Handbooks in European Public Law, Vol. III. Constitutional Adjudication: Institutions* (2020) 120, at 122 ff.

Nitti did not get his way for the constitution of 1947 provides for a constitutional court. Yet constitutional adjudication remained a rarity in Europe for decades.[19] The Conference of European Constitutional Courts was founded in 1972 with only four members—the German Federal Constitutional Court and the Italian, Yugoslavian, and Austrian Constitutional Courts.[20]

Then, a grand transformation began.[21] Today, the Conference of European Constitutional Courts has 40 members, many of which decide important controversies and shape society. This transformation has proved popular: in rankings of public confidence, constitutional courts generally come out very well and far ahead of political actors.[22] And while the judiciary once used to be anonymous and somewhat invisible, today, apex courts, and even individual judges, often communicate with the public, explaining, justifying, and defending their courts' judgments.[23] Sometimes, they even lecture on how to interpret their judgments.

B. Multiple Modernities

This transformation is anything but uniform. It comes in many forms and shades. The many institutions of constitutional adjudication in European society exhibit manifold differences. Their diversity explains why I study the phenomenon of *constitutional adjudication* rather than simply constitutional courts. Only 19 EU Member States have a specific constitutional court, if we consider the *Conseil constitutionnel* as such,[24] but 8 EU Member States (namely, Denmark, Estonia, Finland, Greece, Ireland, the Netherlands, Sweden, and Cyprus) do not.[25] The diversity of constitutional adjudication validates the theorem of multiple modernities even for the small group of countries that form European society (see 3.1.D). The idea of one modernity exemplarily realized in one society (as Hegel propagated for Prussia) is obsolete.

[19] On the Yugoslav Constitutional Court, see Grewe, 'Constitutional Jurisdiction in Ex-Yugoslavia in the Perspective of the European Legal Space', in von Bogdandy, Huber, and Grabenwarter (n. 10), at 51.

[20] See http://www.confeuconstco.org (last visited 29 July 2022).

[21] This is a global phenomenon. See Kennedy, 'Three Globalizations of Law and Legal Thought: 1850–2000', in D. Trubek and A. Santos (eds), *The New Law and Economic Development—A Critical Appraisal* (2006) 19, at 63.

[22] Landfried, 'Constitutional Review in the European Legal Space: A Political Science Perspective', in von Bogdandy, Huber, and Grabenwarter (n. 10), at 591.

[23] On the legal problems, see J. Jahn, *Die Medienöffentlichkeit der Rechtsprechung und ihre Grenzen* (2021) 60 ff.

[24] Jouanjan, 'Constitutional Justice in France', in von Bogdandy, Grabenwarter, and Huber, *The Max Planck Handbooks in European Public Law, Vol. III* (n. 18) 223, at 235–237.

[25] On the reasons, see Tuori, 'Constitutional Review in Finland', in von Bogdandy, Grabenwarter, and Huber, *The Max Planck Handbooks in European Public Law, Vol. III* (n. 18) 183, at 204, 207–209, 219; Besselink, 'Constitutional Adjudication in the Netherlands', in von Bogdandy, Grabenwarter, and Huber, *The Max Planck Handbooks in European Public Law, Vol. III* (n. 18) 565, at 578 ff.

The European level reproduces the difference between an apex court and a constitutional court: on the one hand, the CJEU, like an apex court, has the power to render final decisions on all matters of law, as do the Estonian, the Irish, and the US Supreme Court. On the other hand, the ECtHR focuses on the specific protection of individual rights, the main business of most constitutional courts. The many paths of European constitutional adjudication do not follow any one model, especially not the so-called European (i.e. Kelsenian) model of constitutional adjudication.[26]

There are many reasons for the diversity of the Member States' constitutional adjudication. One is that the relevant institutions were established at different times in different contexts and then developed accordingly, as historical institutionalism explains with the concepts of critical junctures and path dependency.[27] The spectrum ranges from the Dutch *Hoge Raad*, established after the Napoleonic wars by the Constitution of 1815, to the Austrian Constitutional Court of 1920, to the post-socialist constitutional courts of the Central and Eastern European Member States of the 1990s.[28]

We may identify three contexts to which national constitutional adjudication primarily owes its existence. In some states (in particular in Austria, Cyprus, and Belgium, but also in Switzerland), it reflected a federal settlement. In many other states, experiences with authoritarianism and the concern to protect democracy led to a court's creation, for instance, in Italy, Germany, Portugal, Spain, and many post-socialist states. In a third group, such as France, the Netherlands, or the Nordic states, constitutional adjudication owes a lot to the general strengthening of individual rights from the 1970s onwards, a strengthening institutionally embedded in the ECtHR.

The courts' powers differ accordingly.[29] In some legal orders, judicial review of legislation is limited to the disapplication of a law in the individual case. In others,

[26] On this model, see V. Ferreres Comella, *Constitutional Courts and Democratic Values. A European Perspective* (2009) 111 ff.; Mezzetti, 'Sistemi e modelli di giustizia costituzionale', in L. Mezzetti (ed.), *Sistemi e modelli di giustizia costituzionale* (2009) 1, at 1, 5 ff.

[27] Capoccia, 'Critical Junctures', in O. Fioretos, T. G. Falleti, and A. Sheingate (eds), *The Oxford Handbook of Historical Institutionalism* (2016) 89; Grosche and Wagner, 'Einführung in das Tagungsthema. Pfadabhängigkeit hoheitlicher Ordnungsmodelle', in Mainzer Assistententagung Öffentliches Recht e.V. (ed.), *Pfadabhängigkeit hoheitlicher Ordnungsmodelle: 56. Assistententagung Öffentliches Recht* (2016) 11.

[28] J. A. Frowein and T. Marauhn (eds), *Grundfragen der Verfassungsgerichtsbarkeit in Mittel- und Osteuropa* (1998); O. Luchterhandt, C. Starck, and A. Weber, *Verfassungsgerichtsbarkeit in Mittel- und Osteuropa* (2007); Grewe, 'Constitutional Jurisdiction in Ex-Yugoslavia' (n. 19).

[29] Cruz Villalón (n. 10); in detail on the individual states (in alphabetical order), see Amaral and Pereira, 'The Portuguese Constitutional Court', in von Bogdandy, Grabenwarter, and Huber, *The Max Planck Handbooks in European Public Law, Vol. III* (n. 18) 673; Behrendt, 'The Belgian Constitutional Court', in von Bogdandy, Grabenwarter, and Huber, *The Max Planck Handbooks in European Public Law, Vol. III* (n. 18) 71; Besselink (n. 25); Biaggini, 'Constitutional Adjudication in Switzerland', in von Bogdandy, Grabenwarter, and Huber, *The Max Planck Handbooks in European Public Law, Vol. III* (n. 18) 779; Bifulco and Paris (n. 18); Farahat, 'The German Federal Constitutional Court', in von Bogdandy, Grabenwarter, and Huber, *The Max Planck Handbooks in European Public Law, Vol. III* (n. 18) 279; Grabenwarter, 'The Austrian Constitutional Court', in von Bogdandy, Grabenwarter, and

the courts have the power, akin to a 'negative legislator', to invalidate the statute under review. Some courts have the additional power to pass substitute legislation. The protection of individual rights can take the shape of mere interlocutory proceedings, in which the concerned individual plays almost no role (such as in Italy or the EU), or that of separate proceedings instituted by the concerned person (such as the constitutional complaint in Germany and Poland or the individual complaint before the ECtHR). Even greater diversity reigns with respect to proceedings for disputes between political bodies.

Given this spectrum, we may ask whether any particular court embodies a model for all. Proposals include the *Conseil constitutionnel*[30] as well as the German Constitutional Court, given the power and authority the latter enjoys.[31] A model, however, is something that can be reproduced, which means that the Karlsruhe Court cannot serve as such. The German Court's role originated in a unique combination of circumstances: the lost war, the experience with totalitarianism, the German trust in authority, clever judicial politics, and many decades of stable government majorities.[32] Its little use as a model also becomes evident from the fact that some constitutional courts that followed the example of Karlsruhe have encountered enormous difficulties.[33] All things considered, conceptions of a 'European model' remain unpersuasive.[34]

C. The Lever for Transformation

Montesquieu, Hamilton, and Kelsen, the triumvirate of judicial theory, did not see courts as institutions that shape and transform a society. In Montesquieu's view, the power of the courts was 'en quelque façon nulle', while Hamilton considered them the weakest of the three branches. Kelsen conceived constitutional courts only as a 'negative legislator'. On his model, they can void a statute but should not engage

Huber, *The Max Planck Handbooks in European Public Law, Vol. III* (n. 18) 19; Jouanjan, 'Constitutional Justice in France' (n. 24); Murkens (n. 13); Requejo Pagés, 'The Spanish Constitutional Tribunal', in von Bogdandy, Grabenwarter, and Huber, *The Max Planck Handbooks in European Public Law, Vol. III* (n. 18) 719; Sólyom, 'The Constitutional Court of Hungary', in von Bogdandy, Grabenwarter, and Huber, *The Max Planck Handbooks in European Public Law, Vol. III* (n. 18) 357; Tuleja, 'The Polish Constitutional Tribunal', in von Bogdandy, Grabenwarter, and Huber, *The Max Planck Handbooks in European Public Law, Vol. III* (n. 18) 619; Tuori (n. 25).

30 É. Zoller, *Introduction au droit public* (2nd edn, 2013) esp. at 197 ff.

31 S. Issacharoff, *Fragile Democracies. Contested Power in the Era of Constitutional Courts* (2015) 138 ff.

32 Schönberger, 'Karlsruhe: Notes on a Court', in M. Jestaedt *et al.* (eds), *The German Federal Constitutional Court: The Court without Limits* (2020) 1, at 7 ff.

33 On the crises in Spain and Hungary, see Requejo Pagés, 'The Spanish Constitutional Tribunal' (n. 29), and Sólyom (n. 29).

34 Voßkuhle, 'Die Zukunft der Verfassungsgerichtsbarkeit in Deutschland und Europa', 47 *Europäische Grundrechte-Zeitschrift* (2020) 165.

in law-making. To be sure, courts do not issue abstract norms but, instead, decide concrete disputes. But that does not prevent them from shaping a society. Their main instrument in doing so is the law-making that flows from their reasoning.[35]

The duty to give reasons when adjudicating concrete disputes is an eighteenth-century innovation meant to control the courts.[36] For Hegel, this duty is as important as the promulgation of laws and the publicity of judgments,[37] but he certainly does not consider it a springboard for judicial law-making, which he rejects.[38] Yet, today, judicial reasoning is probably constitutional courts' most important instrument for shaping social structures. Once again, transformation is the unintended and unforeseen consequence of an innovation: a duty intended to limit judicial power has transformed into its most powerful instrument.

The meaning that a constitutional court assigns to a provision through interpretation often sets a new standard that not only justifies the decision at hand but also prejudges future cases. Subsequent legal reasoning is expected to build on previous relevant decisions and to make this connection transparent.[39] Participants in legal discourse can hardly avoid such precedent, even if they consider it erroneous, as previous case law often serves as a court's most important argument.[40] In particular, a constitutional or supreme court's published decision becomes an authoritative benchmark for subsequent legal discourse. Legal services in public institutions and a lot of legal scholarship devote themselves to embedding these precedents in the legal order. A constitution's integrative effect on society, which Talleyrand precociously intuited (see 2.1.B), follows mainly from the diffusion of precedents and not from a constitution's black letter.[41]

A crucial tool of judicial power is the principle of proportionality, arguably the most important German contribution to the European and global constitutional culture.[42] If an issue is contested within society, the criteria of 'suitability', 'necessity', and 'adequacy' enable a court to decide on virtually any of its relevant aspects. As the constitutional provisions are often vague, the justices have great leeway. Today, it is evident to everyone that the constitutional text hardly ever determines a decision by a constitutional court. Many participants deliberately cultivate the impression that the pending decision is open, thus creating a tension that generates publicity and highlights a court's power. As a result, a supreme or constitutional

[35] M. Shapiro, *Courts. A Comparative and Political Analysis* (1981) 28 ff.

[36] Werkmüller, 'Urteilsbegründung', in A. Erler, E. Kaufmann, and D. Werkmüller (eds), *Handwörterbuch zur Deutschen Rechtsgeschichte, V. Band: Straftheorie—Zycha* (1998) 611–614.

[37] Hegel, *Elements of the Philosophy of Right* (n. 4) paras 224 f.

[38] Ibid. Para. 211.

[39] Effer-Uhe, 'Präjudizienbindung, Rechtssicherheit und Vertrauensschutz', 68 *Jahrbuch des öffentlichen Rechts* (2020) 37, at 38 ff.

[40] Jakab, 'The Reasoning of Constitutional Courts in Europe', in von Bogdandy, Huber, and Grabenwarter (n. 10), 169–221. See also below 4.3.D.

[41] H. Vorländer, *Die Deutungsmacht der Verfassungsgerichtsbarkeit* (2006).

[42] B. Schlink, *Abwägung im Verfassungsrecht* (1976) 48 ff., 203 ff.; Cohen-Eliya and Porat, 'Proportionality and the Culture of Justification', 59 *American Journal of Comparative Law* (2011) 463.

court becomes the ultimate authority for a concrete social controversy as well as for all similar cases in the future. Constitutional adjudication is particularly powerful because the legislature can only correct the court's law-making (i.e. its precedent) by means of constitutional amendment, which is difficult by design as it mostly requires the cooperation of the political opposition.

The constitutional courts' law-making is political because it affects the general public, has tremendous leeway, and often connotes a specific world view.[43] Nevertheless, the distinction between the world of politics and that of law, one of the most important differentiations in contemporary societies, remains meaningful as judicial law-making differs from political law-making. Precedent operates differently from statutes. Moreover, the organization, staff, competences, procedures, instruments, accountability, and logic of reasoning differ fundamentally between courts, on the one hand, and the parliament and executive, on the other hand. A court perceived as deciding along party-political lines or, worse, as a political instrument ceases to be a court (see 5.4.A).

The power of courts requires more than formal competences, namely, authoritativeness. To gain the latter, a court must be perceived as independent for it requires widespread societal recognition. Moreover, judicial authority presupposes the support and work of the legal profession, such as the legal services of public institutions and the professional public with its many judges, lawyers, bureaucrats, legal scholars, journalists reporting on legal matters, and lawyers in non-governmental organizations. On this basis, many courts have contributed to democratic transformations.

D. On the Acquisition of Power

To understand judicial power, we must comprehend how it is acquired. Given our eventual interest in the transformation brought about by the CJEU and the ECtHR, two aspects are of particular interest: the expansion of a constitutional court's competences and its relationship to other courts. The German Constitutional Court (*Bundesverfassungsgericht*), the Italian Constitutional Court (*Corte costituzionale*, *Corte*), and the French Constitutional Council (*Conseil constitutionnel, Conseil*) will serve as examples.

They do so because they are the constitutional courts of the three most populous Member States. Perhaps as a result, they have influenced the creation and jurisprudence of constitutional courts established later (in Portugal, Spain, or former socialist states). Moreover, the German and the Italian court symbolize the potential

[43] Huber, 'Constitutional Courts and Politics in the European Legal Space', in von Bogdandy, Huber, and Grabenwarter (n. 10), 547–590; A. von Bogdandy and I. Venzke, *In Whose Name? A Public Law Theory of International Adjudication* (2014) 21, 101 ff.

judicial contribution to a society's democratic transformation.[44] Since this was the great topic of European constitutionalism in the second half of the twentieth century, the two post-authoritarian courts became exemplary. France, on the other hand, has the most influential tradition of public law defined by democratic continuity.

Neither the German nor the French or Italian constitutional framers conceptualized these three courts as enjoying the power they have today. In Italy, the establishment of the constitutional court was, as described, controversial until the very end. In Germany, the establishment was not disputed (as the Allies required it), but the framers certainly did not envision today's powerful institution either.[45] The introduction of a constitutional court played a subordinate role in the deliberations. The Basic Law regulates only a few issues pertaining to the constitutional court, and in many respects, it does so inadequately. For instance, it does not require a qualified majority for the selection of new justices. Consequently, a determined majority could take over the *Bundesverfassungsgericht* in much the same way as the Polish majority took over the Polish Constitutional Tribunal in 2015 (see 3.6.A). Only one additional step would be required as the majority would first have to abrogate the qualified-majority requirement in the statute regulating the justices' selection (see 2.1.B–C, *Bundesverfassungsgerichtsgesetz*); that, however, only requires a simple majority. Of course, the need for such an amendment offers a form of defence of which the Polish Tribunal could not avail itself in 2015. Given the self-understanding of the German court and the general support it enjoys, it would probably strike down such a change if the situation became similar to that in Poland in 2015.

In the case of the *Conseil constitutionnel*, it is even clearer that the framers of the Constitution of the Fifth Republic did not envision a law-making institution. Indeed, they called this body a Council rather than a Court because they did not want a constitutional court such as the ones in Austria, Germany, or Italy.[46] The *Conseil constitutionnel* was not conceived as the institution of a post-authoritarian society. Instead, the framers of 1958 intended the court to protect the separation of powers, above all by protecting the executive power against legislative encroachments. This was a reaction to the parliamentary centralism of the Third and Fourth Republics that the Constitution of the Fifth Republic is meant to overcome. For that reason, the *Conseil's raison d'être* in 1958 was not to develop fundamental rights or a democratic society.[47] Accordingly, the subsequent transformation of the

[44] Cruz Villalón (n. 10).

[45] In detail, see Walter, 'Art. 93 GG', in T. Maunz and G. Dürig (eds), *Grundgesetz Kommentar I* (2018) paras 46 ff., with further references.

[46] Jouanjan, 'Constitutional Justice in France' (n. 24) 235.

[47] D. Rousseau, P.-Y. Gahdoun, and J. Bonnet, *Droit du contentieux constitutionnel* (12th edn, 2020) 29 ff.

Conseil constitutionnel into a court that also protects fundamental rights was considered nothing less than a 'constitutional miracle'.[48]

It is almost as miraculous how the *Bundesverfassungsgericht* and the *Corte* extended their powers, establishing themselves as an engine of a democratic society. The fundamental judgments of all three courts are remembered today as transformative steps towards social democratization:[49] the German *Lüth* judgment, the Italian judgment 1/1956,[50] and the French *Liberté d'association* decision.[51] Their common denominator is that they all tremendously expanded the scope of constitutional provisions and, thus, of judicial powers. The *Lüth* judgment includes what is perhaps the most important and most frequently cited sentence of the *Bundesverfassungsgericht*, with the Court holding that 'the Basic Law [. . .] has also established an objective system of values in its section on fundamental rights' and that this system of fundamental values must 'apply to all areas of law as a fundamental constitutional decision'.[52] Consequently, the Court can ultimately adjudicate controversies in all areas of society. The *Corte*'s judgment 1/1956 ascribed a legal character to fundamental rights, thereby contradicting the supreme court, the *Corte di Cassazione*, which had held that fundamental rights have a purely programmatic function.[53] In doing so, the *Corte* also extended its reach tremendously.

The *Conseil constitutionnel*, in its 1971 decision *Liberté d'association*, took an even greater step in expanding its jurisdiction to individual rights. That is because the Constitution of the Fifth Republic of 1958 is almost devoid of fundamental rights. Only its preamble insinuates rights protection by proclaiming the 'attachment' of the French people to the 'Rights of Man' as defined by the Declaration of 1789 and as 'confirmed and complemented by the Preamble to the Constitution of 1946'.[54] This minimalism was obviously insufficient 13 years later, for the Rights Revolution had begun in the meantime (see 4.3.C). Therefore, the *Conseil* simply postulated that the rights mentioned in the preamble were legally binding. The legal argument was weak, given that preambles do not establish binding law, but that did not diminish the transformation of an institution intended to protect the executive power into an—initially embryonic—fundamental rights court.

48 Jouanjan, 'Constitutional Justice in France' (n. 24) 235.

49 Of course, there are also other voices. See Depenheuer, 'Grenzenlos gefährlich. Selbstermächtigung des Bundesverfassungsgerichts', in C. Hillgruber (ed.), *Gouvernement des juges. Fluch oder Segen* (2014) 79.

50 BVerfGE, 7, 198, *Lüth*; Corte costituzionale, sentenza n. 11/1965; on its importance, see V. Barsotti *et al.*, *Italian Constitutional Justice in Global Context* (2016) 30.

51 Conseil constitutionnel, Decision No. 71-44 DC of 16 July 1971, *Law completing the provisions of Articles 5 and 7 of the Law of 1 July 1901 on association agreements*; Haimbaugh, 'Was It France's Marbury v. Madison?', 35 *Ohio State Law Journal* (1974) 910.

52 BVerfGE, 7, 198, *Lüth*, 205; on this, see Jestaedt, 'The Karlsruhe Phenomenon: What Makes the Court What It Is', in Jestaedt *et al.*, *The German Federal Constitutional Court* (n. 32) 32, at 48 ff.

53 Bifulco and Paris (n. 18) 454.

54 In detail, see Jouanjan, 'Frankreich. § 2', in A. von Bogdandy, P. Cruz Villalón, and P. M. Huber (eds), *Handbuch Ius Publicum Europaeum, Bd. I. Grundlagen und Grundzüge staatlichen Verfassungsrechts* (2007) 87.

Why did these three courts engage in such transformations? Hardly any legal scholar will claim that legal texts, legal doctrine, or interpretive theories guided the court's decision-making.[55] Consequently, the courts' true reasons are the object of much speculation. Some claim to have isolated a chief motivating factor. Ran Hirschl argues that judges act like 'any other economic actor: as self-interested individuals'.[56] Accordingly, the judges' concern for their power is sometimes perceived as motivating some constitutional courts to resist transnational courts' case law, such as the Second Senate of the *Bundesverfassungsgericht* in its *Public Sector Purchase Programme* (*PSPP*) judgment.[57] However, this theory's explanatory power is limited as it is also used to explain the antithetical orientation of the First Senate's *Right to Be Forgotten I and II* decisions.[58]

Much more comes to mind: ideologies and world views, cultural patterns, character, and the constraints of collective decision-making but also the call for justice, established protocols of legal argumentation, the established meaning of the law, and, not least, the ethos of fidelity to the law. All these factors seem relevant to me and are deeply interwoven, making it impossible to isolate individual factors and thereby explain judicial decision-making. Thus, the following discussion purports not to explain the development but simply to further its understanding.

While all three courts have become powerful, they play fundamentally different roles within their national legal order.[59] The *Bundesverfassungsgericht* accomplished what no other constitutional court has yet achieved: it established itself as the apex of the German legal system. Through its *Lüth* judgment, it supplanted the Federal Supreme Court (the *Bundesgerichtshof*) which, as successor to the *Reichsgericht*, considered itself the highest German court. The judgment, which overturned a decision by the *Bundesgerichtshof*, made clear that the *Bundesverfassungsgericht* does not cooperate with the specialized courts but rather corrects them.[60] Accordingly, the Court sets the admissibility standards for concrete judicial review (Article 100(1) of the Basic Law)—which implies cooperating

[55] H. Kelsen, *Pure Theory of Law* (1967 [1934]) 236 ff.; Neumann, 'Theorie der juristischen Argumentation', in W. Brugger, U. Neumann, and S. Kirste (eds), *Rechtsphilosophie im 21. Jahrhundert* (2008) 233, at 241.

[56] R. Hirschl, *Comparative Matters. The Renaissance of Comparative Constitutional Law* (2014) 168.

[57] Wolf, 'German Court Decides to Take Back Control with ECB Ruling', *Financial Times* (13 May 2020) 17, https://www.ft.com/content/37825304-9428-11ea-af4b-499244625ac4 (last visited 21 July 2022); Dorr, 'Why Is a German Court Undermining the European Union?', *The Irish Times* (28 May 2020), https://www.irishtimes.com/opinion/why-is-a-german-court-undermining-the-european-union-1.4263978 (last visited 21 July 2022); Dubarry, 'Prendre la Constitution au sérieux. Regard franco-allemand sur l'enchevêtrement des discours juridique et politique au prisme de la proportionnalité', 27 *Recueil Dalloz* (2020) 1525.

[58] BVerfGE 152, 152, *Right to Be Forgotten I* and BVerfGE 152, 216, *Right to Be Forgotten II*; on this, see Wendel, 'Das Bundesverfassungsgericht als Garant der Unionsgrundrechte', 75 *JuristenZeitung* (2020) 157.

[59] This section is based on von Bogdandy and Paris, 'Power Is Perfected in Weakness. On the Authority of the Italian Constitutional Court', in V. Barsotti *et al.* (eds), *Dialogues on Italian Constitutional Justice. A Comparative Perspective* (2021) 263.

[60] *Lüth* (n. 52).

with the ordinary courts instead of controlling them—very high. Consequently, the courts are deterred from making use of it. Under the Italian constitution, by contrast, concrete judicial review represents almost the only way for the Italian Constitutional Court to interpret and apply rights.[61]

Thus, the *Bundesverfassungsgericht*, unlike the *Corte*, has the power to make the final decision at the apex of the judicial system. Since almost any controversy can be brought before a court in Germany (Article 19(4) of the Basic Law), the constitutional complaint is, first and foremost, a legal remedy against a court judgment. Not least for this reason, the *Bundesverfassungsgericht* represents an exception rather than the rule: very few other legal orders allow for a constitutional complaint against judgments.[62] In the vast majority of cases, the *Bundesverfassungsgericht* reviews whether another German court has violated the individual rights enshrined in the Constitution.[63] While it overturns only a tiny percentage of the courts' decisions,[64] this does not detract from its august role.

Furthermore, the two courts have different addressees and audiences in mind. The Italian Constitutional Court, similar to the CJEU, mainly addresses the other courts on which it depends, whereas the German Constitutional Court, much like the ECtHR, primarily addresses the citizenry. The proverbial expression of 'going to Karlsruhe'[65] articulates the citizens' expectation of finding justice before the *Bundesverfassungsgericht* at the end of a long judicial process.

The *Corte* never gained such a role vis-à-vis the other courts. In its Judgment 1/1956, it initially scored a win against the *Cassazione*. In this case, which concerned the freedom of expression, it declared a law unconstitutional that the *Cassazione* had previously considered constitutional. In doing so, the *Corte* sided with the lower court that had referred the case, rebelling against the *Cassazione*'s interpretation and, worse, its authority.

Ten years after the Constitutional Court's decision, the so-called first 'war of the Courts' forced the *Corte* to relinquish a lot of ground. The dispute revolved around its attempt to impose its interpretation of a law on the *Cassazione*, which would have served to constitutionalize the legal order, as exemplified by the *Lüth* judgment of the *Bundesverfassungsgericht*.

Yet, the *Corte*'s attempt failed, revealing an important structural element of Italian constitutional adjudication: the *Corte* can only bring its authority to bear in

[61] J. Luther, *Die italienische Verfassungsgerichtsbarkeit* (1990) 82 ff.

[62] Vašek, 'Constitutional Jurisdiction and Protection of Fundamental Rights in Europe', in von Bogdandy, Huber, and Grabenwarter (n. 10). The Orbán Constitution (see 3.6.A) introduced this remedy to control the ordinary courts through the captured constitutional court.

[63] See Bundesverfassungsgericht, *Annual Statistics 2020*, 33, https://www.bundesverfassungsgericht.de/DE/Verfahren/Jahresstatistiken/2020/gb2020/Gesamtstatistik%202020.pdf?__blob=publicationFile&v=2 (last visited 7 July 2022).

[64] See ibid. 24.

[65] U. Wesel, *Der Gang nach Karlsruhe. Das Bundesverfassungsgericht in der Geschichte der Bundesrepublik* (2004).

conjunction with another court. Hardly conceivable from a German point of view, it is a constitutional court without a constitutional complaint or any other form of direct access for citizens.[66] Instead, the *Corte*'s most important power, that of concrete judicial review, depends on other courts' willingness to refer to it questions of statutory constitutionality. Unlike the *Bundesverfassungsgericht*, the *Corte* does not impose individual rights on recalcitrant courts; instead, it protects rights by acting together with them. Cooperation, not correction, is its tenet. In Italy, no book is entitled anything akin to 'Going to Karlsruhe'.

The *Corte* digested its defeat with the new doctrine of *diritto vivente*.[67] According to this doctrine, it no longer inquires whether the *Cassazione* could have developed a better (i.e. a constitutional) interpretation of the law. In doing so, it defuses the conflict between the two courts. The *Corte* considers the *Cassazione*'s interpretation mandated by the law in question and limits itself to reviewing statutes for constitutionality following the *Cassazione*'s interpretation. Thus, the *Corte*'s normative authority is much more limited than that of the *Bundesverfassungsgericht*. After all, imposing a certain understanding of a statute by means of an 'interpretation that conforms with the constitution' is an important tool of judicial law-making.[68]

This weakness prompted the *Corte* to closely cooperate with the other courts. It developed an 'interjudicial relationality' that has become paradigmatic of Italian constitutional adjudication.[69] Thus, the concept of judicial dialogue, with which German lawyers describe the interaction of the *Bundesverfassungsgericht* with the European courts, grasps the relationship of the Constitutional Court with all other courts.

The *Conseil constitutionnel* found it even more difficult than the *Corte* to establish an authoritative role beside the highest civil court, the *Cour de Cassation*, and the highest administrative court, the *Conseil d'État*. For many decades, it simply was not a court that protected citizens. This remained true even after the 1971 constitutional revolution, which brought rights protection into its remit. The constitutional reform of 1974 expanded standing rights, but this only benefited the parliamentary opposition (*saisine parlementaire*). What remained unchanged was that the *Conseil constitutionnel* could only review a statute before it entered into force and only at the request of political institutions. Litigation involving citizens had to wait for the constitutional reform of 2008 to find its way to the *Conseil constitutionnel*. But the new proceeding, the preliminary ruling procedure (*question prioritaire de constitutionnalité*) is even more circumscribed than Italian

[66] From a comparative perspective, this is also an exception: most legal order provide for some access, Vašek (n. 62).

[67] Corte costituzionale, sentenza n. 11/1965 and sentenza n. 52/1965 as well as sentenza n. 127/1966 and sentenza n. 49/1970; Bifulco and Paris (n. 18) 478.

[68] Farahat, 'Constitutional Jurisdiction and the Separation of Powers in the European Legal Space: A Comparative Analysis', in von Bogdandy, Huber, and Grabenwarter (n. 10).

[69] Barsotti *et al.*, *Italian Constitutional Justice in Global Context* (n. 50) 236.

concrete review for only the *Cour de Cassation* and the *Conseil d'État* can initiate it. Accordingly, the *Conseil constitutionnel* can do little to alter their powerful position.[70] Unlike the *Corte* in Italy or the CJEU, the Constitutional Council thus cannot become the ally of rebellious lower courts.[71] Nevertheless, concrete judicial review is beginning to play a role in the French legal system. Ten years after its introduction, the *Conseil constitutionnel* noted that 80 per cent of its decisions result from these proceedings.[72]

The three constitutional courts also wield different forms of authority over political institutions. The tremendous authority that the *Bundesverfassungsgericht* quickly claimed is summed up by a famous phrase attributed to Konrad Adenauer: 'That is not how we thought it would be' ('*Dat ham wir uns so nich vorjestellt*').[73] These words go to the heart of how the *Bundesverfassungsgericht* has evolved: it has built its authority by confronting political power, establishing itself as a visible counterweight to the government majority.

The Court's founding decade is remembered as a decade of epic victories. One need only recall its 'status struggle', in which it overcame its dependence on the Ministry of Justice, still pervaded by a national socialist presence. Through that struggle, it established itself as one of the five constitutional institutions alongside the Federal President, the *Bundesrat*, the *Bundestag*, and the federal government.[74] In the First Broadcasting Judgment (the so-called *Zweites Deutsches Fernsehen* (*ZDF*) judgment), the *Bundesverfassungsgericht*, responding to a complaint by Social Democratic Party (SPD)-led *Länder*, prevented the establishment of a pro-government television channel,[75] an important project of the Christian Democratic Union (CDU)-led federal government.

Things went differently in Italy in this respect, too. There is no public memory of anything akin to Adenauer's remark. Considering how controversial the *Corte costituzionale* was in the Constituent Assembly, it is hardly surprising that it approached, and continues to approach, its work far more cautiously than the German court. Its landmark decision 1/1956 concerned not the democratic legislature but a statute from fascist times that restricted the freedom of expression.

[70] Gay, 'Le double filtrage des QPC: Une spécificité française en question? Modalités et incidences de la sélection des questions de constitutionnalité en France, Allemagne, Italie et Espagne', in L. Gay (ed.), *La question prioritaire de constitutionnalité. Approche de droit comparé* (2014) 51, at 53, 72 ff.

[71] Santolini, 'La question prioritaire de constitutionnalité au regard du droit comparé', 93 *Revue française de droit constitutionnel* (2013) 83, at 94.

[72] Fabius, 'QPC 2020—Les 10 ans de la question citoyenne', *Titre VII, Les cahiers du Conseil constiutionell* (Octobre 2020), https://www.conseil-constitutionnel.fr/publications/titre-vii/avant-propos-du-president-laurent-fabius (last visited 8 July 2022).

[73] Quoted from Schönberger, 'Karlsruhe' (n. 32) 10. The German quote is from Schönberger, 'Anmerkungen zu Karlsruhe', in M. Jestaedt *et al.* (eds), *Das entgrenzte Gericht. Eine kritische Bilanz nach sechzig Jahren Bundesverfassungsgericht* (2011) 9, at 26.

[74] In detail, Wesel (n. 65) 54–82; Walter, 'Art. 93 GG' (n. 45) paras 93 ff.; on Gerhard Leibholz, the author of the memorandum, see 1.3.

[75] BVerfGE 12, 205, *Rundfunk*.

While the executive branch of democratic Italy continued to use this and similar repressive statutes, it did not actually wish to defend them. By declaring the statute unconstitutional, the Constitutional Court attested to its democratic anti-fascism. In its review of such statutes, the *Corte* discovered a field in which it could develop its case law and authority while avoiding major conflicts with the political sphere.[76] The self-confident Karlsruhe Court, which did not need to proceed with such caution, left such statutes to the ordinary courts.[77] The *Conseil constitutionnel* is even more restrained when reviewing legislation in substantive terms.[78] However, in the spirit of its original role as guardian of the separation of powers, its scrutiny of the legislature's compliance with parliamentary procedure is more strict than that of the other two courts.[79]

The abortion issue illustrates how differently the three courts relate to the legislature. These decisions date back to 1975 and, thus, to the time when individual rights protection was gaining strength in many societies. In its long, innovative, and doctrinally elaborate first decision on abortion rights, the *Bundesverfassungsgericht* rejected the full decriminalization of abortion, a key legislative project of the social–liberal coalition. Here, a powerful court confronted a powerful government (with its parliamentary majority). The *Bundesverfassungsgericht* established when human life begins and how it must be protected.[80]

In the same year, the *Corte* was confronted with the question of whether the general criminalization of abortion without exceptions violates the constitution.[81] Parliamentary attempts at liberalization had failed because of the Christian Democrats' resistance. In this context, a criminal court asked the *Corte* whether punishing a woman for terminating her pregnancy was constitutional if the pregnancy endangered her health. The *Corte*'s very brief decision refrained from determining when life begins and the nature of unborn life. Its terse decision states that unborn life is constitutionally protected in principle but that a criminal court cannot punish a woman for an abortion if her health was in danger.

The *Conseil constitutionnel* also faced the issue in 1975. The context resembled the German one for decriminalizing abortion constituted an important project of Valéry Giscard d'Estaing's liberal presidency and majority. Opposing MPs brought it before the *Conseil constitutionnel* by means of a *saisine parlementaire*. The *Conseil* pursued a third way. Its brief decision clarified that it does not question such decisions of the parliamentary majority.[82] It also developed the formula

[76] E. Malfatti, S. Panizza, and R. Romboli, *Giustizia costituzionale* (6th edn, 2018) 357.

[77] BVerfGE 2, 124, *Normenkontrolle II*.

[78] Bergougnous, 'Le Conseil constitutionnel et le législateur', 38 *Les Nouveaux Cahiers du Conseil constitutionnel* (2013) 5, at 18.

[79] Benetti, 'La procédure parlementaire en question dans les saisines parlementaires', 49 *Les Nouveaux Cahiers du Conseil constitutionnel* (2015) 87.

[80] BVerfGE 39, 1, *Schwangerschaftsabbruch I*.

[81] Corte costituzionale, sentenza n. 27/1975.

[82] Conseil constitutionnel, Decision No. 74-54 DC of 15 January 1975, *Law on Abortion I*; the following quote is from § 1 of the decision, in the English version on the website of the Conseil

it would henceforth use in dealing with such cases. According to this formula, the Constitution 'does not confer on the Constitutional Council a general or particular discretion identical with that of Parliament, but simply empowers it to rule on the constitutionality of statutes referred to it'. In other words, the *Conseil* avoided the matter altogether.

Important differences between the three courts also become apparent in their style of reasoning. The *Bundesverfassungsgericht* often dedicates a separate section to constitutional interpretation, the famous 'C.I.' section,[83] which is neatly separated from the subsequent application of the interpretation to the concrete case. This separation helps the Court develop extensive interpretations that transcend the case in question. Indeed, most commentators focus on the C.I. section's peculiar mix of sermon, political theory, and elaborate doctrine. To ensure that nobody overlooks the directives developed in that part, the Court prefixes them to the decision in so-called *Leitsätze*, which often read like statutory provisions.

The Italian Constitutional Court employs a far more minimalist style of reasoning. The *Corte* does not formulate general directives resembling those of the *Bundesverfassungsgericht*. Moreover, it employs the so-called absorption technique. Thus, the lower courts often include multiple possible grounds for unconstitutionality of a statute they refer to the *Corte*. If the latter holds that one of these grounds is sufficient to render the law unconstitutional, it declares the other grounds 'absorbed' without reviewing them.[84] The *Corte* is usually adamant in avoiding pronouncements that are not strictly necessary. The *Bundesverfassungsgericht*, by contrast, often indulges in *obiter dicta*, namely, in general statements that are not required to decide the case but are meant to have great impact nevertheless.[85] This might surprise a reader from a common law country, where *dicta* do not form part of a precedent. German lawyers and courts do not make this distinction, thereby expanding enormously the *Bundesverfassungsgericht*'s law-making powers. Because of its minimalist approach, the *Corte* exercises much less of a directive function vis-à-vis the legislature and society.

This is even more true of the *Conseil constitutionnel*, whose particularly apodictic and cryptic style of reasoning has traditionally been hostile to generalization.[86] However, things are changing. In 2016, the *Conseil* abandoned its

constitutionnel, https://www.conseil-constitutionnel.fr/en/decision/1975/7454DC.htm (last visited 12 September 2022).

[83] Lepsius, 'The Standard-Setting Power', in Jestaedt *et al.*, *The German Federal Constitutional Court* (n. 32) 70.

[84] Bonomi, *L'assorbimento dei vizi nel giudizio di costituzionalità in via incidentale* (2013).

[85] For a recent example, see BVerfG, Decision of 18 November 2020, 2 BvR 477/17, *State Liability for Foreign Deployments of the Bundeswehr*: the statements on liability are obiter, but they stand at the heart of the Court's reasoning.

[86] Dyèvre, 'The French Constitutional Council', in A. Jakab, A. Dyèvre, and G. Itzcovich (eds), *Comparative Constitutional Reasoning* (2017) 323.

practice of formulating its decision as a single sentence.[87] Its reasoning, however, remains very brief. The *Conseil* provides more orientation, though indirectly as its Secretary General usually publishes a commentary that serves the function of the *Bundesverfassungsgericht*'s C.I.[88]

The *Bundesverfassungsgericht*, on the one hand, and the *Corte* and the *Conseil*, on the other, embody two different forms of logic—*maximalist* or *minimalist*—that determine how a constitutional court shapes a democratic society's structures. The terms 'maximalist' and 'minimalist' are not contradictory but comparative for they describe a difference of degree, not of kind. They are meant analytically rather than evaluatively. Maximalist does not mean activist or *ultra vires*, and minimalist does not mean lethargic or captured.

Both orientations are propagated by renowned scholars.[89] The *Bundesverfassungsgericht* is extolled as the heart of the Republic.[90] The *Corte* is considered one of the most stable institutions in Italy besides the president,[91] and the *Conseil constitutionnel* is even praised as a new incarnation of the European model of constitutional adjudication.[92] These three courts are incommensurable with each other. This helps understand why neither French nor Italian mainstream scholars advocate introducing a constitutional complaint that many German academics regard as the procedural core of democratic constitutionalism.

The transformation of all three courts can be traced back to farsighted judges but also to a general understanding that democratic societies do better with constitutional adjudication. As we will see, this also holds true for European society. Indeed, it depends on judicial law-making (see 2.4.A). Before elaborating on this assertive claim, I shall delineate the Europeanization of the Member States' courts. After all, the two European courts' success much depends on that transformation.

2. Europeanizing Constitutional Adjudication

The rise of constitutional adjudication (see 3.3.C) is not specific to Europe. It is a global development that occurred, above all, in the two decades around the turn of

[87] Conseil constitutionnel, Decision No. 2016-540 QPC of 10 May 2016, *Société civile Groupement foncier rural Namin et Co.* and Conseil constitutionnel, Decision No. 2016-539 QPC, *Mme Ève G.*; Belloubet, 'La motivation des décisions du Conseil constitutionnel: justifier et réformer', 55–56 *Les Nouveaux Cahiers du Conseil constitutionnel* (2017) 5.

[88] R. K. Weber, *Der Begründungsstil von Conseil constitutionnel und Bundesverfassungsgericht. Eine vergleichende Analyse der Spruchpraxis* (2019) 120–127.

[89] On the one hand, C. R. Sunstein, *One Case at a Time. Judicial Minimalism on the Supreme Court* (1999) 3–72, 259–263; on the other hand, Kumm, 'Who Is Afraid of the Total Constitution? Constitutional Rights as Principles and the Constitutionalization of Private Law', 7 *German Law Journal* (2006) 341.

[90] See Stolleis, *Herzkammern der Republik* (n. 11).

[91] Cruz Villalón (n. 10).

[92] Zoller (n. 30).

the millennium.[93] Most states now feature some form of constitutional adjudication, exercised either by an apex court or by a specific constitutional court.[94] The judicial guarantee and development of constitutional legality has been a central component of the democratic rule of law since the fall of the Iron Curtain in 1989.[95]

Constitutional jurisdiction in European society is part of a global phenomenon. But, at the same time, it is very distinctive.[96] One distinctive feature is that European constitutional adjudication is not governed by a single apex court (as in most societies) but is instead exercised by many institutions: the CJEU, the ECtHR, the Member States' apex courts, and, frequently, lower courts entrusted with this task by European law. European society's pluralism is reflected in the pluralism of its institutions of constitutional adjudication.

The European embedding of national courts affects their doctrines, practices, outlooks, authority, and image.[97] I will examine three levers of that embedding: the duty under European law to provide for constitutional adjudication, the constitutional role of European legal sources, and the multilevel cooperation of constitutional courts. The crucial duty to refer cases to the CJEU will be tackled later (see 4.3.B, 4.4.B).

A. Europeanizing the Courts' Mandates

All Member States' constitutions determine, in very different ways, which courts have a mandate for constitutional adjudication and how they ought to exercise it (see 4.1.B). Over the past 50 years, the CJEU and the ECtHR have transformed these mandates by broadening them. Today, all Member State courts exercise some constitutional adjudication, and they do so on a common basis.

The *Simmenthal* decision of 1978, which empowered all courts to exercise a specific European form of decentralized constitutional adjudication, is perhaps the most paradigmatic example of the transformation prompted by the CJEU.[98] As is often the case, that transformation was not the CJEU's primary intention.

[93] Lustig and Weiler, 'Judicial Review in the Contemporary World. Retrospective and Prospective', 16 *International Journal of Constitutional Law* (2018) 315; L. Pegoraro, *Giustizia costituzionale comparata. Dai modelli ai sistemi* (2nd edn, 2015); M. Fromont, *Justice constitutionnelle comparée* (2013).

[94] Cassese, 'Fine della solitudine delle corti costituzionali, ovvero il dilemma del porcospino', in Accademia delle Scienze di Torino (ed.), *Inaugurazione del 232° anno accademico dell'Accademia delle Scienze di Torino* (2014) 20.

[95] Ackerman, 'The Rise of World Constitutionalism', 83 *Virginia Law Review* (1997) 771.

[96] The following section draws on von Bogdandy, Grabenwarter, and Huber, 'Constitutional Adjudication in the European Legal Space', in von Bogdandy, Grabenwarter, and Huber, *The Max Planck Handbooks in European Public Law, Vol. III* (n. 18) 1.

[97] Torres Pérez, 'The Challenges for Constitutional Courts as Guardians of Fundamental Rights in the European Union', in P. Popelier, A. Mazmanyan, and W. Vandenbruwaene (eds), *The Role of Constitutional Courts in Multilevel Governance* (2013) 49, at 53.

[98] CJEU, Case 106/77, *Amministrazione delle finanze dello Stato v. Simmenthal* (EU:C:1978:49).

Its objective was not to introduce decentralized constitutional adjudication but to ensure the primacy, and thus the effectiveness, of Union law (see 3.3.C). Structural transformation occurred almost incidentally.

The subject of the dispute seems downright trivial. It centred on fees for the public health inspection of imported canned meat. Somewhat unusually, these fees had been laid down by the Italian legislature in a statute. The reason constitutional adjudication enters the equation is that the CJEU granted the *Pretore di Susa*, a first-instance judge, the power to disapply that statute for being contrary to Union law. Under the Italian Constitution, as under the German, Polish, or Spanish ones, this decision is reserved to the constitutional court. However, the CJEU maintained that even in Member States with centralized judicial review, all courts can disapply the law if a violation of Union law is at issue. Hence, the CJEU curtailed what was perhaps the constitutional courts' most specific power.

Initially, this transformation led to few conflicts with constitutional courts since controlling fees for meat imports does not belong to their core mandate. However, the relationship became more conflictual once the constitutional dimension of EU primary law deepened with the Treaty of Amsterdam (1997), the Charter of Fundamental Rights (2000), and the Treaty of Lisbon (2007), which increasingly affected the role of the constitutional courts.[99] In such conflicts, the CJEU has staunchly defended the power of all courts to disapply statutes and thereby exercise some constitutional adjudication. It repeatedly held that the constitutional courts may limit neither the lower courts' power of review[100] nor their authority to submit a reference on the matter to the Luxembourg court.[101]

This CJEU case law advances European unity, which is a prerequisite for European democracy (see 4.3.B). Beyond the systemic level, today it also safeguards democracy in more concrete cases, as the Polish rule-of-law crisis demonstrates. Since 2018, Polish courts have brought preliminary proceedings before the CJEU, requesting that it help stymie the executive's attempt to capture the judiciary (see 3.6.A). To counteract this, the Polish Minister of Justice called on the Polish Constitutional Tribunal to declare Article 267 of the Treaty on the Functioning of the European Union (TFEU) unconstitutional inasmuch as it allows preliminary

99 Cruz Villalón (n. 10); Farahat, 'The German Federal Constitutional Court' (n. 29) 294–299; Martín y Pérez de Nanclares, 'The Cooperation of Constitutional Courts in the European Legal Space', in von Bogdandy, Huber, and Grabenwarter (n. 10); Paris, 'The Impact of EU Law and the ECHR on National Constitutional Adjudication in the European Legal Space', in von Bogdandy, Huber, and Grabenwarter (n. 10); Claes and de Witte, 'The Roles of Constitutional Courts in the European Legal Space', in von Bogdandy, Huber, and Grabenwarter (n. 10); Requejo Pagés, 'The Decline of the Traditional Model of European Constitutional Jurisdiction', in von Bogdandy, Huber, and Grabenwarter (n. 10); Vašek (n. 62).

100 CJEU, Case C-617/10, *Åkerberg Fransson* (EU:C:2013:280) para. 48.

101 CJEU, Joined Cases C-188/10 and C-189/10, *Melki and Abdeli* (EU:C:2010:363); Case C-112/13, *A* (EU:C:2014:2195).

rulings on this capture.[102] The European reactions bear witness to how deeply decentralized constitutional adjudication is anchored in the European legal fabric.

The Strasbourg Convention system also transforms the national constitutional courts, though in a less invasive way. So far, the ECtHR does not call on national courts to disapply laws that violate the Convention. However, doctrine of review for conventionality of the Inter-American Court of Human Rights (IACtHR) demonstrates that this step is conceivable.[103] In any event, the Convention requires the Convention States to respect the ECtHR's case law, remedy violations thereof, and prevent future infringements.[104] Because these requirements are substantial, they have met considerable resistance; nevertheless, the Convention states confirmed them.[105] According to these specifications, all national courts must do everything within their power to comply with the European Convention on Human Rights (ECHR) requirements as interpreted by the ECtHR.[106] This includes interpreting national law in compliance with the Convention. UK Supreme Court Justice Brenda Hale, who became an icon of the English rule of law for checking the Johnson government during the Brexit process, emphasized that 'it is amazing how much can be done in this way'.[107]

If European law has done a lot to advance constitutional adjudication, so far it does not require to establish a constitutional court or to empower its courts to annul legislation. But it has established, within the Polish rule-of-law crisis, a prohibition of regression. The impetus came from the Council of Europe's Venice Commission.

Until the Polish crisis, the Venice Commission's policy was to only recommend 'providing for a constitutional court or equivalent body'; in other words, it did not to consider it a legal requirement.[108] But then, in its opinion on the reform of the

[102] Biernat and Kawczyńska, 'Though This Be Madness, Yet There's Method In't: Pitting the Polish Constitutional Tribunal against the Luxembourg Court', *Verfassungsblog* (26 October 2019).

[103] Ferrer Mac-Gregor, 'The Conventionality Control as a Core Mechanism of the Ius Constitutionale Commune', in A. von Bogdandy *et al.* (eds), *Transformative Constitutionalism in Latin America. The Emergence of a New Ius Commune* (2017) 321. Such a duty exists in some European states because of national constitutional law. See, e.g. Jouanjan, 'Constitutional Justice in France' (n. 24) 256.

[104] Gerards, 'The European Court of Human Rights and the National Courts. Giving Shape to the Notion of "Shared Responsibility"', in J. Gerards and J. Fleuren (eds), *Implementation of the European Convention on Human Rights and of the Judgments of the ECtHR in National Case Law. A Comparative Analysis* (2014) 13, at 27; R. Kunz, *Richter über internationale Gerichte? Die Rolle innerstaatlicher Gerichte bei der Umsetzung der Entscheidungen von EGMR und IAGMR* (2020).

[105] Council of Europe, Copenhagen Declaration of 12–13 April 2018, paras 14, 17, 41, http://rm.coe.int/copenhagen-declaration/16807b915chttp://rm.coe.int/copenhagen-declaration/16807b915c%3e (last visited 8 July 2022). On the Declaration, see Polakiewicz and Suominen-Picht, 'Aktuelle Herausforderungen für Europarat und EMRK', *Europäische Grundrechte-Zeitschrift* (2018) 383.

[106] Copenhagen Declaration (n. 105) paras 3, 8, 14, 26 ff.; Arnardóttir, '*Res Interpretata, Erga Omnes Effect* and the Role of the Margin of Appreciation in Giving Domestic Effect to the Judgments of the European Court of Human Rights', 28 *European Journal of International Law* (2017) 819.

[107] Lady Hale, *The Bryce Lecture 2015: The Supreme Court in the United Kingdom Constitution* (5 February 2015) 12, http://www.supremecourt.uk/docs/speech-150205.pdf (last visited 11 July 2022).

[108] European Commission for Democracy through Law (Venice Commission), Rule of Law Checklist, 106th Plenary Session (Venice, 11–12 March 2016) para. 108.

Polish Constitutional Tribunal, the Commission emphasized that 'where a constitutional court has been established, one of the central elements for ensuring checks and balances is the independent constitutional court' and that 'as long as the situation of constitutional crisis related to the Constitutional Tribunal remains unsettled and as long as the Constitutional Tribunal cannot carry out its work in an efficient manner, not only is the rule of law in danger, but so is democracy and human rights'.[109]

Under this standard, it is almost impossible to disassemble an operative constitutional court. Certainly, the Venice Commission does not have the instruments to enforce this understanding against a determined government majority. However, its opinions enjoy much authority because they help determine what is legally acceptable in European society. The Article 7 TEU proceedings against Poland show that many actors rely on them (see 4.4.C).

It remains to be seen to what extent European law will secure the independence of Polish constitutional adjudication. But it clearly proves that constitutional adjudication is no longer a mere constitutional 'accessory', unlike before the fall of the Iron Curtain. Rather, it forms part of the constitutional core of European society.

B. Europeanizing the Sources

Constitutional adjudication rests on the idea of hierarchy: all legislation and further legal acts are subordinated to constitutional law, as seminally theorized by Hans Kelsen.[110] For a long time, constitutional law was conceived of as a single and national source of law. The only task of constitutional adjudication was to ensure that all national legal acts respect the national constitution, its sole source and focus.[111]

This understanding of constitutional adjudication does not fit constitutional law in European society, given the composite structure of its law (see 2.2.C). Today, even national constitutional courts have to deal with the constitutional provisions of other legal orders as interpreted and applied by the CJEU, the ECtHR, and other constitutional courts. Constitutional adjudication in Europe is faced with a plurality of constitutional sources.[112] Across the world, only Latin America shows somewhat comparable structures (see 2.6.C).

[109] European Commission for Democracy through Law (Venice Commission), Opinion on Amendments to the Act of 25 June 2015 on the Constitutional Tribunal, 106th Plenary Session (Venice, 11–12 March 2016) para. 135.

[110] Kelsen, 'Wesen und Entwicklung der Staatsgerichtsbarkeit', 5 *Veröffentlichungen der Vereinigung der Deutschen Staatsrechtslehrer* (1929) 30, at 37.

[111] As remains true for the US Supreme Court. See its decisions regarding Guantanamo, e.g. *Rasul v. Bush*, 542 U.S. 466 (2004).

[112] Barsotti *et al.*, 'Introduction. Dialogue as a Method', in V. Barsotti *et al.* (eds), *Dialogues on Italian Constitutional Justice. A Comparative Perspective* (2021) 1; Martín y Pérez de Nanclares (n. 99).

The primacy of EU law is an EU obligation and hence imposes itself on domestic constitutional adjudication as a relevant source (see 3.3.C, 4.4.B). The situation is more open when it comes to the ECHR, and the national courts refer to it in different ways: some commit to it but do not address it.[113] While the French *Conseil constitutionnel* does not cite the ECHR in its decisions, analyses show that it considers the Strasbourg Court's case law and generally follows it.[114] In some legal orders, the ECHR is deeply integrated into constitutional law, notably in Austria, where it has constitutional status.[115] In Italy, Article 117(1) of the Constitution requires the legislature to respect Italy's duties under EU and international law, thereby entrenching the respective duty under EU and international law.[116] The Spanish *Tribunal Constitucional* comes to the same conclusion by interpreting Article 10(2) of the Constitution accordingly.[117]

Article 1(2) of the Basic Law would allow the same solution for Germany.[118] However, the German Constitutional Court assigns the ECHR and the ECtHR a lower position by positing that Article 59(2) of the Basic Law constitutes the key provision. According to this provision, the Convention only enjoys statutory rank. This does not mean that the Court disregards the Convention. Rather, 'the guarantees of the Convention influence the interpretation of the fundamental rights and constitutional principles of the Basic Law' and '[t]he text of the Convention and the case law of the European Court of Human Rights serve, on the level of constitutional law, as guides to interpretation in determining the content and scope of fundamental rights and constitutional principles of the Basic Law'.[119] This has helped the Court avoid permanent conflict with Strasbourg.

At the same time, the Convention and the Strasbourg case law are less integrated into the German constitutional order than into other legal orders. Unlike for most other courts, the ECHR only plays a supplementary—even a subordinate—role for the German Constitutional Court. This becomes readily apparent in the Second Senate's decision on the ban on strikes by civil servants as well as judgments that serve as a lead case. The Basic Law provides the primary standard of review, whereas the ban's compliance with the Convention is presented as a mere confirmation of the already-established conclusion.[120]

113 See Vašek (n. 62).

114 Jouanjan, 'Constitutional Justice in France' (n. 24) 274 f.

115 Grabenwarter, 'The Austrian Constitutional Court' (n. 29) 66.

116 Bifulco and Paris (n. 18) 494 f.

117 Requejo Pagés, 'The Spanish Constitutional Tribunal' (n. 29) 751.

118 N. Sternberg, *Der Rang von Menschenrechtsverträgen im deutschen Recht unter besonderer Berücksichtigung von Art. 1 Abs. 2 GG* (1999) 227.

119 BVerfGE 111, 307, *Görgülü*, para. 32.

120 BVerfGE 148, 296, *Ban on Strike Action for Civil Servants*; Hering, 'Beamtenstreik zwischen Karlsruhe und Straßburg: Art. 11 EMRK und die konventionskonforme Auslegung durch das BVerfG. Anmerkungen und Überlegungen zu BVerfG, Urt. v. 12.6.2018, Az. 2 BvR 1738/12', 79 *Zeitschrift für ausländisches öffentliches Recht und Völkerrecht* (2019) 241, at 256.

Thus, the various institutions of constitutional adjudication practice the pluralism of constitutional sources in very different modes. What are identical are the common norms and institutions as well as the overall complexity. To deal with this complexity and the many challenges it entails, the courts resort to multilevel cooperation, another transformative factor.

C. Europeanizing through Multilevel Cooperation

Like many other public institutions in European society, the apex courts of the various legal orders interact not only with courts in their own legal order but also with other legal orders' apex courts, thereby weaving the very fabric of European society. Such interaction is often referred to as networking.[121] For the courts tasked with constitutional adjudication, however, it has become customary to call it 'multi-level cooperation of constitutional courts'.[122] Initially, this referred mostly to the conflict-prone interaction of constitutional courts with the CJEU and the ECtHR. By now, it has also come to designate the interaction with other national courts.

While claims of a 'global community of judges' have remained mostly speculative,[123] the close-knit networks in European society are well documented. Many judges are in constant, and sometimes even close, contact with colleagues from other legal orders.[124] That these interactions are publicly financed evinces the depth of the transformation. In the end, the judges' task is to decide pending cases. It should come as a surprise that this endeavour includes visiting colleagues in foreign countries to discuss general topics (although pending cases are off-limits) and that public funds are used to finance these trips. And yet, such visits and joint events serve the judicial function because they help the courts live up to their complex mandate. Sociologically, such reiterated, or even recurrent, interaction can be interpreted as an institutionalized network. Methodologically, it represents comparative law. Legally, this multilevel cooperation constitutes one aspect of the 'union among the peoples of Europe' (Article 1(2) TEU).

The multilevel cooperation goes to the core of constitutional activity. Christoph Grabenwarter, now President of the Austrian Constitutional Court, states that

[121] Claes and de Visser, 'Courts United? On European Judicial Networks', in A. Vauchez and B. de Witte (eds), *Lawyering Europe. European Law as a Transnational Social Field* (2013) 75.

[122] Voßkuhle, 'Der europäische Verfassungsgerichtsverbund', 29 *Neue Zeitschrift für Verwaltungsrecht* (2010) 1.

[123] Wiener and Liste, 'Lost without Translation? Cross-Referencing and a New Global Community of Courts', 21 *Indiana Journal of Global Legal Studies* (2014) 263.

[124] S. Cassese, *Dentro la Corte. Diario di un giudice costituzionale* (2015); Martini, 'Lifting the Constitutional Curtain? The Use of Foreign Precedent by the German Federal Constitutional Court', in T. Groppi and M.-C. Ponthoreau (eds), *The Use of Foreign Precedents by Constitutional Judges* (2013) 229.

today's practice of constitutional adjudication no longer constitutes the isolated activity of apex-court judges who must interpret a clearly delimited body of law. Rather, it is based on a complex and integrative process of interpreting and applying provisions and precedents of various legal orders.[125] Tellingly, courts want to be heard beyond the borders of their legal order. Many apex courts now use public funds to publish important judgments online and in English in order to reach foreign audiences.[126] Some believe that a constitutional court's domestic position increasingly depends on its international recognition and reputation.[127]

The *Conference of European Constitutional Courts* provides an institutionalized forum for this cooperation. It was originally intended to strengthen constitutional adjudication in Yugoslavia[128] but then changed completely. Today, it represents a network that brings together institutions performing tasks of constitutional adjudication from all over Europe. Reflecting European diversity, the participating courts do not merely include constitutional courts. Thus, the *Hoge Rad* of the Netherlands is a member, even though it is neither a constitutional court nor empowered to invalidate statutes. Remarkably, the CJEU and the ECtHR are not members of the conference, making the *Conference* look somewhat defensive.

Since institutionalized encounters are vital for social integration as well as building and maintaining structures, there is also activity at the European level. In 2005, the EU Commission funded the creation of the Network of the Presidents of the Supreme Courts of the European Union. It serves as an interface for the communication between the European institutions and these courts, although not the constitutional courts. An EU-centred network that also includes the latter only emerged in 2017 with the Judicial Network of the European Union.

In 2015, the ECtHR created a Superior Courts Network.[129] It is open to all supreme and constitutional courts. The ECtHR grants the national courts access to its internal tools but requires their support for its comparative work.[130] While the five highest German federal courts (*Bundesgerichtshof* (Karlsruhe, private and criminal law), *Bundesarbeitsgericht* (Erfurt, labour law), *Bundesfinanzhof* (Munich, tax law), *Bundessozialgericht* (Kassel, social security law), and *Bundesverwaltungsgericht* (Leipzig, administrative law)) participate in this network, the Federal

[125] Grabenwarter, 'Zusammenfassung der Ergebnisse der vorangegangenen Sitzungen für den XVI. Kongress der Konferenz der Europäischen Verfassungsgerichte', in Verfassungsgerichtshof der Republik Österreich (ed.), *Die Kooperation der Verfassungsgerichte in Europa. Aktuelle Rahmenbedingungen und Perspektiven* (2014) 174.

[126] Wendel, 'Richterliche Rechtsvergleichung als Dialogform: Die Integrationsrechtsprechung nationaler Verfassungsgerichte in gemeineuropäischer Perspektive', 52 *Der Staat* (2013) 339, at 364.

[127] Huls, 'The Ebb and Flow of Judicial Leadership in the Netherlands', 8 *Utrecht Law Review* (2012) 129.

[128] Sólyom (n. 29) 363 f.

[129] See ECtHR, Cooperation Charter of the Superior Court Network (2015).

[130] Fribergh and Liddell, 'The Interlaken Process and the Jurisconsult', in L. Berg *et al.* (eds), *Cohérence et impact de la jurisprudence de la Cour européenne des droits de l'homme: Liber amicorum Vincent Berger* (2013) 177, at 184.

Constitutional Court does not. By the end of this chapter, this will no longer come as a surprise.

Indeed, the constitutional courts' Europeanization in general, and their multilevel cooperation in particular, is by no means only intended to support the European institutions. Rather, multilevel cooperation also has the task of organizing resistance against the CJEU and the ECtHR. Joint action—whereby several constitutional courts hand down similar rulings—promises to be more effective and appear more legitimate as there will be fewer suspicions that the courts are defending specific national interests. Europeanization does not mean submitting to European institutions. Part of the checks and balances in European society is that national courts keep a watchful eye on the transformation induced by the CJEU and ECtHR.

3. How the CJEU and the ECtHR Forged European Society

Constitutional jurisdiction has grown from a rare and insignificant institution into a force that has helped transform societies in a good number of European countries. The CJEU in Luxembourg and the ECtHR in Strasbourg also wield transformative power. This section pursues the two courts' transformation in greater detail, doing so, as always, in the sense of an objective and a subjective genitive: what is at stake is both the transformation of these courts themselves and the changes they have brought about in European society.

In post-war Germany and Italy, democratic societies would have developed even without the *Bundesverfassungsgericht* and the *Corte costituzionale*, as the North Atlantic Treaty Organization (NATO), the European Economic Community (EEC), and the White House would have stood ready to act as constitutional guardians. Matters are different when it comes to European society. It is hard to imagine that the European society invoked by Article 2 TEU would exist today without the case law of the CJEU and the ECtHR. Even more so than the national constitutional courts, the CJEU and the ECtHR are protagonists of social transformation. With regard to the CJEU, Eric Stein, a professor at the University of Michigan Law School, expressed this in arguably the most famous dictum on European law. He maintains that the CJEU 'has fashioned a constitutional framework for a federal-type structure in Europe'.[131] And with regard to the ECHR and its institutions, Jochen Frowein stated, shortly after Stein, that it was a 'sleeping beauty' that he, among others, had awakened with his kiss as a member and Vice-President of the Convention's Commission.[132]

[131] Stein, 'Lawyers, Judges, and the Making of a Transnational Constitution', 75 *American Journal of International Law* (1981) 1.

[132] Frowein, 'European Integration through Fundamental Rights', 18 *University of Michigan Journal of Law Reform* (1984) 5, at 8.

A. The Original Mandate

The authors of the Treaties assigned a transformative mandate to neither the CJEU nor the ECtHR.[133] Instead, they thought that the Courts would assume more of a subordinate role. The CJEU was established to protect Member State interests vis-à-vis a newly created supranational administrative authority, while the ECHR was supposed to provide a backstop against totalitarianism. Their current role is as unanticipated as that of the *Bundesverfassungsgericht*, the *Conseil constitutionnel*, and the *Corte costituzionale*, and it testifies to a transformation in European public law.

1. The CJEU: A European Administrative Tribunal

The early plans for European economic integration bore a French signature. In keeping with the idea of French administration at the time, an expertocratic administrative authority—not a supranational legislature, and certainly not a court—should advance integration (see 2.4.A). This idea underlies the Schuman Plan, which the French government presented on 9 May 1950 to advance European economic integration in the area of coal and steel.[134] The High Authority, the predecessor of the European Commission, was vested with broad powers to monitor the coal and steel sector, forge the national markets, and expand the production of coal and steel.[135] The administrative understanding of integration developed accordingly (see 2.4.A–C).

The creation of what is today the CJEU responded to concerns about Member State sovereignty. Belgium and the Netherlands pushed for a counterweight to the High Authority's powers of intervention and regulation. Thus, the CJEU's original task was to oversee supranational administrative activity in order to protect Member State interests, not to build a new legal order.[136]

The Court of Justice, which began operating in 1952, was a compromise between the French plan for a strong European executive and the concerns of smaller states that European authority would become overbearing. Therefore, the primary issue was to offer judicial protection against administrative action, which explains why the French *Conseil d'État*,[137] the archetype of an administrative court, served as a model (see 2.4.B). The procedural core of the ECSC's Court of Justice was the action for annulment, which features today in the almost identically worded Article

[133] The following remarks draw on von Bogdandy and Krenn, 'ECJ and ECtHR: Two Senates of Europe's Constitutional Jurisdiction', in von Bogdandy, Huber, and Grabenwarter (n. 10).

[134] T. Tohidipur, *Europäische Gerichtsbarkeit im Institutionensystem der EU. Zu Genese und Zustand justizieller Konstitutionalisierung* (2008) 17–23.

[135] Mosler, 'Der Vertrag über die Europäische Gemeinschaft für Kohle und Stahl. Entstehung und Qualifizierung', 14 *Zeitschrift für ausländisches öffentliches Recht und Völkerrecht* (1951) 1, at 10.

[136] Boerger-De Smedt, 'La Cour de Justice dans les négociations du traité de Paris instituant la CECA', 14 *Journal of European Integration History* (2008) 7, at 13.

[137] Reuter, 'Quelques aspects institutionnels du Plan Schuman', *Revue du droit public et de la science politique en France et à l'étranger* (1951) 105, at 120.

263 TFEU. Modelled on the French *recours pour excès de pouvoir*, it nonetheless differed from it in essential aspects.[138] Compared to the *Conseil d'État*, access to the Court of Justice was extremely restricted, and the economic grounds of the High Authority's decisions were excluded from judicial review. Thus, there was a '*discordance totale*'[139] in comparison to the power of the *Conseil d'État*. Furthermore, the Court of Justice's task was limited to adjudicating individual cases and did not include establishing a legal system, a task that characterizes the *Conseil d'État*.[140]

In the early years, the Court of Justice did not review Member State action. This task was reserved for the High Authority, which could impose sanctions on states that had breached the Treaty (Article 88 ECSC Treaty). The Court of Justice only came into play when a Member State objected to the High Authority's actions. Above all, the ECSC Treaty's preliminary ruling proceedings—with which the CJEU would later Europeanize the Member States' legal orders—only allowed for the review of supranational acts. The only questions that could be raised concerned the validity of the Community institutions' acts; contrary to today, questions about their interpretation, which represent the true levers of change (see 4.1.C), were inadmissible.

Of course, some actors in the ECSC Court and in its academic and political environment wished for the Court to play a more far-reaching role. Federalists pointed out the first signs of the Court's constitutional adjudication early on.[141] Some decisions show the seeds of later, constitutionally significant rulings.[142] But the ECSC Court mostly stuck to its task of only reviewing the High Authority's administrative acts.[143] In a nutshell, the ECSC Court was minimalist and, for that reason, close to oblivion.

2. The ECtHR: A Backstop against Authoritarian Regression

Like the ECSC Court, the ECtHR is a post-war phenomenon. The ECHR entered into force on 3 September 1953, and the Strasbourg Court took up its work on 23 February 1959. Unlike the CJEU, with its more administrative bent, the ECtHR was closely linked to the development of constitutional adjudication from the

[138] In detail, Drewes, *Entstehen und Entwicklung des Rechtsschutzes vor den Gerichten der Europäischen Gemeinschaften. Am Beispiel der Nichtigkeitsklage* (2000).

[139] L'Huillier, 'Une conquête du droit administratif français. Le contentieux de la Communauté européenne du charbon et de l'acier', 13 *Recueil Dalloz* (1953) 63, at 65.

[140] E. Steindorff, *Die Nichtigkeitsklage im Recht der Europäischen Gemeinschaft für Kohle und Stahl* (1952) 116.

[141] See Lagrange, 'La Cour de justice des Communautés européennes du Plan Schuman à l'Union européenne', in P.-H. Teitgen (ed.), *Mélanges Fernand Dehousse. Tome II. La construction européenne* (1979) 127, at 127–129.

[142] A. K. Mangold, *Gemeinschaftsrecht und deutsches Recht. Die Europäisierung der deutschen Rechtsordnung in historisch-empirischer Sicht* (2011) 97–106.

[143] The function of an administrative court remains important. See Hering, 'Der Gerichtshof der Europäischen Union als Verwaltungsgericht. § 153', in A. von Bogdandy, C. Grabenwarter, and P. M. Huber (eds), *Handbuch Ius Publicum Europaeum, Bd. IX. Verwaltungsgerichtsbarkeit in Europa: Gemeineuropäische Perspektiven und supranationaler Rechtsschutz* (2021) 645.

very beginning[144] insofar as it was tasked—much like the national constitutional courts—with protecting individual rights.

Yet, the ECtHR was conceived as a mere backstop against a regression into authoritarianism.[145] The Convention's human rights guarantees merely codified its Members' national standards. Moreover, the Convention only provided for a weak court, one that also lacked mandatory jurisdiction.[146] More progressive proposals, such as the draft of the federalist 'European Movement', which proposed a Court that permitted direct complaints from affected individuals and could invalidate national statutes, did not prevail.[147]

It was not until 1959 that eight Treaty states had made the necessary declarations for the ECtHR to begin its work. Both the Court's relevance and its competences were scant. The Human Rights Commission, which sought amicable settlements, tightly controlled access to the Court. Moreover, only the Commission or an involved state party—but not the parties concerned—could seize the Court. The Court's prospects for making a difference seemed bleak, as Henri Rolin, the Court's vice-president, and later president, made clear in a speech in 1965 that received much attention.[148] While the Commission received almost 2,700 complaints between 1955 and 1965, only a few were considered admissible, and almost all were rejected as manifestly ill-founded. Between 1955 and 1965, the Court decided all of two cases.[149]

By contrast, the ECtHR adjudicated 40,667 submissions in 2019. Undoubtedly, it had become an active court. This is also true of the CJEU, which settled a total of 1,739 cases.[150] Both have become large institutions: In 2021, the ECtHR had 47 judges, a staff of 640 people, and an annual budget of almost €74 million, while the CJEU had a total of 76 judges, 11 advocates general, 2,235 staff members, and an annual budget of €444 million.[151] Both courts have become powerful actors of European transformation and exercise functions of constitutional adjudication. The judges mingle naturally, though not always harmoniously, with their

144 Moravcsik, 'The Origins of Human Rights Regimes. Democratic Delegation in Postwar Europe', 54 *International Organization* (2000) 217.

145 Wildhaber, 'Changing Ideas about the Tasks of the European Court of Human Rights', in L. Wildhaber (ed.), *The European Court of Human Rights. 1998–2006. History, Achievements, Reform* (2006) 136.

146 Madsen, 'The Protracted Institutionalization of the Strasbourg Court. From Legal Diplomacy to Integrationist Jurisprudence', in J. Christoffersen and M. R. Madsen (eds), *The European Court of Human Rights between Law and Politics* (2011) 43.

147 E. Bates, *The Evolution of the European Convention on Human Rights. From its Inception to the Creation of a Permanent Court of Human Rights* (2010) 54 ff.

148 Rolin, 'Has the European Court of Human Rights a Future?', 11 *Howard Law Journal* (1965) 442.

149 ECtHR, *Lawless v. Ireland (No. 3)*, Appl. no. 332/57, Judgment of 1 July 1961, Series A, No. 3; *De Becker v. Belgium*, Appl. no. 214/56, Judgment of 27 March 1962, Series A, No. 4.

150 ECtHR, *Analysis of Statistics 2019* (2020) 4; CJEU, *Annual Report 2019: Judicial Activity: Synopsis of the Judicial Activity of the Court of Justice and the General Court of the European Union* (2019) 5, 54.

151 ECtHR, *ECHR Budget* (2020), https://echr.coe.int/Pages/home.aspx?p=court/howitworks&c (last visited 15 July 2022); CJEU, *The Court in Figures* (updated 31 December 2022), https://curia.europa.eu/jcms/jcms/P_80908/en (last visited 15 July 2022).

colleagues from the national apex courts. Today, the CJEU and the ECtHR are ingrained in European society's consciousness as the European judiciary, even though many citizens, and even some lawyers, struggle to distinguish between the Luxembourg and the Strasbourg Court. How did this come about?

B. Building Unity: The CJEU

According to widely accepted opinion, international society is anarchic and, for that reason, undemocratic.[152] A democratic society requires exiting from anarchy; in other words, it requires political unity. More than anything else, political unity implies common institutions that are authoritative and wield effective instruments for law-making and law enforcement.

It is hard to imagine today's political unity in Europe without the CJEU's case law. Although that case law certainly represents but one of several pillars, it is an essential one. For over 60 years, the CJEU has advanced European political unity by supporting the emergence of a European political system that makes a difference. The prevailing interpretation, whereby this case law has merely served to juridify politics, fails to grasp the Court's defining achievement:[153] a genuinely European politicization of European issues (see 2.2.B).

The transformative case law began as a response to a deep crisis. In the early 1960s, European integration faced a difficult situation. The ECSC had fallen short of expectations, while the memory of the European Political Community's failure in the French National Assembly was still fresh. Given this situation, the French government, which had played a decisive role in propagating the supranational design of the ECSC, championed much greater intergovernmentalism.[154] Thus, the EEC took on a new institutional form, compared to the ECSC. No longer did a supranational administrative authority constitute its institutional centre. This task now fell to the Council, which comprised members of the Member States' governments and was supposed to advance integration with regulations and directives. However, this project did not unfold as planned either because it became clear that this form of law-making would not suffice to achieve a common market, the EEC Treaty's main goal.

Consequently, the young community was stuck in a crisis that transformed into a *critical juncture*, to use the vivid terminology of historical institutionalism.[155] The

[152] H. Bull, *The Anarchical Society. A Study of Order in World Politics* (1977).

[153] This is the fundamental criticism that Dieter Grimm tends to put forward. See, e.g. Grimm, 'Staat und Verfassung vor 60 Jahren und heute', in S. Bretthauer *et al.* (eds), *Wandlungen im Öffentlichen Recht. Festschrift zu 60 Jahren Assistententagung—Junge Tagung Öffentliches Recht* (2020) 95, at 111.

[154] Boerger-De Smedt, 'Negotiating the Foundations of European Law, 1950–57. The Legal History of the Treaties of Paris and Rome', 21 *Contemporary European History* (2012) 339.

[155] On the concept, see Capoccia and Kelemen, 'The Study of Critical Junctures: Theory, Narrative, and Counterfactuals in Historical Institutionsalism', 59 *World Politics* (2007) 341.

future path emerged in the Court's response to this crisis. The transformative character of its case law was completely unexpected.[156] It helped unfold the two central aspects of political unity: the formation of a political will and its enforcement. As early as 1966, Jean-Pierre Colin identified a 'gouvernement des juges dans les Communautés européennes'.[157] Given this title's reference to Édouard Lambert's famous and highly critical book (see 4.5.A), one might have expected resistance.[158] But there was almost none, either in Colin's book or in political and legal circles; instead, the Court's reaction drew praise.

In hindsight, we can reconstruct this case law as crucial to the development of a democratic European society. I have already discussed how the Court hardened Community law in order to allow for true government (see 3.3). Now, I will elaborate on further aspects of how the Court created unity, aspects that also reveal its institutional path.

1. Promoting European Law-Making

Ever since the 1960s, the CJEU's case law has strengthened the ability of the Community's political bodies to govern. The mainstream narrative obscures this fact by presenting the CJEU as a surrogate legislature, especially because of its liberalizing case law on the four market freedoms. But it has always been clear that case law can never replace politics or policies. Therefore, the basic thrust of the Court's case law has always been to induce Member States to legislate by means of the EEC's political institutions.[159]

The paradigmatic case law on the free movement of goods (now Articles 28–37 TFEU) vividly illustrates as much. At stake in the 1974 *Dassonville* judgment was a Belgium regulation that restricted the marketing of Scotch whisky in Belgium to certain dealers, thereby protecting their profits. The CJEU imposed a duty of justification on this as on practically every national regulation of the movement of goods: 'All trading rules enacted by Member States which are capable of hindering, directly or indirectly, actually or potentially, intra-Community trade are to be considered as measures having an effect equivalent to quantitative restrictions.'[160] This encompasses environmental standards as well as bans on Sunday trading.[161]

[156] W. Hallstein, *Die echten Probleme der europäischen Integration* (1965) 9; Schlochauer, 'Der Gerichtshof der Europäischen Gemeinschaften als Integrationsfaktor', in E. von Caemmerer, H.-J. Schlochauer, and E. Steindorff (eds), *Probleme des europäischen Rechts. Festschrift für Walter Hallstein zu seinem 65. Geburtstag* (1966) 431; Pescatore, 'La carence du législateur communautaire et le devoir du juge', in G. Lüke, G. Ress, and M. R. Will (eds), *Rechtsvergleichung, Europarecht und Staatenintegration. Gedächtnisschrift für Léontin-Jean Constantinesco* (1983) 559.

[157] J.-P. Colin, *Le gouvernement des juges dans les Communautés européennes* (1966).

[158] Lambert (n. 17).

[159] Snell, 'The Internal Market and the Philosophies of Market Integration', in C. Barnard and S. Peers (eds), *European Union Law* (2017) 310, at 319 ff.

[160] CJEU, Case 8/74, *Dassonville* (EU:C:1974:82) para. 5.

[161] Sharpston, 'About that Sunday Trading Mess . . .', in F. Amtenbrink *et al.* (eds), *The Internal Market and the Future of European Integration. Essays in Honour of Laurence W. Gormley* (2019) 150.

The CJEU has never been anarchist or libertarian. National regulations have always been permissible under Community law if they promote a public interest and are proportionate. Importantly, the CJEU claims the authority to decide on this. Its decisions sometimes show more sympathy for a free market and sometimes more understanding for public interests. Overall, its case law did away with many national regulatory measures. As a result, many refer to it with the pejorative term 'negative integration'. Some even depict it as an instrument of capitalism,[162] as neoliberal deregulation, as an attack on the social compromise in post-war Europe.[163]

We understand this case law better if we reconstruct it as promoting not neoliberalism but Europe's political unity. This becomes evident in the proviso, which can be found in many judgments, whereby the fundamental freedoms only apply if there is no EEC legislation.[164] Thus, the European legislature can regulate the movement of goods, services, capital, and the freedom of establishment differently than the Court of Justice's market freedom jurisprudence.[165] Some attribute this differentiation to the CJEU's bias in favour of the Union's institutions.[166] I think that the objective of strengthening the European political process, and thereby advancing European unity, is more convincing, not least because it responds to the mandate of 'ever closer union'.

Further lines of the Court's case law—such as its tame review of the European legislator (Article 263 TFEU), which initially consisted only of the Council and later came to encompass both the Council and the Parliament—are also premised on the inclination to promote European law-making and thus the emergence of a genuinely European political will. Critics have accused the CJEU of not enforcing the limits of the Union's competences,[167] not taking fundamental rights seriously when they bear upon the Union's institutions,[168] and interpreting the action for

[162] J. Galtung, *Europe in the Making* (1989).

[163] F. W. Scharpf, *Governing in Europe: Effective and Democratic?* (1999) 43 ff. But see the redefinition in Höpner and Schmidt, 'Can We Make the European Fundamental Freedoms Less Constraining? A Literature Review', in K. Armstrong (ed.), *Cambridge Yearbook of European Legal Studies* (2020) 1, at 5 ff.

[164] CJEU, Case 120/78, *Cassis de Dijon* (EU:C:1979:42) para. 8; Case C-573/12, *Ålands Vindkraft* (EU:C:2014:2037) para. 57; Kingreen, 'Art. 36 AEUV', in C. Calliess and M. Ruffert (eds), *EUV/AEUV. Das Verfassungsrecht der Europäischen Union mit Europäischer Grundrechtecharta. Kommentar* (2016) 395, at para. 18 with further references. For more details on the Court's complex jurisprudence, see Syrpis, 'The Relationship between Primary and Secondary Law in the EU', 52 *Common Market Law Review* (2015) 461.

[165] The free movement of workers constitutes an exception because the CJEU—probably in response to being accused of a capitalist bias—interprets it as a fundamental right that protects dependent employees: CJEU, Case C-415/93, *Bosman* (EU:C:1995:463) para. 129; O'Leary, 'Free Movement of Persons and Services', in P. Craig and G. de Búrca (eds), *The Evolution of EU Law* (2011) 499, at 505 ff.

[166] But see G. Beck, *The Legal Reasoning of the Court of Justice of the EU* (2012) 318 ff.

[167] Huber, 'Europa am Scheideweg—Zur Notwendigkeit einer realistischen und nachhaltigen Fortentwicklung der Europäischen Union, deutschen "Hausaufgaben" und der Bedeutung eines Narrativs', in C. Franzius, F. C. Mayer, and J. Neyer (eds), *Die Neuerfindung Europas* (2019) 215, at 225 ff.

[168] Coppel and O'Neill, 'The European Court of Justice. Taking Rights Seriously?', 12 *Legal Studies* (1992) 227.

annulment restrictively, thereby making it overly difficult for citizens to challenge the Union's institutions.[169]

The constitutional adjudication of the CJEU may, indeed, appear deficient from the perspective of some legal orders when it comes to policing the Union's law-making. This is especially true of the German legal order, whose Constitutional Court generally does not pull punches. Things look different from the perspective of European society, however, since the primary objective is to provide this society with functioning institutions and the necessary instruments. By contrast, the *Bundesverfassungsgericht* was never confronted with a situation in which German institutions lacked authority, federal law was systematically disapplied by the *Länder*, and a close union between the *Länder* was still to be achieved.

Since political unity presupposes the exercise of competences, no debate is more instructive than that about the Union's competences. It initially focused on three provisions. Article 352 TFEU, the so-called flexibility clause, allows action by unanimous Council decision if European policymakers deem this necessary to achieve the Treaty objectives, but the action in question does not fall within the ambit of the specific competences. The Council frequently availed itself of this competence to implement the heads of state and government's decision in the early 1970s to use the EEC's institutions as a framework for coordinating matters that clearly transcend economic questions.[170] Thus, the Community advanced into areas such as environmental, social, research, and regional policy. For a long time, the Court tolerated all submitted uses of this competence.[171] While it drew criticism for this jurisprudence, it did the same when it opined that Article 352 TFEU could not help the Community accede to the ECHR, given the constitutional dimension of this accession.[172]

The second debate centred on Article 114 TFEU, the most frequently used competence for harmonizing legislation relevant to the internal market.[173] It was only in the late 1990s, in its judgment on the Tobacco Advertising Directive, that the Court declared the limits of this power infringed. For the very first time, it struck down a legislative act for lack of competence.[174] Because this remained an exception, the

[169] Kühling, 'Fundamental Rights', in von Bogdandy and Bast (n. 1) 479, 512.

[170] Declaration of the first Summit Conference of the enlarged Community held in Paris on 19 and 20 October 1972, Bull. EC 10-1972, 14.

[171] Seminal CJEU, Case 8/73, *Hauptzollamt Bremerhaven v. Massey Ferguson* (EU:C:1973:90) paras 3 f.

[172] CJEU, Opinion 2/94, *Adhésion de la Communauté à la CEDH* (EU:C:1996:140) paras 28 f.; G. Gaja, 'Opinion 2/94, Accession by the Community to the European Convention for the Protection of Human Rights and Fundamental Freedoms, Given on 28 March 1996, Not Yet Reported', 33 *Common Market Law Review* (1996) 973, at 981 ff.; Ruffert, 'Anmerkung zu EuGH, 28. 3. 1996—Gutachten 2/94. Beitritt der Gemeinschaft zur EMRK', 51 *JuristenZeitung* (1996) 623.

[173] See, e.g. the establishment of agencies. See CJEU, Case C-66/04, *United Kingdom v. Parliament and Council* (EU:C:2005:743). In detail, see van Cleynenbreugel, 'Meroni Circumvented? Article 114 TFEU and EU Regulatory Agencies', 21 *Maastricht Journal of European and Comparative Law* (2014) 64, at 64 f.

[174] CJEU, Case C-376/98, *Germany v. Parliament and Council* (EU:C:2000:544) paras 83 f.

criticism has not abated,[175] culminating in the *Bundesverfassungsgericht's* PSPP judgment (see 4.3.B, 5.2.C).

The third discussion concerns the competences for establishing the economic and monetary Union. In response to the serious monetary and economic crisis of 2008, the Union adopted measures that, in all likelihood, exceeded the Treaty legislator's intentions, given that they transformed the European economic constitution.[176] By permitting the use of the economic and monetary competences set out in the Treaties,[177] the Court triggered its most serious conflict with the *Bundesverfassungsgericht* to date,[178] with the Second Senate demanding that the ECB and the CJEU be more responsive to economic policy concerns, such as government debt, savings, pensions, real estate prices, and the survival of non-viable companies. The German court's stance is ironic because it was upon German insistence that the governing provision, Article 127 TFEU, establishes price stability as the ECB's primary objective.[179] Beyond that, the German decision also exposes the fact that Europe's neoliberal orientation is, by and large, a thing of the past.[180]

The CJEU's case law on fundamental rights corroborates the account of a court whose main objective is to promote unity. The Court has introduced and advanced the protection of fundamental rights to much acclaim.[181] But it did so out of federal, not human rights, concerns. The German and the Italian constitutional court had conditioned their acceptance of the primacy of Union law on EU fundamental rights. Therefore, the CJEU's transformative case law originated in an attempt to safeguard the autonomy of the Community legal order.[182] Given this logic, it is unsurprising that the Court's review of Union legislation for fundamental rights compliance was timid for a long time.

Recently, however, the CJEU has hardened its approach in matters of fundamental rights.[183] After the Charter of Fundamental Rights came into force in 2009, the Court intensified its review and invalidated some Union legislative acts, with *Digital Rights Ireland* representing the lodestar of the new approach.[184]

[175] Garben and Govaere, 'The Division of Competences between the EU and the Member States. Reflections on the Past, the Present and the Future', in S. Garben and I. Govaere (eds), *The Division of Competences between the EU and the Member States. Reflections on the Past, the Present and the Future* (2017) 3, at 7.

[176] Ioannidis, 'Europe's New Transformations. How the EU Economic Constitution Changed during the Eurozone Crisis', 53 *Common Market Law Review* (2016) 1237.

[177] CJEU, Case C-493/17, *Weiss et al.* (EU:C:2018:1000).

[178] BVerfGE 154, 17, *Public Sector Purchase Programme—PSPP*, paras 138 ff.

[179] Ibid. paras 165 ff.

[180] Goldmann, 'The European Economic Constitution after the PSPP Judgment. Towards Integrative Liberalism?', 21 *German Law Journal* (2020) 1058.

[181] De Witte, 'The Past and Future Role of the European Court of Justice in the Protection of Human Rights', in P. Alston (ed.), *The EU and Human Rights* (1999) 859.

[182] In detail, Claes and de Witte (n. 99).

[183] See Rosas, 'Five Years of Charter Case Law. Some Observations', in S. A. de Vries, U. Bernitz, and S. Weatherill (eds), *The EU Charter of Fundamental Rights as a Binding Instrument. Five Years Old and Growing* (2015) 11.

[184] CJEU, Joined Cases C-293/12 and C-594/12, *Digital Rights Ireland and Seitlinger et al.* (EU:C:2014:238) para. 47.

Nevertheless, the CJEU continues to adjudicate fundamental rights questions differently than most constitutional courts and the ECtHR. Its main objective is still that Union law have a uniform effect. This orientation is enshrined in perhaps the most important provision of the Charter of Fundamental Rights, Article 51. The Treaty legislator does not wish for the CJEU to set general human rights standards for European society.

The CJEU further cultivates European unity by insisting that the Commission, the Council, and the Parliament cooperate with one another.[185] As already pointed out in the introduction to this chapter, the cooperation between—rather than the separation of—powers can act as a meaningful guiding principle for a political system. For EU legislation to be legitimate and effective, cooperation between the actors involved in the legislative process is essential. The principle of sincere cooperation between EU institutions, which was codified for the first time by the Lisbon Treaty in Article 13(2) TEU, underscores this. To advance such cooperation, the CJEU has developed Article 263(2) TFEU into a procedure that allows the EU institutions to settle conflicts that could jeopardize political decision-making. The *Bundesverfassungsgericht* has a specific procedure for this, the so-called *Organstreit* proceedings (Article 93(1) no. 1 Basic Law). The procedure allows the CJEU to support the Union's parliamentarization as a core element of European unity.[186] The best-known example is the ruling that granted the European Parliament standing rights.[187] While it was legally dubious at the time, the Member States confirmed it by amending Article 263(2) TFEU accordingly.

Summing up, building unity by politicizing Europe in a genuinely European way, rather than merely juridifying it, lies at the heart of the CJEU's case law. Such a stance is common among federal courts. The objective of federal unity explains much of the case law of the apex courts of Switzerland,[188] the United States,[189] and Austria, particularly in the federations' formational period.

2. Enforcing European Law

However, political unity requires more than just the formation of a common political will. That will must also be enforced, thereby entrenching normative expectations (see 3.3.A). This is a chronic problem for a political will formed under international law, be it set out in treaties or the product of international organizations. The modern nation state often pays little respect to international rules,

[185] See, e.g. CJEU, Case C-409/13, *Council v. Commission* (EU:C:2015:217) paras 76 ff.

[186] Ninatti and Arcari, 'Patterns of Democracy in the Case Law of the EU Court of Justice and the European Court of Human Rights', 35 *Polish Yearbook of International Law* (2015) 171.

[187] CJEU, Case 70/88, *Parliament v. Council* (ECLI:EU:C:1990:217) para. 26.

[188] Biaggini (n. 29).

[189] M. Höreth, *Die Selbstautorisierung des Agenten. Der Europäische Gerichtshof im Vergleich zum U.S. Supreme Court* (2008) 191–237.

particularly when they interfere with its policies. For that reason, some even call international law's legal character into question.

Enforcing Community law, the common European political will, has been a central issue since the early 1960s.[190] The pertinent doctrines on autonomy, primacy, and direct effect (see 3.3.C) emerged from what is arguably the most famous line of the CJEU's case law. The most famous narrative about European law, whereby these doctrines constitutionalize the Founding Treaties, is evidence of this.[191]

This narrative begins in 1963 with *Van Gend en Loos*, a case constructed by pro-European forces.[192] Here, the CJEU postulated that a provision of the EEC Treaty had direct effect within national law, meaning that individuals could invoke it before national courts. The subject matter of the dispute was rather harmless, thus facilitating the transformative step. At issue was an import duty of 8 instead of 3 per cent on a chemical substance. That the CJEU marked the ruling's fiftieth anniversary with a grand celebration despite the triviality of the subject matter bears witness to its significance, however.[193] Shortly after *Van Gend en Loos*, *Costa v. ENEL*[194]—a case also strategically litigated for policy reasons[195]—established the primacy of Union law over national law. To this day, these judgments symbolize the very nature of Union law as well as the CJEU's transformative thrust.[196]

The key idea is very simple. At stake is the effectiveness of Union law in regulating societal relations.[197] With the two doctrines of direct effect and primacy, Community law overcame international law's chronic weakness and became relevant to everyday life.[198]

This evolution did not occur overnight. Realizing it took time and proved protracted.[199] Even within the CJEU, these doctrines were initially contested: only four of the seven judges voted in favour of Van Gend en Loos.[200] What is more, *Van Gend en Loos* was a comparatively easy decision for many reasons, including the underlying dispute, the affected country (the Netherlands are particularly open

[190] Vauchez, 'The Transnational Politics of Judicialization. Van Gend en Loos and the Making of EU Polity', 16 *European Law Journal* (2010) 1.

[191] Stein (n. 131); Weiler, 'The Transformation of Europe', 100 *Yale Law Journal* (1991) 2403.

[192] CJEU, Case 26/62, *Van Gend en Loos v. Administratie der Belastingen* (EU:C:1963:1).

[193] CJEU, *50th Anniversary of the Judgment in Van Gend en Loos 1963–2013* (2013); expressive images at https://curia.europa.eu/jcms/jcms/P_101113 (last visited 19 July 2022).

[194] CJEU, Case 6/64, *Costa v. E.N.E.L.* (EU:C:1964:66).

[195] For details on the case's political background, see Arena, 'From an Unpaid Electricity Bill to the Primacy of EU Law. Gian Galeazzo Stendardi and the Making of *Costa v. ENEL*', 30 *European Journal of International Law* (2019) 1017.

[196] But see CJEU, Opinion 2/13, *ECHR Accession II* (EU:C:2014:2454) para. 166.

[197] Pescatore, 'The Doctrine of "Direct Effect". An Infant Disease of Community Law', 8 *European Law Review* (1983) 155.

[198] Lecourt, 'Quel eut été le droit des communautés sans les arrêts de 1963 et 1964?', in *L'Europe et le droit. Mélanges en hommage à Jean Boulouis* (1991) 349, at 360.

[199] K. J. Alter, *Establishing the Supremacy of European Law. The Making of an International Rule of Law in Europe* (2001) 64–181.

[200] For details, see Rasmussen, 'Revolutionizing European Law. A History of the Van Gend en Loos Judgment', 12 *International Journal of Constitutional Law* (2014) 136.

to international law), and the preciseness of the applied provision. The Court expanded the doctrine of direct effect cautiously and in close touch with the European institutions, Member State governments, and national courts. Only in 2016 did a study argue that the direct effect of Union law could be presumed.[201] Union law must be applied, enforced, and sanctioned like national law.

While direct effect is no longer a subject of dispute today, primacy is. The question of its scope lies at the heart of what is arguably the most famous dispute in European law: does primacy of EU law apply without exception (which is what the CJEU maintains) or only within limits that are defined and monitored by the Member States (which is what some national apex courts postulate)?[202] This conflict represents but one aspect of the debate about the structure of European democracy.

The Member States legitimized the CJEU's case law on primacy most prominently in 2009. The Declaration No. 17 concerning primacy, attached to the Treaty of Lisbon, reads:

> The Conference recalls that, in accordance with well settled case law of the Court of Justice of the European Union, the Treaties and the law adopted by the Union on the basis of the Treaties have primacy over the law of Member States, under the conditions laid down by the said case law.' This statement is so clear that the Second Senate of the German Constitutional Court prudently avoids any mention of it.[203]

3. The Procedural Lever

The preliminary ruling proceedings (Article 267 TFEU) represent the CJEU's main mechanism to pursue unity. Most of the decisions mentioned in this book originated in these proceedings. Here, the Court of Justice settles a question of Union law in an interlocutory procedure initiated by a Member State court, which then adjudicates the underlying dispute. The proceedings link the CJEU to the Member State courts, which imbues its interpretations with the national courts' legitimacy and authoritativeness. It forms the bedrock of the union between EU and national courts, which consists of their multilevel cooperation (see 4.2.C). Because of these proceedings, Member State courts double as Union courts. Accordingly, no provision was likely as significant for Europe's judicial transformation as Article 267 TFEU.

[201] C. Wohlfahrt, *Die Vermutung unmittelbarer Wirkung des Unionsrechts. Ein Plädoyer für die Aufgabe der Kriterien hinreichender Genauigkeit und Unbedingtheit* (2016). For a different view, see D. Gallo, *L'efficacia diretta del diritto dell'Unione europea negli ordinamenti nazionali. Evoluzione di una dottrina ancora controversa* (2018).

[202] Schill and Krenn, 'Art. 4 EUV. Prinzipien der föderativen Grundstruktur', in E. Grabitz, M. Hilf, and M. Nettesheim (eds), *Das Recht der Europäischen Union* (2020) paras 24–38.

[203] *Public Sector Purchase Programme—PSPP* (n. 178) paras 234 ff.

The ECSC Treaty of 1951 already included one dimension of these proceedings, namely, the review of the High Authority's acts. The Treaties of Rome then added a further dimension, one that allowed the CJEU to write history. Thanks to this amendment, the CJEU can not only review but also interpret Union law. Given the above remarks on courts' power resources (see 4.1.D), it should come as no surprise that this is the CJEU's most important power. Without it, present-day Europe would look different.

This impact exemplifies how an unanticipated interpretation can open up new horizons. The new dimension of the preliminary reference proceedings originated in the so-called *groupe juridique*, which played an important role in negotiating the Rome Treaties. As Pierre Pescatore, a Luxembourgian member of the group who would later become a CJEU judge, reports, they discussed the preliminary ruling proceedings with reference to the referral procedure before the Italian and German Constitutional Courts (see 4.1.D). Thus, its constitutional dimension was obvious.[204] Nevertheless, the group did not consider that interpreting EU law could allow the CJEU to review Member State law. The group's only concern was the uniform interpretation of the Council's legal acts. No one anticipated the interpretation that the CJEU was to develop in 1963 in the *Van Gend en Loos* judgment, on which European law rests today.

The *Van Gend en Loos* and *Costa v. ENEL* judgments transformed the preliminary reference proceedings into a remedy for scrutinizing Member State legal acts. This has empowered the Member States' lower-instance courts. They can now review legislation and the case law of their apex courts with the help of the CJEU.[205] Given the delicacy of this endeavour, it is helpful that it constitutes a joint enterprise. The CJEU interprets Union law but does not apply it, whereas national courts disapply national legislation but adhere to the CJEU's judgment.[206] The joining of the various resources of legitimacy is a core feature of the European union of courts.

As the proceedings under Article 267 TFEU operate similarly to concrete judicial review in Italy (see 4.1.D), lower-instance courts are the CJEU's most common interlocutors. Only recently have apex and constitutional courts noticeably increased the number of references for preliminary rulings.[207] Nevertheless, the CJEU is determined to keep access open to all courts. An interlocutory procedure in which only apex courts can bring a question before the CJEU, as is the case for access to the *Conseil constitutionnel* (see 4.1.D), does not comply with Union law. There are not many other issues about which the CJEU is so adamant.[208]

[204] Pescatore, 'Les travaux du "groupe juridique" dans la négotiation des traités de Rome', 34 *Revue d'histoire luxembourgeoise* (1982) 145, at 157 f.

[205] Weiler, 'The Transformation of Europe' (n. 191) 2426.

[206] On this relationship, see A.-M. Slaughter, A. Stone Sweet, and J. H. H. Weiler, *The European Court and National Courts. Doctrine & Jurisprudence: Legal Change in its Social Context* (1998).

[207] See Claes and de Witte (n. 99).

[208] *Melki and Abdeli* (n. 101).

The CJEU sets admissibility hurdles low. Similar to the Italian *Corte*, and unlike the German *Bundesverfassungsgericht*, the CJEU only demands that the national court plausibly describe why a reference is relevant to the dispute before it. Hence, many important questions reach the Court of Justice and allow it to shape the legal structures of European society and intervene in crucial debates.[209] The attempt of Polish authoritarian forces to prohibit Polish judges from making such references underscores how significant this openness is not only for European unity but also for European democracy (see 3.6.A, 4.6.C).

C. Human Rights Juridification: The ECtHR

1. The European Rights Revolution

The ECtHR is the other genuinely European court in European society. Its transformation is different to the CJEU's but just as important. Its core contribution is embedding human rights in Europe's legal structure.[210] This is significant because respecting individual rights has become a paramount requirement for public authority to be legitimate.[211] Some have called this, somewhat hyperbolically, the rights revolution.[212] We have already encountered this development in Latin America, where human rights even served to fight extreme forms of repression (see 2.6.C). In Europe, the human rights proclaimed in the 1975 Helsinki Final Act helped overcome authoritarian socialism.[213] But human rights also had a role in transforming Western societies, and this is where the ECtHR comes in.

The ECtHR expanded individual rights throughout Europe, thus democratizing and also Europeanizing national societies. The ECtHR's role lends itself to various interpretations: we can consider it inspiration for human rights protection,[214] a law-making constitutional court,[215] or the final instance for protecting the individual.[216] From the perspective of a democratic European society, what is

[209] Consider the example of Brexit and CJEU, Case C-621/18, *Wightman et al.* (EU:C:2018:999) paras 20–36.

[210] Helfer, 'Redesigning the European Court of Human Rights. Embeddedness as a Deep Structural Principle of the European Human Rights Regime', 19 *European Journal of International Law* (2008) 125; F. J. García Roca, *La transformación del Convenio Europeo de Derechos Humanos* (2019) 69 f.

[211] On the reasons, see Kennedy (n. 21) 61 ff; S. Moyn, *The Last Utopia. Human Rights in History* (2010) 8.

[212] C. R. Epp, *The Rights Revolution. Lawyers, Activists, and Supreme Courts in Comparative Perspective* (1998); M. de S.-O.-l'E. Lasser, *Judicial Transformations. The Rights Revolution in the Courts of Europe* (2009).

[213] J. Eckel, *The Ambivalence of Good: Human Rights in International Politics since the 1940s* (2019) 292 ff.

[214] Çalı, 'The Purposes of the European Human Rights System. One or Many?', 3 *European Human Rights Law Review* (2008) 299, at 303.

[215] Walter, 'Art. 93 GG' (n. 45) paras 84 ff.

[216] ECtHR, High Level Conference on the Future of the European Court of Human Rights: Brighton Declaration, 19–20 April 2012, para. 35c.

especially significant is that it imposes a duty of justification on any exercise of authority. I propose calling this the human rights juridification.[217]

The ECtHR is relevant to European democratic society in three ways. First, it has brought human rights, which have become constitutive for a democratic society, to all corners of Europe.[218] Second, it conceives the Convention rights so broadly that virtually any exercise of authority is subject to justification, including authority under private law, provided a private relationship exhibits vast asymmetries of power.[219] While rights restrictions certainly remain permissible, they must be justified: they must be based in democratic law, sufficiently determinate, and proportionate. The right to justification can be reconstructed, as does Rainer Forst, as the essence of a democratic society. The third contribution of the ECtHR's case law to European democratic society lies in supplying basic concepts for discourses in which this society produces itself (see 1.2).[220]

The ECtHR could assume this role because many Convention states lacked, at that time, a modern rights catalogue or institutions truly exercising constitutional adjudication.[221] These deficiencies provided the ECtHR and the (former) Commission on Human Rights with an opportunity to become relevant. They exploited it by beginning to support the rights revolution in many countries, thereby taking on a task comparable to a constitutional court. In the wake of EEC integration,[222] the ECtHR mustered the support of many actors and gained a key role in the democratic rule of law in Europe. Today, it is identified with this role.[223]

The Court's assumption of this role was not simple.[224] Rather, it had to prudently accumulate authoritativeness and legitimacy. A first step was convincing States to ratify the protocols that provided for the individual complaint to the Human Rights Commission and for the Court's jurisdiction. Therefore, the Commission

[217] I owe this notion to Jürgen Bast.

[218] Stone Sweet and Keller, 'The Reception of the ECHR in National Legal Orders', in A. Stone Sweet and H. Keller (eds), *A Europe of Rights. The Impact of the ECHR on National Legal Systems* (2008) 3.

[219] Krieger, 'Funktionen von Grund- und Menschenrechten', in O. Dörr, R. Grote, and T. Marauhn (eds), *EMRK/GG. Konkordanzkommentar zum europäischen und deutschen Grundrechtsschutz* (2013) 287.

[220] Forst, 'The Justification of Basic Rights: A Discourse-Theoretical Approach', 45 *Netherlands Journal of Legal Philosophy* (2016) 7, at 8 ff.; Forst, 'The Nature of Human Rights', in D. Held and P. Maffettone (eds), *Global Political Theory* (2016) 22.

[221] For the Netherlands, see, e.g. Wessel and van de Griendt, 'Niederlande. § 19', in A. von Bogdandy, P. Cruz Villalón, and P. M. Huber (eds), *Handbuch Ius Publicum Europaeum, Bd. II. Offene Staatlichkeit—Wissenschaft vom Verfassungsrecht* (2008) 177, at paras 52 ff.; for Austria, see Grabenwarter, 'Österreich. § 20', in A. von Bogdandy, P. Cruz Villalón, and P. M. Huber (eds), *Handbuch Ius Publicum Europaeum, Bd. II. Offene Staatlichkeit—Wissenschaft vom Verfassungsrecht* (2008) 211, at paras 64 ff.

[222] Madsen, 'The Challenging Authority of the European Court of Human Rights: From Cold War Legal Diplomacy to the Brighton Declaration and Backlash', 70 *Law and Contemporary Problems* (2016) 141, at 152.

[223] Copenhagen Declaration (n. 105) para. 2.

[224] In detail, see Madsen, 'From Cold War Instrument to Supreme European Court. The European Court of Human Rights at the Crossroads of International and National Law and Politics', 32 *Law & Social Inquiry* (2007) 137.

on Human Rights' and the ECtHR's minimalist interpretations in the 1960s are hardly surprising for respecting sovereignty was their focus.

The 1967 Greek military coup brought the European human rights system to a critical juncture. The Commission had to decide whether the Convention should remain primarily symbolic, as the antithesis of Soviet socialism, or should begin to play a practical role in the West. Much like the Inter-American Commission a few years later, the Human Rights Commission was wise enough to seize the opportunity.[225]

On this basis, the ECtHR likewise began to change its cautious stance from the mid-1970s onwards. By then, all 18 members of the Council of Europe had ratified the Convention, and 13 of them had consented to the jurisdiction of the ECtHR. They included France and the United Kingdom, the two dominant states that were initially very sceptical about submitting to the ECtHR. In the phase of growing acceptance and authoritativeness, the central question was how the Convention should be interpreted: in terms of traditional international law (i.e. with due respect to state sovereignty) or in constitutional terms, which would serve to limit state power. This question came to a head in *Golder v. United Kingdom*,[226] which plays a similar role in the narrative about the ECtHR as *Van Gend en Loos* does for the CJEU.

Golder v. United Kingdom concerned the rights of a prison inmate, Sidney Elmer Golder, who sought to bring proceedings against a prison warden for defamation and wished to seek legal counsel. When his request was refused, he lodged a complaint with the ECHR Commission. The United Kingdom argued that the Convention should be interpreted narrowly, it being a treaty between sovereign states. The Commission took a different view, and the Court followed suit. It found that the right to a fair trial guaranteed access to a court, although Article 6 ECHR does not explicitly state as much. According to the Court's core argument, every interpretation must take into account the Convention's objective and purpose if it wishes to be of any use to the aggrieved individual.[227] The critical-juncture cases of the ECtHR and the CJEU could not be more different: the former featured a prisoner's right to a fair trial, the latter a large company's right to a lower tariff rate.

Much like *Van Gend en Loos*, *Golder* was a disputed decision within the court. It was issued by nine votes to three, and the three dissenting votes were vehement. Thus, the famous Austrian judge Verdross, a student of Kelsen and one of the fathers of international constitutionalism, pointed out that the ECtHR was special among international courts because it had to adjudicate conflicts arising not

[225] Becket, 'The Greek Case before the European Human Rights Commission', 1 *Human Rights* (1970) 91.

[226] ECtHR, *Golder v. United Kingdom*, Appl. no. 4451/70, Judgment of 21 February 1975, Series A, No. 18, paras 26–36.

[227] Ibid. paras 34–36.

between but *within* contracting states. Therefore, he argued, the majority had got it wrong, and the Convention had to be interpreted narrowly.[228]

Verdross did not convince his fellow judges, and the Court moved forward. It argued that any interpretation of the Convention must recognize that it contains rights that are meant to be 'practical and effective' rather than 'theoretical or illusory'.[229] Moreover, the Court conceived the Convention as a living instrument that must be interpreted according to the changing challenges of evolving societies.[230] Thus, the ECtHR's interpretation moved away from the standards of international law.[231] This was decisive for the Convention's societal embedding for its rights became autonomous, relevant, and dynamic.

Today, the ECtHR's decisions are hardly distinguishable from the decisions of constitutional courts.[232] One of the Court's most famous statements, whereby the Convention is a 'constitutional instrument of European public order',[233] clearly expresses its constitutional self-conception. The ECtHR cannot be said to merely adjudicate individual cases because its decisions set precedents that claim authority throughout Europe.[234]

Since this claim drew criticism, the ECtHR granted the Member States a so-called margin of appreciation. This ingenious doctrine[235] mitigated the resistance without altering the ECtHR's constitutional, and indeed transformative, thrust. As a matter of fact, constitutional courts utilize similar doctrines, for example, legislative discretion.[236]

The *procedural* margin of appreciation constitutes a remarkable development of this doctrine.[237] It allows the ECtHR to review whether domestic judicial and parliamentary procedures consider and process the Convention rights, that is, whether the latter are sufficiently entrenched. Thus, the ECtHR is more likely to

[228] *Golder v. United Kingdom* (n. 226) separate Opinion of Judge Verdross.

[229] ECtHR, *Airey v. Ireland*, Appl. no. 6289/73, Judgment of 9 October 1979, Series A, No. 32, para. 24.

[230] ECtHR, *Tyrer v. United Kingdom*, Appl. no. 5856/72, Judgment of 25 April 1978, Series A, No. 26, para. 31.

[231] Letsas, 'The ECHR as a Living Instrument: Its Meaning and Legitimacy', in A. Føllesdal, B. Peters, and G. Ulfstein (eds), *Constituting Europe. The European Court of Human Rights in a National, European and Global Context* (2013) 106.

[232] Walter, 'Die Europäische Menschenrechtskonvention als Konstitutionalisierungsprozeß', 59 *Zeitschrift für ausländisches öffentliches Recht und Völkerrecht* (1999) 961.

[233] ECtHR, *Loizidou v. Turkey*, Appl. no. 15318/89, (Preliminary Objections) Judgment of 23 March 1995, Series A, No. 310, para. 75.

[234] See ECtHR, *Ireland v. United Kingdom*, Appl. no. 5310/71, Judgment of 18 January 1978, Series A, No. 25, para. 154.

[235] J. Asche, *Die Margin of Appreciation. Entwurf einer Dogmatik monokausaler richterlicher Zurückhaltung für den europäischen Menschenrechtsschutz* (2018) 13 ff.

[236] Grewe, 'Vergleich zwischen den Interpretationsmethoden europäischer Verfassungsgerichte und des Europäischen Gerichtshofes für Menschenrechte', 61 *Zeitschrift für ausländisches öffentliches Recht und Völkerrecht* (2001) 459, at 465.

[237] J. Gerards, 'Procedural Review by the ECtHR: A Typology', in J. Gerards and E. Brems (eds), *Procedural Review in European Fundamental Rights Cases* (2017) 127.

accept national judgments if they demonstrate that the Court's case law served as their guide.[238] The same applies to parliamentary procedures.

The procedural margin of appreciation has great potential for entrenching European human rights. It promotes the Convention and the ECtHR's case law while respecting constitutional diversity.[239] Nevertheless, it faces challenges, particularly when it comes to parliamentary procedures. It is questionable whether the ECtHR can adequately evaluate parliamentary debates. Moreover, seeing an international court tell MPs which arguments to use can be difficult to stomach. This becomes evident in the United Kingdom's sharp criticism of the ECtHR's finding that Parliament's debate on prisoners' human rights missed the mark.[240]

The ECtHR developed its role primarily with regard to states parties that lacked constitutional adjudication or a modern catalogue of fundamental rights. One may wonder what role the ECtHR plays for states that, like Germany or Italy, have both; their constitutional courts ensure individual rights and do not need the Strasbourg Court's help to do so. Accordingly, the Court plays a somewhat different role here: it primarily embeds cases from these countries in the European rights discourse, thus reinforcing these states and societies' Europeanness. Thanks to the decisions of the Strasbourg Court, German and Italian fundamental rights protection is embedded in a pan-European human rights system that has a common vocabulary, a common case-based doctrine, and even the beginnings of a common legal culture. Of course, this achievement requires the Strasbourg Court to review these constitutional courts.[241]

The ECtHR's transformative case law has provoked resistance.[242] Beginning in 2010, the states parties started reviewing the ECtHR's performance in the so-called Interlaken Process, accompanied by lively scholarly debate.[243] The outcome of that process, which was laid down in the Copenhagen Declaration of April 2018, confirms, in principle, the Court's mandate as developed over more than a generation.[244] The Court continues to enjoy the support of many important actors.[245]

[238] Spano, 'The Future of the European Court of Human Rights – Subsidiarity, Process-Based Review and the Rule of Law', 18 *European Human Rights Law Review* (2018) 473, at 487–488.

[239] Kleinlein, 'The Procedural Approach of the European Court of Human Rights. Between Subsidiarity and Dynamic Evolution', 68 *International & Comparative Law Quarterly* (2019) 91.

[240] Nußberger, 'Procedural Review by the ECHR. View from the Court', in Gerards and Brems (n. 237) 161, at 163.

[241] Paris, 'Allies and Counterbalances. Constitutional Courts and the European Court of Human Rights. A Comparative Perspective', 77 *Zeitschrift für ausländisches öffentliches Recht und Völkerrecht* (2017) 623.

[242] M. Breuer (ed.), *Principled Resistance to ECtHR Judgments. A New Paradigm?* (2019).

[243] Çalı (n. 214); Keller, Fischer, and Kühne, 'Debating the Future of the European Court of Human Rights after the Interlaken Conference. Two Innovative Proposals', 21 *European Journal of International Law* (2010) 1025.

[244] Copenhagen Declaration (n. 105) paras 26 ff.

[245] Council of Europe, *The Interlaken Process: Measures Taken from 2010 to 2019 to Secure the Effective Implementation of the European Convention on Human Rights* (2020).

The Declaration confirms that every state party has the fundamental duty to enforce its judgments.[246]

The Interlaken Process, which many considered a threat to the ECtHR's authority, thus strengthened the Court's role for the democratic rule of law in Europe.[247] It proved that the voices of systemic criticism are much more isolated than they sometimes appear. In the end, then, the Court's politicization supported human rights juridification.

2. The Procedural Lever

The individual complaint (Article 34 ECHR) constitutes the Convention system's procedural lever,[248] providing for the human rights juridification of European society. Article 34 ECHR ensures that there is a steady stream of cases, and individuals have direct access. This certainly was not always so; it represents an achievement of the second period of European public law. Until 1994, there was only the individual complaint to the European Commission of Human Rights. Protocol No. 9 then allowed complainants to transfer their claim from the Commission to the Court. Protocol No. 11, in force since 1998, abolished the Commission altogether and provided for direct access.[249]

Today, the individual complaint before the Strasbourg Court has a scope similar to that of the constitutional complaint in Germany[250] or Spain.[251] Since the Convention does not distinguish between public bodies, the Court exercises its review over the administration, judiciary, legislature,[252] and even constitutional law.[253] At the same time, the ECtHR is far weaker than constitutional courts because it cannot strike down an act in violation of the Convention.[254] Sometimes, however, the Court determines how a violation should be remedied.[255]

An individual complaint can only be lodged once the domestic legal proceedings have been concluded (Article 35(1) ECHR). It is not an interlocutory procedure like the preliminary reference proceedings before the CJEU under Article

[246] See Copenhagen Declaration (n. 105) paras 19 ff.

[247] Ibid. para. 2.

[248] On inter-state complaints, which have recently become more important, see Ulfstein and Risini, 'Inter-State Applications under the European Convention on Human Rights. Strengths and Challenges', *EJIL:Talk!* (24 January 2020).

[249] Schlette, 'Europäischer Menschenrechtsschutz nach der Reform der EMRK', 54 *JuristenZeitung* (1999) 219.

[250] Farahat, 'The German Federal Constitutional Court' (n. 29) 313–324.

[251] Requejo Pagés, 'The Spanish Constitutional Tribunal' (n. 29) 745–749.

[252] ECtHR, *Marckx v. Belgium*, Appl. no. 6833/74, Judgment of 13 June 1979, Series A, No. 31, para. 58.

[253] ECtHR, *Baka v. Hungary*, Appl. no. 20261/12, Judgment of 23 June 2016, ECHR 2016.

[254] Frowein, 'Art. 46 EMRK', in J. A. Frowein and W. Peukert (eds), *Europäische Menschenrechtskonvention* (2009) 602.

[255] See the dissenting Opinion of Judge Pinto de Albuquerque (joined by Judges Karakaş, Sajó, Lazarova Trajkovska, Tsotsoria, Vehabović, and Kūros) in ECtHR, *Moreira Ferreira v. Portugal (No. 2)*, Appl. no. 19867/12, Judgment of 11 July 2017, ECHR 2017, paras 2–18.

267 TFEU, which has proved so useful for providing a close link to the national judiciary. Therefore, it is no wonder that many advocate its introduction in the Convention system. Indeed, Protocol No. 16 has provided for an interlocutory procedure since 2018. However, it allows only national apex courts to involve the ECtHR, and the Court's decisions are only advisory.[256] The ECtHR's leverage, and thus its transformative power, remain much weaker than that of the CJEU.[257]

Nevertheless, the individual complaint ties the ECtHR to national courts. The requirement of exhausting all domestic legal recourse often (though not always) means that a constitutional court decides on the case prior to the ECtHR. This creates some interaction between the national constitutional court and the ECtHR.[258] Forms of dialogue have developed, and they often lead to the resolution of a juridical conflict.[259] In Germany, the detention conditions of potential criminals provide an example.[260] Of course, such dialogue only works if all institutions involved are willing to cooperate (see 4.4.B).

In this way, the ECHR and the ECtHR have become embedded in European society. The 44,500 complaints that reached the Court in 2019 prove as much. Today, the compulsory canon of legal training mostly includes the Strasbourg system. When the ECtHR refers to itself as 'the conscience of Europe',[261] it solemnly articulates a European societal fact. It also represents European society's principles to the rest of the world, being Europe's most cited court in foreign judgments.[262]

D. The Power of European Precedent

The CJEU and the ECtHR can only shape European society if their decisions have precedential effects, that is, if their case law has a law-making function (see 4.1.C). While the details remain controversial, some cornerstones are largely undisputed. Most importantly, the precedential effect of CJEU and ECtHR judgments is generally recognized, even though there is no equivalent to the Anglo-American

[256] Protocol No. 16 to the Convention for the Protection of Human Rights and Fundamental Freedoms.

[257] See also Lemmens, 'Protocol No. 16 to the ECHR: Managing Backlog through Complex Judicial Dialogue', 15 *European Constitutional Law Review* (2019) 691.

[258] See Van de Heyning, 'Constitutional Courts as Guardians of Fundamental Rights. The Constitutionalisation of the Convention through Domestic Constitutional Adjudication', in Popelier, Mazmanyan, and Vandenbruwaene (n. 97) 19, at 21.

[259] See Gerards, 'The European Court of Human Rights and the National Courts' (n. 104) 75–82.

[260] Pollähne, 'Europäische Rechtssicherheit gegen Deutsches Sicherheitsrecht? Zur EGMR-Entscheidung in Sachen nachträgliche (Verlängerung der) Sicherungsverwahrung', 43 *Kritische Justiz* (2010) 255.

[261] Council of Europe, *The Conscience of Europe: 50 Years of the European Court of Human Rights* (2010); critically, see Dzehtsiarou and Tzevelekos, 'The Conscience of Europe That Landed in Strasbourg. A Circle of Life of the European Court of Human Rights', 1 *ECHR Law Review* (2020) 1.

[262] Jakab (n. 40).

doctrine of *stare decisis*.[263] Both courts can speak, as a matter of course, of their case *law*.

The general recognition of the European courts' law-making is facilitated greatly by the fact that all Member State apex courts engage in precedential law-making as well (see 4.1.C): all courts employ their previous decisions as the most important argument to justify new decisions. Accordingly, most lawyers take the courts' precedent into account when crafting their arguments. From the first term of their university studies onwards, prospective lawyers are trained to work with the decisions by the judges of national, and now also European, apex courts. This practice is key to European legal culture and the courts' power to shape society.

The specific authoritativeness of apex courts' law-making turns on them being apex courts, that is, the final recourse once all legal remedies have been exhausted. Such remedies do not exist between the national courts and the ECtHR or CJEU. Though there are procedures that link the latter two to the national courts (namely, the preliminary ruling proceedings (CJEU) and the individual complaint (ECtHR)), neither is conceived as a legal remedy that can quash the decision of the adjudicating domestic court. Nevertheless, both courts have invented strategies that turn their decisions into influential precedents, though with considerable differences.

The CJEU has been more successful in that respect than the ECtHR, with the doctrine established in the *CILFIT* judgment proving integral.[264] Once again, a deep transformation took place in a restrained manner. The judgment concerned rather trivial fees for health inspections, and the Court formulated its doctrine cautiously. It postulated that its judgments serve as a precedent for national courts purely in procedural terms, for the *CILFIT* doctrine only determines when a final national court can dispense with a reference for a preliminary ruling. This is the case when 'previous decisions of the Court have already dealt with the point in question' and the national court follows them. This can hardly be contested as *ultra vires*. However, the very point of this principle is that it implies the domestic court's duty to refer in all other cases. As a result, national courts are firmly bound to the CJEU's precedents, a tie secured by procedural law. With this ingenious move, the Court evaded the difficult question of which legal ground justified its rulings' precedential effect. And it proved successful throughout Europe.[265] The German

[263] M. Jacob, *Precedents and Case-Based Reasoning in the European Court of Justice. Unfinished Business* (2014) 218 ff.; M. Payandeh, *Judikative Rechtserzeugung. Theorie, Dogmatik und Methodik der Wirkung von Präjudizien* (2017) 11 ff.

[264] CJEU, Case 283/81, *CILFIT v. Ministero della Sanità* (EU:C:1982:335); U. Haltern, *Europarecht. Dogmatik im Kontext, Bd. 2. Rule of Law—Verbunddogmatik—Grundrechte* (3rd edn, 2017) 129 ff. On the need to adapt the doctrine, see Case C-561/19, *Consorzio Italian Management and Catania Multiservizi SpA v. Rete Ferroviaria Italiana SpA*, Opinion of AG Bobek (EU:C:2021:291).

[265] CJEU, *Research Note: Application of the Cilfit Case-Law by National Courts or Tribunals against Whose Decisions There Is No Judicial Remedy under National Law* (2019); Bobek, 'Europeanization of Public Law', in von Bogdandy, Huber, and Cassese (n. 16) 631, at 640 ff., 649 ff.

Constitutional Court supports this doctrine explicitly, holding that any German court that does not comply with the doctrine violates the Basic Law.[266]

The ECtHR also attributes precedential effect to its decisions.[267] In principle, its claim is widely recognized.[268] It enjoys the backing of the Convention states.[269] However, reservations are more common regarding the ECtHR than the CJEU. The case law of the *Bundesverfassungsgericht* and the Italian *Corte* demonstrate as much.

The German Constitutional Court ascribes a 'factual function of direction and guidance' to the Strasbourg Court's case law.[270] All German courts must therefore give 'due consideration' to relevant ECtHR judgments in their decision-making process. Although the Convention only has the rank of a federal statute (Article 59(2) of the Basic Law), the ECtHR's case law serves as an 'interpretative aid' when it comes to fundamental rights and rule-of-law principles contained in the Basic Law. Moreover, a constitutional complaint can be based on a violation of the Convention.[271] However, the German Constitutional Court continues interpreting German fundamental rights rather independently of the Strasbourg Court's case law.[272]

The *Corte costituzionale*, by contrast, often uses the ECHR, as interpreted by the ECtHR, as the primary yardstick for its constitutional review.[273] With its decisions no. 348 and 349 from 2007, the so-called twin decisions,[274] the *Corte* assumed the power to review Italian statutes for compliance with the Convention. It did so by referring to Article 117(1) of the Italian Constitution, which mandates that statutes must respect international obligations. Daniel Thym has coined a fitting slogan: 'Unite all fundamental rights!'[275]

In Italy, the ECHR, as interpreted by the Strasbourg Court, provides the main standard of review for constitutionality, and the interpretation of Italian

266 BVerfGE 73, 339, *Solange II*, 366 f.; Britz, 'Verfassungsrechtliche Effektivierung des Vorabentscheidungsverfahrens', 19 *Neue Juristische Wochenschrift* (2012) 1313; comparatively X. Arzoz Santisteban, *La garantía constitucional del deber de reenvío prejudicial* (2020).

267 See, e.g. *Ireland v. United Kingdom* (n. 234) para. 154; *Opuz v. Turkey*, Appl. no. 33401/02, Judgment of 9 June 2006, ECHR 2009, para. 163. The following passage is based on A. von Bogdandy and L. Hering, 'In the Name of the European Club of Liberal Democracies. On the Identity, Mandate and National Buffering of the ECTHR's Case Law', in H. Ruiz Fabri *et al.* (eds), *International Judicial Legitimacy: New Voices and Approaches* (2020) 2710.

268 M. Payandeh, 'Die Präjudizienwirkung der Entscheidungen des Europäischen Gerichtshofs für Menschenrechte', 68 *Jahrbuch des öffentlichen Rechts* (2020) 1.

269 See Copenhagen Declaration (n. 105) para. 26.

270 *Ban on Strike Action for Civil Servants* (n. 120) para. 129, with further references. For a seminal account, see Mosler, 'Schlußbericht', in I. Maier (ed.), *Europäischer Menschenrechtsschutz. Schranken und Wirkungen* (1982) 333, at 355, 366.

271 *Görgülü* (n. 119).

272 Exemplarily presented in *Ban on Strike Action for Civil Servants* (n. 120) paras 172 ff.

273 On the development, see Bifulco and Paris (n. 18) 494 f.

274 Corte costituzionale, sentenze n. 348 and 349/2007. On the so-called twin decisions, see Barsotti *et al.*, *Italian Constitutional Justice in Global Context* (n. 50) 226.

275 Thym, 'Vereinigt die Grundrechte!', 70 *JuristenZeitung* (2015) 53. In detail, see T. Kleinlein, *Grundrechtsföderalismus* (2020) 335 ff.

fundamental rights is closely linked to Convention rights. This serves the ECtHR but also the *Corte*. Importantly, the *Corte* prohibits the ordinary courts from declaring statutes violative of the Convention, which had seemed possible under Article 117(1) of the Italian Constitution and was practised by some courts.[276] The *Corte* claims this power for itself alone.[277] Thus, it avoids losing vast ground to the *Corte di Cassazione* and the *Consiglio di Stato*. The *Bundesverfassungsgericht* preempts any such development by granting the Convention merely statutory rank.

Conflicts arise when the CJEU and ECtHR claim authority beyond what the national courts are willing to accept. Once again, the *Bundesverfassungsgericht* and the *Corte* provide insightful examples. Both articulate the limits of the precedential effect of CJEU judgments, applying their general doctrines on supranational public authority. Thus, the *Bundesverfassungsgericht* applies its *Solange*, *ultra vires*, and identity doctrines, while the *Corte* applies its *controlimiti* doctrine.[278] Since these doctrines only target exceptional cases, both courts largely recognize the precedential effect of CJEU judgments in the sense of the *CILFIT* doctrine.

The ECtHR's claim that its judgments have precedential effects is similarly categorical.[279] It does not differentiate between the decision of a panel of 3, a chamber of 7, or the Grand Chamber of 17 judges; neither does it distinguish between new developments and case law that has been consolidated in different constellations by several decisions.[280]

Many courts, including the German Constitutional Court and the *Corte costituzionale*, do not accept the ECtHR's categorical claim. The judgment of the Second Senate on the ban on strike action by civil servants limits the precedential effect for German courts. Thus, the latter must only 'identify [the ECtHR's] statements regarding principal values enshrined in the Convention and address them'.[281] Furthermore, German law can only be interpreted in accordance with the Convention '[i]f German courts have latitude for interpreting and balancing within the scope of recognized methods of the interpretation of laws'. And even within this framework, German courts may never proceed 'schematically' but must carefully 'integrate' the ECtHR's case law into the domestic constitutional order and the 'existing, dogmatically differentiated national legal system'. This is particularly true for the reception of ECtHR decisions not issued against Germany. The *Bundesverfassungsgericht* thus limits the precedential effect of ECtHR case law

[276] Martinico, 'Judicial Disobedience and the ECtHR. The Italian Case', in Breuer (n. 242) 137, at 139 ff.

[277] Paris and Oellers-Frahm, 'Zwei weitere völkerrechts, unfreundliche' Entscheidungen des italienischen Verfassungsgerichthofs aus dem Jahr 2015 (Nr. 49 und 50)', *Europäische Grundrechte-Zeitschrift* (2016) 245, at 246.

[278] See 3.2.D and, for a recent example, BVerfGE 156, 182, *European Arrest Warrant II*, para. 40; Corte costituzionale, ordinanza n. 24/2017, *Taricco*.

[279] CJEU, *Research Note* (n. 265) 29 ff, 158 ff.

[280] ECtHR, *G.I.E.M. S.R.L. a.o. v. Italy*, Appl. nos 1828/06, 34163/07, 19029/11, Judgment of 28 June 2018, para. 252.

[281] *Ban on Strike Action for Civil Servants* (n. 120) paras 132.

by requiring national courts to critically assess its possible impact. In other words, it institutes a buffer. This is a far cry from the precedential effect that the Karlsruhe Court assigns to its own decisions but also to the decisions of the CJEU.[282]

The *Corte*'s case law provides for a similar buffering. In 2015, the *Corte* decided that Italian courts need only follow the ECtHR's pilot judgments or consolidated case law.[283] Criteria for the latter include whether the decision in question was handed down by the Grand Chamber, whether it is settled case law, and whether there are dissenting opinions, but also whether the case law fits the Italian legal order.

These buffering doctrines have drawn sharp criticism.[284] They undermine the ECtHR's authoritativeness, they are vague, they might promote arbitrariness, and they are simply impractical for the average judge. At the same time, the buffering implies that the national courts—and the apex courts, in particular—share the burden of legitimizing the ECtHR's case law. This, in turn, supports the difficult business of human rights juridification. The democratic legitimation of ECtHR decisions is weak, especially when it comes to adjudicating societally contested matters.

The opening of national legal orders to ECtHR precedent places an immense burden of legitimation on the Court. Contrary to the Luxembourg Court, there is no corresponding legislature. Against that background, the supposed weakening of the ECtHR through national buffering turns out to provide justificatory relief. If the domestic courts are not strictly bound to Strasbourg precedent, they assume responsibility and contribute their own democratic legitimation to the Court's case law. This leads to a general feature of European public law: the common but differentiated responsibility of all courts.

4. Common but Differentiated Responsibility

The pluralistic nature of European society is reflected in the pluralism of its institutions. European law is not subject to an apex court as in India or the United States. Ultimate responsibility is shared by various institutions that are each integrated into different contexts. This already shows in the various institutions' legal bases: the CJEU's lies in the EU Treaty, the ECtHR's in the ECHR, and the Member State courts' in their respective constitutions. Similarly, the judges swear different oaths of office. At the same time, they all serve the union of the peoples of Europe (see 2.2.D). Thus, all courts have a common but differentiated responsibility for

282 Payandeh, *Judikative Rechtserzeugung* (n. 263) 373 ff.

283 Corte costituzionale, sentenza n. 49/2015, para. 7; Paris and Oellers-Frahm (n. 277) 247 ff.

284 Viganò, 'La Consulta e la tela di Penelope', 2 *Diritto Penale Contemporaneo* (2015) 333; Keller and Walther, 'The Bell of Görgülü Can't Be Unrung—Can It?', 19 *Global Community Yearbook of International Law and Jurisprudence* (2020) 83.

European law. In what follows, I will address three aspects of this responsibility: the relationship between the CJEU and the ECtHR (see 4.4.A), the relationship of these two courts to the constitutional courts (see 4.4.B), and their shared positioning against authoritarian structures (see 4.4.C).

A. The CJEU and ECtHR's Complementarity

Many European citizens, and even some lawyers, have difficulty distinguishing between the Luxembourg and the Strasbourg courts. The two institutions are often mistaken for one another. Common wisdom says that disenchantment with the ECtHR caused much of Brexit. But if we only smile smugly in response, we overlook a deep truth that becomes apparent in this mix-up.

The ECtHR and the CJEU pursue different mandates: while the ECtHR seeks to juridify power relations by means of human rights juridification, the CJEU aims to cultivate European unity (see 3.3.A). However, we can give these different orientations a constructive turn for the two mandates can be understood as complementary in the emergence and democratization of European society. The ECtHR strives for a society within which any exercise of power must be justified, while the CJEU is primarily orientated towards a common public authority that makes a European democratic society possible in the first place. Thus, they have differentiated tasks but a common purpose.

We can describe this complementarity with a metaphor that depicts the two courts as the two senates of European society's apex court.[285] This metaphor is inspired by the German Constitutional Court, which is divided into two senates, with the First Senate focusing on fundamental rights and the Second on institutional issues. In the light of this metaphor, I will now compare how the ECtHR and the CJEU contribute to European society. In substance, I submit a doctrinal reconstruction that reflects their common responsibility.

I conceive the metaphor of the two senates from the perspective of Union law. This understanding is supported by Articles 2 and 6(3) TEU and Article 52(3) of the EU Charter of Fundamental Rights (CFR). These provisions establish that the ECHR and the ECtHR's case law are foundational for the EU.

Article 2 TEU bases the Union on human rights and not on fundamental rights, that is, not on the CFR. Human rights are conceived as universal and are guaranteed by international law. By contrast, fundamental rights are guarantees under constitutional law and are specific to a polity. Since Article 2 TEU bases the Union on human rights, it embeds the Union in a broader normative framework than just its own constitutional order. The role that the EU Treaty thus assigns to the ECHR,

[285] The idea emerged from a conversation with Juan Luis Requejo Pagés. It was first elaborated in von Bogdandy and Krenn (n. 133).

and by extension to the ECtHR, secures this orientation institutionally. European society, organized in the EU, ascribes a constitutional role to the ECtHR. Thus, it installs a powerful safeguard against EU particularism, all the more so because the ECtHR's case law reflects universal human rights.[286] That the ECtHR has a broader geographic remit than the CJEU is not a weakness of European public law, then, but an expression of its universalist orientation.

Discussing the objections that come to mind helps clarify my proposal. The first objection concerns the territorial discrepancy between the two courts' jurisdiction. The CJEU's jurisdiction is limited to the 27 EU Member States, while the ECtHR's includes a further 20 states parties. Yet, the fuzziness that results from this discrepancy is part and parcel of the meaningful fuzziness of European society (see 3.2.D). Admittedly, it is a problem that judges sent from authoritarian states such as Azerbaijan, Russia, and Turkey participate in interpreting the ECHR. Should the ECtHR, due to the membership of such states, increasingly hand down rulings that are incompatible with Article 2 TEU, the synthesis of the two courts propagated here would no longer hold. However, there are no signs of such a takeover.

Combining the CJEU and the ECtHR in this way does not deny their differences. The two courts are based on different legal foundations. They are embedded in different organizations: the CJEU in the rich EU, and the ECtHR in the chronically underfunded Council of Europe. Accordingly, CJEU judges are driven around by chauffeurs in luxury cars, while you may run into ECtHR judges in public transport. Procedurally, the two courts are not yet linked to one another.

Nor does my reconstruction claim that the two courts always cooperate.[287] For a long time, the two courts simply co-existed. When the CFR entered into force in 2009, the relationship turned uncooperative. The Luxembourg Court began to develop its own case law on fundamental rights, which threatened to marginalize the ECtHR.[288] Then the CJEU halted the EU's accession to the ECHR for the second time in December 2014, a move interpreted as a hostile act.[289] Its opinion in this matter was awkward because the Treaty legislator had responded to the CJEU's first negative opinion by introducing, in 2009, an explicit mandate to join the ECHR (Article 6(2) TEU).[290] The CJEU's attitude towards the ECtHR is somewhat

[286] Sicilianos, 'The European Court of Human Rights Facing the Security Council. Towards Systemic Harmonization', 66 *International & Comparative Law Quarterly* (2017) 783, at 804.

[287] On tensions between the Senates of the German Constitutional Court, see Eschelbach, '§ 14. Zuständigkeit der Senate und Einberufung des Plenums', in D. Umbach, T. Clemens, and F.-W. Dollinger (eds), *Bundesverfassungsgerichtsgesetz. Mitarbeiterkommentar und Handbuch* (2005) 260, at 264.

[288] De Búrca, 'After the EU Charter of Fundamental Rights. The Court of Justice as a Human Rights Adjudicator?', 20 *Maastricht Journal of European and Comparative Law* (2013) 168, at 174–178; Krommendijk, 'The Use of ECtHR Case Law by the Court of Justice after Lisbon', 6 *Maastricht Journal of European and Comparative Law* (2015) 812, at 832 f.

[289] *ECHR Accession II* (n. 196); see, e.g. Peers, 'The EU's Accession to the ECHR. The Dream Becomes a Nightmare', 16 *German Law Journal* (2015) 213, at 221 f.

[290] But see Halberstam, '"It's the Autonomy, Stupid!" A Modest Defense of Opinion 2/13 on EU Accession to the ECHR, and the Way Forward', 16 *German Law Journal* (2015) 105; Krenn, 'Autonomy

reminiscent of the German Constitutional Court's Second Senate vis-à-vis the CJEU (see 3.2.C).

Nor do I claim that the two courts operate according to the same logic. There are vast differences between the two, given their different paths, memberships, contexts, procedures, and standards. The principle of subsidiarity is integral to the ECtHR's jurisdiction, which only kicks in when all state organs have failed to provide the sort of protection that meets the ECHR guarantees.[291] By contrast, the CJEU's path follows the idea of legal unity within one polity and society, an idea that does not inform the Council of Europe. This difference emerges vividly in the contrasting interpretation of a twin provision of Convention and Union law, Article 53 ECHR and Article 53 CFR. Both provisions establish that the Convention and the Charter, respectively, are compatible with national fundamental rights that grant a higher level of protection. While Article 53 ECHR is understood as an expression of the diversity of fundamental rights and is practised as such,[292] the CJEU has imposed narrow limits on such diversity. Within the scope of Union law, it allows for higher national fundamental rights standards 'provided that the level of protection provided for by the Charter, as interpreted by the Court, and the primacy, unity and effectiveness of Union law are not thereby compromised'.[293] Consequently, fundamental rights standards in the EU can only diverge within narrow limits.[294]

Nevertheless, if one looks at the broader picture, the intimate connection between the two courts, as articulated by the metaphor of the two senates, is evident. Two embryonic institutions of international dispute resolution, created in response to the Second World War, have grown into powerful actors by adopting the techniques of constitutional courts. Both shape European society and are committed to Europe (Article 1 of the Statute of the Council of Europe and Article 1 TEU). Both bring a continental dimension to the democratic rule of law. Both adjudicate from a genuinely European perspective, thanks to their composition and procedures. And both courts depend on each other. Thus, the CJEU's cultivation of European unity strengthens the compliance pull of the ECtHR's case law (see 1.6.D). Conversely, because the CJEU's jurisdiction is functionally limited in the vital area of fundamental rights (Article 51 CFR), European public law relies heavily on the ECtHR.

and Effectiveness as Common Concerns. A Path to ECHR Accession after Opinion 2/13', 16 *German Law Journal* (2015) 147.

[291] ECtHR, *Handyside v. United Kingdom*, Appl. no. 5493/72, Judgment of 7 December 1976, Series A, No. 24, para. 48; R. Spano, 'Universality or Diversity of Human Rights? Strasbourg in the Age of Subsidiarity', 14 *Human Rights Law Review* (2014) 487.

[292] Frowein, 'Art. 53 EMRK', in Frowein and Peukert (n. 254) 619.

[293] CJEU, Case C-399/11, *Melloni* (EU:C:2013:107) para. 60.

[294] CJEU, Case C-42/17, *M.A.S. and M.B.* (EU:C:2017:936) para 47; C. Rauchegger, 'National Constitutional Rights and the Primacy of EU Law: M.A.S.', 55 *Common Market Law Review* (2018) 1521.

B. Growing Forests and Falling Trees

The CJEU and the ECtHR share a common, albeit differentiated, responsibility for European law and European society. The same applies to the Member States' courts. The legal basis for their European responsibility is contained in Article 4(3) TEU, the mandate of the Member State courts under European law (see 4.2.A), and the 'Europe clauses' of the Member State constitutions.[295] It also follows from the rule of law (principle): often, a decision by the Luxembourg or Strasbourg court requires a further decision by a national court if it is to be realized within society, given that the CJEU and ECtHR cannot void national decisions.[296] Common responsibility also results from a court's responsibility for its own legal order since the latter is closely interwoven with the other legal orders.

The constitutional courts are of particular interest in this regard because the CJEU and ECtHR's case law has affected their role more than that of all other courts. While the powers and importance of most Member State courts has increased as a result of their Europeanization, the monopoly of the constitutional courts is under threat (see 4.2). Scholars of European law have put a lot of effort into researching the resulting conflict.[297] Ideal-typically, the constitutional courts have two options: to resist[298] or to cooperate.[299]

Many have accepted, and even supported, the CJEU and ECtHR's transformative case law, not least by recognizing, in principle, their precedential effect (see 4.3.D). Specifically with regard to the CJEU, many constitutional courts moderate their review and sanction violations of the duty to refer cases to the CJEU. The apotheosis of this support is when a constitutional court itself refers a critical case to the CJEU and abides by the latter's decision.[300]

At the same time, some Member State constitutional courts have positioned themselves as review bodies vis-à-vis the ECtHR and the CJEU, usually by invoking the democratic principle (see 3.2.C). The dispute about the scope of EU law's primacy is well known. The CJEU's doctrine assumes Union law's unconditional

[295] M. Wendel, *Permeabilität im europäischen Verfassungsrecht. Verfassungsrechtliche Integrationsnormen auf Staats- und Unionsebene im Vergleich* (2011); D. Burchardt, *Die Rangfrage im europäischen Normenverbund. Theoretische Grundlagen und dogmatische Grundzüge des Verhältnisses von Unionsrecht und nationalem Recht* (2015) 199 ff.

[296] There is an exception for Central Banks: CJEU, Joined Cases C-202/18 and C-238/18, *Rimšēvičs* (EU:C:2019:139) paras 69 ff.; Hinarejos, 'The Court of Justice Annuls a National Measure Directly to Protect ECB Independence: *Rimšēvičs*', 56 *Common Market Law Review* (2019) 1649.

[297] Claes and de Witte (n. 99).

[298] Paradigmatically, see Komárek, 'Why National Constitutional Courts Should Not Embrace EU Fundamental Rights', in de Vries, Bernitz, and Weatherill (n. 183) 75.

[299] Paradigmatically, see Paris, 'Constitutional Courts as European Union Courts. The Current and Potential Use of EU Law as a Yardstick for Constitutional Review', 24 *Maastricht Journal of European and Comparative Law* (2017) 792; Balaguer Callejón *et al.*, 'Encuesta sobre el TJUE como actor de constitucionalidad', 39 *Teoría y Realidad Constitucional* (2017) 13.

[300] Claes, 'Luxembourg, Here We Come? Constitutional Courts and the Preliminary Reference Procedure', 16 *German Law Journal* (2015) 1331.

primacy over all constitutional law of the Member States (see 3.3.C).[301] While the Member State constitutional courts recognize primacy in principle, they impose provisos that enable them to check the CJEU.[302]

This dispute is so defining for European public law that it belongs to basic legal knowledge. That is why legal education engraves European pluralism into the legal world view of future generations, just as they were previously schooled in Kelsen's pyramid of norms. They learn that not every important question must be definitively resolved in European society and that its controversial nature can be part of a democratic society.

Apparently, the politicians have learned to live with this openness. On the one hand, they have refrained from correcting the CJEU's case law on primacy, although the many amendments to the Treaties granted them numerous opportunities to do so.[303] They have never complied with the demand, advocated by prominent voices, that a court of competences replace, or even review, the CJEU.[304] To the contrary, they have explicitly supported its case law on primacy, for example, in the 2009 Declaration No. 17 concerning provisions of the Lisbon Treaty. On the other hand, they never established the remedy of appeal, which would allow the CJEU (or ECtHR) to overturn a national court's judgment. Neither have politicians taken up proposals to entrench, in national law, the constitutional courts' duty to refer critical cases to the CJEU.[305] Schmitt has made the fitting observation that there is no final say in a genuine federation.[306]

Following Grabenwarter, the responsibility of constitutional courts can be summarized as encompassing three functions, namely, connection, legitimation, and review.[307] The *function of connection* expresses that the constitutional courts form a specific link between the domestic and the European courts. The requirement that all domestic remedies must have been exhausted before a complaint can be brought before the ECtHR even entails that often a case has been decided by competent constitutional court. Frequently, constitutional courts are also the first courts to engage with new, constitutionally relevant case law from the CJEU and

[301] Lenaerts, Gutiérrez Fons, and Adam, 'Exploring the Autonomy of the European Legal Order', 81 *Zeitschrift für ausländisches öffentliches Recht und Völkerrecht* (2021) 47.

[302] On the state of the discussion, see Schill and Krenn (n. 202) paras 14–38.

[303] Alter, 'Who Are the "Masters of the Treaty"? European Governments and the European Court of Justice', in K. J. Alter (ed.), *The European Court's Political Power* (2009) 109, at 128 f.

[304] Weiler *et al.*, 'Certain Rectangular Problems of European Integration', *Project IV/95/02, European Parliament Directorate General for Research* (1996) 1, at 69; Wegener, 'Karlsruher Unheil—Das Urteil des Bundesverfassungsgerichts vom 5. Mai 2020 (2 BvR 859/15) in Sachen Staatsanleihekäufe der Europäischen Zentralbank', 55 *Europarecht* (2020) 347, at 360 f.

[305] Bergmann and Karpenstein, 'Identitäts- und Ultra vires-Kontrolle durch das Bundesverfassungsgericht. Zur Notwendigkeit einer gesetzlichen Vorlageverpflichtung', 4 *Zeitschrift für Europarechtliche Studien* (2009) 529.

[306] C. Schmitt, *Constitutional Theory (1928)* (2008) 387 ff.

[307] Grabenwarter, 'Zusammenfassung' (n. 125).

ECtHR and thus introduce it into domestic legal discourse. In other words, there are many channels of communication.

Furthermore, constitutional courts have a *function of legitimation*. By processing European decisions and citing them affirmatively, they provide additional legitimation, which supports domestic reception (see 4.3.D). The *function of review* is closely related to that of legitimation. Thus, constitutional courts review CJEU and ECtHR decisions and claim the power to prohibit their effects within the domestic legal order. This function can serve the European checks and balances but can also facilitate constitutional protectionism. In both respects, the arguments mostly revolve around constitutional identity (see 3.2.C).

Consequently, conflicts are bound to occur and can serve the European constitutional core. It is important, however, that they do not escalate. Any conflict must be managed in the light of the courts' common responsibility. Fortunately, the interaction between them is very flexible.[308] This flexibility reflects a remarkable development. The Kelsenian model of constitutional adjudication offers only limited decision-making possibilities since it only provides for the nullity of the act found to be unlawful. By contrast, there are many options within the framework of European multilevel cooperation, but there is almost never the hard consequence of nullity.[309]

The ECtHR's judgments are essentially declaratory in nature, which grants the states parties leeway in remedying a declared violation. The possibility of appealing an ECtHR decision before the Grand Chamber of the ECtHR also contributes to this flexibility. Accordingly, the ECtHR, acting in its most authoritative composition, can correct chamber decisions that have proved conflictual.[310]

The CJEU is more authoritative than the ECHR. Nevertheless, it, too, demonstrates flexibility. Its doctrine of primacy shows as much. In the 1960s, it was disputed whether the primacy over national law established in the *Costa/ENEL* case should be conceived as a primacy of validity, with the consequence of nullity, or as a softer form of primacy, resulting only in disapplication. The softer solution prevailed.[311] Furthermore, the operative part of CJEU judgments (i.e. the decision's holding) offers possibilities to handle conflicts constructively. The CJEU often limits itself to guiding the national courts, leaving it to them to balance the conflicting interests in the individual case.[312] The *Taricco* case shows that Article 267

[308] Claes and de Witte (n. 99); Requejo Pagés, 'The Decline of the Traditional Model of European Constitutional Jurisdiction' (n. 99).

[309] F. Schorkopf, *Staatsrecht der internationalen Beziehungen* (2017) 40 ff.

[310] Consider, e.g. the *Horncastle Saga*, ECtHR, *Al-Khawaja and Tahery v. United Kingdom*, Appl. no. 26766/05 and 22228/06, Judgment of 20 January 2009, ECHR 2009–IV; *R v. Horncastle and others* (2009), UKSC 14; *Al-Khawaja and Tahery v. United Kingdom*, Appl. nos 26766/05 and 22228/06, Judgment of 15 December 2011.

[311] See, on the one hand, E. Grabitz, *Gemeinschaftsrecht bricht nationales Recht* (1966) 113; on the other hand, M. Zuleeg, *Das Recht der Europäischen Gemeinschaften im innerstaatlichen Bereich* (1969) 140 ff.

[312] Tridimas, 'Constitutional Review of Member State Action. The Virtues and Vices of an Incomplete Jurisdiction', 9 *International Journal of Constitutional Law* (2011) 737; Sarmiento, 'Half a Case at

TFEU can even serve as a kind of legal remedy against a CJEU decision, meaning that the CJEU can correct it in the light of the constitutional courts' objections.[313]

The relevant doctrines (*controlimiti*, *ultra vires*, etc.) are similarly flexible. It is only a slight exaggeration to view them as jokers in a power game.[314] At the same time, the fact that these jokers are only very rarely played reflects the courts' common responsibility. It is widely held that Union law should remain unapplied only as a means of last resort. A constitutional court has to justify such a move by pointing to a grave threat to constitutional principles; moreover, it should first give the CJEU the opportunity to address and manage the conflict.[315]

Common responsibility is enacted in different ways. Ideal-typically, we can distinguish between a maximalist style, which insists on a right to the final say, and a minimalist style, which is relational (see 4.1.D). The German Constitutional Court above all employs the former and the Italian Constitutional Court the latter.

When the German Constitutional Court perceives a conflict between EU and German constitutional law, it tends to instruct the European Court of Justice (ECJ) about the limits of EU primacy in pithy terms. The reaction of the Karlsruhe Court to the broad interpretation of the Charter's scope in *Åkerberg Fransson* provides a famous example.[316] Two months after the CJEU's judgment, it stated—and did so, moreover, in an *obiter dictum* (i.e. without cause)—that the *Åkerberg Fransson* decision

> must not be read in a way that would view it as an apparent ultra vires act [...]. The decision must thus not be understood and applied in such a way that absolutely any connection of a provision's subject matter to the merely abstract scope of Union law, or merely incidental effects on Union law, would be sufficient for binding the Member States by the Union's fundamental rights set forth in the EUCFR.[317]

As a rule, the German Constitutional Court leaves little room for interpretation, as is the case here: the CJEU must interpret the precedent of *Åkerberg Fransson*

a Time. Dealing with Judicial Minimalism at the European Court of Justice', in M. Claes *et al.* (eds), *Constitutional Conversations in Europe. Actors, Topics and Procedures* (2012) 13.

[313] Bonelli, 'The Taricco Saga and the Consolidation of Judicial Dialogue in the European Union. CJEU, C-105/14 Ivo Taricco and Others, ECLI:EU:C:2015:555; and C-42/17 M.A.S., M.B., ECLI:EU:C:2017:936 Italian Constitutional Court, Order no. 24/2017', 25 *Maastricht Journal of European and Comparative Law* (2018) 357; Rossi, 'M.A.S. e M.B. e la torre di Babele: alla fine le Corti si comprendono ... pur parlando lingue diverse', in C. Amalfitano (ed.), *Primato del Diritto dell'Unione Europea e Controlimiti alla Prova della 'Saga Taricco'* (2017) 153.

[314] See the critique in CJEU, Case C-62/14, *Gauweiler et al.*, Opinion of AG Cruz Villalón (EU:C:2015:7) paras 59 f.

[315] In detail, see von Bogdandy, Grabenwarter, and Huber, 'Constitutional Adjudication in the European Legal Space' (n. 96).

[316] *Åkerberg Fransson* (n. 100).

[317] BVerfGE 133, 277, *Counter-Terrorism Database*, para. 91, my translation.

narrowly if it wishes to avoid serious conflict.[318] In this vein, the German Constitutional Court established a detailed catalogue of non-transferable issues in the Lisbon judgment (see 3.2.C). Its formulation in the *OMT* case is similarly categorical.[319] The German Constitutional Court assumes common responsibility by clearly articulating its position.

In *Taricco*, the Italian Constitutional Court chose virtually the opposite approach. The case concerns the punishment of tax fraud to the detriment of the EU budget. Since the Italian judiciary often works slowly, such offences frequently become statute-barred. The ensuing impunity harms European financial interests considerably. Therefore, the CJEU held that the Italian criminal court had to disapply the statute of limitations in order not to impede the effectiveness of Union law.[320] Said court then asked the *Corte* whether to comply with this CJEU judgment. The *Corte*, in turn, again referred the question to the CJEU, pointing out that sentencing the defendant would violate the constitutional prohibition of retroactivity.

The order for reference 24/2017 to the ECJ undoubtedly contained a threat. The *Corte* made it clear that it would likely use its strongest weapon, the *controlimiti* doctrine, if the CJEU were to uphold its *Taricco* judgment. Unlike the *Bundesverfassungsgericht*, however, it did not outline the decision it expected the CJEU to make. Rather, in a minimalistic move, it limited itself to declaring a conflict between a CJEU judgment and one of the Italian Constitution's highest principles. And, unlike the *Bundesverfassungsgericht*, it also did not elaborate on the principle's scope in the order for reference, leaving open what it would ultimately consider acceptable. Thus, it did not shy away from a conflict that would affect its constitutional authoritativeness significantly. However, it also kept almost all its options open.

Both the German and the Italian approaches allow for conflicts to be managed constructively.[321] The CJEU has adjusted its standards pursuant to the preliminary reference of the Italian Constitutional Court.[322] The same applies to the *Åkerberg-Fransson* doctrine, which has taken into account the German Court's criticism.[323] However, I hold that the relational Italian style better suits the courts' common responsibility because it seems more dialogic.

[318] Thym, 'Die Reichweite der EU-Grundrechte-Charta. Zu viel Grundrechtsschutz?', 32 *Neue Zeitschrift für Verwaltungsrecht* (2013) 889; Fontanelli, '*Hic Sunt Nationes*. The Elusive Limits of the EU Charter and the German Constitutional Watchdog. Court of Justice of the European Union: Judgment of 26 February 2013, Case C-617/10 *Åklagaren v. Hans Åkerberg Fransson*', 9 *European Constitutional Law Review* (2013) 315, at 327 ff.

[319] BVerfGE 134, 366, *OMT Decision*.

[320] CJEU, Case C-105/14, *Taricco* (EU:C:2015:555) paras 35–44.

[321] von Bogdandy and Paris (n. 59).

[322] *M.A.S. and M.B.* (n. 294).

[323] See *Siragusa* (n. 293); Case C-265/13, *Torralbo Marcos* (EU:C:2014:187); Case C-198/13, *Julian Hernández* (EU:C:2014:2055).

The courts' common responsibility brings with it considerable costs to legal certainty and the length of judicial proceedings.[324] But they seem an acceptable price to pay. No one should overlook the civilizational gain that inheres in the way the pluralistic European society manages, cabins, and often resolves its conflicts by judicial means. This civilizational achievement shows that most judges have a shared conception of their functions, are aware of their common responsibility, and rely on common principles.[325]

Davide Paris summarizes this achievement with the metaphor of a silently growing forest in which, every now and then, a tree crashes loudly to the ground.[326] For 60 years now, a forest of European judicial cooperation has been growing under common responsibility. It has helped European society process its differences, which is why conflicts attract a lot of attention. We are right to be concerned when we think we see a squad of judges with axe in hand.[327]

While the established culture of common responsibility helps prevent conflicts from escalating,[328] we should, nevertheless, be concerned when a tree falls with a crash. The ECtHR, in particular, has had to struggle with cases of non-compliance.[329] But the CJEU, too, has had such cases, especially the *PSPP* judgment of the German Constitutional Court's Second Senate.[330] In that case, the courts involved were no longer able to hedge the conflict. Therefore, German politicians had to act. They settled the problem with the least amount of fuss: in a resolution

[324] Burchardt, 'Kehrtwende in der Grundrechts- und Vorrangrechtsprechung des EuGH? Anmerkung zum Urteil des EuGH vom 5.12.2017 in der Rechtssache M.A.S. und M.B. (C-42/17, "Taricco II")', 53 *Europarecht* (2018) 248; Albi, 'An Essay on How the Discourse on Sovereignty and on the Cooperativeness of National Courts Has Diverted Attention from the Erosion of Classical Constitutional Rights in the EU', in Claes *et al.* (n. 312) 41.

[325] See Cartabia, 'Courts' Relations', 18 *International Journal of Constitutional Law* (2020) 3.

[326] Paris, 'A Falling Tree Makes More Noise Than a Growing Forest. On the Constitutional Courts' Underestimated Contribution to the Domestic Enforcement of the European Convention on Human Rights', 77 *Zeitschrift für ausländisches öffentliches Recht und Völkerrecht* (2017) 581.

[327] Mayer, 'Auf dem Weg zum Richterfaustrecht? Zum PSPP-Urteil des BVerfG' *Verfassungsblog* (7 May 2020).

[328] Dyèvre, 'Domestic Judicial Defiance in the European Union. A Systemic Threat to the Authority of EU Law?', 35 *Yearbook of European Law* (2016) 106; Goldmann, 'Constitutional Pluralism as Mutually Assured Discretion. The Court of Justice, the German Federal Constitutional Court, and the ECB', 23 *Maastricht Journal of European and Comparative Law* (2016) 119.

[329] But see ECtHR, *Hirst v. United Kingdom (No. 2)*, Appl. no. 74025/01, Judgment of 6 October 2005, ECHR 2005-IX; A. von Staaden, *Strategies of Compliance with the European Court of Human Rights* (2018); Panke, 'The European Court of Human Rights under Scrutiny: Explaining Variation in Non-compliance', 18 *Comparative European Politics* (2020) 151; P. Popelier, S. Lambrecht, and K. Lemmens, *Criticism of the European Court of Human Rights* (2017).

[330] Cassese, 'Il guinzaglio tedesco', *Il Foglio* (19 May 2020), https://images.irpa.eu/wp-content/uploads/2020/05/Cassese_190520_il-Foglio.pdf (last visited 21 July 2022); Imad, 'Nicolas Goetzmann: "L'Allemagne cherche à germaniser le droit européen"', *Le Figaro* (6 May 2020), https://www.lefigaro.fr/vox/economie/nicolas-goetzmann-l-allemagne-cherche-a-germaniser-le-droit-europeen-20200506 (last visited 21 July 2022); O'Leary, 'How a German Court Fired a Shot That Could Unravel the EU', *The Irish Times* (13 May 2020), https://www.irishtimes.com/news/world/europe/how-a-german-court-fired-a-shot-that-could-unravel-the-eu-1.4252763 (last visited 21 July 2022); Reiermann, 'Dieses Urteil ist ein Attentat', *Der Spiegel* (8 February 2020); Wefing, 'Die Rechthaber', *Die Zeit* (6 May 2020).

against which only the parliamentary group of the *Alternative für Deutschland* voted, the *Bundestag* declared that, unlike the Second Senate, it did not doubt the lawfulness of European action.[331] Thus, it resolved the conflict in favour of Germany's European responsibility.

C. Closing Ranks to Counteract a Common Threat

The authoritarian developments in some Member States provide a test case for the courts' common responsibility. The more institutions identify and react to such developments, the more promising and legitimate the fight against them becomes. Here, common responsibility implies that the various courts come together to form a unified front.

The finding that a particular course of events violates a fundamental principle and amounts to a systemic deficiency usually comes with an *evaluative overall assessment* of a series of detailed measures (*wertende Gesamteinschätzung*) (see 3.6.B).[332] This practice responds to the difficulty of grasping authoritarian structures in juridical terms. Judicial proceedings normally focus on a concrete, individualized action. But to grasp the systemic deficiency that inheres in authoritarian developments, a series of actions frequently need to be examined in their *entirety*; individual statutes or measures may appear quite harmless.[333] The evaluation of the Polish judiciary's restructuring is instructive in this regard (see 3.6.A). The statement that there is a 'clear risk of a serious breach' of one of the values mentioned in Article 2 TEU is based on an overall view of all measures concerning the judiciary. It takes into account the country's political and social conditions, including the actions against the parliamentary opposition, media, academia, and non-governmental organizations. Because such an assessment of various measures, events, and statements entails great leeway, it can easily be denounced as political, partisan, and hence unlawful and illegitimate.

Given these challenges, an evaluative overall assessment becomes more legitimate if it is shared by various independent and authoritative institutions. The more institutions are united in determining a systemic deficiency, the greater the legitimacy of this finding. That is why the CJEU, the ECtHR, the EU Commission, and the Venice Commission refer to one another in their decisions[334] as

[331] Online services of the German *Bundestag*: Bundestag, *Bundestag: EZB hat Karlsruher Vorgaben zu Anleihekäufen erfüllt* (2020), https://www.bundestag.de/dokumente/textarchiv/2020/kw27-de-anleihekaeufe-703660 (last visited 21 July 2022).

[332] See European Commission, Proposal for a Council Decision on the determination of a clear risk of a serious breach by the Republic of Poland of the Rule of Law, COM(2017) 835 final, at paras 109, 173.

[333] CJEU, Joined Cases C-585/18–C-625/18, *A.K. (Independence of the Disciplinary Chamber of the Supreme Court)* (EU:C:2019:982) para. 142.

[334] But see European Commission, Proposal for a Council Decision on the determination of a clear risk of a serious breach by the Republic of Poland of the Rule of Law (n. 332) paras 18, 32, 95, 116 ff.;

well as to assessments by international bodies and recognized civil society organizations.[335]

In this chapter, the cooperation between the CJEU and the ECtHR in discharging their responsibilities is of particular interest. Given the uneasy relationship between the two (see 4.4.A), it was by no means certain that they would support each other's decisions. However, the most recent judgments attest a closing of ranks. In *Commission v. Hungary*, the CJEU concretized the EU fundamental right to freedom of assembly on the basis of the relevant ECtHR case law. In *Guðmundur Andri Ástráðsson*, the ECtHR, in turn, concretized the Convention right to a fair trial on the basis of the CJEU's case law on the Polish judicial reform.[336]

The logic of this evaluative union also applies to Member State courts confronted with authoritarian structures in another Member State. This affects the choice of which standard a domestic court ought to apply: national constitutional principles, international standards, or the principles of Article 2 TEU. The latter has the great advantage of allowing the Member State court to make a preliminary reference to the CJEU, thereby strengthening the evaluative union. Involving the CJEU also helps lessen the risk of bilateral escalation. Moreover, seizing the CJEU helps defend liberal democracy and its principles in one fell swoop. Finally, the rule of law demands a fair trial, which means that the incriminated Member State must be involved. But while the state is sure to be heard before the CJEU, it is difficult for a domestic court to formally involve another state in such a sensitive proceeding.

This path requires constitutional courts to interpret and apply the principles of Article 2 TEU (see 3.1.C). Europeanizing their mandate in such a manner has long encountered resistance, especially within the *Bundesverfassungsgericht*. That its First Senate has pursued this course since 2019 represents a milestone, then.[337] Henceforth, the Court's review will be based solely on the Union's fundamental rights whenever the subject matter is subject to full Union law harmonization. In all other cases, it will consider both Union and German constitutional law in parallel and may interpret German fundamental rights in the light of the Charter.[338]

CJEU, Joined Cases C-404/15 and C-659/15 PPU, *Aranyosi and Căldăraru* (EU:C:2016:198); Case C-216/18 PPU, *LM*, Opinion of AG Tanchev (EU:C:2018:517). In detail, see Bustos Gisbert, 'La influencia de los textos no vinculantes del Consejo de Europa sobre independencia judicial en el TEDH y en la UE', 47 *Teoría y Realidad Constitucional* (2021) 161.

[335] European Commission, Proposal for a Council Decision on the determination of a clear risk of a serious breach by the Republic of Poland of the Rule of Law (n. 332) paras 33, 63, 76, 80, 82.

[336] CJEU, Case C-78/18, *Commission v. Hungary (Transparency of Associations)* (EU:C:2020:476) para. 112; ECtHR, *Guðmundur Andri Ástráðsson v. Iceland*, Appl. no. 26374/18, Judgment of 1 December 2020; Nußberger, 'La prise en compte de la Charte des droits fondamentaux de l'Union par la Cour européenne des droits de l'homme', in A. Iliopoulou-Penot and L. Xenou (eds), *La charte des droits fondamentaux, source de renouveau constitutionnel européen?* (2020) 69.

[337] *Right to Be Forgotten I* and *Right to Be Forgotten II* (n. 58). On the other courts' role in implementing fundamental rights, see the contributions in M. Bobek and J. Adams-Prassl (eds), *The EU Charter of Fundamental Rights in the Member States* (2020).

[338] On the following, see *Right to Be Forgotten II* (n. 58) paras 53 ff., 67.

This logic jibes with the courts' common responsibility in confronting systemic deficiencies.

The First Senate's decision to change tack in the middle of the Polish rule-of-law crisis has met with approval.[339] The Senate abandoned the concept of separate fundamental rights spheres and positioned itself as a European court that helps develop EU constitutional law. By emphasizing the primacy of Union law, it strengthens the position of the Polish judges who defend the European constitutional core (see 3.6.A, 5.4.A) and supports the CJEU's specific role in that struggle.[340] In doing so, it sets an example for how courts exercise their common but differentiated responsibility for European public law.

5. Democratic Courts

A. The Mandate for Structural Transformation

Courts have become actors of societal mediation. While they always had that role concerning individual controversies, today, they also shape general structures between competing societal forces. Therefore, the question arises of whether such judicial law-making compromises democracy, or, in our case, the democratic character of European society. In what is arguably the most famous European study on constitutional adjudication, Lambert cautioned against giving courts such power, which he considered akin to a *gouvernement des juges*.[341] Since then, few topics of public law have been the object of similar academic passion and theoretical effort.[342] Once again, we can turn to Schmitt for a poignant observation. In his view,

339 Wendel, 'Das Bundesverfassungsgericht als Garant der Unionsgrundrechte' (n. 58); Karpenstein and Kottmann, 'Vom Gegen- zum Mitspieler. Das BVerfG und die Unionsgrundrechte', 31 *Europäische Zeitschrift für Wirtschaftsrecht* (2020) 185; Kühling, 'Das "Recht auf Vergessenwerden" vor dem BVerfG. November(r)evolution für die Grundrechtsarchitektur im Mehrebenensystem', 73 *Neue Juristische Wochenschrift* (2020) 275; Hofmann, Heger, and Gharibyan, 'Die Wandlung des Grundrechtsschutzes durch das Bundesverfassungsgericht. Recht auf Vergessen I und II als "Solange III"?', 102 *Kritische Vierteljahresschrift für Gesetzgebung und Rechtswissenschaft* (2019) 277; Avbelj, 'The Federal Constitutional Court Rules for a Bright Future of Constitutional Pluralism', 21 *German Law Journal* (2020) 27.

340 Goldmann, 'As Darkness Deepens. The Right to Be Forgotten in the Context of Authoritarian Constitutionalism', 21 *German Law Journal* (2020) 45.

341 Lambert (n. 17). On this influence, see Quint, 'The Influence of the United States Supreme Court on Judicial Review in Europe', in von Bogdandy, Grabenwarter, and Huber, *The Max Planck Handbooks in European Public Law, Vol. III* (n. 18) 841, at 852 ff.

342 On the debate, see Canivet, 'Les limites de la mission du juge constitutionnel', 69 *Cités* (2017) 41; Murillo de la Cueva, 'La independencia y el gobierno de los jueces. Un debate constitucional', 40 *Teoría y Realidad Constitucional* (2017) 351; Barroso, 'Countermajoritarian, Representative, and Enlightened: The Roles of Constitutional Courts in Democracies', 67 *American Journal of Comparative Law* (2019) 109; Cruz Villalón (n. 10); Grewe, 'Constitutional Jurisdiction in Ex-Yugoslavia' (n. 19); de Visser, 'Constitutional Courts Securing Their Legitimacy: An Institutional-Procedural Analysis', in von Bogdandy, Huber, and Grabenwarter (n. 10); Farahat, 'Constitutional Jurisdiction and the Separation of Powers' (n. 68); Landfried (n. 22).

a law-making jurisdiction blurs the fundamental distinction between law and politics and moralizes societal controversies, especially in matters of constitutional rights.[343] Again, I beg to differ.

Let me start by contextualizing my answer. By the 1980s, the debate had become more or less academic because independent, impartial, and societally relevant constitutional adjudication had become a generally recognized component of democracy (see 4.1.A). Critical voices did not pose a real challenge. This has changed over the past 10 years, particularly in Hungary and Poland. Orbán's *illiberal democracy* is arguably the first idea of constitutional policy from Central and Eastern Europe that has garnered attention throughout Europe.[344] It emphasizes democratic immediacy and thus calls current European public law, with its logic of mediations, into question. *Illiberal democracy* represents a European challenge: 'The peripheries [are] the "hotter" zones of production of new meaning compared to the conservatism of the centre.'[345]

Béla Pokol, a Humboldt Fellow with Niklas Luhmann,[346] Professor of Legal Theory and Sociology of Law at the University of Szeged, Chairman of the Parliamentary Committee on Constitutional and Justice Matters (1998–2002), and Justice of the Hungarian Constitutional Court since 2011, has articulated this position in his scholarly work.[347] One of his central theorems is the 'dual state'. Unlike Ernst Fraenkel's famous book of the same title on national socialism, Pokol does not address the dual structure of a state that terrorizes its internal opponents while it follows the rule of law for compliant citizens.[348] The duplication Pokol identifies consists of the democratic majority's parliamentary legislation bowing to judges' undemocratic and ideological case law.

Despite Pokol's decided anticommunism, there are remarkable parallels between his view and the conception of constitutional adjudication in socialist legal scholarship, which interpreted it as an undemocratic instrument of class rule.[349] For Pokol, too, judges are part of a social class, although he defines the latter more in ideological than economic terms. He sees the constitutional justices as part of an

343 Schmitt, *Der Hüter der Verfassung* (n. 10); C. Schmitt, *The Tyranny of Values* (1996).

344 See 2.6.D. The term, including its pejorative connotation, was coined by Zakaria, 'The Rise of Illiberal Democracy', 76 *Foreign Affairs* (1997) 22.

345 A. Koschorke, *Hegel und wir* (2015) 162 (trans. Naomi Shulman).

346 B. Pokol, *Theoretische Soziologie und Rechtstheorie. Kritik und Korrigierung der Theorie von Niklas Luhmann* (2013).

347 B. Pokol, *Double State and the Doubling of the Legal System: Constitutional Law and the Duplication of the Branches of Law* (2020); Pokol, 'The Gradual Duplication of the Legal System through Constitutional Adjudication', *SSRN Electronic Journal* (2019), https://papers.ssrn.com/sol3/papers.cfm?abstract_id=3482521 (last visited 21 August 2022). See also C. E. Parau, *Transnational Networking and Elite Self-Empowerment: The Making of the Judiciary in Contemporary Europe and Beyond* (2018). On this, see Gearty, 'The Courts in Europe Today: Subverting or Saving Democracy?', 16 *European Constitutional Law Review* (2020) 770.

348 E. Fraenkel, *The Dual State. A Contribution to the Theory of Dictatorship* (1941); E. Fraenkel, *Der Doppelstaat. Recht und Justiz im 'Dritten Reich'* (1974).

349 Tuleja (n. 29) 621.

international elite that wants to impose what are ultimately left-liberal doctrines on society, thereby transforming it according to their worldview.

Pokol's emphasis is novel. For Lambert, constitutional adjudication perpetuated the conceptions of the old national elite.[350] Like Hermann Heller,[351] Lambert combatted it as an obstacle to democratic social legislation.[352] Similarly, Hirschl declared court-centred constitutionalization a conservative strategy of those who fear for their social hegemony.[353] Pokol, by contrast, perceives constitutional adjudication not as a conserving but as a transformative force: he argues that it transforms society according to the left-liberal standards of a global group. He is not alone in this: David Kosař, who certainly does not share Pokol's world view, also considers a liberalizing constitutional court an imposition, one that explains the success of Viktor Orbán and Jarosław Kaczyński.[354]

Discussing the democratic legitimacy of constitutional adjudication requires a concept of democracy.[355] It strikes me as particularly important that a democratic society requires more than a freely elected majority; it must also abide by many other standards. Article 2 TEU articulates these standards for European society, referring to 'pluralism, non-discrimination, tolerance, justice, solidarity and equality between women and men' and the values of 'respect for human dignity, freedom, democracy, equality, the rule of law and respect for human rights, including the rights of persons belonging to minorities'.

A democratic society implies that every exercise of power must be justified in the light of these standards. To be meaningful, a justification must be subject to review.[356] To be credible, such review ultimately requires a body that is independent and impartial, that is, judicial.[357] Since the standards of this review are open, the democratic mandate to adjudicate includes developing them interpretatively in light of current-day challenges. This simple logic explains the basic legitimacy of constitutional adjudication.

We can substantiate this approach with Böckenförde's influential doctrine of the chain of legitimation. It has a critical thrust because Böckenförde, following Schmitt, considered the Federal Republic in danger of becoming a jurisdictional state (*Jurisdiktionsstaat*), in particular because of the Constitutional Court's

[350] Lambert (n. 17) 220 ff.
[351] H. Heller, *Rechtsstaat oder Diktatur?* (1930) 9.
[352] Lambert (n. 17) 220 ff.
[353] Hirschl (n. 56) 264.
[354] Kosař, Baroš, and Dufek, 'The Twin Challenges to Separation of Powers in Central Europe. Technocratic Governance and Populism', 15 *European Constitutional Law Review* (2019) 427. On this, see 2.6.D.
[355] A. Farahat, *Transnationale Solidaritätskonflikte. Eine vergleichende Analyse verfassungsgerichtlicher Konfliktbearbeitung in der Eurokrise* (2021) para. 3.
[356] Madison, 'Federalist No. 10', in *The Federalist Papers* (1787) 51; R. Forst, *The Right to Justification. Elements of a Constructivist Theory of Justice* (2011).
[357] Kelsen, 'Wesen und Entwicklung der Staatsgerichtsbarkeit' (n. 110) 55.

power.[358] Böckenförde analysed courts' democratic legitimation[359] concerning a court's nature as an institution (*institutional* legitimation), the source it interprets and applies (*substantive* legitimation), and the judge who is ultimately in charge of adjudicating the case at hand (*personal* legitimation).

If we consider constitutional adjudication in European society from this angle, we can conclude that it enjoys solid democratic legitimation. As for *institutional* and *substantive* legitimation, it bears emphasizing that the European Treaties and the Member State constitutions, including those of the Central and Eastern European Member States, were enacted or reformed by freely elected parliaments or in free referendums. To be sure, the Council of Europe and the EU were involved, too. But I do not consider this the kind of undemocratic foreign imposition that accompanied constitution-making in Bosnia and Herzegovina or Iraq (see 2.6.D). If there are legitimate doubts, they concern the Hungarian Basic Law that Orbán's majority passed in 2011 without bothering seriously to involve the opposition.[360]

Democratic legitimacy requires the possibility of democratic change. In the United States, whose debate on the *counter-majoritarian difficulty* has an outsize influence on academic thought, the constitution more or less cannot be changed. This is different in European society. For the most part, the Member States' constitutions are easier to amend.[361] Of course, the Union Treaties or the ECHR may only be amended unanimously (Article 48 TEU, Article 39 Vienna Convention on the Law of Treaties). But there is the possibility of withdrawal (Article 50 TEU, Article 58 ECHR). In the United States, no state can evade the Supreme Court in this way.

What remains is the question of personal legitimation. Parliaments usually play a role in the selection of constitutional justices, albeit in different forms. Furthermore, constitutional justices in Europe have far shorter mandates than in the United States,[362] which aids democratic legitimation.[363] The fact that appointment procedures can certainly be improved (see 4.5.B), that they can be abused, and that their results are not always unanimously celebrated does not controvert this chain of democratic legitimation.

[358] Böckenförde, 'Grundrechte als Grundsatznormen. Zur gegenwärtigen Lage der Grundrechtsdogmatik', 29 *Der Staat* (1990) 1, at 29. See also B. Rüthers, *Die heimliche Revolution vom Rechtsstaat zum Richterstaat. Verfassung und Methoden. Ein Essay* (2016) 29 ff., 79 ff., whose criticism is more vehement still.

[359] E.-W. Böckenförde, *Verfassungsfragen der Richterwahl* (1974); for background, see Böckenförde, 'Demokratie als Verfassungsprinzip', in J. Isensee and P. Kirchhof (eds), *Handbuch des Staatsrechts der Bundesrepublik Deutschland, Bd. II.* (2004) 429.

[360] On this, see Jakab and Sonnevend, 'Kontinuität mit Mängeln: Das neue ungarische Grundgesetz', 72 *Zeitschrift für ausländisches öffentliches Recht und Völkerrecht* (2012) 79 (still hoping for continuity, albeit in vain).

[361] S. Ragone, *I controlli giurisdizionali sulle revisioni costituzionali. Profili teorici e comparativi* (2011) 29 ff., 125 ff.

[362] Grabenwarter, 'Judicial Appointments in Comparative Perspective', in von Bogdandy, Huber, and Grabenwarter (n. 10); Landfried (n. 22).

[363] Ferreres Comella (n. 26) 96.

Proving a chain of legitimation does not resolve the democratic question. Rather, the chain must produce *sufficient* democratic legitimation.[364] This becomes especially important when courts make law and shape society. Renowned scholars already doubt whether the justices of the *Bundesverfassungsgericht* have sufficient democratic legitimacy for this task.[365] Matters are even more complicated for the ECtHR and the CJEU since their chains of legitimation are longer and more convoluted.[366]

Indeed, neither the Treaty legislator nor any constitutional framer has explicitly conferred on any court the mandate they exercise today. The major judgments that today symbolize their mandates go beyond the legislator's expectations (see 4.1, 4.3.A–C). And yet, even such decisions, sometimes described as revolutionary,[367] can be construed as democratically legitimate when understood within the framework of complex democracies.

Societal complexity is widely acknowledged today.[368] Accordingly, the doctrine that only the national assembly's majority decision should shape society has faded.[369] Hence, many democratic societies have set up powerful institutions alongside parliament and endowed them with open mandates. This applies to apex courts as much as to central banks.

The mandate is open, but there are many constraints; judicial power is anything but unlimited. The constraints include the requirement that a majority of judges from a pluralistic bench vote for the decision; the expectation that the ruling will honour established standards of reasoning; concerns about maintaining—and, indeed, developing—authoritativeness and legitimacy; and, finally, review by other courts (see 4.4.B). Moreover, parliaments continue to play a major role. They can amend the constitution or the Treaties, although that is difficult by design. Other interventions face fewer constraints: the legislators can select judges with different outlooks or participate in later proceedings in order to change a particular line of jurisprudence. Moreover, it takes a long time for a decision to strengthen into the kind of precedent that casts a long shadow; many actors, including academics, judges of other courts, and—last but not least—later compositions of the adjudicating court, must refer to the ruling.[370] Recognizing judicial law-making

364 Böckenförde, *Verfassungsfragen der Richterwahl* (n. 359) 75 f., 141.

365 Voßkuhle and Sydow, 'Die demokratische Legitimation des Richters', 57 *JuristenZeitung* (2002) 673, at 676–679.

366 Zamaria, 'Democratic Legitimacy and Non-Majoritarian Institutions: Reflections on the Functional and Democratic Legitimacy of International Adjudicative Bodies and Independent Regulatory Agencies', in Ruiz Fabri *et al.* (n. 267) 19, at 24 ff.

367 Weiler, 'A Quiet Revolution: The European Court of Justice and its Interlocutors', 26 *Comparative Political Studies* (1994) 510; Rasmussen (n. 200).

368 P. Rosanvallon, *Le siècle du populisme. Histoire, théorie, critique* (2020) 37 ff.

369 P. Rosanvallon, *La légitimité démocratique. Impartialité, réflexivité, proximité* (2008) 116 ff., 222 ff. Comparatively, see von Bogdandy (n. 8) 41 ff.

370 N. Yang, *Die Leitentscheidung. Zur Grundlegung eines Begriffs und seiner Erforschung im Unionsrecht anhand des EuGH-Urteils Kadi* (2018) esp. at 37 ff.; Torres Pérez, 'In Nobody's Name. A Checks and Balances Approach to International Judicial Independence', in Ruiz Fabri *et al.* (n. 267) 45.

authority does not mean that every decision must be accepted as an example thereof. To the contrary, reviewing a decision's justification (i.e. criticism) is essential to the courts' democratic embedding.

Béla Pokol is right to argue that constitutional adjudication can miss its democratic mandate. However, the most important examples are not found among courts that decide against the government majority. Instead, they include courts who become a government's tractable servant. A prime example is the Constitutional Senate of the Venezuelan Supreme Court, which transformed into a weapon of Presidents Chavez and Maduro.[371] The Polish and Hungarian constitutional courts also pursue this downhill course.[372]

The Venezuelan, Polish, and Hungarian examples provide another insight about constitutional adjudication. They underscore that a constitutional court often does not present a major obstacle for a determined government that seeks to evade its scrutiny.[373] If the core mandate of constitutional courts truly consisted of counteracting authoritarian tendencies, they would lose much of their legitimacy and appear rather insignificant.[374] The opposite is true if we construe the core mandate of constitutional courts, as of constitutional adjudication in general, as that of developing a complex society characterized by 'pluralism, non-discrimination, tolerance, justice, solidarity and equality between women and men' and 'respect for human dignity, freedom, democracy, equality, the rule of law and respect for human rights, including the rights of persons belonging to minorities'. Judicial law-making that places these principles front and centre does not compromise the democratic character of European society. Instead, it contributes to it.

B. Democratic Selection Procedures

The democratic development of European society must likewise come to characterize the selection of ECtHR and CJEU judges.[375] Contrary to widespread

[371] A. R. Brewer Carías, *La consolidación de la tiranía judicial. El juez constitucional controlado por el poder ejecutivo asumiendo el poder absoluto* (2017); J. M. Casal Hernández, 'The Constitutional Chamber and the Erosion of Democracy in Venezuela', 80 *Zeitschrift für ausländisches öffentliches Recht und Völkerrecht* (2020) 913.

[372] Sadurski, 'Polish Constitutional Tribunal Under PiS: From an Activist Court, to a Paralysed Tribunal, to a Governmental Enabler', 11 *Hague Journal on the Rule of Law* (2018) 63; Bakó, 'Hungary's Latest Experiences with Article 2 TEU: The Need for "Informed" EU Sanctions', in A. von Bogdandy *et al.* (eds), *Defending Checks and Balances in EU Member States. Taking Stock of Europe's Actions* (2021) 35, at 48 ff.

[373] G. Frankenberg, *Autoritarismus. Verfassungstheoretische Perspektiven* (2020) 165–169.

[374] But the Colombian Constitutional Court is different. See Issacharoff, García-Jaramillo, and Benítez-Rojas, 'Judicial Review of Presidential Re- Election Amendments in Colombia', in R. Grote, F. Lachenmann, and R. Wolfrum (eds), *Max Planck Encyclopedia of Comparative Constitutional Law* (2020).

[375] See the contributions in M. Bobek (ed.), *Selecting Europe's Judges: A Critical Review of the Appointment Procedures to the European Courts* (2015); Epping, 'Die demokratische Legitimation der dritten Gewalt der Europäischen Gemeinschaften', 36 *Der Staat* (1997) 349.

understanding, this selection is not a solely technical affair[376] but has political substance and is, for that reason, democratically relevant. Closer analysis reveals deficiencies and suggests a need for transformation.

The Treaties outline judicial selection only loosely. The TFEU requires independence and professional expertise (Articles 251(1) and 254(2) TFEU), while the ECHR requires 'high moral character' and legal competence (Article 21(1) ECHR). This allows for different conceptions of the judicial office. Some consider the judicial task a mainly cognitive affair, while others think of it as normative and creative. Some might suggest restraint and minimalism, others engagement and maximalism. Some conceptualize the Union as a federal commonwealth, others as an instrument of interstate cooperation. These different understandings lead to different conceptions of the judicial office. The same holds true for political convictions and normative world views that inevitably inform the judges' work.[377]

It seems obvious that these important points should be addressed in the selection procedures if these wish to be meaningful. Moreover, the allocation of influential, prestigious, and well-paid judgeships is often an important political tool, which adds to the need for democratic scrutiny. For all these reasons, most parliaments today have a role in the judicial selection of constitutional or apex courts. Such politicization does not equate judges with politicians.[378] Nor does the politicization of judicial selection as such call their impartiality and independence into question. It is beyond question that independence and impartiality are essential elements of the courts' democratic mandate. However, parliamentary involvement is no more a threat than government fiat or the internal logic of judicial self-government.

Reconstructing judicial selection in the light of the principle of democracy does not equal a vote for sweeping politicization. Having the people elect the judges, as occurs in some US states or in Bolivia,[379] is not desirable. Specifically, two points are at stake: first, that representative institutions openly and cooperatively determine the legislative aspect of judicial selection and, second, that the previously elaborated criteria are applied transparently in the selection procedures (Article 11(2 and 3) TEU).

Let us begin with the legislative aspect: the vague Treaty requirements are concretized in strikingly different ways in the EU and the Council of Europe. In Strasbourg, the Consultative Assembly of the Council of Europe, a parliamentary

376 See Sauvé, 'Selecting the European Union's Judges: The Practice of the Article 255 Panel', in Bobek, *Selecting Europe's Judges* (n. 375) 78.

377 Rodríguez Iglesias, 'The Judge Confronts Himself as Judge—Presentation', in R. Badinter and S. Breyer (eds), *Judges in Contemporary Democracy. An International Conversation* (2004) 275, at 281.

378 Möllers, 'Legality, Legitimacy, and Legitimation of the Federal Constitutional Court', in Jestaedt *et al.*, *The German Federal Constitutional Court* (n. 32) 131, at 146 ff.

379 On the United States, see Wheeler, 'Judicial Independence in the United States of America', in A. Seibert-Fohr (ed.), *Judicial Independence in Transition* (2012) 521, at 528 ff. On the direct election of judges pursuant to the Bolivian constitutional reform that came into force in 2009, see Driscoll and Nelson, 'The 2011 Judicial Elections in Bolivia', 31 *Electoral Studies* (2012) 628.

body composed of national representatives (Articles 22 ff. of the Statute of the Council of Europe), is the driving force. In an open and deliberative process, it has established the requisite criteria and settled controversial issues. In Brussels, things are much more reserved. The so-called *Comité 255*, the Committee on Article 255 TFEU, has established selection criteria in its activity reports.[380]

One of the most visible and important powers of the Council of Europe's Consultative (Parliamentary) Assembly is selecting the judges for the ECtHR. Under Article 22 ECHR, it selects a candidate from the national shortlist of three. It requires the prior national selection process to be democratic, transparent, and non-discriminatory.[381] Since the national and transnational components of the selection are closely intertwined, the interaction of national and transnational institutions determines the success and legitimacy of the process.[382]

Since the mid-1990s, the Parliamentary Assembly has actively shaped the selection process. It has set out requirements in a series of legal acts, recommendations, resolutions, and reports.[383] Thus, the bench should be composed of individuals who are competent and communicative, recognize the socio-political dimension of their task, and demonstrate humanity and a commitment to public service. Moreover, multilingualism is important.[384] Because of the need for gender equality, at least 40 per cent of the judges should be women.

We can disagree about whether all these criteria are convincing. But the procedure is impressive from a democratic perspective, as proven by the gender equality requirement.[385] After intensive debates, the Assembly established that national nomination lists (Article 22 ECHR) must always include female candidates.[386] To do so, it came to an agreement with the Committee of Ministers—that addressed the ECtHR's legal opinion on the matter, and responded to national governments' concerns. This process has cooperative, deliberative elements across various levels, which is laudable in democratic terms.

[380] Most recently, *Sixth Activity Report of the Panel Provided for by Article 255 of the Treaty on the Functioning of the European Union* (2019), https://curia.europa.eu/jcms/upload/docs/application/pdf/2020-01/qcar19002enn_002_-_public.pdf (last visited 21 August 2022).

[381] Council of Europe (Parliamentary Assembly), Resolution 1646 (2009), at para. 2. See the earlier Council of Europe (Parliamentary Assembly), Recommendation 1649 (2004). This may include public notices of vacancies and hearings of the national parliaments. The Committee of Ministers supports these demands. See Council of Europe (Committee of Ministers), CM (2012) 40 final (29 March 2012).

[382] Resolution 1646 (2009) (n. 381) para. 1.

[383] Council of Europe (Parliamentary Assembly), Report of the Assembly Committee on Legal Affairs and Human Rights on the Procedure for electing judges to the European Court of Human Rights of 7 December 2012 (AS/Jur/Inf (2012) 02 rev4).

[384] Council of Europe (Parliamentary Assembly), Report of the Committee on Legal Affairs and Human Rights on the Candidates for the European Court of Human Rights of 7 October 2003 (Doc. 9963), para. 56.

[385] Hennette-Vauchez, 'More Women—But Which Women? The Rule and the Politics of Gender Balance at the European Court of Human Rights', 26 *European Journal of International Law* (2015) 195; F. Baetens (ed.), *Identity and Diversity on the International Bench* (2021).

[386] Council of Europe (Parliamentary Assembly), Resolution 1366 (2004), amended by Resolution 1426 (2005), Resolution 1627 (2008), and Resolution 1841 (2011).

In the EU, the development of criteria for judicial selection takes a different path. The Comité *255*, established by the Lisbon Treaty, is the most visible actor.[387] Its main task is to prepare the decision of the Member State governments by evaluating individual candidates. In its activity reports, this committee has established the criteria it uses for evaluation. The mode for appointing its members is cooptative since the president of the CJEU proposes the composition of the Comité 255.[388]

The establishment of this committee represents a valuable development in the evaluation of the candidates' professional qualifications. If we consider judicial selection from the perspective of democratic principles, however, it becomes clear that experts can only play a limited role,[389] especially when it comes to developing the requisite procedures and criteria. The Committee has recognized as much. It emphasizes, for instance, that it is not its task to consider the overall composition of the bench.[390] Questions of social representativeness or equal gender representation on the bench are outside its remit.

It could help to involve the European Parliament. Since the Spinelli Report,[391] it has repeatedly demanded an active role in the selection of CJEU judges.[392] Its participation would reflect the logic of Article 10 TEU and offers a promising way to enhance the democratic quality and public perception of the process. Moreover, it does not require a Treaty amendment: the European Parliament, advised by the *Comité 255*, could establish general criteria for judicial selection in the form of resolutions or recommendations.[393]

The second aspect concerns the appointment of individual judges.[394] In the EU and the Council of Europe, the selection begins with the Member States' governments proposing suitable candidates. These proposals are no longer rubber-stamped. Rather, both systems have established committees of experts to ensure compliance with the requirements. The equivalent of the EU's *Comité 255* in the Council of Europe is a committee of seven experts informally named after its first president, Luzius Wildhaber. It is meant to advise any Convention State on its candidates' suitability before the state sends its list of three candidates to the

[387] Council Decision 2010/124/EU relating to the operating rules of the panel provided for in Article 255 of the Treaty on the Functioning of the European Union, OJ 2010 L 50/18.

[388] See de Waele, 'Not Quite the Bed That Procrustes Built. Dissecting the System for Selecting Judges at the Court of Justice of the European Union', in Bobek, *Selecting Europe's Judges* (n. 375) 24.

[389] Voßkuhle and Sydow (n. 365) 677.

[390] *Activity Report of the Panel Provided for by Article 255 of the Treaty on the Functioning of the European Union*, Second Activity Report (26 December 2012), 7, http://register.consilium.europa.eu/pdf/en/13/st05/st05091.en13.pdf (last visited 21 July 2022).

[391] EP Resolution on the draft Treaty establishing the European Union, OJ 1984 C 77/33, Art. 30 para. 2.

[392] Clariana, 'Le rôle du Parlement européen dans le développement de la Cour de justice', in N. Colneric *et al.* (eds), *Festschrift für Gil Carlos Rodríguez Iglesias* (2003) 21, at 25 ff.

[393] Article 120 of the Rules of Procedure of the European Parliament.

[394] On the criticism, see de Waele (n. 388); Kosař, 'Selecting Strasbourg Judges. A Critique', in Bobek, *Selecting Europe's Judges* (n. 375) 120.

Parliamentary Assembly.[395] Involving experts in this way is desirable. Often, their personal and professional experience helps gather, organize, and evaluate information, for instance, when assessing candidates' professional qualifications, independence, and impartiality.[396] Hence, it is problematic that most Convention states ignore the Committee's assessment and propose candidates whom the panel has rejected.[397] It is especially deplorable that the Parliamentary Assembly goes along with this.

In the EU, the governments of the Member States decide who shall join the bench pursuant to Articles 253 and 254 TFEU. This seems anachronistic for two reasons. First, the procedure of judicial selection in the EU is not subject to any judicial review, which is odd, given the role of judicial review in the EU. Second, the decision not to involve the European Parliament sits uneasily with the logic of Article 10 TEU. After all, the Parliament plays at least an advisory role in selection procedures for other independent Union institutions (Articles 283(2) and 286(2) TFEU).

If we apply the classificatory dimension of the concept of democracy, the CJEU and the ECtHR are democratic institutions, then. However, the comparative dimension reveals deficiencies as well as potential for improvement (see 3.5.C). The same holds true for the courts' proceedings as well as for their reasoning.[398]

C. In Whose Name?

Like any mandate, the judicial mandate requires that someone grant the mandatary its mandate. Reconstructing the European courts' mandate leads to the question of who that is. Many national courts answer this question by adjudicating a case *In the Name of the People* or *the Republic*.[399] The CJEU and the ECHR do not provide any such information in their judgments.[400] The difference also becomes apparent in the oath of office. Under section 11 of the German Constitutional Court Act, a new justice must swear that, 'I shall, as an impartial judge, at all times faithfully observe

[395] Council of Europe (Committee of Ministers), Resolution CM/Res(2010)26.

[396] Steering Committee for Human Rights, Draft CDDH report on the review of the functioning of the Advisory Panel of experts on candidates for election as judge to the European Court of Human Rights, GT-GDR-E(2013)R2 Addendum II (19 September 2013).

[397] Steering Committee for Human Rights, *Selection and Election of Judges of the European Court of Human Rights* (2018) 34–43.

[398] For my reflections on this matter, see von Bogdandy and Venzke (n. 43) 171 ff. See also, Farahat, *Transnationale Solidaritätskonflikte* (n. 355) para. 3 B.

[399] See sec. 25 para. 4 of the German Constitutional Court Act; Art. 454 of the French Civil Procedure Act; Art. 101 para. 1 of the Italian Constitution; Art. 202 para. 1 of the Portuguese Constitution; Art. 82 para. 2 of the Austrian Federal Constitutional Law; Art. 49 para. 10 of the Czech Code of Administrative Procedure. For more on the formula, see P.-C. Müller-Graff, 'Zur Geschichte der Formel "Im Namen des Volkes"', 88 *Zeitschrift für Zivilprozess* (1975) 442; M. Stolleis, *Im Namen des Gesetzes* (2004) 7 ff.

[400] On the wisdom of this silence, see Clausen, 'In the Name of the European Union, the Member States and/or the European Citizens?', in Ruiz Fabri *et al.* (n. 267) 249.

the Basic Law of the Federal Republic of Germany.' In Austria, according to section 29 para. 1 of the Act on the Service of Judges and Prosecutors, judges must swear to serve the Republic with all their might. But under Article 4 of the Court of Justice's Rules of Procedure, the only oath required is the promise to 'perform my duties impartially and conscientiously [and to] preserve the secrecy of the deliberations of the Court of Justice'. The oath of office for the ECtHR under Rule 3 of the Rules of the Court is similarly meagre. This reflects how uncertain their structures of accountability are.

Which formula could serve to introduce a CJEU or ECtHR decision to convey an idea of its democratic legitimation? The following reconstruction will culminate in two proposals that enrich my understanding of the two courts' mandate, their relationship, and of European society.

I shall turn first to the ECtHR. Which formulation could articulate its democratic legitimation similarly to the formulation *In the Name of the People*?[401] For a start, we might imagine a reference to the Convention. In that case, an ECtHR decision would begin with the words 'In the Name of the European Convention on Human Rights', like a national decision that used 'In the Name of the Law' as its opening formula.[402] But this would fail to recognize that the parliamentary decision to make the law, not the law itself, constitutes the decision's source of democratic legitimation.

Many international courts ground their legitimacy in the consent of the disputing states before it. Accordingly, they rule *In the Name of the Disputing States*. But this suits the International Court of Justice, not the Strasbourg Court, whose disputes involve a state and an individual (often of that state itself), not two states in conflict with one another.

The democratic legitimacy of the Strasbourg Court flows from the ratification of the Convention by *all* states parties. Therefore, it decides *In the Name of all States Parties*. The holistic *all* expresses that an ECtHR judgment decides not only the case at hand but also a concern common to all states parties. The preamble of the ECHR speaks of an 'effective political democracy' throughout Europe; the Convention goes far beyond international law's traditional bilateralism because the ECtHR's decisions pursue an interest common to the Convention states.

The formula *In the Name of all States Parties* can be refined, however. The ECHR overcomes not only traditional bilateralism but also international law's traditional value relativism. The states parties must follow the principles of *the rule of law and democracy*.[403] Certainly, not all states fulfilled all requirements when they acceded

[401] The following section is based on von Bogdandy and Hering (n. 267).

[402] For a similar suggestion for the CJEU, see L. van Middelaar, *The Passage to Europe. How a Continent Became a Union* (2014) 27: 'on behalf of the European treaty'.

[403] See Preamble and Art. 3 of the Statute of the Council of Europe; Zand, 'The Concept of Democracy and the European Convention on Human Rights', 5 *University of Baltimore Journal of International Law* (2017) 195.

to the ECHR. But deficient states were admitted under the proviso that they develop in accordance with the Convention.[404]

The Convention's requirements regarding the rule of law and democracy take on clearer contours in their threefold contrast to the totalitarian systems of the Axis powers, Soviet communism,[405] and authoritarian regimes such as that of the Greek colonels.[406] In addition to effective fundamental rights protection, it demands political pluralism and a functioning system for separating the government powers.[407] The Convention seeks not only to 'defend [the] people' 'against dictatorship' but also—vitally, in the current context—to strengthen 'the resistance in all [. . .] countries against insidious attempts to undermine [the] democratic way of life'.[408]

The Convention not only concerns the state apparatus and public authority but is also a pioneering treaty because it overcomes traditional international law in a third respect. It endows individuals with rights and allows them to become transnational actors by means of the individual complaint. The Convention also strengthens individuals as political subjects. The protection of democratic rights represents one of the Court's central lines of jurisprudence; it includes decisions on the political freedom of association under Article 11 ECHR,[409] political freedom of expression under Article 10 ECHR,[410] and the right to free elections under Article 3 of the First Additional Protocol.[411]

The significance of this achievement should become apparent in the formula. Indeed, national courts do not decide *In the Name of the State* but precisely in that *of the People* or *the Republic*. This can be articulated by shortening the formula to *In the Name of European Democracies*. Sublating *states* in *democracies* expresses that the citizenry is included. The plural form of 'democracies' denotes that the ECtHR does not speak in the name of an abstract idea of political order. Accordingly, the formula underscores that the Court's democratic legitimacy derives from the democratically organized peoples of the Convention States.

Finally, the formula should express that the Court's democratic legitimacy represents European democracies' common achievement. This leads to the concept of *community*.[412] European democracies have come together under the statute of

[404] Council of Europe (Parliamentary Assembly), Application by Russia for membership of the Council of Europe, Opinion 192 (1996), No. 7.

[405] Madsen, 'From Cold War Instrument to Supreme European Court' (n. 224).

[406] H. A. Richter, *Griechenland 1950–1974. Zwischen Demokratie und Diktatur* (2013) 323 ff.

[407] ECtHR, *Campbell and Fell v. United Kingdom*, Appl. no. 7819/77, Judgment of 28 June 1984, Series A No. 80, para. 78.

[408] See Council of Europe, 5 *Collected Edition of the 'Travaux préparatoires'* (1979) 332; Council of Europe, 1 *Collected Edition of the 'Travaux préparatoires'* (1979) 30.

[409] ECtHR, *Vona v. Hungary*, Appl. no. 35943/10, Judgment of 9 July 2013, para. 58.

[410] *Handyside v. United Kingdom* (n. 291) para. 49.

[411] ECtHR, *Matthews v. United Kingdom*, Appl. no. 24833/94, Judgment of 18 February 1999, ECHR 1999-1, para. 42.

[412] Bellamy, 'The Democratic Legitimacy of International Human Rights Conventions: Political Constitutionalism and the European Convention on Human Rights', 25 *European Journal of International Law* (2015) 1019, at 1031 ff.

the Council of Europe and the Convention to pursue objectives that they cannot achieve alone. The most important objective is a regional human rights system that secures their democratic constitutionalism.[413] To this end, the Convention states have set up common institutions endowed with public authority, most importantly the ECtHR, whose judges they jointly select by parliamentary procedure. Therefore, the Court rules *In the Name of the European Community of Democracies.*

All observations concerning the ECtHR apply to the CJEU. The EU, even more than the Council of Europe, is a *community of European democracies.* The requirements of Article 48 TEU take up the criteria of Article 4 of the Statute of the Council of Europe but are more demanding. Furthermore, the Union's internal structure differs markedly from that of the Council of Europe. As befits its far greater power, the Union has its own citizenship, direct elections, and democratic life. Articles 9–12 TEU set down 'provisions on democratic principles' that apply to all institutions of the EU (Article 13 TEU), including the CJEU.

Because there is no European people (see 2.3.A), the CJEU cannot decide *In the Name of the People* but only, at best, *In the Name of its Peoples* (see 3.5.A). But this would obscure a great innovation of Union law: Union citizenship (see 2.3.A).

The introductory article of Title II of the Treaties on EU democracy begins with Union citizenship. On this basis, we should consider articulating the CJEU's democratic mandate with the words *In the Name of Union Citizens.*[414] However, it would misconstrue the Union's democracy to focus *solely* on Union citizens. Union law recognizes that all Union citizens are organized by the Member States. To create the EU's democracy, the Treaties combine the peoples of the Member States with the Union citizens. The Union is based on a *dual structure of legitimacy*: the totality of Union citizens *and* the peoples of the Member States (see 3.5.A).

The dual structure of legitimacy expresses European transformation. What formula could get to the heart of this? The formula *In the Name of Union Citizens and the Peoples of the Member States* is one option. This understanding shows up in Article I-1(1) of the failed Constitutional Treaty of 2004.

But there is another option. According to Article 1(2) TEU, the objective of European Union is *a union of the peoples of Europe*. The indefinite article *a* indicates that the union of Article 1(2) TEU is more than the organization of the *European Union* invoked by Article 1(3) TEU, that is, the organization that is a legal entity (Article 47 TEU). Article 1(2) TEU articulates the overall union between the legal entity of the *European Union* and the Member States, that is, the association (or polity) upheld by all the members of European society that are simultaneously Union citizens and the Member States' nationals (see 2.2.D). This echoes Jean

[413] Bates (n. 147) 5.

[414] In this sense, see Wernicke, 'Au nom de qui? The European Court of Justice between Member States, Civil Society and Union Citizens', 13 *European Law Journal* (2007) 380, at 406 ff.

Monnet's famous dictum about the purpose of integration: 'We are not forming coalitions of states, we are uniting people.'[415]

Consequently, the CJEU ought to decide *In the Name of the Union*. This formula fits the CJEU's mandate to promote the Union, the citizens, and Member States' values, objectives, and interests (Article 13(1) TEU). In critical situations, this may include the mandate of transformative constitutionalism.

6. Transformative Constitutionalism

Constitutional jurisdiction has shaped European public law at least since 1990, contributing to the emergence and democratization of European society. Some of its cases amount to transformative constitutionalism (see 2.6.B). To deepen this dimension, I will again turn to Latin American experiences, which exemplify how a court can contribute to democratic transitions. Then, I will address the relevant jurisprudence of the two European courts. I will begin with the ECtHR, which has been making such decisions for over two decades, unlike the CJEU, which only started doing so on 27 February 2018.

A. New Responses to Old Challenges

Owing to the binary logic of the law, every judgment produces a loser. Many consider the loser's acquiescence the real crux of the judicial function: why and when does the loser acquiesce in the court's ruling?[416] This question is especially pertinent when a court decision is difficult, or even impossible, to enforce, as in the case of a constitutional court that rules against its government or an international court that rules against a state. Acquiescence is especially uncertain when courts demand transformations. In the following, I address three related challenges that courts face in any event: coping with politicization, creating a supportive social field, and tackling the problem of non-compliance.

Political resistance against courts in general and transformative decisions in particular has been a major issue in recent years.[417] It often leads to politicization in the sense that political actors question the legality and legitimacy of a decision, a line of jurisprudence, or even of a court as such. This endangers a court's

[415] J. Monnet, *Mémoires* (1976) 7: 'Nous ne coalisons pas des États, nous unissons des hommes.'

[416] N. Luhmann, *Legitimation durch Verfahren* (1969) esp. at 57 ff.; Shapiro (n. 35) 2.

[417] Soley and Steininger, 'Parting Ways or Lashing Back? Withdrawals, Backlash and the Inter-American Court of Human Rights', 14 *International Journal of Law in Context* (2018) 237; Madsen, 'From Boom to Backlash? The European Court of Human Rights and the Transformation of Europe', in H. Aust and E. Demir (eds), *The European Court of Human Rights: Current Challenges in Historical and Comparative Perspective* (2020) 21.

authoritativeness and, thus, perhaps its most important resource. But it also presents an opportunity.

The letter of the law alone does not make a court authoritative. Authoritativeness is also taken, conquered, often in a situation of conflict. Therefore, political resistance offers a court the chance to build or strengthen its authoritativeness (see 4.1.D). Of course, it takes acumen, courage, and political skill to make good use of any such opportunity. Scholarly analysis cannot provide for any of these faculties, but it can determine when courts have been successful. Latin American experiences illustrate this point.

In 2017, the IACtHR issued an opinion, at the request of the Costa Rican government, that Convention states must treat same-sex couples equally to heterosexual couples.[418] The government had made this request to have a trump card that it could play against the reluctant legislature. Implementing the opinion became a central issue in the subsequent election campaign; the two candidates in the second round of elections defined themselves by their opposing positions on this opinion. The candidate who supported it won the election.[419] Indeed, the entire election turned out to be something like a referendum on the authority of the Inter-American Court in Costa Rica.

Even more interesting is a public letter that the presidents of Argentina, Brazil, Chile, Colombia, and Paraguay—Mauricio Macri, Jair Bolsonaro, Sebastián Piñera, Iván Duque, and Mario Abdo Benítez—sent to the Inter-American Commission on Human Rights in April 2019.[420] All these presidents can be categorized as being on the right side of the political spectrum. They also represented 70 per cent of the region's population and 80 per cent of its gross domestic product (GDP). While the letter recognized the importance of the Inter-American human rights system, it demanded that its institutions show greater respect for the principle of subsidiarity, apply restrictive methods of interpretation, and work with 'due knowledge and consideration of the political, economic and social realities of the States'.

These requests called into question the transformative constitutionalism of the Inter-American human rights system. As a result, more than 200 non-governmental organizations (NGOs) mobilized against the letter.[421] They

[418] Inter-American Court of Human Rights, *Advisory Opinion OC-24/17: Gender Identity, and Equality and Non-discrimination of Same-Sex Couples* (2017); Urueña, 'Reclaiming the Keys to the Kingdom (of the World): Evangelicals and Human Rights in Latin America', in J. E. Nijman and W. G. Werner (eds), *Netherlands Yearbook of International Law 2018: Populism and International Law* (2019) 175.

[419] Semple, 'Costa Rica Election Hands Presidency to Governing Party Stalwart', *New York Times* (1 April 2018), https://www.nytimes.com/2018/04/01/world/americas/costa-rica-election-alvarado-quesada.html (last visited 21 July 2022).

[420] La República Argentina, la República Federativa del Brasil, la República de Chile, la República de Colombia y la República del Paraguay, Declaración Sobre el Sistema Interamericano de Derechos Humanos (2019), https://repositorio.uca.edu.ar/handle/123456789/8628 (last visited 21 July 2022).

[421] See ASILEGAL, *Embates al Sistema Interamericano de Derechos Humanos vulneran la protección regional de los DD.HH* (2 May 2019), https://asilegal.org.mx/comunicados/embates-al-sistema-interamericano-ddhh (last visited 21 July 2022).

portrayed it as an attack on the very system that symbolizes and safeguards the restoration of democracy in Latin America.[422] Their mobilization proved successful and the coalition of the five presidents fell apart. Thus, there was no concerted attempt to undermine the system, for example, by agreeing on a particular staffing policy for commissioners or judges. The only such candidate failed in the General Assembly of the Organization of American States.[423] The Chilean government, which had initiated the letter, soon put forward Antonia Urrejola Noguera and Patricia Pérez Goldberg, who are committed to the Inter-American system.

We can compare the letter of the five presidents with the Interlaken Process on the ECtHR (see 4.3.C), which was also the result of political resistance. For a long time, voices that were critical of the ECtHR dominated this process. Ultimately, however, the far more numerous actors who view the ECtHR's case law as lawful and legitimate mobilized. Thus, the politicization confirmed, and indeed promoted, the Court's legitimacy.

Something similar is occurring in Poland. There, the government is mobilizing against the European courts that support Polish judges fighting for their independence. But the government's politicization appears to be backfiring because it soon became apparent that vast parts of Polish society support the European courts.[424]

The second challenge concerns the need for a supportive social field.[425] Transformative constitutionalism is not a solitary judicial activity. It requires numerous other actors who identify suitable facts, prepare them as legal cases, take them to court, litigate them, accompany the process of implementation, and then use the decisions as precedents in later controversies.[426] Court decisions are only the tip of an iceberg of social practice. Often, the formation of such a field parallels that of a court.[427] In the end, they depend on each other.

In Latin America, many civil society organizations have only developed thanks to the possibilities of the Inter-American system. This serves to democratize

[422] On this role, see C. S. Nino, *Radical Evil on Trial* (1996) 68 f.

[423] García, 'Derrotada la iniciativa encabezada por Colombia para reformar la defensa de Derechos Humanos en la OEA', *El País* (28 June 2019), https://elpais.com/internacional/2019/06/27/america/1561672485_548623.html (last visited 22 July 2022); Acosta *et al.*, *Informe del Panel Independiente de Expertos y Expertas para la evaluación de candidatos y candidatas a la Comisión Interamericana de Derechos Humanos* (5 June 2019), https://www.wcl.american.edu/impact/initiatives-programs/center/documents/2019-informe-del-panel-independiente-de-expertos (last visited 22 July 2022).

[424] Pankowska, *Majority of Poles take EU Court of Justice Side in Fighting PiS Attack on Courts*, *ruleoflaw.pl* (19 November 2019), https://ruleoflaw.pl/majority-of-poles-take-eu-court-of-justice-side-in-fighting-pis-attack-on-courts (last visited 22 July 2022).

[425] Vauchez, 'Introduction. Euro-Lawyering, Transnational Social Fields and European Polity-Building', in Vauchez and de Witte (n. 121) 1; fundamentally, Bourdieu, 'The Force of Law. Toward a Sociology of the Juridical Field', 38 *Hastings Law Journal* (1986) 814.

[426] In detail, M. Neves, *Verfassung und Positivität des Rechts in der peripheren Moderne. Eine theoretische Betrachtung und Interpretation des Falls Brasilien* (1992) 37 ff., 160 ff.; Vauchez, 'Communities of International Litigators', in C. P. R. Romano, K. J. Alter, and Y. Shany (eds), *The Oxford Handbook of International Adjudication* (201) 655, at 656 f.

[427] Hennette-Vauchez, 'The ECHR and the Birth of (European) Human Rights Law as an Academic Discipline', in Vauchez and de Witte (n. 121) 122, at 123.

the region.[428] The same is true in Central and Eastern Europe. We may think of NGOs such as Amnesty International, the Stefan Batory Foundation, the Helsinki Foundation for Human Rights, the Centre for Legal Resources, or the Wolne Sądy (Free Courts) initiative but also of associations such as the Polish judicial organizations Iustitia and Themis or the association of prosecutors Lex Super Omnia or Asociația Forumul Judecătorilor din România.[429] The Hungarian government's actions against civil society organizations such as the Open Society Foundation and the Central European University confirm that the latter are relevant societal forces.[430]

This field goes beyond actors who Karen Alter and Laurence Helfer describe as advocatory lawyers,[431] such as human rights activists or activist legal scholarship. It includes the representatives of the state institutions involved and, in particular, domestic courts. It involves iterative interactions between the actors, allows for mutual learning, and develops shared normative expectations. It thereby affects the world view, interests, and strategies of all actors involved—of activists, the responsible authorities, scholarship, and (last but not least) the judges.[432]

Transnational case law that shapes structures requires reception by domestic courts.[433] Therefore, it is a great success for the European or the Inter-American courts when domestic judges identify as European or Inter-American judges. This also underscores the cultural significance of the CJEU's doctrine that every Member State court is also a Union court (see 2.2.C, 4.4.B).

Conflicts can foster such identities. In 2012, the Inter-American Court ruled against the Costa Rican Supreme Court's decision declaring in vitro fertilization unconstitutional.[434] The Costa Rican legislature then legalized the treatment, following which evangelical groups brought the statute before the Costa Rican Supreme Court. It maintained its previous jurisprudence and declared the statute unconstitutional despite the Inter-American Court's decision.[435] The IACtHR immediately responded with a decision reaffirming the legality of in vitro fertilization

[428] P. Engstrom (ed.), *The Inter-American Human Rights System. Impact Beyond Compliance* (2019).

[429] Konrad Adenauer Stiftung and Asociația Forumul Judecătorilor din România, *900 Days of Uninterrupted Siege upon the Romanian Magistracy. A Survival Guide* (2020).

[430] The CJEU has declared both laws to be contrary to Union law: *Commission v. Hungary (Transparency of Associations)* (n. 336); Case C-66/18, *Commission v. Hungary (Enseignement supérieur)* (EU:C:2020:792); Spieker, 'Werteverteidigung im Binnenmarkt? Das ungarische Transparenzgesetz auf dem Prüfstand des EuGH', 31 *Europäische Zeitschrift für Wirtschaftsrecht* (2020) 854.

[431] K. J. Alter and L. R. Helfer, *Transplanting International Courts. The Law and Politics of the Andean Tribunal of Justice* (2017) 230–233.

[432] Wendt, 'The Agent-Structure Problem in International Relations Theory', 41 *International Organization* (1987) 335.

[433] D. Guarnizo-Peralta, 'Cortes pasivas, cortes activas, o cortes dialógicas? Comentarios en torno al caso Cuscul Pivaral y otros v. Guatemala', in M. Morales Antoniazzi, L. Ronconi, and L. Clérico (eds), *Interamericanización de los DESCA. El caso Cuscul Pivaral de la Corte IDH* (2020) 429; see also 4.5.

[434] Inter-American Court of Human Rights, *Artavia Murillo et al. ('In Vitro Fertilization') v. Costa Rica*, Decision of 28 November 2012 (Merits), Series C, No. 257.

[435] Sala Constitucional de la Corte Suprema de Costa Rica, Sentencia No. 2016-01692 of 3 February 2016.

in Costa Rica.[436] At this level of escalation, the Costa Rican justices accepted the authority of the IACtHR.[437] Shortly thereafter, the President of the Supreme Court, Carmenmaría Escoto, explicitly confirmed that her court, all controversies notwithstanding, was committed to Inter-Americanization.[438]

For the CJEU, the ECtHR, and the IACtHR, this suggests attending to actors who support their case law and help it enter social reality. Judicial cooperation constitutes one important building block (see 4.2.C, 4.4.B), the larger field of societal actors another one. That civil society organizations play a minor role before the CJEU and the ECtHR, compared to the Inter-American Court, suggests a potential for development.[439]

A challenge also presents itself when a state does not comply with a decision. The ruling might then be pointless, even harmful. The question is particularly relevant when a judgment strives for transformation because the ruling is devoid of meaning if it cannot engender effects within society. Moreover, the compliance rate is particularly low in these cases. Compliance means that the state remedies the violation and adjusts the social field.[440]

A high rate of compliance often seems to indicate that a court triggers transformative effects and is authoritative.[441] The ECtHR faces considerable difficulties in this regard.[442] But the CJEU also confronts challenges (see 3.2.C, 4.6.C). The importance of compliance could suggest that courts should not address structural problems so as not to jeopardize their authority. Studying the opposite course, which was chosen by the Inter-American Court, is hence instructive for Europe.

[436] IACtHR, *Artavia Murillo et al ('In Vitro Fertilization') v. Costa Rica*, Decision of 26 February 2016 (Resolution on compliance, paras 26, 36.

[437] Avendaño, 'Magistrado Luis Fernando Salazar: Es momento de que la Sala IV se haga a un lado', *La Nación* (1 March 2016), https://www.nacion.com/el-pais/salud/magistrado-luis-fernando-salazar-es-momento-de-que-la-sala-iv-se-haga-a-un-lado/KXMCQE7VEZGW7PQPFTGDR25JKU/story (last visited 22 July 2022).

[438] See Poder Judicial—República de Costa Rica, *Presidenta de la Corte en ejercicio destaca labor de la Corte IDH* (2018), https://pj.poder-judicial.go.cr/index.php/prensa/389-cme-corteidh (last visited 22 July 2022). On the concept of inter-Americanization, see Morales Antoniazzi, 'Interamericanización. Fundamentos e impactos', in E. Ferrer Mac-Gregor *et al.* (eds), *Cumplimiento e impacto de las sentencias de la Corte Interamericana y el Tribunal Europeo de Derechos Humanos. Transformando realidades* (2019) 57.

[439] Dothan, 'Luring NGOs to International Courts: A Comment on *CLR v. Romania*', 75 *Zeitschrift für ausländisches öffentliches Recht und Völkerrecht* (2015) 635; Erken, 'The Participation of Non-Governmental Organisations and National Human Rights Institutions in the Execution of Judgments of the Strasbourg Court. Exploring Rule 9 Communications at the Committee of Ministers', 2 *ECHR Law Review* (2020) 248.

[440] Huneeus, 'Compliance with Judgments and Decisions', in C. P. R. Romano, K. J. Alter, and Y. Shany (eds), *The Oxford Handbook of International Adjudication* (2014) 438.

[441] Alter, Helfer, and Madsen, 'How Context Shapes the Authority of International Courts', in K. J. Alter, L. R. Helfer, and M. R. Madsen (eds), *International Court Authority* (2018) 24.

[442] See, e.g. Council of Europe (Committee of Ministers), *Annual Report 2018, Supervision of the Execution of Judgments and Decisions of the European Court of Human Rights* (2018) 71 ff.

The Inter-American Court suffers from an especially low compliance rate.[443] But we overlook many transformative effects if we focus on this alone. Thus, the very process of promoting compliance can be useful, too. Thus, the Inter-American Court insists on duties of disclosure, conducts site visits, and organizes hearings at which state authorities, victims, and stakeholders—who often have never met—exchange opinions and discuss strategies.[444]

States' compliance with an international judgment differs from the question of whether a civil judgment against a delinquent debtor is enforced. To further compliance, international decisions are often vague; only during the implementation process, and in dialogue with the states involved, do they take on more precise contours.[445] What is more, the context of implementation is rarely static, and the Inter-American Court often tries to influence it. Frequently, one objective of its rulings is to allow other actors to use the decision to promote a supportive context: how can *this* international decision help the national judiciary promote compliance with its own decisions? How can an international decision help civil society mobilize for the issue at hand? This is how compliance partnerships emerge.[446]

Moreover, a court exerts its influence not just through the eye of the needle by ensuring full compliance with its rulings.[447] Again, Latin America helps us understand this more clearly. Until the 1980s, human rights, beyond symbolism, hardly played a role in most Latin American states. Today, by contrast, inter-American provisions, decisions, and institutions are present in the entire region, even though the compliance rate is low. They are interwoven with national provisions to form a shared law of human rights, creating a new social field of possibilities for structural transformation.[448] There are many actors in this field. Transformative constitutionalism means that intractable social problems that once appeared to be manageable only in political or even revolutionary terms are now also articulated as legal issues and dealt with in the forms of law. This can have far-reaching effects. The transformative case law of the Colombian Constitutional Court, for example,

[443] Gonzalez-Salzberg, 'Do States Comply with the Compulsory Judgments of the Inter-American Court of Human Rights? An Empirical Study of the Compliance with 330 Measures of Reparation', 13 *Revista do Instituto Brasileiro de Direitos Humanos* (2013) 93.

[444] In detail, see von Bogdandy and Urueña, 'International Transformative Constitutionalism in Latin America', 114 *American Journal of International Law* (2020) 403, at 425 ff.

[445] On the CJEU, see Börzel *et al.*, 'Obstinate and Inefficient: Why Member States Do Not Comply with European Law', 43 *Comparative Political Studies* (2010) 1363; Tridimas (n. 312).

[446] Huneeus, 'Constitutional Lawyers and the Inter-American Court's Varied Authority', 79 *Law and Contemporary Problems* (2016) 179; L. J. Conant, *Justice Contained* (2002) 214 ff.

[447] Parra Verra, 'The Impact of Inter-American Judgments by Institutional Empowerment', in von Bogdandy *et al.*, *Transformative Constitutionalism in Latin America* (n. 103) 357; Engstrom, 'Introduction: Rethinking the Impact of the Inter-American Human Rights System', in Engstrom, *The Inter-American Human Rights System* (n. 428) 1.

[448] For the appropriate theory, see C. Möllers, *Die Möglichkeit der Normen. Über eine Praxis jenseits von Moralität und Kausalität* (2018) 127 f., 131 ff.

contributed to the peace process that won the Nobel Peace Prize in 2016.[449] Of course, human rights continue to be violated systematically in many countries, but no lawyer should overlook that decisions by the Inter-American Court help address many deficiencies.

The Latin American experience suggests focusing on the bigger picture regarding the CJEU and ECtHR's possibilities in addressing systemic deficiencies. There is legal value in judgments that identify deficient situations as such, publicly state what needs to be done, and strengthen social forces committed to remedying the deficiency. If domestic institutions—namely, the government, its parliamentary majority, or a captured court—do not comply with a judgment issued by the ECtHR or the CJEU, Europeans should consider this the problem of the deviant domestic institution and not of the ECtHR or the CJEU.

B. The Requirements Set Out by the ECtHR

Since the 1980s, the ECtHR has brought about a human rights juridification of European society (see 4.3.C). This can be interpreted as transformative.[450] However, the Court hardly addressed systemic deficiencies.[451] It only started doing so when the so-called transformation states acceded to the Council of Europe and the ECHR in the 1990s and the ECtHR began to accompany them in their constitutional transformation.[452]

In this context, new lines of jurisprudence emerged that restricted national autonomy far more than before. One such line concerns the structure of the national judiciary as well as the many delicate issues of transitional justice.[453] Moreover, the ECtHR indicates the domestic measures required to remedy a violation of the Convention.[454] It orders the resumption of criminal proceedings, restitution in cases of expropriation, or release from prison. What is even more important from the perspective of transformation is that the Court orders general measures, in particular in so-called pilot judgments.[455] There, the Court identifies a systemic

[449] Agreement of 24 November 2016, Fuerzas Armadas Revolucionarias de Colombia, Ejército del Pueblo—FARC-EP y Gobierno de Colombia, Acuerdo Final Para La Terminación Del Conflicto y La Construcción de Una Paz Estable y Duradera.

[450] Madsen, 'From Cold War Instrument to Supreme European Court' (n. 224).

[451] But see the case law regarding the excessive length of judicial proceedings (3.3.D).

[452] I. Motoc and I. Ziemele (eds), *The Impact of the ECHR on Democratic Change in Central and Eastern Europe. Judicial Perspectives* (2016). On the qualification as transformative constitutionalism, see Sonnevend, 'Preserving the Acquis of Transformative Constitutionalism in Times of Constitutional Crisis. Lessons from the Hungarian Case', in von Bogdandy *et al.*, *Transformative Constitutionalism in Latin America* (n. 103) 123.

[453] Brems, 'Transitional Justice in the Case Law of the European Court of Human Rights', 5 *International Journal of Transitional Justice* (2011) 282.

[454] Keller and Kühne, 'Zur Verfassungsgerichtsbarkeit des Europäischen Gerichtshofs für Menschenrechte', 76 *Zeitschrift für ausländisches öffentliches Recht und Völkerrecht* (2016) 245.

[455] ECtHR, *Broniowski v. Poland*, Appl. no. 31443/96, Judgment of 22 June 2004.

problem, indicates the necessary steps to remedy it, and sets a deadline for doing so. In substance, it demands that the requisite legislation be enacted.[456]

When the ECtHR's transformative case law began in the 1990s, it was still expected that the democratic rule of law would eventually prevail in all Convention states (see 2.6.D). When this hope became ever more elusive, the ECtHR had to recalibrate its transformative constitutionalism.[457] Now, jurisprudence aims to define core human rights requirements and to demand that they be enforced. Most of these judgments concern states outside the EU. Nevertheless, they are significant for these states: a violation of the ECHR's core substance indicates that the constitutional core of Article 2 TEU has been violated, too.[458] This ECtHR case law can be understood as transformative constitutionalism because it addresses structural deficiencies, much like the case law of the Inter-American Court. In what follows, I will sketch out this transformative constitutionalism based on the case law concerning the state of emergency, the core substance of rights, and the abuse of law.[459]

Article 15 ECHR allows the states parties to suspend Convention rights in a state of emergency. The Court acts cautiously in this matter and grants the states parties a broad margin of appreciation.[460] By now, however, it has specified its definition of a 'strict requirement', introduced a review for proportionality, and thereby subjected emergency measures to a duty of justification under its oversight.[461]

The situation in Turkey that began in 2016 poses an especially great challenge for the ECtHR.[462] On the one hand, its help was urgently required. On the other hand, the Turkish government proved extremely recalcitrant, which means that the ECtHR risked becoming less authoritative. It accepted the challenge: in the *Altan* and *Alpay* cases, it examined, for the first time, the significance of freedom of expression (Article 10 ECHR) in the context of a state of emergency. It held that the right may be derogated, but only in truly exceptional cases.[463] Furthermore, it emphasized that freedom of expression is vital to a vibrant democracy and pointed out that a state of emergency may not be used as a pretext to restrict the freedom of political debate, which lies at the heart of a democratic society.

456 Fyrnys, 'Expanding Competences by Judicial Lawmaking. The Pilot Judgment Procedure of the European Court of Human Rights', 12 *German Law Journal* (2011) 1231, at 1231, 1244, 1254.

457 This section is based on von Bogdandy and Hering (n. 267).

458 *Aranyosi and Căldăraru* (n. 334) paras 87.

459 However, there are also indications that the Court is retreating. See Helfer and Voeten, 'Walking Back Human Rights in Europe?', 31 *European Journal of International Law* (2020) 797.

460 von Bogdandy and Spieker, 'Protecting Fundamental Rights beyond the Charter. Repositioning the Reverse Solange Doctrine in Light of the CJEU's Article 2 TEU Case-Law', in Bobek and Adams-Prassl (n. 337) 525.

461 ECtHR, *A and others v. United Kingdom*, Appl. no. 3455/05, Judgment of 19 February 2009, paras 182 ff.; *Mehmet Hasan Altan v. Turkey*, Appl. no. 13237/17, Judgment of 20 March 2018.

462 Weber, 'Die Europäische Menschenrechtskonvention und die Türkei – Zum Notstand sowie zur Möglichkeit der Wiedereinführung der Todesstrafe', 69 *Die Öffentliche Verwaltung* (2016) 921.

463 *Mehmet Hasan Altan v. Turkey* (n. 461) paras 206 ff.; *Şahin Alpay v. Turkey*, Appl. no. 16538/17, Judgment of 20 March 2018, paras 176 ff.

The ECtHR's case law clearly mirrors the distinction between constitutional law and the constitutional core. Like most constitutional courts, the ECtHR, given its mandate to support the *rights revolution* in Europe (see 4.3.C), interprets individual rights a broadly. Yet, it also allows any restrictions that can withstand a review for proportionality. Consequently, it seems that any restrictive measure can, if necessary, be justified.

However, the concept of core substance,[464] which parallels that of the constitutional core (see 3.1.C), counteracts any attempts at total relativization. Today, it is clear that Convention rights consist of two spheres, with the core substance being more important and worthy of protection.[465] When a state interferes with a core substance, the ECtHR's reasoning becomes more categorical. In doing so, it establishes red lines because it largely foregoes balancing the rights and interests that are at stake in the individual case.

The protection of a right's core substance is particularly evident in the prohibitions of torture (Article 3 ECHR) and slavery (Article 4 ECHR), where the Court does not engage in balancing at all.[466] The core of the prohibition against the deprivation of one's life (Article 2(2) ECHR) only includes narrow exceptions that are not subject to balancing.[467] Categorical forms of reasoning are more difficult to apply when the human right at stake is subject to broadly defined limitations, such as privacy or the freedom of religion, expression, or assembly (Articles 8–11 ECHR). Yet, the doctrine of the core (or essential) substance allows for differentiation. Thus, expressions of opinion that are critical of the government can only be restricted if they incite violence.[468] Political communication is highly protected because it plays a key role for democracy.[469]

For some years now, the Court has been developing another instrument that responds to systemic deficiencies: the prohibition of the abuse of law, as manifested in the persecution of the political opposition.[470] In 2004, in the *Gusinskiy* case, the Court for the first time found a violation of Article 18 (which limits the ways in which the government can use rights restrictions) in conjunction with Article 5 ECHR (right to liberty and security).[471] Later cases dealt with prominent

[464] von Bernstorff, 'Kerngehaltsschutz durch den UN-Menschenrechtsausschuss und den EGMR. Vom Wert kategorialer Argumentationsformen', 50 *Der Staat* (2011) 165.

[465] I. Leijten, *Core Socio-Economic Rights and the European Court of Human Rights* (2018) 2, 11.

[466] See e.g. ECtHR, *Gäfgen v. Germany*, Appl. no. 22978/05, Judgment of 1 June 2010, paras 101 ff, especially para. 107.

[467] ECtHR, *McCann and others v. United Kingdom*, Appl. no. 18984/91, Judgment of 27 September 1995, Series A, No. 324, para. 150.

[468] See, e.g. ECtHR, *Zana v. Turkey*, Appl. no. 18954/91, Judgment of 25 November 1997, ECHR 1997-VII; *Sürek and Özdemir v. Turkey*, Appl. no. 23927/94 and 24277/94, Judgment of 8 July 1999.

[469] Fundamentally, ECtHR, *Lingens v. Austria*, Appl. no. 9815/82, Judgment of 8 July 1986, Series A, No. 103.

[470] Heri, 'Loyalty, Subsidiarity, and Article 18 ECHR: How the ECtHR Deals with Mala Fide Limitations of Rights', 1 *ECHR Law Review* (2020) 25.

[471] ECtHR, *Gusinsky v. Russia*, Appl. no. 70276/01, Judgment of 19 May 2004, ECHR 2004-IV.

opposition politicians in Russia and Turkey, such as Alexei Navalny and Selahattin Demirtaş.[472] In the first *Mammadov* judgment, the Court required the national authorities to acquit the complainant. By ordering the opposition politician to be released from prison, the ECtHR strengthened political pluralism, which is indispensable for democratic transformation.

The Chamber decision in *Mammadov v. Azerbaijan* led to the first proceedings under Article 46(4) ECHR. In its unanimous decision, the Grand Chamber declared that Azerbaijan had failed to enforce this judgment, thereby violating its duties under the Convention.[473] Fiona de Londras and Kanstantsin Dzehtsiarou question whether this decision is useful as it is unlikely to promote the prior judgment's implementation.[474] But the Latin American experience shows that such a decision is, nonetheless, meaningful. Even if the government refuses to yield, the decision clearly articulates what is required, strengthens the domestic opposition, and confirms the self-image of the states parties united in the Council of Europe as a community of democracies (see 4.5.C). Of course, this does not solve the difficult question of how to deal with deviant states.[475]

The ECtHR's transformative power works primarily through the levers of the Union (see 2.6.D). These levers have a weaker impact on Azerbaijan, Russia, and Turkey than on (true) candidate countries (see 2.6.D) and EU Member States. Moreover, levers only work when they are used. Two of the Union's quasi-iconic levers vis-à-vis its Member States—infringement and preliminary ruling proceedings—were not used in this regard for a long time. Only in its judgment of 27 February 2018 did the ECJ signal its willingness to active the two proceedings and, in doing so, fulfil its mandate under Article 13(1) TEU to 'aim to promote its [European] values' (see 3.6.C).

C. The CJEU's Mobilization

Since 1963, the CJEU's jurisprudence has been transformative. It is constitutive for the emergence of today's European society (see 4.3.B). Since many scholars interpret it not only as transformative but also as constitutionalist or

472 ECtHR, *Navalnyy v. Russia*, Appl. no. 29580/12, Judgment of 15 November 2018; *Selahattin Demirtaş v. Turkey (No. 2)*, Appl. no. 14305/17, Judgment of 22 December 2020.

473 ECtHR, *Ilgar Mammadov v. Azerbaijan*, Appl. no. 15172/13, Judgment of 29 May 2019; Çalı, 'No Going Nuclear in Strasbourg: The Infringement Decision in Ilgar Mammadov v. Azerbaijan by the European Court of Human Rights' *Verfassungsblog* (30 September 2019).

474 De Londras and Dzehtsiarou, 'Mission Impossible? Addressing Non-Execution through Infringement Proceedings in the European Court of Human Rights', 66 *International & Comparative Law Quarterly* (2017) 467, at 486 ff.

475 See Steininger, 'With or Without You: Suspension, Expulsion, and the Limits of Membership Sanctions in Regional Human Rights Regimes', 81 *Zeitschrift für ausländisches öffentliches Recht und Völkerrecht* (2021) 539.

constitutionalizing,[476] the *Van Gend en Loos* decision of 1963 inaugurated what could be described as transformative constitutionalism.

However, this would obscure that the path of integration was not constitutional but economic in the first phase of European public law (see 2.6.A). There were constitutionalist elements insofar as the CJEU introduced fundamental rights, strengthened the European Parliament, and prohibited some instances of gender discrimination.[477] But these innovations are better understood as providing constitutionalist support for market integration than as transformative constitutionalism that addresses systemic deficiencies in the light of Article 2 TEU.

It was only during the second period of European public law that the Treaty legislator established the foundations of true constitutional adjudication. It first appeared in the 1992 Maastricht Treaty, albeit cryptically, before emerging more clearly in the 1997 Amsterdam Treaty. Since 2007, the European constitutional core is set out in Article 2 TEU (see 2.5.A, 3.1.C). But even then, the CJEU remained hesitant 'to go constitutional' (see 2.5.B), and systemic deficiencies in the Member States initially remained completely outside its remit. This corresponded to a kind of European division of labour, with the Council of Europe attending to constitutional democracy in the EU Member States.

This hesitation can be justified doctrinally if we consider the values of Article 2 TEU too abstract and indeterminate for judicial operationalization.[478] The principle of the separation of powers can support this view: the judicial application of these values extends the CJEU's sphere to highly political conflicts and greatly increases its powers, which some consider too great anyway. Operationalizing Article 2 TEU means trouble—trouble that can be avoided if the values are understood as non-justiciable.

The CJEU's reaction to the restructuring of the Hungarian judiciary, which the newly elected Orbán government propelled by retiring judges, is emblematic of this early approach. When the Commission brought infringement proceedings against Hungary in 2012, the CJEU treated the judiciary's disempowerment solely as a matter of inadmissible age discrimination, thus sidestepping the constitutional and systemic dimension.[479]

[476] But see Stein (n. 131); Tohidipur (n. 134).

[477] Maduro, 'Reforming the Market or the State? Article 30 and the European Constitution: Economic Freedom and Political Rights', 3 *European Law Journal* (1997) 55.

[478] Kochenov and Pech, 'Monitoring and Enforcement of the Rule of Law in the EU: Rhetoric and Reality', 11 *European Constitutional Law Review* (2015) 512, at 520; Nicolosi, 'The Contribution of the Court of Justice to the Codification of the Founding Values of the European Union', 51 *Revista de Derecho Comunitario Europeo* (2015) 613, at 643; Martenczuk, 'Art. 7 EUV und der Rechtsstaatsrahmen als Instrumente der Wahrung der Grundwerte der Union', in S. Kadelbach (ed.), *Verfassungskrisen in der Europäischen Union* (2018) 41, at 46.

[479] CJEU, Case C-286/12, *Commission v. Hungary* (EU:C:2012:687) paras 24 ff.; Halmai, 'The Early Retirement Age of the Hungarian Judges', in F. Nicola and B. Davies (eds), *EU Law Stories: Contextual and Critical Histories of European Jurisprudence* (2017) 471.

Its judgment did not save the Hungarian judiciary's independence. On the contrary, the situation steadily worsened. Other states followed Hungary's path. Since European politics seemed as paralysed during the crisis of values as it had been during the monetary crisis, the CJEU ultimately mobilized, just like the ECB did during the monetary crisis (see 3.5.C). In both cases, this mobilization was enabled by a transformative interpretation of the institutions' mandate.[480] Thus, in 2018, the CJEU made a constitutional quantum leap in its response to authoritarian tendencies in Poland, operationalizing Article 2 TEU with a view to systemic deficiencies in the Polish judicial system (see 3.6.A).

The ECJ laid the doctrinal groundwork for this case law in the *Associação Sindical dos Juízes Portugueses (ASJP)* case (see 3.6.C). The decision deduced requirements for the Member State courts' independence from Article 19 TEU in conjunction with Article 2 TEU.[481] The *LM* decision (*Deficiencies in the system of justice*), which addressed the execution of a Polish arrest warrant by Irish authorities, followed shortly thereafter. It suggested that individuals can invoke European values in connection with their fundamental rights.[482] The constitutional principles at stake were the separation of powers, an independent judiciary, and the fundamental right to an impartial court and a fair trial.

The two decisions complement each other. With the *Associação Sindical dos Juízes Portugueses (ASJP)* case, the CJEU developed the decentralized system of EU judicial protection into a system that also serves constitutional oversight. Every Member State court can now review, in cooperation with the CJEU, whether other Member State institutions abide by Article 2 TEU. With the *LM* case, the CJEU mobilized 'the vigilance of individuals concerned to protect their rights', as famously put in the *Van Gend en Loos* judgment, in order to realize not only the internal market but also the European constitutional core.[483] A flood of references for preliminary rulings shows that EU citizens and domestic courts are willing to play this role. As the history of integration and the Latin American experience illustrate, this constitutes a transformative step.

The Court of Justice cumulates different provisions as a mediating response to the argument, which is even shared by some CJEU judges, that it cannot apply the standards of Article 2 TEU because they are too vague.[484] Methodologically speaking, this qualifies as a systematic interpretation. The Court applies the

[480] On a reconstruction of Union law from this perspective, see A. Vauchez, *Démocratiser l'Europe* (2014).

[481] CJEU, Case C-64/16, *Associação Sindical dos Juízes Portugueses* (EU:C:2018:117).

[482] *LM* (n. 334) paras 47 ff. For more on the judgment, see the contributions by S. Biernat, P. Bogdanowicz, M. Bonelli, I. Canor, C. Dupré, P. Filipek, A. Frackowiak-Adamska, G. Rugge, and M. Taborowski in von Bogdandy *et al.*, *Defending Checks and Balances in EU Member States* (n. 372).

[483] *Van Gend en Loos* (n. 192).

[484] Levits, 'Die Europäische Union als Wertegemeinschaft. Art 2 iVm Art 7 des Vertrages über die Europäische Union als Grundlage und Begrenzung des Staatsordnungsmodells des demokratischen Verfassungsstaates der Mitgliedstaaten', in T. Jaeger (ed.), *Europa 4.0? Die EU im Angesicht politischer und technologischer Herausforderungen* (2018) 239, at 262.

constitutional core only in conjunction with other Treaty provisions, which gain in scope and substance by being related to the principles of Article 2 TEU.[485] Nevertheless, this allows the CJEU to review almost all constellations that were previously considered beyond its reach.[486]

The *LM* decision held that the Irish authorities had to execute the challenged Polish arrest warrant as there was no concrete danger to the person concerned. But shortly thereafter, the Court intervened with sanctions and declared part of the Polish judicial reforms contrary to EU law (see 5.4.A).[487] The dispute over the Polish Disciplinary Chamber (see 3.6.A) has turned particularly confrontational. With the CJEU's backing,[488] a senate of the Polish Supreme Court (still composed of independent judges) declared the Disciplinary Chamber unlawful.[489] Nevertheless, the Chamber did not cease operations. The CJEU then issued an interim order requiring Poland to suspend the statute.[490] The Disciplinary Chamber complied, inasmuch as it no longer conducted disciplinary proceedings, but it still maintained that it had the power to waive judicial immunity with similar effect.[491] In addition, it turned to the Polish Constitutional Tribunal, referring to it the question of whether the Polish constitution prohibits the execution of the CJEU's interim order. The Polish Constitutional Tribunal issued a judgment to this effect, employing the *PSPP* judgment of the German Constitutional Court's Second Senate as its blueprint and justificatory backing.[492]

The conflict between the CJEU and the Polish government majority, as well as the judges it appointed, is without precedent. Overcoming the Polish deficiencies (i.e. returning to a situation in which the Polish judiciary satisfies the European constitutional core) will be a long process, and it is evident that the CJEU plays an important role in it. This is why transformative constitutionalism provides a useful lens for its mobilization.

Many observers consider the situation in Hungary even more deficient than that in Poland since the government's control over independent institutions and society

[485] von Bogdandy and Spieker, 'Countering the Judicial Silencing of Critics: Article 2 TEU Values, Reverse Solange, and the Responsibilities of National Judges', 15 *European Constitutional Law Review* (2019) 391, at 409 ff.; Rossi, 'La valeur juridique des valeurs. L'article 2 TUE: Relations avec d'autres dispositions de droit primaire de l'UE et remèdes juridictionnels', 3 *Revue trimestrielle de droit européen* (2020) 639, at 650.

[486] Consider, however, the procedural limitations established in CJEU, Case C-558/18, *Miasto Łowicz (Régime disciplinaire concernant les magistrats)* (EU:C:2020:234).

[487] CJEU, Case C-619/18, *Commission v. Poland (Independence of the Supreme Court)* (EU:C:2019:531); Case C-192/18, *Commission v. Poland (Independence of the Ordinary Courts)* (EU:C:2019:924).

[488] *A.K. (Independence of the Disciplinary Chamber of the Supreme Court)* (n. 333).

[489] Supreme Court (Poland), Judgment of 5 December 2019, Case III PO 7/18; Orders of 15 January 2020, Cases III PO 8/18 and III PO 9/18; Order of 23 January 2020, Case BSA I-4110-1/20.

[490] CJEU, Case C-791/19, *Commission v. Poland (Régime disciplinaire des juges)* (EU:C:2020:147).

[491] Bodnar and Filipek, 'Time Is of the Essence' *Verfassungsblog* (30 November 2020).

[492] Biernat, 'How Far Is It from Warsaw to Luxembourg and Karlsruhe: The Impact of the PSPP Judgment on Poland', 21 *German Law Journal* (2020) 1104.

is far more advanced there. In 2020, the Commission brought an action against a Hungarian statute that imposed sanctionable duties of registration, reporting, and disclosure on civil society organizations that receive support from abroad.[493] Such statutes are an effective means to weaken democracy-promoting forces. Given that the problem has worsened, and perhaps also thanks to a new CJEU president, the Court now no longer ducks such issues, unlike in 2012.

Quoting the ECtHR, the CJEU states that 'the right to freedom of association constitutes one of the essential bases of a democratic and pluralist society, inasmuch as it allows citizens to act collectively in fields of mutual interest and in doing so to contribute to the proper functioning of public life'.[494] Its judgment declares the Hungarian statute unlawful and thus protects the agents of democratic transformation. The Court uses the economic freedoms to argue for the applicability of the Charter of Fundamental Rights, thus putting the economic constitution at the service of the constitutional core (see 3.5.C). Since Hungarian authoritarian structures are even more entrenched than in Poland, some at the constitutional level, the lens of transformative constitutionalism also fits the jurisprudence that addresses these deficiencies.

The CJEU's transformative constitutionalism rests on a transformative interpretation of its mandate. While it expands the Court's power, it is not *ultra vires*. Theoretically, it remains in the remit of what Hegel calls 'the continued upholding and development of earlier decisions', albeit under circumstances that the Treaty legislator most likely did not imagine. At issue are systemic deficiencies that threaten the Union (see 3.6.A) as well as the political branch's paralysis. Doctrinally, the CJEU has the mandate to 'promote its values' (Article 13(1) TEU), and the grounds for their justiciability are sound (see 3.1.B). The political proceedings established in Article 7 TEU are no obstacle to infringement and preliminary ruling proceedings (Articles 258, 259, and 267 TFEU).[495]

Two final considerations support the legitimacy of this judicial mobilization. First, the CJEU limits itself to drawing red lines.[496] It only prohibits particularly problematic measures and identifies systemic deficiencies; it does not dictate the precise structure of Member State institutions. Because the focus lies on what is *not* permissible, the CJEU follows a minimalist approach in this regard.[497] It abstains

[493] *Commission v. Hungary (Transparency of Associations)* (n. 336). In detail, Spieker (n. 430).

[494] *Commission v. Hungary (Transparency of Associations)* (n. 336) para. 112.

[495] Bogdanowicz and Schmidt, 'The Infringement Procedure in the Rule of Law Crisis: How to Make Effective Use of Article 258 TFEU', *Common Market Law Review* (2018) 1061, at 1069–1073; Hillion, 'Overseeing the Rule of Law in the EU: Legal Mandate and Means', in C. Closa and D. Kochenov (eds), *Reinforcing Rule of Law Oversight in the European Union* (2016) 59.

[496] von Bogdandy *et al.*, 'A Potential Constitutional Moment for the European Rule of Law. The Importance of Red Lines', 55 *Common Market Law Review* (2018) 963.

[497] This is confirmed by its decision on judicial independence in Malta. See CJEU, Case C-896/19, *Repubblika* (EU:C:2021:311).

from developing interpretative standards that could restrict the Member States' constitutional autonomy and identity (see 3.2.C and 3.2.D).

The ECtHR Grand Chamber confirmed this approach in the *Guðmundur Andri Ástráðsson* case.[498] While the judgment addresses Iceland, it has developments such as in Poland and Hungary in mind as well. At issue was a comprehensive reform of the Icelandic judicial system, during which the Minister of Justice had intervened in judicial appointments. The Court declared that these interventions violate Article 6 ECHR. While careful not to deduce a model for judicial selection from Article 6 ECHR, it emphasizes the significance both of a trustworthy judiciary and of its own power of review.[499]

The legitimacy of the CJEU's transformative constitutionalism is aided by the fact that it does not represent a solitary operation but is part of a broader European operation, as the ECtHR *Guðmundur Andri Ástráðsson* case shows. The Court's interpretations are, moreover, embedded in a process that also involves the Commission, Council, and Parliament as European legislators as well as the Venice Commission of the Council of Europe (see 3.1.C). The same holds true for the finding that the constitutional core has been violated because such a finding usually rests on a collective evaluation conducted by various independent institutions (see 4.4.C).

These processes of interpretation and evaluation include more than public institutions. Legal scholars also have a role to play. Indeed, it seems to me that their reactions to authoritarian tendencies are part of European society's self-production. In this respect, the role played by Max Steinbeis's *Verfassungsblog* (*On Matters Constitutional*) strikes me as paradigmatic.

The role of legal scholarship goes even further. Many of the judgments addressed in this book bear the mark of judges who are also professors of public law. Put hyperbolically, much of European society's jurisprudence is the work of professors. The fourth part of this book uncovers the truth that lies in this hyperbole.

[498] *Guðmundur Andri Ástráðsson v. Iceland* (n. 336).

[499] Ibid. paras 207 ff.; *Thiam v. France*, Appl. no. 80018/12, Judgment of 18 October 2018, paras 49, 72 ff.; *Xero Flor v. Poland*, Appl. no. 4907/18, Judgment of 7 May 2021, para. 252.

5
Scholarship

1. The *Gestalt* of European Jurisprudence

A. Agency

Scholarly reconstructions of the social world play their own social role (see 1.4). Recall Hegel's quintessential statement: 'I am ever more convinced that theoretical work accomplishes more in the world than practical work. Once the realm of ideas (*Vorstellungen*) is revolutionized, reality (*Wirklichkeit*) will not hold out.'[1] This view is widely shared. According to the sociologist Ernest Gellner, '[a]t the base of the modern social order stands not the executioner but the professor'.[2] For the economist John Maynard Keynes, any idea that shaped the world came from an 'academic scribbler'.[3] Carl Schmitt, in perhaps the most famous book on European jurisprudence, portrays legal scholarship as 'the first-born child of the modern European culture (*Geist*), of the "occidental rationalism" of the modern age'. On his view, legal scholarship (*Jurisprudenz*) enjoys an 'almost legislative dignity' and, when worst comes to worst, serves as the 'last refuge of legal consciousness'.[4]

These are the statements of dead white men sugar-coating their profession, but not just that. We may refuse Hegel's idealism, Gellner's radicalism, Keynes' complacency, and Schmitt's hyperbole. However, we can hardly deny that legal scholars play their own social role: more than simply describing *their* legal systems from without, they often mould them from within. They shape the concepts and principles (see 2.1A–2.6.B, 3.1.A–3.5.B), construct, explain, and legitimize legal and political structures, and inspire, support, and criticize the development of the law. Legal scholars forge the next generation of the legal staff that will formalize,

[1] G. W. F. Hegel, *Hegel, the Letters* (1984) 179.

[2] E. Gellner, *Nations and Nationalism* (1983) 34.

[3] J. M. Keynes, *The General Theory of Employment, Interest and Money* (2018 [1935]) 383.

[4] Schmitt, 'The Situation of European Jurisprudence', in A. von Bogdandy, R. Mehring, and A. Hussain (eds), *Carl Schmitt's European Jurisprudence* (2022 [1950]) 29 f., 26, 46 f. On Schmitt's text, see M. Barberis, *Europa del diritto. Sull'identità giuridica europea* (2008) 15 ff., 25; L. Garofalo, *Intrecci schmittiani* (2020). For historical contextualization, see Mehring, 'Savigny or Hegel? History of Origin, Context, Motives and Impact', in A. von Bogdandy, R. Mehring, and A. Hussain (eds), *Carl Schmitt's European Jurisprudence* (2022) 65, at 69 ff. The following considerations are based on von Bogdandy, 'The Current Situation of European Jurisprudence in the Light of Carl Schmitt's Homonymous Text', in A. von Bogdandy, R. Mehring, and A. Hussain (eds), *Carl Schmitt's European Jurisprudence* (2022) 113.

The Emergence of European Society through Public Law. First Edition. Armin von Bogdandy, Oxford University Press.
 DOI: 10.1093/oso/9780198909347.003.0005

and even shape, many societal operations. Many scholars, by propagating their concepts, doctrines, theories, or interpretations, address the academic, the professional, and the general public. They do so in their capacities as academics but also as legal counsel, experts in political processes, or—crowning their academic career—as judges.

Therefore, I now depict the structural transformation of European public law by reconstructing the transformation of its scholarship. Since I have been working in the field for more than 30 years, this endeavour presents evident challenges, vividly described by Ulrich Haltern.[5] But Haltern also shows how to face them: by being transparent about one's positionality. In the following, I present my understanding of a holistic, reconstructive, and transformative scholarship that promotes the democratic project of Article 2 of the Treaty on the European Union (TEU). As in the previous sections, the transformation *of* legal scholarship implies both an objective and a subjective genitive (see 1.4): on the one hand, societal forces exert great influence on what scholars do; on the other hand, legal scholars play a role of their own—they have agency.

The case of *Professor Carl Schmitt* demonstrates what that can mean. Karl Löwenstein had him arrested for his academic writings, which, in his view, had supported German crimes (see 3.6.A). However, the American prosecutor Robert Kempner, formerly a brave Prussian prosecutor who had tried to bring Hitler to the dock in 1932, saw no way to build a criminal case against Schmitt on these grounds; to his chagrin, he had Schmitt released instead.[6] Nevertheless, the ostracism that Schmitt felt so painfully in the following years shows that mechanisms beyond criminal law can likewise sanction agency.

If legal scholarship plays a vital role in society, then European society requires European jurisprudence. This suggests structural transformation for most scholarship is national[7] and often characterized by epistemic nationalism.[8] I shall outline the role and *Gestalt* of European legal scholarship in three respects, with and against Schmitt's 'The Situation of European Jurisprudence'. Schmitt conceptualizes a European jurisprudence without European institutions, whereas current legal scholarship depends on them (see 5.1.B). Schmitt then raises the spectre of

[5] Haltern, 'Europarecht und ich', 68 *Jahrbuch des öffentlichen Rechts* (2020) 439, at 440 f.

[6] R. M. W. Kempner, *Das Dritte Reich im Kreuzverhör. Aus den unveröffentlichten Vernehmungsprotokollen des Anklägers* (1969) 293 ff. See also H. Quaritsch (ed.), *Carl Schmitt—Antworten in Nürnberg* (2000) 27 ff.

[7] A. Jakab, *European Constitutional Language* (2016) 83 f.; D. Thym, 'Zustand und Zukunft der Europarechtswissenschaft in Deutschland', 50 *Europarecht* (2015) 671; Hatje and Mankowski, '"Nationale Unionsrechte". Sprachgrenzen, Traditionsgrenzen, Systemgrenzen, Denkgrenzen', 49 *Europarecht* (2014) 155; de Witte, 'European Union Law. A Unified Academic Discipline?', in A. Vauchez and B. de Witte (eds), *Lawyering Europe. European Law as a Transnational Social Field* (2013) 101, at 114 f.

[8] Peters, 'Die Zukunft der Völkerrechtswissenschaft: Wider den epistemischen Nationalismus', 67 *Zeitschrift für ausländisches öffentliches Recht und Völkerrecht* (2007) 721.

hegemonic structures (see 5.1.C). To oppose them, academic identities must be Europeanized (see 5.1.D).

B. Schmitt and We

Contemporary European jurisprudence takes on sharp contours when considered in the light of Schmitt's essay, although the latter had nothing to do with the new integration project. Of course, in 1950, there was no European law like today's Union law. Yet, Schmitt published his *Situation* in the year of the Schuman Declaration (see 2.2.A), and the Statute of the Council of Europe of 5 May 1949 had already been in force for a year.[9] One might have expected Schmitt to make his work topical by referring to the beginnings of European integration, not least as he intended for the essay to relaunch his career in post-war Germany. After the Second World War, many a Nazi reinvented himself as an advocate of European integration.[10] It is surprising, then, that Schmitt does not refer to the post-war project at all.

Schmitt's silence on post-war integration efforts speaks volumes about his view, which was one of deep disrespect. The one time he described it explicitly, he depicts European political unity as at best 'a byproduct, if not a leftover' of the geopolitical situation, that is, the antagonism between the United States and the Union of Soviet Socialist Republics (USSR).[11] He never warmed to the Federal Republic, its integration into the West in general, and its participation in the European project in particular. He wore his heart on his sleeve in the last sentence of *The Situation*: '[T]he confusion of tongues will prove to be better than the Babylonian unity'.[12]

Schmitt's European jurisprudence builds not on political integration but on an entirely different foundation. That foundation becomes clear already from the title's powerful statement that a European jurisprudence existed five years after the Second World War and had even existed during the war. (We can deduce the latter from the fact that Schmitt had presented the text's main ideas in lectures he gave during the war years.)

Schmitt bolsters his claim about the existence of a European jurisprudence with three main arguments. The first is polemical and *ex negativo*: for him, to deny the

[9] For his understanding of the geopolitics of that time, see Schmitt, 'Die geschichtliche Struktur des heutigen Welt-Gegensatzes von Ost und West', in A. Mohler (ed.), *Freundschaftliche Begegnungen. FS für Ernst Jünger zum 60. Geburtstag* (1955) 135, at 137.

[10] Consider Hanno F. Konopath's metamorphosis from race theorist into the creator of the European flag. See Mogge, '"Wir lieben Balder, den Lichten ...". Völkisch-religiöse Jugendbünde vom Wilhelminischen Reich zum "Dritten Reich"', in U. Puschner and C. Vollnhals (eds), *Die völkisch-religiöse Bewegung im Nationalsozialismus. Eine Beziehungs- und Konfliktgeschichte* (2012) 45, at 56 f. The authorship is disputed and is also attributed to Holocaust survivor Paul Lévy and Arsène Heitz: M. Göldner, *Politische Symbole der europäischen Integration. Fahne, Hymne, Hauptstadt, Pass, Briefmarke, Auszeichnungen* (1988) 58 ff.

[11] Schmitt, 'The Legal World Revolution (1978)', *Télos* (1987) 73, at 85; on this see 2.4.C.

[12] Schmitt, 'The Situation of European Jurisprudence' (n. 4) 46 f.

existence of a European jurisprudence is evidence of narrow-minded legal positivism.[13] The second argument is phenomenological. Thus, Schmitt claims that the various European legal orders often operate with similar concepts and institutions. This holds true for individual rules as well as the 'systematic structure of the whole' 'in every legal discipline'.[14] He does not offer proof for his claim, maintaining that this congruence is 'known to every expert in the field'.[15] The result is a 'very strong European legal community', 'a genuine European community characterised by a true common law'.[16] His third argument then explains this congruence with a millennium of 'reciprocal receptions'. Thus, the many national bodies of jurisprudence are but aspects of one European jurisprudence, even if legal scholars are not aware of its existence.

Schmitt's conceptualization is highly problematic. First of all, one cannot conceptualize scholarship without taking institutions into account. This holds true for scholarship on national law as well as for international law; consider institutions such as the *Institut de droit international*, the *International Law Association*, and the Hague Academy of International Law.[17] For European law, such institutions developed only slowly. In 1990, Helmut Coing, founding director of the Max Planck Institute for European Legal History in Frankfurt and advocate of a new European *Ius Commune*, still considered the Europeanization of legal scholarship a project for the future.[18] The lack of institutions in Schmitt's essay is all the more telling because he often wrote as an institutionalist. Thus, he should have known better.

Furthermore, many scholars from other European countries would have resisted being merged with German scholars five years after the end of the Second World War. Many of the latter had been complicit with the Nazi regime and violated the standards Schmitt himself preaches in *The Situation*: 'a recognition of the individual based on mutual respect even in a conflict situation' and 'a sense for reciprocity and the minimum of an orderly procedure'.[19] Indeed, German legal scholarship had to earn its recognition anew after the Second World War.[20] Schmitt's terminological coup—*European* jurisprudence—was probably intended to help shorten this path, but it could not do so. No victim of the German war of aggression could accept the apologetic second sentence of Schmitt's text, which describes the Second World War as having 'torn Europe apart'.[21]

[13] Ibid. 9 ff.
[14] Ibid. 13 f.
[15] Ibid. 13.
[16] Ibid.
[17] M. Koskenniemi, *The Gentle Civilizer of Nations. The Rise and Fall of International Law 1870–1960* (2001) 11 ff.
[18] Coing, 'Europäisierung der Rechtswissenschaft', 15 *Neue Juristische Wochenschrift* (1990) 937.
[19] Schmitt, 'The Situation of European Jurisprudence' (n. 4) 43 f.
[20] F. Lange, *Praxisorientierung und Gemeinschaftskonzeption. Hermann Mosler als Wegbereiter der westdeutschen Völkerrechtswissenschaft nach 1945* (2017) 41 ff.
[21] Schmitt, 'The Situation of European Jurisprudence' (n. 4) 9.

Schmitt's conceptualization is even more unsuitable for our time. If we follow its logic, legal scholarship dissolves from a European into a global one.[22] There is truth in his argument that many of the 'essential legal concepts and legal institutions' can be found in all European legal orders. Today, however, this does not lead to a European but to a global jurisprudence as we encounter these legal concepts and legal institutions in nearly all legal orders throughout the world.[23] This even applies to China, the country perhaps most likely to shape social order in a way that runs counter to the 'West' or the 'Global North'.[24] The essential legal concepts and institutions originating in the European tradition constitute global phenomena today.

At first glance, Schmitt's argument that the 'inner-European process of encounter and mutual influence' constitutes a specifically European jurisprudence might be more convincing. Schmitt conjures the atmosphere of a European republic of scholars, one to which voices from all European nations contribute on an equal footing. However, such a republic existed neither in his time nor now. Schmitt's *The Situation* itself proves the point because it represents a conversation within German legal scholarship, embellished with some largely irrelevant references to foreign authors. Ultimately, Schmitt draws a line from Friedrich Carl von Savigny to himself within the framework of Hegelian thought.[25]

If there is more transnational interaction today, much of that goes beyond Europe, finding its points of reference at US law schools. Europeans might play a leading role when it comes to Roman law, canon law, or substantive criminal law, but when it comes to the global economy, global order, the internet, or global security, 'every expert in these disciplines is familiar' with the scholarship produced at a handful of US institutions.[26] Some hold that US scholarship is hegemonic even in European law.[27]

Schmitt's understanding of European jurisprudence is thus highly deficient. Contrary to what he asserts on the very first page of *The Situation*, such scholarship requires a European political will and European legislation. Indeed, today's European scholarship owes its existence to European institutions. The Court of Justice of the European Union (CJEU) and the Commission created the *Fédération*

[22] Cassese, 'La globalisation du droit', in P. Titiun (ed.), *La conscience des droits. Mélanges en l'honneur de Jean-Paul Costa* (2011) 113.

[23] For constitutional law, see Frankenberg, 'Constitutions as Commodities: Notes on a Theory of Transfer', in G. Frankenberg (ed.), *Order from Transfer. Comparative Constitutional Design and Legal Culture* (2013) 1.

[24] U. Kischel, *Comparative Law* (2019) 756 f., 774, 784 ff., 699 f., 715, 724 ff.

[25] C. Schmitt, *Verfassungsrechtliche Aufsätze aus den Jahren 1924–1925. Materialien zu einer Verfassungslehre* (1958) 427 ff.

[26] Reimann, 'The American Advantage in Global Lawyering', 78 *Rabels Zeitschrift für ausländisches und internationales Privatrecht* (2014) 1.

[27] Arnull, 'The Americanization of EU Law Scholarship', in A. Arnull, P. Eeckhout, and T. Tridimas (eds), *Continuity and Change in EU Law. Essays in Honour of Sir Francis Jacobs* (2008) 415; A. Sandulli, *Il ruolo del diritto in Europa. L'integrazione europea dalla prospettiva del diritto amministrativo* (2018) 193 f.

Internationale pour le Droit Européen (*FIDE*) in 1961 as an instrument of integration policy.[28] The *Collège d'Europe*, with campuses in Bruges and Natolin, is perhaps the most important educational establishment for the next generation of European civil servants. This reflects a time-proven European tradition: since early European modernity, many rulers have promoted legal scholarship to support their policy goals.[29]

The founding of the European University Institute in Florence in 1972 represents a very significant academic project.[30] European politics had got what it wanted. Already in the late 1970s, Mauro Cappelletti and Joseph Weiler positioned the Institute as a leading site of European legal scholarship, creating the concept of *integration through law* and a group that reconstructed the law accordingly.[31] The volumes published under this title centred on Community law's transformative power and on the legal comparison to the United States. No other project has achieved similar visibility.

Because European legal scholarship must be practised throughout Europe, national legal scholarship must be Europeanized. Accordingly, the Union has long funded dedicated Jean Monnet Chairs at many universities as well as relevant academic projects. With its conclusions of Lisbon (2000) and Barcelona (2002), the European Council gave tremendous impetus to the Europeanization of research; by now, it is a fully fledged EU policy field under Article 179(1) of the Treaty on the Functioning of the European Union (TFEU).[32] One outcome is the European Research Council (ERC)[33] and its associated executive agency, the European Research Council Executive Agency (ERCEA).[34] Their grants have established a European reputational hierarchy, thus Europeanizing a driving force for academic work.[35]

[28] On FIDE., Laffranque, 'FIDE—Uniting Great Minds of European Law. 50 Years of the International Federation for European Law', 18 *Juridica International* (2011) 173; Vauchez, 'The Transnational Politics of Judicialization. Van Gend en Loos and the Making of EU Polity', 16 *European Law Journal* (2010) 1, at 10.

[29] Pauly, 'Deutschland. § 58', in A. von Bogdandy, S. Cassese, and P. M. Huber (eds), *Handbuch Ius Publicum Europaeum, Bd. IV. Verwaltungsrecht in Europa: Wissenschaft* (2011) 41, at para. 1; Leitl-Staudinger, 'Österreich. § 62', in A. von Bogdandy, S. Cassese, and P. M. Huber (eds), *Handbuch Ius Publicum Europaeum, Bd. IV. Verwaltungsrecht in Europa: Wissenschaft* (2011) 195, at para. 3; Jakab, 'Ungarn. § 67', in A. von Bogdandy, S. Cassese, and P. M. Huber (eds), *Handbuch Ius Publicum Europaeum, Bd. IV. Verwaltungsrecht in Europa: Wissenschaft* (2011) 365, at para. 2.

[30] Preamble, Art. 2 para. 1 sub-para. 1 of the Convention Setting up a European University Institute.

[31] M. Cappelletti, M. Seccombe, and J. H. H. Weiler (eds), *Integration through Law. Europe and the American Federal Experience* (1985–1988).

[32] De Elera, 'The European Research Area. On the Way towards a European Scientific Community?', 12 *European Law Journal* (2006) 559.

[33] Commission Decision 2013/C 373/09 of 12 December 2013 establishing the European Research Council, OJ 2013 C 373/23.

[34] Commission Implementing Decision 2013/779/EU of 17 December 2013 establishing the European Research Council Executive Agency and repealing Decision 2008/37/EC, OJ 2013 L 346/58.

[35] On the role of reputation, see N. Luhmann, *Die Wissenschaft der Gesellschaft* (1990) 245–251; Goerlich, 'Die Rolle von Reputation in der Rechtswissenschaft', in E. Hilgendorf and H. Schulze-Fielitz (eds), *Selbstreflexion der Rechtswissenschaft* (2021) 207.

National research policy operates along these lines, too.[36] Even the Polish government redesigned its incentives so that Polish legal scholars would speak to a European audience.[37] This was a remarkable act—all the more so because a national-conservative government was Europeanizing Polish legal scholarship.[38]

C. The Problem of Hegemony

The process of integration, including the Europeanization of legal scholarship, promises a Europe united in equality.[39] Yet, integration has always met the suspicion that it might promote dominance. Daniel Halberstam, Eric Stein's successor at the University of Michigan, has conceptualized this suspicion by distinguishing between two types of hegemony. Hegemony can flow from cultural resources, such as scholarly prowess, or from hard power, a powerful military, a strong economy, or—relevant to our context—decision-making powers.[40] Halberstam cites Schmitt's *The Situation of European Jurisprudence* as a study on cultural hegemony and Heinrich Triepel's 1938 text *Hegemony* as one on hard hegemony.[41]

Over the past 30 years, Anglo-American scholarship has served as a model for shaping the European research space, and research at elite US law schools has played a key role in doing so. Cappelletti and Weiler's *Integration through Law Project* (see 5.1.A) are testament to that as well. Moreover, nothing matches the power of the English language, replete with concepts coined by Anglo-American scholars.[42]

Schmitt's *The Situation of European Jurisprudence* suggests considering Germany as well. Although the text invokes *European jurisprudence* in its title, it propagates the cultural hegemony of *German jurisprudence*, claiming that the latter sowed the

[36] Wissenschaftsrat, *Perspektiven der Rechtswissenschaft in Deutschland. Situation, Analysen, Empfehlungen* (2012).

[37] That is, in English and in the major transnational journals. See the Polish Ministry of Science and Higher Education (Ministerstwo Nauki i Szkolnictwa Wyższego) (20 December 2019), https://www.gov.pl/web/nauka/nowe-rozszerzone-wykazy-czasopism-naukowych-i-recenzowanych-materialow-z-konferencji-miedzynarodowych-oraz-wydawnictw-monografii-naukowych (last visited 11 July 2022).

[38] On the role of public law scholarship for Polish identity, see Lipowicz, 'Polen. § 34', in A. von Bogdandy, P. Cruz Villalón, and P. M. Huber (eds), *Handbuch Ius Publicum Europaeum, Bd. II. Offene Staatlichkeit—Wissenschaft vom Verfassungsrecht* (2008) 663, at paras 10 ff.; Wasilewski, 'Polen. § 63', in von Bogdandy, Cassese, and Huber (n. 29) 229, at para. 21.

[39] Lenaerts, 'No Member State is More Equal Than Others. The Primacy of EU law and the Principle of the Equality of the Member States before the Treaties', *Verfassungsblog* (8 October 2020).

[40] Halberstam, 'Anti-Hegemony and Its Discontents. On Germany in Europe', *Verfassungsblog* (14 October 2020).

[41] H. Triepel, *Die Hegemonie. Ein Buch von führenden Staaten* (1938). It predicted Hitler's failure, albeit between the lines, of course.

[42] Tomuschat, 'The (Hegemonic?) Role of the English Language', 86 *Nordic Journal of International Law* (2017) 196; Cartabia, 'La lingua inglese e lo studio del diritto pubblico', 3 *Rivista trimestrale di diritto pubblico* (2018) 907.

'seeds of its spirit' of European jurisprudence. Schmitt dismisses both French and English legal thought as inadequate[43] and ultimately posits that there are only two authoritative legal scholars: explicitly, Savigny, and implicitly, himself. Schmitt's Europeanism thus represents covert nationalism. Indeed, the text of 1950 repeats much of his *The Historic Situation of German Jurisprudence*, which was published in 1936.[44]

Does the very process of European integration that Schmitt rejected realize, in an ironic turn, his objective? Time and again, European integration has been interpreted as advancing German domination (see 2.3.C). Even irreproachable authors have detected German hegemony in Europe and have even propagated it as necessary and desirable.[45] For others, that prospect has served as a good reason to reject Union policies or even the Union as a whole (see 2.3.C).

How dominant is German legal scholarship? Non-German lawyers working in European institutions avow that the German legal mindset, shaped by German legal scholarship, has great assertive power. The index of Daniel Innerarity's book *Democracy in Europe* lists only one Member State—Germany—but cites it 13 times. The Italian scholar Aldo Sandulli, certainly not a Germanophile, sees European administrative law as a product of German scholarship.[46] If British legal scholarship exerts less and less influence post-Brexit, the role of German jurisprudence could become even more prominent. In fact, this very book could be part of such a development.

Germany is the European state that arguably invests the most resources in legal scholarship. And unlike the Netherlands, Switzerland, or the United Kingdom, it largely restricts the use of these resources to nationals. The usual requirement of two German state exams (the state administers the exam because law is considered too important to leave the exam to the universities) casts long shadows on who can become a professor of law. Thus, even German research committed to a European perspective is often deeply Germanic and, for that reason alone, propagates German positions and patterns of thought.[47] This book is certainly rooted in this tradition. Its focus on Article 2 TEU might be evidence of German hypertextualism[48] and its Hegelian stance the 'true nucleus of the "German approach"'.[49]

[43] Schmitt, 'The Situation of European Jurisprudence' (n. 4) 35 f.

[44] Schmitt, 'The Historical Situation of German Jurisprudence' (1936), in von Bogdandy, Mehring, and Hussain (n. 4) 49.

[45] Schönberger, 'Hegemon wider Willen. Zur Stellung Deutschlands in der Europäischen Union', 66 *Merkur* (2012) 1; A. Bolaffi, *Cuore tedesco. Il modello Germania, l'Italia e la crisi europea* (2013); Minton Beddoes, 'Europe's Reluctant Hegemon: Special Report', *The Economist* (15 June 2013); S. Bulmer and W. E. Paterson, *Germany and the European Union. Europe's Reluctant Hegemon?* (2019).

[46] Sandulli (n. 27) 165. He also notes, however, that the author of the most famous book in this field (namely, Paul Craig) is English.

[47] Çalı, 'The Two Faces of German Legal Hegemony?', *Verfassungsblog* (7 October 2020).

[48] Miller, 'The Ugly German', *Verfassungsblog* (13 October 2020).

[49] C. Schönberger, *Der 'German Approach'. Die deutsche Staatsrechtslehre im Wissenschaftsvergleich* (2015) 2.

Being rooted in a national tradition does not indicate hegemonial aspirations, however. It can also express the pluralism of European society. In this sense, I understand this book as a legitimate proposal in the European marketplace of juridical ideas.[50]

In this marketplace, there is no German hegemony.[51] A look at the publishers, editors, and authors of the leading journals on the topics addressed in this book (such as the *Common Market Law Review*, the *European Constitutional Law Review*, the *European Law Journal*,[52] the *European Journal of International Law*, the *Maastricht Journal of Comparative and European Law*, and the *International Journal of Constitutional Law*) reveals diverse and mostly transnational orientations. Academics who wish to make themselves heard throughout European society must submit to the transnational logic of these media. If we can describe any particular scholarly tradition as prevalent, it would have to be the understandings, institutions, and persons shaped by Anglo-American legal scholarship.

In the entire European legal space, there are only two regular publications with a German bent that play a relevant role: the *German Law Journal* and the *Verfassungsblog*. However, their idea and practice relate to a *Europeanized Germany*, not to a *German Europe*.[53] Like this book, they stand for a European democratic society characterized by the principles of Article 2 TEU.[54]

While German academics do not have cultural hegemony in the Schmittian sense, German professorial law might be hegemonic in the Triepelian sense. Much of that law comes from the *Bundesverfassungsgericht*, where half of the judges tend to be career academics. They are often the reporting judges for significant cases. Thus, almost all cases on European integration carry signs of academic ambition. The professors' power resource lies in the position of the *Bundesverfassungsgericht* within European law. The Second Senate, in particular, has vastly extended its decision-making purview with the aim of becoming the final arbiter in questions of European law (see 3.4.B). The power resources of the Federal Republic of Germany—the Union's most populous and economically strongest Member State—Europeanize the impact of the Court's case law (see 3.2.C, 3.4.B, 3.5.B, 4.4.B).

The German Constitutional Court's unique role draws German academics along in its wake. In the Court's slipstream, their scholarship structures the European

[50] Formulated as a research programme in Jestaedt, 'Wissenschaft im Recht. Rechtsdogmatik im Wissenschaftsvergleich', 69 *JuristenZeitung* (2014) 1, at 12.

[51] Jakab, 'The Fading International Influence of German Constitutional Thinking', *Verfassungsblog* (9 October 2020); Jiménez, 'Influence Yes, Hegemony No. German Legal Science Viewed from Spain', *Verfassungsblog* (11 October 2020); Sarmiento, 'On the Road to German Hegemony in EU Law?', *Verfassungsblog* (7 October 2020).

[52] But only until its fall in 2020. See Arcuri, Costamagna, and Vauchez, 'In Defense of Academic Freedom and Autonomy', *Verfassungsblog* (6 February 2020).

[53] U. Beck, *German Europe* (2013) vii, takes up this play on words by Thomas Mann.

[54] But see Iancu, 'Status Quo Hegemony? Conflicting Narratives about the "Rule of Law"', *Verfassungsblog* (6 October 2020).

discourse, as Antoine Vauchez sharply observes. This applies to scholars in agreement with the Court's decisions as well as to those in disagreement.[55] According to Vauchez, the German Court germanizes European conflicts. It does so by deciding such conflicts (e.g. on European solidarity) on the basis of German legal standards and a German mindset. Simultaneously, the Court Europeanizes the German discussion formats on how to deal with these conflicts as scholars in other legal orders can hardly avoid engaging with the Court.

The Second Senate's *Public Sector Purchase Programme (PSPP)* judgment of 5 May 2020 fuelled the suspicion that the Court was striving for hegemony. Sabino Cassese, the doyen of European public law, argued on the front page of the Italian daily *Il Foglio* on 19 May 2020 that the Senate wanted to put the Union on a German leash.[56] Pál Sonnevend understood the judgment as an act, hardly concealed by doctrinal considerations, to advance certain German interests.[57] Oreste Pollicino even held that the German Court had abused its dominant position.[58]

How can we address this concern? The Second Senate can certainly modify its case law of its own volition. After the severe criticism directed against the *PSPP* judgment, there are signs pointing in this direction.[59] Furthermore, the Plenary of the German Constitutional Court could bring the Second Senate's case law into agreement with the First Senate's more cooperative line (see 4.4.C). A more fundamental response would be to further Europeanize German legal academia, which supplies the judiciary with new recruits, provides fresh ideas, and serves as an interlocutor. Finally, the further Europeanization of scholars' identities would prove particularly transformational.

D. Scholarly Identities

A transformation towards a European jurisprudence implicates the actors' self-understanding (see 3.2.B). Such transformation is difficult to grasp. One indicator is to look at what scholars study, and how. New topics and approaches can influence how scholars understand themselves. Examples include the study of legal issues across various legal orders, be it on democracy, fundamental rights, regulatory policies, legal protection, or mutual trust. *National* identity became a topic for *European law*. All of these topics arise from the interaction between legal orders that the holistic concept of European law articulates (see 2.2.D). Nowadays, legal

[55] Vauchez, 'Vicarious Hegemony. The German Crisis of European Law', *Verfassungsblog* (6 October 2020).

[56] Cassese, 'The Paths of European Legal Scholarship', *Verfassungsblog* (5 October 2020).

[57] Sonnevend, 'How Not to Become Hegemonial. Self-Preservation through Verfassungsdogmatik', *Verfassungsblog* (13 October 2020).

[58] Pollicino, 'The European "Market" for Constitutional Ideas. Abuse of a Judicial Dominant Position?', *Verfassungsblog* (9 October 2020).

[59] BVerfGE 156, 182, *Romania II*.

scholars who only work on *their* national law without considering anything *outside* seem almost anachronistic.[60]

New topics do not always engender a transformation of disciplinary identities. Nevertheless, the aforementioned topics loosen scholars' ties to the legal order in which they, as individuals, were primarily socialized. This reveals transformation because legal scholars traditionally conceive of their identity within national boundaries: they think of their own law versus foreign law or versus international law. Epistemic nationalism shapes one's identity. While my holistic approach does not dismiss such formative forces, it embeds them in the broader context of European law (see 3.2.C).

The dynamics of the European space of legal research also transform disciplinary identities by changing how scholars pose questions as well as cultures of attention, styles, and methods. Its dynamics affect how authority and scholarship are organized as well as the media, career paths, academic loyalties, structures of equality, and the question of how to gain (and lose) one's reputation. Questions of method are particularly significant.

Methodology often determines a discipline's identity. In the case of Continental jurisprudence, the so-called legal method has pride of place (see 5.3.D). Yet, it has come under pressure. Visibility in the European research area—the thing most heads of academic institutions expect above all else from their academic staff—is based primarily on problem-orientated, theoretical, or interdisciplinary research. The comparative method has likewise become increasingly important, broadening the horizons of jurisprudence (see 5.2.C). Today, a scholar can hardly gain a European-wide reputation by making doctrinal contributions to individual questions or writing textbooks or commentaries, all of which has constituted the bulk of academic work in past decades.

Another transformative dimension lies in the changing structures of academic power. Since many upcoming scholars seek high European visibility by publishing in international journals that feature anonymous peer review, the power of the old guard in most national systems has weakened. The *FIDE* provides a telling example. An association of national European law societies, it has been influenced significantly by the national societies' presidents. *FIDE* was almost immediately surpassed in academic importance by the *International Society of Public Law*, which was founded in 2014 and is much more welcoming of promising new scholars. We have Sabino Cassese and Joseph Weiler to thank for this diverse and open marketplace of ideas.[61]

[60] Ackermann, 'Eine "ungeheure Jurisprudenz"? Die Europarechtswissenschaft und die Europäisierung des Rechts', 68 *Jahrbuch des öffentlichen Rechts* (2020) 471.

[61] On their programme, see S. Cassese, *An International Society of Public Law* (2015); Weiler, 'The International Society for Public Law—Call for Papers and Panels', 12 *International Journal of Constitutional Law* (2014) 1.

New career options abroad, particularly those offered by English, Irish, Dutch, Norwegian, Scottish, and Swiss faculties, also have a transformative effect. Foreigners who work at these institutions often feel that they had virtually no career opportunities in their home country's system. It is striking that many of the voices we hear throughout Europe are those of migrant workers speaking from such institutions. The European research area reinforces the freedom to pursue a career autonomously, based on one's own academic interests. We can assume that this group of migrant workers takes on a vital role in a genuinely European scholarly community. This brings us to the most important point.

There is a developed European public law, but a European academic legal community is still in its beginnings. Most legal scholars articulate their self-understanding primarily in terms of the national community in which their professional future unfolds. This is hardly convincing: if national systems of legal scholarship want to accompany the course of European society, they must find and reflect their place in this society.

To Europeanize legal scholarship is a difficult undertaking, given the plurality of languages, the complexity of the research and publication landscape, and the cultural diversity that legal research often reflects.[62] But if multilingualism, a comparative approach, transnational cooperation, and a European publication profile open doors to attractive positions, many scholars will make the effort and support structural transformation.[63]

Such developments are perhaps easier to detect outside Germany. In 2012, I presented my ideas on European legal scholarship in Leiden at the *Staatsrechtconferentie*, the annual conference of the *Staatsrechtkring*, the Dutch Association of Constitutional Law.[64] Unlike the Association of German Professors of Public Law (see 3.1.A), the Dutch Association admits scholars who, in the German system, are called—strangely enough—*Nachwuchs*, offspring.[65] The latter categorically opposed my assertion that national identities continue to dominate academic identities. For many, the fact that they belonged to the Dutch or Belgian, or even Flemish, community constituted only one of several identities. While that identity remains important, it is not paramount, being embedded instead in the wider European as well as international context. I saw them as self-confident citizens of European society.

[62] A look at the authors included in many of these journals reveals, however, that editors often make considerable efforts to reflect this diversity.

[63] For proposals, see Sydow, 'Die Europarechtswissenschaft europäisieren? Überlegungen zur Strukturentwicklung der juristischen Fakultäten und zur Lehre des Europarechts', 68 *Jahrbuch des öffentlichen Rechts* (2020) 545; C. Jamin, *La cuisine du droit. L'École de Droit de Sciences Po: une expérimentation française* (2012) 171 ff.

[64] The conference proceedings are published in M. Diamant *et al.* (eds), *The Powers That Be. Op zoek naar nieuwe Checks and Balances in de verhouding tussen wetgever, bestuur, rechter en media in de veellagige rechtsorde* (2013).

[65] Wissenschaftsrat (n. 36) 13 ff.

2. An Autonomous Voice of Reason

A. Autonomy and Democracy

If legal scholarship is to play a role in a democratic society, it must be democratic.[66] This seems to require a kind of positivism that serves the will of parliament. While I consider that important, I nevertheless maintain, with Hegel, Gellner, Keynes, and Schmitt, that other tasks are significant as well, such as supporting European society in an autonomous, constructive, and dedicated way (see 5.1.A).

Let me elaborate on this understanding by turning once more to Schmitt's *The Situation*. A positivistic subordination to parliamentary law-making has always been anathema to Schmitt. He would have despised even more research that pursues the European research policy's objective of turning the European Union (EU) into 'the most competitive and dynamic knowledge-based economy in the world'.[67]

Schmitt's idea of European jurisprudence goes against such subservience. His text propagates 'maintaining distance'. For Schmitt, jurisprudence is in crisis because it has largely lost its autonomy: on the one hand, he maintains, it has surrendered to the rationality of other disciplines and, on the other hand, as a science of positive law, it merely escorts law-making.[68] Schmitt insists that what is needed instead is autonomous jurisprudence.

He emphasizes autonomy as the guiding criterion of jurisprudential research: 'European jurisprudence […] has always been determined by two great oppositions: on the one side, to theology, metaphysics and philosophy; on the other, to mere technical craft.'[69] More recently, the social sciences have to be added to that list.[70] If jurisprudence goes down that road, it will 'be merged with other faculties, and the achievement of half a millennium would be lost'.[71] In this respect, the jurist Schmitt does not follow Hegel, who claims all socially relevant legal questions for his philosophy of law, thus relegating jurisprudence to a historical and instrumental science.[72] It is only consistent, then, for Schmitt's *The Situation* to centre on a legal scholar—namely, Friedrich Carl von Savigny, the titan of German legal scholarship.

[66] N. Bobbio, *Teoria della scienza giuridica* (1950) 137 f.; Lepsius, 'Rechtswissenschaft in der Demokratie', 52 *Der Staat* (2013) 157, at 178 ff.

[67] European Council Conclusions of 24 March 2000, para. 5. It is slowly liberating itself from this grasp. See Patel, 'Kooperation und Konkurrenz. Die Entstehung der europäischen Wissenschafts- und Forschungspolitik seit 1945', 69 *Vierteljahrshefte für Zeitgeschichte* (2021) 183, at 207 f.

[68] Schmitt, 'The Situation of European Jurisprudence' (n. 4) 40.

[69] Ibid. 41.

[70] Ibid. 12.

[71] Ibid. 41.

[72] G. W. F. Hegel, *Elements of the Philosophy of Right* (1991 [1821]) paras 2, 212.

While I agree with Schmitt's insistence on autonomy, my motive is different. Thus, a democratic European society can hardly forego autonomous legal scholarship. This follows from the constitutive role that scholarship's specific use of reason plays for a legal order (see 1.2, 5.1.A). Furthermore, autonomous scholarship responds to representative democracies as systems of mediation (see 1.1, 3.5.A–B). A mediating scholarship is needed because the different principles of Article 2 TEU realize the democratic project only through their interplay. This is the essence of doctrines of principles (see 3.1.A).

This form of reason is compatible with a democratic society, as Mauro Barberis, Jürgen Habermas, and Alexander Somek demonstrate.[73] An external perspective helps better gauge this point.[74] Mauro Bussani, who teaches law in Trieste and Macao, concludes the *Cambridge Companion to Comparative Law* with the observation that Western democracy, indeed all of Western culture, depends on the autonomy of the law.[75]

Without a legal scholarship that has a 'sense for the logic and consistency of concepts and institutions', there is no meaningful law.[76] Schmitt maintains that the juridical form of reason even constitutes 'the basis of a rational human existence'.[77] He holds that it is endangered by the 'motorized legislature',[78] which includes the law-making executive. While he did not concern himself with judicial law-making (see 4), which is highly significant today, it would only be grist to his mill. Schmitt understands the acceleration of norm creation as part of the general acceleration of societal transformation, which, in turn, has a lot to do with the dynamics of an advanced economy.[79] Schmitt strikes a nerve central to EU jurisprudence as its original task was to develop a European common market (see 2.2.A, 4.3.B, 5.1.B).

Schmitt's stress on jurisprudence's autonomy—his defence of juridical rationality against pure economic rationality—is part of his general conservative critique of capitalism. But there is more to it than that. Aldo Sandulli, a representative of the democratic school of Italian administrative law, also stresses that European legal scholarship should defy the hegemony of economic rationality.[80] His point

[73] Barberis (n. 4) 10 ff.; Habermas, 'Discourse Theory and International Law. An Interview with Jürgen Habermas', 4, https://esil-sedi.eu/wp-content/uploads/2018/04/2013InterviewHabermas.pdf (last visited 12 July 2022); A. Somek, 'The Indelible Science of Law', 7 *International Journal of Constitutional Law* (2009) 424, at 431 ff.

[74] M. Neves, *Verfassung und Positivität des Rechts in der peripheren Moderne. Eine theoretische Betrachtung und Interpretation des Falls Brasilien* (1992).

[75] Bussani, 'Democracy and the Western Legal Tradition', in M. Bussani and U. Mattei (eds), *The Cambridge Companion to Comparative Law* (2012) 384, at 392 f.

[76] Schmitt, 'The Situation of European Jurisprudence' (n. 4) 44.

[77] Ibid. 43. On the natural law dimension of this statement, see 'Stolleis, 'Carl Schmitt', in M. J. Sattler (ed.), *Staat und Recht. Die deutsche Staatslehre im 19. und 20. Jahrhundert* (1972) 123, at 145.

[78] For more details, see Schmitt, 'Vergleichender Überblick über die neueste Entwicklung des Problems der gesetzgeberischen Ermächtigungen (Legislative Delegationen)', 6 *Zeitschrift für ausländisches öffentliches Recht und Völkerrecht* (1936) 252.

[79] See also Schmitt, 'Die geschichtliche Struktur' (n. 9) 155.

[80] Sandulli (n. 27). He relies heavily on Goldmann, 'The Great Recurrence. Karl Polanyi and the Crises of the European Union', 23 *European Law Journal* (2017) 272.

of departure is not a conservative critique but the widely lamented end of embedded liberalism. This corresponds with Heller's analysis (see 3.4.C) and articulates the post-war social consensus that stabilized democracy in Western Europe.[81] Today, even forces that were previously decidedly neoliberal pine after embedded liberalism.[82] On Sandulli's view, European jurisprudence can help embed liberalism anew if it succeeds in making social relations comply better with democratic principles.

Sandulli holds that the rationality of other societal spheres should be strengthened vis-à-vis strong economic actors in order to support social cohesion. He argues that legal scholarship has a prominent role to play in this process:[83] in the light of legal values, it should construct an order that mediates between the different spheres' rationalities. This programme addresses European jurisprudence in particular because the demise of embedded liberalism in Europe is not least the fault of Union law.

In this way, European jurisprudence helps realize a democratic society as an independent voice of reason (see 2.6.D, 3.5.C). It serves the democratic project by providing the necessary concepts, systematizing the legal material accordingly, identifying deficiencies, and—last but not least—imagining ways to advance the project of Article 2 TEU (see 1.2, 1.4, 3.1.A, 3.2.B, 5.1.A). In this jurisprudential process, mediation plays a crucial role (see 1.1). European jurisprudence must synthesize the specific rationalities of other disciplines in the medium of law and endow this synthesis with real power.[84] This recalls one of Schmitt's central points: in *The Situation*, Schmitt describes the true role of jurisprudence as 'a system of mediations'.[85]

In this process, Sandulli assigns legal scholarship primacy over the other sciences (*interdisciplinarietà a primazia giuridica*).[86] He even attributes it a jurisgenerative role,[87] reminiscent of the quasi-legislative dignity with which Schmitt ennobled jurisprudence. I reject such understandings since there are reasonable concerns that jurists might wield too much power.[88] Legal scholars' authority differs from authoritative sources that originate in the democratic process.

[81] See Ruggie, 'International Regimes, Transactions, and Change. Embedded Liberalism in the Postwar Economic Order', 36 *International Organization* (1982) 379; T. Judt, *Postwar. A History of Europe since 1945* (2005) 324 ff.

[82] Emblematically, Charlemagne, 'The New Nationalism', *The Economist* (19 November 2016). See also 2.6.D.

[83] Sandulli (n. 27) 188, 195.

[84] Ibid. 197–210, esp. 209.

[85] Schmitt, *Verfassungsrechtliche Aufsätze* (n. 25) 429. See also A. Somek, *Rechtssystem und Republik. Über die politische Funktion des systematischen Rechtsdenkens* (1992) 20 ff.

[86] Sandulli (n. 27) 202.

[87] Ibid. Hence, such ambition is not a 'specifically German' phenomenon, contrary to what Schönberger writes: Schönberger, *Der 'German Approach'* (n. 49).

[88] E. Fraenkel, *Zur Soziologie der Klassenjustiz* (1927).

B. Comparative Law with Eduard Gans

European jurisprudence embraces various legal orders. This makes comparison a building block of its reasoning, which, in turn, implies mediating between the various orders.[89] Such mediations contribute to a law that dovetails with European society. This conception of comparative law was first developed by Eduard Gans, one of Hegel's foremost students. He became a pioneer of the Vormärz (which led to the revolution of 1848), a link between Hegel and Marx, and a progressive antipode of the conservative Savigny.[90] Wikipedia presents Gans as a 'liberal pragmatist with a very early perspective on a Europe united in peace'.

In terms of scholarship, Gans enhanced the Hegelian reconstruction of reason with systematic legal comparison.[91] He was the first, as Stefan Vogenauer maintains, to practice systematic comparative law.[92] This counteracts abstract essentialism, anaemic models, and the uncontrolled generalization of national doctrines as universal reason.

Gans' major comparative work is his four-volume *The Law of Succession in the Development of World History: A Treatise of World History* (*Erbrecht in weltgeschichtlicher Entwicklung: Eine Abhandlung der Universalrechtsgeschichte*), published between 1824 and 1835.[93] As in Hegel's work, it deals with overcoming abstractions.[94] In a tremendous tour de force, Gans surveys the Chinese, Indian, Mosaic-Talmudic, Islamic, and Greek as well as the ancient and medieval Roman law of succession. In each case, he discusses the same aspects that are integral to concrete freedom: family, property, volition, and testament. Compared to Hagemeier's descriptive approach to comparative law (see 2.1.A), Gans' undertaking evinces enormous progress.

Again and again, later scholars have demanded that comparative law play the central role advocated by Gans. Konrad Zweigert, the founder of the functional method of comparative law, presented it as a 'universal interpretive method'.[95] In

[89] Cassese, 'The "Constitutional Traditions Common to the Member States" of the European Union', 67 *Rivista trimestrale di diritto pubblico* (2017) 939; P. Ridola, *Diritto comparato e diritto costituzionale europeo* (2010) 52 f.

[90] Braun, 'Eduard Gans (1797–1839): Ein homo politicus zwischen Hegel und Savigny', in H. Heinrichs *et al.* (eds), *Deutsche Juristen jüdischer Herkunft* (1993) 45, at 53.

[91] Mohnhaupt, 'Universalrechtsgeschichte und Vergleichung bei Eduard Gans', in R. Blänkner, G. Göhler, and N. Waszek (eds), *Eduard Gans (1797–1839). Politischer Professor zwischen Restauration und Vormärz* (2001) 339.

[92] Vogenauer, 'Rechtsgeschichte und Rechtsvergleichung um 1900: Die Geschichte einer anderen "Emanzipation durch Auseinanderdenken"', 76 *Rabels Zeitschrift für ausländisches und internationales Privatrecht* (2012) 1122, at 1127.

[93] Bertani, 'Das Erbrecht in weltgeschichtlicher Entwickelung (1824–1835) von Eduard Gans. Das erste Zeugnis vom Einfluss Hegels auf die Privatrechtsgeschichtsschreibung', 11 *Rechtsgeschichte* (2007) 110.

[94] Beyer, 'Gans' Vorrede zur Hegelschen Rechtsphilosophie', 45 *Archiv für Rechts- und Sozialphilosophie* (1959) 257, at 261.

[95] Zweigert, 'Rechtsvergleichung als universale Interpretationsmethode', 15 *Zeitschrift für ausländisches und internationales Privatrecht* (1949) 5. To be sure, Zweigert's universalism only applied to what is now the Global North.

1989, Peter Häberle declared comparative law the 'fifth' method of interpretation.[96] In 2016, Jürgen Basedow even considered it 'obligatory'.[97]

Yet, the comparative approach has not become mainstream, for good reason.[98] Its legal foundations are too sparse for supporting a strong legal argument. Following Hegel, Gans believed in a universal reason that would assert itself in history. Today's equivalent might be a global constitutionalism that posits the United Nations Charter of 1945 or the International Covenants of 1966 as the constitutional basis for a global law of humankind. In my opinion, such constitutionalism lacks a legal, political, and societal basis.[99] World society, if that is a meaningful concept, is not based on the principles of the United Nations Charter or the two Covenants of 1966 (see 1.2). Accordingly, I agree with those contemporary public law comparativists who do not consider that global comparisons are embedded in, or leading to, a general law that rules the various legal orders. Vicki Jackson sums it up well. This leading advocate of global comparison suggests 'engagements' between legal orders to argue for the relevance of global comparisons.[100]

European comparative law's potential is entirely different and goes far beyond engagements. It compares legal orders that are linked by a common law with constitutional features. Moreover, these orders serve a legally constituted society. All legal acts of any public authority in the Union are bound by the common constitutional core (see 3.1.C). Thus, European legal comparison has a legal basis, contrary even to comparisons with other democracies, such as Australia, Canada, Israel, the United Kingdom, or the United States. Comparative law under Article 2 TEU can be put to doctrinal use. One important aspect regards precisely the principles of Article 2 TEU as they are informed by the principles of the Member States' constitutions (see 3.1.D, 3.2.C).

Today, the comparative argument is an established and ever more expected element of legal scholarship in European society (on judicial interactions, see 4.2.C, 4.4.B, 4.4.C). This helps European legal culture. By common culture, I mean that all legal actors operate within a shared framework of knowledge, arguments, practices, values, and mutual understanding.[101] Claus-Dieter Ehlermann has

[96] Häberle, 'Grundrechtsgeltung und Grundrechtsinterpretation im Verfassungsstaat—Zugleich zur Rechtsvergleichung als "fünfter" Auslegungsmethode', 44 *JuristenZeitung* (1989) 913, at 916 ff.

[97] Basedow, 'Hundert Jahre Rechtsvergleichung. Von wissenschaftlicher Erkenntnisquelle zur obligatorischen Methode der Rechtsanwendung', 71 *JuristenZeitung* (2016) 269.

[98] Riesenhuber, 'Rechtsvergleichung als Methode der Rechtsfindung?', 218 *Archiv für die civilistische Praxis* (2018) 693.

[99] von Bogdandy, Goldmann, and Venzke, 'From Public International to International Public Law. Translating World Public Opinion into International Public Authority', 28 *European Journal of International Law* (2017) 115, at 126 f.

[100] V. C. Jackson, *Constitutional Engagement in a Transnational Era* (2010).

[101] S. de la Sierra, *Una metodología para el Derecho comparado europeo: Derecho público comparado y Derecho administrativo europeo* (2004) 67 ff.; P. Häberle and M. Kotzur, *Europäische Verfassungslehre* (2016) 104–111.

taught me that comprehending the arguments, interests, and constraints of actors from the other Member States is the mark of a proficient European jurist.

C. Comparative Law in European Society

European comparative law is by now an established academic field.[102] Article 2 TEU answers the difficult question of whether the different legal orders are fundamentally comparable (see 5.2.B). The first question is whether to consider all 27 Member States. The idea of equality seems to suggest that this is necessary. However, such research requires library, financial, human, and time resources that only the European institutions can usually provide.[103]

Scholarly practice is generally selective, and I have never heard that a selective study is flawed in principle. After all, selective comparison is a standard method of human insight and normative argumentation.[104] However, a selection requires justification. At the current incipient state of European comparative law, many justifications are accepted (see 4.1.D), not least that of limited language proficiency. At the same time, it is understood that comparative research is deficient if it is only orientated towards confirming the desired result or deliberately avoids contradictory findings. As Antonio Scalia put it in what is arguably the most famous statement on the comparative method, 'To invoke alien law when it agrees with one's own thinking, and ignore it otherwise, is not reasoned decision-making, but sophistry.'[105]

Comparative law is even more objectionable when it suggests something that does not exist, as did the CJEU's *Mangold* judgment on age discrimination.[106] Similarly objectionable is the comparative argument in the Second Senate's judgment of 5 May 2020, which implies that its decision is representative of the

[102] C. D. Classen, *Nationales Verfassungsrecht in der Europäischen Union. Eine integrierte Darstellung von 27 Verfassungsordnungen* (2021); E. Di Salvatore (ed.), *Sistemi costituzionali europei* (2021); A. Weber, *European Constitutions Compared* (2019); C. Grewe and H. Ruiz Fabri, *Droits constitutionnels européens* (1995).

[103] On the CJEU's comparative approach, see Lenaerts, 'Discovering the Law of the EU: The European Court of Justice and the Comparative Law Method', in T. Perišin and S. Rodin (eds), *The Transformation or Reconstitution of Europe. The Critical Legal Studies Perspective on the Role of the Courts in the European Union* (2018) 61. On the ECtHR's comparative approach, see Ambrus, 'Comparative Law Method in the Jurisprudence of the European Court of Human Rights in the Light of the Rule of Law', 2 *Erasmus Law Review* (2009) 353.

[104] Ruffert, 'The Transformation of Administrative Law as a Transnational Methodological Project', in M. Ruffert (ed.), *The Transformation of Administrative Law in Europe* (2007) 3, at 5.

[105] USSC, *Roper v. Simmons*, 543 U.S. 551, 627 (2005) (Scalia, J, dissenting). For criticism of the CJEU along these lines, see Bardin, 'Depuis l'arrêt Algera, retour sur une utilisation "discrète" du droit comparé par la Cour de justice de l'Union européenne', in T. D. Manno (ed.), *Le recours au droit comparé par le juge* (2014) 97, at 97 ff., esp. at 101.

[106] CJEU, Case C-144/04, *Mangold* (EU:C:2005:709) para. 74; see Basedow (n. 97) 275; Preis, 'Verbot der Altersdiskriminierung als Gemeinschaftsgrundrecht. Der Fall "Mangold" und die Folgen', *Neue Zeitschrift für Arbeitsrecht* (2006) 401, at 401, 406.

European mainstream.[107] This statement does not withstand scrutiny[108] for no other constitutional court reviews, in a constitutional complaint based on the right to vote, whether a central bank's decision has adequately considered government debt, savings, pensions, real estate prices, and the survival of economically non-viable companies (see 3.4.B).

Like any argument, comparative legal arguments can serve many purposes, even flawed ones. The Hungarian Constitutional Court provides a particularly crass example with the way it uses the Second Senate's case law to arrive at decisions that strengthen authoritarian tendencies.[109] Justices of the Second Senate themselves have lamented this use.[110]

Beyond such objectionable practices, there are many good uses of comparative argument. Three appear dominant: confirming a statement, highlighting a contrast, and developing a broader conceptual framework.[111] In order to avoid Scalia's reproach, European scholars must, to the extent that they are capable of doing so, plumb the breadth and depth of European pluralism, searching for typical patterns as well as divergences.[112] Importantly, they must contextualize their findings, as abstract rules and doctrines can play out very differently in concrete relationships.[113] Conducted in this way, comparative law can play a role similar to that of experimentation in other disciplines.[114]

[107] BVerfGE 154, 17, *Public Sector Purchase Programme—PSPP*, paras 124 ff.

[108] Galetta, 'Karlsruhe über Alles? The Reasoning on the Principle of Proportionality in the Judgment of 5 May 2020 of the German BVerfG and Its Consequences', 14 *federalismi.it.* (2020) 173, at 174 ff.

[109] Bakó, 'The Zauberlehrling Unchained? The Recycling of the German Federal Constitutional Court's Case Law on Identity-, *Ultra Vires-* and Fundamental Rights Review in Hungary', 78 *Zeitschrift für ausländisches öffentliches Recht und Völkerrecht* (2018) 863.

[110] Di Lorenzo and Wefing, 'Andreas Voßkuhle: "Erfolg ist eher kalt". Der scheidende Präsident des Bundesverfassungsgerichts zieht Bilanz. Ein Gespräch mit Andreas Voßkuhle über bedrohte Richter, die Gefahren für die Freiheit in der Corona-Krise und Fehler der liberalen Eliten', *Die Zeit* (14 May 2020) 6; Janisch and Kornelius, 'Huber: "Wir haben Applaus von der falschen Seite bekommen"', *Süddeutsche Zeitung* (13 May 2020); Maidowski, 'Anders als die polnische Regierung will das Bundesverfassungsgericht mehr Kontrolle durch den Europäischen Gerichtshof, nicht weniger', *Website of Stowarzyszenie Sędziów Polskich Iustitia* (26 May 2020), https://www.iustitia.pl/en/activity/informations/3856-verfassungsrichter-dr-ulrich-maidowski-erklaert-anders-als-die-polnische-regierung-will-das-bundesverfassungsgericht-mehr-kontrolle-durch-den-europaeischen-gerichtshof (last visited 11 July 2022).

[111] Wendel, 'Richterliche Rechtsvergleichung als Dialogform: Die Integrationsrechtsprechung nationaler Verfassungsgerichte in gemeineuropäischer Perspektive', 52 *Der Staat* (2013) 339, at 344 ff.; Groppi and Ponthoreau, 'The Use of Foreign Precedents by Constitutional Judges. A Limited Practice, An Uncertain Future', in T. Groppi and M.-C. Ponthoreau (eds), *The Use of Foreign Precedents by Constitutional Judges* (2013) 411, at 424 ff.; Benvenisti, 'Reclaiming Democracy: The Strategic Uses of Foreign and International Law by National Courts', 102 *American Journal of International Law* (2008) 241, at 241 ff.

[112] Vincze, 'Europäisierung des nationalen Verwaltungsrechts. Eine rechtsvergleichende Annäherung', 77 *Zeitschrift für ausländisches öffentliches Recht und Völkerrecht* (2017) 235, at 246 ff.

[113] For convincing criticism on this basis, see Muszyński, 'Comparative Legal Argument in the Polish Discussion on Changes in the Judiciary', 68 *Jahrbuch des öffentlichen Rechts* (2020) 705.

[114] M. Shapiro, *Courts. A Comparative and Political Analysis* (1981) viii.

As a judgment by the Corte costituzionale illustrates, European comparative law has thus been able to make useful contributions.[115] In judgment 239/2018, the *Corte* decided on the constitutionality of a 4 per cent threshold for the election of the Members of the European Parliament that are assigned to Italy.[116] In 2011 and 2014, the Second Senate of the *Bundesverfassungsgericht* had declared similar threshold clauses unconstitutional under German law, thus encouraging the fragmentation of the European Parliament.[117] The *Corte* and the *Bundesverfassungsgericht* both interpreted the same principle of democratic equality. The *Corte,* responding to the Second Senate's decision, reasoned why it came to the opposite conclusion, thereby advancing the debate on European democracy (see 3.5.B).

Can the comparative method yield an answer that we, as academics, can consider the 'best'? Zweigert seems to suggest as much: after thorough comparison, one solution might emerge that is 'clearly superior'.[118] I consider this as problematic. A more modest but safer role for European comparative reasoning is that of a resource for reflection and construction.[119]

As a means of legal argumentation, European comparative law also demands assessing the externalities of domestic decisions, that is, their impact on other legal orders. Given the interdependence of legal orders within European society, a legislative, administrative, or judicial decision may well have significant repercussions or consequences outside the legal order in which it was made. The consideration of consequences is today accepted as part of legal reasoning, albeit usually only within the framework of the national legal order.[120] In European society, shared responsibility (see 4.4.) implies that this framework extends to all associated legal orders. Thus, a national court must consider whether a possible interpretation of a national provision could lead to the insolvency of the Greek state or encourage authoritarian tendencies in other Member States. Ignoring such potential consequences fails European responsibility and amounts to epistemic nationalism. Looking beyond one's national borders is essential to ensuring reasonable outcomes in European society.

[115] The *Corte* is especially renowned for its practice of comparative law; see the comparative law studies on its webpage, Corte Constituzionale, *Studi di diritto comparator*, https://www.cortecostituzionale.it/actionDirittoComparato.do (last visited 11 July 2022).

[116] Sentenza n. 239/2018; for a comparative review, see Lanchester, 'La soglia di esclusione tra il government e la governance', *Giurisprudenza costituzionale* (2018) 2743.

[117] See BVerfGE 129, 300, *Five-Percent Threshold Clause EuWG*; BVerfGE 135, 259, *Three-Percent Threshold Clause European Elections Act*. See 3.5.A.

[118] K. Zweigert and H. Kötz, *Introduction to Comparative Law* (2011) 46 f.; Zweigert (n. 95) 14.

[119] Dann, 'Thoughts on a Methodology of European Constitutional Law', 6 *German Law Journal* (2005) 1453, esp. at 1427 ff.; Schmidt-Aßmann, 'Zum Standort der Rechtsvergleichung im Verwaltungsrecht', 78 *Zeitschrift für ausländisches öffentliches Recht und Völkerrecht* (2018) 807, esp. at 836 ff., 850 ff.

[120] G. Lübbe-Wolff, *Rechtsfolgen und Realfolgen. Welche Rolle können Folgenerwägungen in der juristischen Regel- und Begriffsbildung spielen?* (1981) 156 f.; Voßkuhle, 'Neue Verwaltungsrechtswissenschaft', in W. Hoffmann-Riem, E. Schmidt-Aßmann, and A. Voßkuhle (eds), *Grundlagen des Verwaltungsrechts, Bd. 1* (2006) § 1, paras 32 ff.

3. Roles

A. Helping Out Legal Practice

Forty years ago, German law books and journals seemed destined simply to aid legal practice by sitting in colourless court libraries, on the shelves of lawyers' consultation rooms, or in university libraries, where they help students 'solve' (not 'argue', as in the United States) practical cases. Their lack of aesthetics seemed a deliberate attempt to demonstrate their practicality. Weiler's dissertation was the first law book I encountered whose very cover conveyed a theoretical, even intellectual claim that went beyond the law books I knew.[121]

This has now changed, underscoring the transformation of German academia. Today, there are far more texts whose artful covers or enigmatic titles convey a claim to scholarly originality and even intellectual sophistication. Nevertheless, German legal scholarship maintains its basic identity of a *praktische Wissenschaft* (practical science); for the most part, it aims to make the law ready to use, learnable, and coherent and to keep legal doctrine in sync with a changing society.[122] More or less the same applies to other continental European countries.[123]

Its doctrinal focus differentiates the mainstream of European scholarship from that shaped by US influence. Robert Post, the former Dean of Yale Law School, maintains that the latter focuses on an *economic* or *policy analysis of law*.[124] Martin Shapiro's perhaps most famous sentence highlights how far removed from European jurisprudence these approaches are. Commenting on a doctrinal contribution by Ami Barav, a well-renowned European law scholar of Israeli origin and US citizenship but with a French *doctorat d'Etat*, he writes, '[It] represents a stage of constitutional scholarship out of which American constitutional law must have passed about seventy years ago [...]. Such an approach has proved fundamentally arid in the study of individual constitutions.'[125]

Shapiro's quote overlooks the value of practical doctrine in the operation of many societies. However, there is no doubt that the role of legal scholarship goes

[121] J. H. H. Weiler, *Il sistema comunitario europeo. Struttura giuridica e processo politico* (1985).

[122] Kahl, 'Dogmatik im EU-Recht', 144 *Archiv des öffentlichen Rechts* (2019) 159.

[123] See the contributions on this subject by M. Fioravanti, M. García-Pechuán, L. Heuschling, A. Jakab, I. Lipowicz, K. Å. Modéer, R. Nehmelman, C. Pilafas, R. J. Schweizer, and A. Somek in von Bogdandy, Cruz Villalón, and Huber, *Handbuch Ius Publicum Europaeum, Bd. II* (n. 38), as well as the contributions by P. Chrétien, G. Edelstam, A. Jakab, B. Leitl-Staudinger, A. Sandulli, J. A. Santamaría Pastor, P. Tschannen, and A. Wasilewski in von Bogdandy, Cassese, and Huber (n. 29). On English legal scholarship, see P. S. Atiyah and R. S. Summers, *Form and Substance in Anglo-American Law. A Comparative Study of Legal Reasoning, Legal Theory, and Legal Institutions* (1987), 403 ff.; M. Loughlin, *Public Law and Political Theory* (1992), at 138 ff.

[124] Post, 'Constitutional Scholarship in the United States', 7 *International Journal of Constitutional Law* (2009) 416, at 421. Critically, see Edwards, 'The Growing Disjunction between Legal Education and the Legal Profession', 91 *Michigan Law Review* (1992) 34.

[125] Shapiro, 'Comparative Law and Comparative Politics', 53 *Southern California Law Review* (1979) 537, at 538.

beyond that of providing aid to legal practice, following up on the insights of Hegel, Gellner, Keynes, and Schmitt (see 5.1.A). In the following, I discuss three major contributions: reasoned critique, the elaboration of theory (conceptual foundations), and new doctrines. This focus is not meant to deny the importance of socio-legal studies.

B. Critique

Reasoned critique is perhaps reason's first form of expression. How can legal scholarship practice scholarly critique? Part of my answer to this question becomes apparent in my discussion of the Second Senate's rulings and of Schmitt's, as well as Weiler's, scholarship. Methodologically speaking, it reconstructs their arguments before searching for weaknesses, such as inconsistencies or hollow premises. For more extensive critique, many turn to standards developed in other disciplines, such as political theory or economics. By contrast, a Hegelian tradition allows for an autonomous, specifically jurisprudential approach (see 1.4). To elucidate this point, let me return to Schmitt.

For Schmitt, *concrete orders*—that is, the normativity of societal institutions—constitute the standard for such critique. This critique operates with an institutional concept of the law that links the latter to the normativity of societal institutions. In consequence, social normativity turns into a standard that is internal to the law. This helps Schmitt criticize liberal legal developments for he operates with traditional, often authoritarian institutions; examples include 'the cohabitation of spouses in marriage, of family members in a family […] of functionaries in the state apparatus, of the priests in a church, of comrades in a work camp'.[126] These traditional institutions provide juridical meaning, writes Schmitt, and respecting them generates political legitimacy for the law.[127] Accordingly, Schmitt recommends that the law be developed slowly and 'unintentionally'.[128] Like Savigny and many other conservatives, he is averse to grand legislation that purports to reform society.[129]

Rejecting such conservatism should not mean discarding the methodological wit of Schmitt's operation, which consists of elaborating an internal critical dimension. This dimension is better served by constitutional principles, which, though clearly part of the law, can easily be interpreted as transcending its *status quo*.[130]

[126] C. Schmitt, *On the Three Types of Juristic Thought* (2004 [1934]) at 54. Schmitt, being a conservative, refers to the *traditional* cohabitation of spouses and to a *paternalistic* family.

[127] Howland, 'Carl Schmitt's Turn to Sovereignty in Jurisprudence', 9 *Beijing Law Review* (2018) 211.

[128] Schmitt, 'The Situation of European Jurisprudence' (n. 4) 33.

[129] This was the prevalent understanding of fundamental rights in the Weimar period. See K. Tanner, *Die fromme Verstaatlichung des Gewissens. Zur Auseinandersetzung um die Legitimität der Weimarer Reichsverfassung in Staatsrechtswissenschaft und Theologie der zwanziger Jahre* (1989) 103 ff., 134 ff.

[130] Reinhardt and Schmalz, 'Ressourcen der Rechtskritik. Kritik als Praxis und Reflexion', 54 *Kritische Justiz* (2021) 131.

Legal scholarship can take on an independent critical role (see 1.4, 2.6.B, 5.1.A) by pointing to democratic constitutions' unfulfilled promises.[131] Article 2 TEU builds on this. It helps throw into relief that the democratic transformation of European society remains unfinished even in strictly legal terms (see 2.6.D, 3.5–6, 4.6, 5.4).

C. Theory

Like any academic work, legal scholarship requires theory. Theoretical inquiries are part and parcel of what is called *Grundlagenforschung* (foundational research) in Germany. In that capacity, they complement legal history, which has been dominant since Savigny's time, legal methodology, socio-legal studies (such as legal sociology, anthropology, and ethnology), law and economics, and legal philosophy (which is close to legal theory but often characterized by more of a historical rather than systematic interest).[132] Theoretical inquiries are often historically embedded and make use of the grand theories and narratives of neighbouring disciplines. This book follows this approach by reconstructing, within the broad framework of Hegelian thought, the transformation of European law in the light of a democratic European society.

Legal theory's contact with other disciplines need not diminish its autonomy. Once again, Schmitt serves as a fruitful interlocutor: theoretical inquiries that feature grand narratives are virtually his trademark. Mostly, a concept provides the main focus. Schmitt's *The Situation*, for example, revolves around the term 'European jurisprudence'. Schmitt explains his understanding of *concepts* in his key work *The Concept of the Political*. Elaborating a concept aims 'to establish ... a framework for certain jurisprudential questions, so as to bring order to a confounding subject matter and to arrive at a topography of its concepts'.[133] In both texts, he develops such a jurisprudential answer using insights from many other disciplines: history, political philosophy, economics, sociology, political science, and theology. He cultivated a way of freewheeling thinking that reaps insights from many fields and has proved remarkably fecund, as his reception in other academic disciplines shows.

If legal scholarship addresses a question that also falls within other disciplines' purview, the question arises of how it can make a specific contribution.[134] The

[131] J. Habermas, *Between Facts and Norms: Contributions to a Discourse Theory of Law and Democracy* (2008 [1992]); Forst and Günther, 'Die Herausbildung normativer Ordnungen. Zur Idee eines interdisziplinären Forschungsprogramms', in R. Forst and K. Günther (eds), *Die Herausbildung normativer Ordnungen. Interdisziplinäre Perspektiven* (2011) 11.

[132] Wissenschaftsrat (n. 36) 25.

[133] C. Schmitt, *Der Begriff des Politischen. Text von 1932 mit einem Vorwort und drei Corollarien* (1963) 9.

[134] For a survey of influential positions, see C. Engel and W. Schön (eds), *Das Proprium der Rechtswissenschaft* (2007).

answer depends on what autonomy means for interdisciplinary research, which has become indispensable for the many topics that European public law scholarship addresses.[135] The ERC is right to propagate interdisciplinarity.[136] But that does not imply subordinating legal research to the knowledge-generating discipline.[137] Rather, interdisciplinarity presupposes that legal scholarship remains autonomous.

Schmitt integrated findings from other disciplines *as a legal scholar*. Thus, he claimed an *intra*disciplinary space—one internal to legal scholarship—within which he practised *inter*disciplinarity. As an academic who was a legal scholar by training, affiliation, and identity, he drew heavily on other disciplines but, in doing so, followed the logic of his discipline. His work does not eradicate disciplinary boundaries. For that reason, it is interdisciplinary and not transdisciplinary.

The intradisciplinary localization of interdisciplinary work is key to jurisprudential autonomy. First, the questions that guide the interaction with other disciplines and the reception of their knowledge emanate from the legal world. Second, given the *intra*disciplinarity, the author's evaluating peers are other legal scholars.

Regarding the first aspect, the topics under investigation usually pertain to the legal world, whose specificities are usually of little interest to other disciplines. They involve law-making, the interpretation or application of the law, the construction of legal doctrine, legal (rather than more general normative) criticism, the law's effects on society, and (as in *The Situation of European Jurisprudence*) scholarly self-understandings. Since these questions are mostly alien to other disciplines, their answers require a discipline-specific approach.

The second aspect is perhaps even more important. If we conceive of theoretical inquiries as an intradisciplinary endeavour, defining and controlling the standards of good scholarship falls to other *legal* scholars.[138] This is important because only rarely does a jurisprudential contribution succeed in appraising the current state of research in other disciplines, let alone in penetrating it fully. Take this study as an example. How can it plumb the depths of the state of research on Hegel and Schmitt in political theory, political science, and history or of all relevant sociological

[135] Schuppert, 'Die Verwaltungsrechtswissenschaft im Kontext der Wissenschaftsdisziplinen. § 70', in von Bogdandy, Cassese, and Huber (n. 29) 461, at paras 8 ff.; von Arnauld, 'Öffnung der öffentlich-rechtlichen Methode durch Internationalität und Interdisziplinarität. Erscheinungsformen, Chancen, Grenzen', 74 *Veröffentlichungen der Vereinigung der Deutschen Staatsrechtslehrer* (2015) 39.

[136] König and Gorman, 'The Challenge of Funding Interdisciplinary Research. A Look Inside Public Research Agencies', in R. Frodeman (ed.), *The Oxford Handbook of Interdisciplinarity* (2017) 513, at 520.

[137] This is Hirschl's proposal. See R. Hirschl, *Comparative Matters. The Renaissance of Comparative Constitutional Law* (2014) 151 ff. But see von Bogdandy, 'Comparative Constitutional Law as a Social Science? A Hegelian Reaction to Ran Hirschl's *Comparative Matters*', 49 *Verfassung und Recht in Übersee/Law and Politics in Africa, Asia and Latin America* (2016) 278.

[138] See the DFG Code 'Leitlinien zur Sicherung guter wissenschaftlicher Praxis' ('Guidelines for Safeguarding Good Scientific Practice'), the Guidelines 'Gute wissenschaftliche Praxis im öffentlichen Recht' ('Good Scientific Practice in Public Law') of the Association of German Professors of Constitutional Law, and the Rules of Good Scientific Practice of the Max Planck Society.

research on a topic as broad as European society? As a rule, reception tends to be syncretic, eclectic, even reductionist.

Nevertheless, such syncretism, eclecticism, or reductionism may result in good legal scholarship. We can even go further: the autonomy I am advocating represents a trump card that allows scholars to make productive use of other disciplines' findings in the light of their own jurisprudential questions.[139] Freedom in theoretical legal scholarship does not equate to a lack of standards. There certainly are standards. A legal scholar should be open about his or her approach as well as about his or her selection and understanding of the results of pertinent research. Moreover, the train of thought—its internal coherence—and the individual arguments must be comprehensible, there should be an argumentative debate with other, divergent approaches, and the relevant legal material should be presented accurately.[140] If we conceptualize these criteria within the framework of truth theory, a syncretic understanding of truth emerges, combining elements of the theories of correspondence, coherence, and consensus.[141]

However, the autonomy of juridical theoretical inquiries comes at a price. Because legal scholarship belongs to the practical sciences, a theoretical proposal should ultimately prove its practical worth. To do so, the natural thing is to translate it into doctrinal scholarship. The more theoretical contributions support doctrinal constructions that prove their worth in the labyrinth of positive law and its operations, of legal policy or legal critique, the greater their academic substance.[142] In this way, theoretical research in the law parallels processes of knowledge generation in the natural sciences, which often begin with a speculative theorem that must then be confirmed by means of empirical research.

The freedom in developing jurisprudential theory comes at the price of remaining dependent on other processes of legal reasoning. The epistemic status of theoretical contributions often resembles that of a hypothesis that must prove its worth in more concrete legal discourses. Otherwise, theoretical inquiries will easily get caught in a maze of blind theories, ideological slogans, and shaky speculations.

This also applies to the development of legal concepts, a major field of jurisprudential theory. Jurisprudential conceptualization must ultimately prove fruitful in legal practice. This book's conceptualization of European public law thus seeks to

[139] Kuntz, 'Auf der Suche nach einem Proprium der Rechtswissenschaft. Sinn und Unsinn des Bemühens um disziplinäre Identität', 219 *Archiv für die civilistische Praxis* (2019) 254, at 298.

[140] Many of these criteria are addressed in Schulze-Fielitz, 'Was macht die Qualität öffentlich-rechtlicher Forschung aus?', 50 *Jahrbuch des öffentlichen Rechts* (2002) 1, at 26 ff.

[141] Habermas, 'Wahrheitstheorien', in H. Fahrenbach (ed.), *Wirklichkeit und Reflexion. Walter Schulz zum 60. Geburtstag* (1973) 211; Lorenz, 'Semantische Wahrheitstheorie', in J. Mittelstraß (ed.), *Enzyklopädie Philosophie und Wissenschaftstheorie, Bd. 4* (1997) 592; Glanzberg, 'Truth', in E. N. Zalta (ed.), Stanford Encyclopedia of Philosophy, http://plato.stanford.edu/entries/truth (last visited 11 July 2022); Deckert, 'Recht und Wahrheit. Zum gegenwärtigen Stand der Diskussion', 82 *Archiv für Rechts- und Sozialphilosophie* (1996) 43.

[142] Volkmann, 'Rechts-Produktion oder: Wie die Theorie der Verfassung ihren Inhalt bestimmt', 54 *Der Staat* (2015) 35, at 60.

help operators of European law understand their subject better, to enrich interpretations of important provisions (above all Article 2 TEU), and to facilitate internal criticism. This understanding suggests taking another look at legal doctrine's specific form of reason.

D. Doctrine

Traditionally, doctrine has made up the core of legal scholarship in Europe. Some even define this scholarship by its doctrinal method.[143] But doctrine's defining role has been fading of late. Critics accuse it of being dogmatic (i.e. irresponsive to a democratic society)[144] or methodologically opaque.[145] Though there is truth in this criticism, I hold that legal doctrine is essential and that it can contribute to a democratic society.[146] Its functional legitimation follows precisely from the doctrines it constructs, for the latter rationalize the law embodied in an almost infinite number of provisions and judgments that are often hard to find, difficult to understand, and related to one another in intricate ways. Law that is rationalized this way helps produce adequate social order.[147] This implies abstraction, conceptualization, and the structuring of vast amounts of material as well as inventing new doctrines.[148]

A look back to the nineteenth century illustrates my point. For a long time, scholarship on public law was viewed with suspicion, especially inasmuch as it addressed political institutions. Its claims were considered either exegetical (and thus not very substantial, historiographical or philosophical) or mere political opinion.

143 Voßkuhle (n. 120) § 1 para. 1. For more detail, see Pauly (n. 29) paras 19 ff.; Napolitano, 'Sul futuro delle scienze del diritto pubblico. Variazioni su una lezione tedesca in terra americana', 60 *Rivista trimestrale di diritto pubblico* (2010) 1, at 3.

144 Sandulli (n. 27) 38 f., 197, 207.

145 Everson, 'Is It Just Me, or Is There an Elephant in the Room?', 13 *European Law Journal* (2007) 136.

146 von Bogdandy, 'The Past and Promise of Doctrinal Constructivism: A Strategy for Responding to the Challenges Facing Constitutional Scholarship in Europe', 7 *International Journal of Constitutional Law* (2009) 364; von Bogdandy, 'National Legal Scholarship in the European Legal Area—A Manifesto', 10 *International Journal of Constitutional Law* (2012) 614. See also Somek, 'The Indelible Science of Law' (n. 73) 431 ff.; Rosenfeld, 'Preface. The Role of Constitutional Scholarship in Comparative Perspective. An Exchange among Armin von Bogdandy, Robert Post, Mattias Kumm, and Alexander Somek', 7 *International Journal of Constitutional Law* (2009) 361; Scoditti, 'Europa e scienza giuridica. La scienza giuridica e i signori del diritto', 135 *Foro Italiano* (2012) 241; Caponi, 'Europa e scienza giuridica. Diritto della scienza e scienza del diritto', 135 *Foro Italiano* (2012) 244; Granieri and Pardolesi, 'Europa e scienza giuridica. Ma i tre signori del diritto sono rimasti in due?', 135 *Foro Italiano* (2012) 247; Palmieri, 'Europa e scienza giuridica. La scienza giuridica europea e le professioni legali: dalla conoscenza alla consapevolezza', 135 *Foro Italiano* (2012) 249; Brutti, 'Per la scienza giuridica europea (riflessioni su un dibattito in corso)', 62 *Rivista trimestrale di diritto pubblico* (2012) 905; Napolitano (n. 143).

147 M. Weber, *Wirtschaft und Gesellschaft. Grundriss der verstehenden Soziologie* (1972) 825 ff.; Wissenschaftsrat (n. 36) 33.

148 Grundmann, '§ 9. Systemdenken und Systembildung', in K. Riesenhuber (ed.), *Europäische Methodenlehre. Handbuch für Ausbildung und Praxis* (2015) 172; Hesselink, 'A European Legal Method? On European Private Law and Scientific Method', 15 *European Law Journal* (2009) 20.

Private law completely overshadowed public law scholarship.[149] Scholars of private law at the University of Paris even sued to prevent the establishment of a chair in constitutional law; they were concerned that its work would tarnish the reputation of legal scholarship as a whole.[150]

In Germany, the public law (*staatsrechtliche*) positivism of the late nineteenth century finally enabled public law to prove its worth by means of the legal method, that is, the production of doctrine. Karl von Gerber (1823–1891) and Paul Laband (1838–1918) personify this transformation.[151] Similar academic transformations happened in many other countries thanks to legal scholars who are also remembered as 'founders': Nikolaos Saripolos in Greece (1817–1887), Vittorio Emanuele Orlando in Italy (1860–1952), Johannes T. Buys in the Netherlands (1828–1893), Antoni Okolski in Poland (1838–1897), Hugo Blomberg in Sweden (1850–1909), and Ernö Nagy in Hungary (1853–1921).[152] Albert V. Dicey (1835–1922) also belongs to this group.[153] In Austria, Kelsen's pure theory of law may have provided the apotheosis of jurisprudential autonomy.[154]

That this programme has proved successful throughout Europe does not mean that scholarly practices developed in an identical way. Under the cheese dome of the nation state, the various national disciplines developed their own signature approaches, practices, and roles. German jurisprudence—not least thanks to the German language's distinctive ability to nominalize and combine nouns—has woven a particularly tight web of doctrinal concepts and a particularly dense layer of public law doctrines.[155] Yet, even the differences between German-speaking countries (i.e. between Kelsenian Austria, thoroughly democratic Switzerland, and Germany) are deep.

[149] Fioravanti, 'Italien. § 31', in von Bogdandy, Cruz Villalón, and Huber, *Handbuch Ius Publicum Europaeum, Bd. II* (n. 38) 585, at para. 13; Nehmelman, 'Niederlande. § 32', in von Bogdandy, Cruz Villalón, and Huber, *Handbuch Ius Publicum Europaeum, Bd. II* (n. 38) 613, at para. 16; Pilafas, 'Griechenland. § 29', in von Bogdandy, Cruz Villalón, and Huber, *Handbuch Ius Publicum Europaeum, Bd. II* (n. 38) 525, at paras 9 ff.

[150] Heuschling, 'Frankreich. § 28', in von Bogdandy, Cruz Villalón, and Huber, *Handbuch Ius Publicum Europaeum, Bd. II* (n. 38) 491, at para. 12.

[151] Pauly, 'Deutschland. § 27', in von Bogdandy, Cruz Villalón, and Huber, *Handbuch Ius Publicum Europaeum, Bd. II* (n. 38) 463, at para. 7. For a comparative perspective, see Jouanjan, 'Die Belle époque des Verwaltungsrechts. Zur Entstehung der modernen Verwaltungsrechtswissenschaft in Europa (1880–1920). § 69', in von Bogdandy, Cassese, and Huber (n. 29) 425.

[152] On Ernö Nagy, see Jakab, 'Ungarn. § 38', in von Bogdandy, Cruz Villalón, and Huber, *Handbuch Ius Publicum Europaeum, Bd. II* (n. 38) 777, at para. 7. On Nikolaos Saripolos, see Pilafas (n. 149) para. 15. On Johannes T. Buys, see Nehmelman (n. 149) para. 16. On Hugo Blomberg, see Modéer, 'Schweden. § 35', in von Bogdandy, Cruz Villalón, and Huber, *Handbuch Ius Publicum Europaeum, Bd. II* (n. 38) 697, at para. 7. On Vittorio Emanuele Orlando, see Fioravanti (n. 149) paras 10, 15.

[153] Loughlin, 'Großbritannien. § 4', in A. von Bogdandy, P. Cruz Villalón, and P. M. Huber (eds), *Handbuch Ius Publicum Europaeum, Bd. I. Grundlagen und Grundzüge staatlichen Verfassungsrechts* (2007) 217, at para. 39.

[154] Somek, 'Österreich. § 33', in von Bogdandy, Cruz Villalón, and Huber, *Handbuch Ius Publicum Europaeum, Bd. II* (n. 38) 637, at paras 4 f.

[155] Jakab, 'Ungarn. § 38' (n. 152) para. 42; Heuschling (n. 150) paras 47, 53.

Nevertheless, doctrine became a dominant factor everywhere. We can interpret this development in different ways: as part of an ideological project to justify government authority, as a means to stabilize a historical compromise between different social groups, as a sign for ever more societal differentiation in the context of industrialization, or as the incorporation of an idea into the social world. I will present it from an internal perspective, that is, public law's autonomy.

As reason requires procedure, I focus on legal doctrine's method. This is not an easy task since the doctrinal method gets by with remarkably little methodological reflection. The seminal German textbook on administrative law throws this point into relief. In Otto Mayer's words, the book's task is 'to present the system of the various institutions of administrative law [...]. We will present the material as it has arranged itself.'[156] Here, as in the entire book, Mayer's actual method, the processes of selection, abstraction, conceptualization, and structuring, remains obscure. It is a testament to the Hegelian legacy that Mayer refers but vaguely to him:

> It [the method] is based on the belief in the power of general ideas of law, which appear and unfold in the various manifestations of real law but at the same time change and progress in history. In my case, it is probably Hegelian legal philosophy [...] that allowed me to pursue such ideas even in German administrative law, disjointed and unfinished as it is.[157]

In the past, many authors were similarly hooked on a crypto-idealistic concept of a system.[158] Their ambition was to display the system that was believed to inhere in the law. The same holds true for the individual doctrines that compose a doctrinal system. This crypto-idealistic understanding has been overcome, together with Hegel's absolute idealism (see 1.4). Schmitt's *The Situation* underscores this point by presenting the system as a regulative idea rather than an ontological fact. The task of jurisprudence, Schmitt holds, is to '*seek* to safeguard the unity and the consistency of law'.[159]

Today, most scholars understand systemic thinking as a tool and doctrinal concepts as constructions for ordering the law. Accordingly, they are more restrained when it comes to the legal authority of doctrines and the impact they should have on legal reasoning.[160] Doctrines are abstract, while legal reasoning must, in the end, prove its worth in the concrete case at hand. But abstract guidance still plays a significant role and so do systematic thinking and doctrines. Accordingly, much of

156 O. Mayer, *Deutsches Verwaltungsrecht, Bd. 1* (1924) 21.
157 Ibid. Preface, VIII.
158 Somek, *Rechtssystem und Republik* (n. 85) 193–221.
159 Schmitt, 'The Situation of European Jurisprudence' (n. 4) 30 (emphasis added).
160 E. Schmidt-Aßmann, *Verwaltungsrechtliche Dogmatik. Eine Zwischenbilanz zu Entwicklung, Reform und künftigen Aufgaben* (2013) 3 ff. On remnants of the systemic thinking of old, see Ackermann (n. 60) 481 ff.

legal scholarship continues to follow the idea of systemic order and pursues juridical functionality through doctrinal work, understanding the law 'as a largely self-referential order'.[161]

The methods of good doctrinal scholarship become clearly apparent in the standards for assessing such scholarship. A good contribution must pursue a meaningful question; be situated in the current state of discussion; offer fitting, comprehensible, and coherent arguments; and link them to the relevant legal material presented systematically, accurately, and circumspectly. If these criteria basically resemble those that apply to theoretical contributions, they differ from the latter in that doctrinal scholarship must attend to positive law more closely and should offer some practical conclusions. This is incompatible with a narrow-minded dogmatism, reality-blind formalism, and hyper-strict textualism. Modern doctrinal work knows many interfaces to other disciplines and can practice interdisciplinarity.[162] Many legal scholars know much about policies and double smoothly as policy experts.

Doctrinal scholarship will continue to play an important role in European jurisprudence. However, one of its forms has probably been exhausted: the 'juridical cathedral'[163] (i.e. the comprehensive treatise), which, in the past, arguably constituted its most prestigious product. The only book on European law I know that is understood in this sense—as a conceptually guided, comprehensive doctrinal account penned by a single author—is Ipsen's *Europäisches Gemeinschaftsrecht* (see 2.4.C). Written half a century ago, it is now regarded as a monument of a bygone era.

Today, productive doctrine takes other forms. Consider the model draft on European administrative law, produced by the Research Network on EU Administrative Law (ReNEUAL),[164] or perhaps the most successful textbook, entitled *EU Law: Text, Cases, and Materials*, written by Paul Craig and Gráinne de Búrca in Oxford and New York.[165] No longer is the ambition of legal doctrine to provide systematic surveys. Instead, it frequently adopts a problem-orientated approach that seeks to advance the democratic project.[166] Article 2 TEU provides its basis in positive law.

[161] C. Bumke, *Rechtsdogmatik. Eine Disziplin und ihre Arbeitsweise. Zugleich eine Studie über das rechtsdogmatische Arbeiten Friedrich Carl von Savignys* (2017) 226.

[162] Cassese, 'New Paths for Administrative Law. A Manifesto', 10 *International Journal of Constitutional Law* (2012) 603, at 603–613; Schmidt-Aßmann, *Verwaltungsrechtliche Dogmatik* (n. 160) 21 ff.

[163] Heuschling (n. 150) paras 22, 24.

[164] See http://www.reneual.eu/index.php/organization (last visited 11 July 2022); J. Ziller, J.-P. Schneider, and H. Hofmann (eds), *La codification de la procédure administrative de l'Union européenne. Le modèle ReNEUAL* (2017).

[165] P. Craig and G. de Búrca, *EU Law. Text, Cases, and Materials* (7th edn, 2020). The first edition was published in 1998.

[166] Ackermann (n. 60) 479 ff.

4. Fighting Fire with Fire

A. Criminal State Organs

Instead of offering a summary or questions for further research, this book ends with a doctrinal proposal for further transformation that exemplifies the ideas expressed in section 5.3.D. I understand legal scholarship as a practical discipline that should go beyond describing, systematizing, theorizing, and criticizing the law and ought also to provide for doctrinal innovation. To innovate doctrinally, scholarship must introduce a new idea, argue for its constitutional legitimacy, identify its legal bases, and introduce it as coherently as possible into the body of law.

I propose reinforcing the European constitutional core with the help of criminal sanctions.[167] This proposal is the result of combining EU and national law. Thus, it is quintessentially a doctrine of European law and not just one of EU law.

To date, violating the European constitutional core is not considered a reason for criminal liability. I dispute that opinion. For a start, prosecuting such acts is legitimate because of the threat that authoritarian tendencies pose to European democratic society (see 2.6.D, 3.6.A).[168] Karl Loewenstein's pioneering contribution of 1937 calls for fighting fire (i.e. authoritarian governments) with fire (i.e. criminal law) as society's most powerful internal weapon.[169] Democratic criminal law protects not only the individual but also the democratic order.[170]

The Nuremberg and Tokyo trials established the relevance of transnational law for criminal sanctions. Such relevance may stem from an explicit act of law-making (e.g. the Rome Statute of the International Criminal Court) but also from court decisions. The Inter-American Court concluded from the American Convention on Human Rights that states parties must punish persons who are responsible for systemic deficiencies such as extrajudicial killings or forced disappearances (see 2.6.B). The European Court of Human Rights (ECtHR) has followed this example.[171] The situation in the EU is far less dramatic than the circumstances that led to those judgments by the Inter-American Court. Unlike in Latin America and in some Convention states that are not members of the EU, state terrorism does

[167] The following is based on von Bogdandy and Spieker, 'Countering the Judicial Silencing of Critics: Article 2 TEU Values, Reverse Solange, and the Responsibilities of National Judges', 15 *European Constitutional Law Review* (2019) 391.

[168] Reinforcing a constitutional core with the help of criminal law represents an established idea. See Hefendehl, 'Politisches Strafrecht zwischen dem Schutz von Staat und Verfassung und einem Kampf gegen die Feinde', in A. Hoyer *et al.* (eds), *Festschrift für Friedrich-Christian Schroeder zum 70. Geburtstag* (2006) 453.

[169] Loewenstein, 'Militant Democracy and Fundamental Rights, II', 31 *American Political Science Review* (1937) 638, at 656. See also 3.6.A.

[170] Appel, 'Rechtsgüterschutz durch Strafrecht? Anmerkungen aus verfassungsrechtlicher Sicht', 82 *Kritische Vierteljahresschrift für Gesetzgebung und Rechtswissenschaft* (1999) 278.

[171] Brems, 'Transitional Justice in the Case Law of the European Court of Human Rights', 5 *International Journal of Transitional Justice* (2011) 282.

not plague European society, although the 2017 murder of the Maltese journalist Daphne Caruana Galizia and the 2018 murders of Slovak journalist Ján Kuciak and his partner Martina Kušnírová raise questions.[172]

The following discussion will show how less serious acts can lead to criminal (or disciplinary) sanctions under European law as part of European transformative constitutionalism. It should be stressed that this represents but one of various ways in which European institutions might aid democratic transitions. I choose to elaborate on criminal liability because it is particularly demanding in legal terms and allows many of this book's holdings to be recapitulated.

The current Polish and Hungarian governments target political opponents, especially by judicial means. Their repression can constitute the criminal offence of perverting justice, prosecuting the innocent, and abusing public office. The use of criminal law in this context has two main goals. First, in keeping with its preventive function, it seeks to reinforce the constitutional core and strengthen red lines, thereby protecting the possibility for democratic change through the ballot box. Second, it can contribute to the replacement of compromised judges, politicians, and officials after a change of government.

A new majority will face the question of whether, and how, to undo the recruitments with which the current Polish and Hungarian governments are entrenching their power and policies. Packed courts, particularly constitutional courts, are key to these governments' strategy. Undoing that strategy is a delicate matter, however, as it might conflict with the principles of judicial independence and thus the rule of law. The doctrine I present demonstrates how the European rule of law, as enshrined in Article 2 TEU, can nevertheless support, rather than prohibit, measures to undo court-packing.[173]

Poland's judicial policy after 2015 serves as the example case for elaborating this proposal. The Polish government (including the legislature) began by weakening and aligning many sectors of the Polish judiciary (see 3.6.A), thereby curtailing the courts' power to act as a check on the other government branches. Then, it availed itself of the courts to stymie its political opponents.

Thus, the legal scholar Wojciech Sadurski is facing a number of court cases because of his vocal and often polemical criticism of the Polish government.[174] The ruling PiS party has brought civil proceedings against him because he allegedly described it as a 'criminal organization'.[175] *Telewizja Polska* (*TVP*), the

[172] M. Schmidt, *Verfassungsaufsicht in der Europäischen Union. Eine akteurszentrierte Analyse der Rechtsstaatlichkeitskrise der Europäischen Union* (2021) 212 ff., 225 ff.

[173] On the importance of the rule of law in such contexts, see Böckenförde, 'Der verdrängte Ausnahmezustand', *Neue Juristische Wochenschrift* (1978) 1881, at 1883; P. Cruz Villalón, *Estados excepcionales y suspensión de garantías* (1984) 23 ff.; Dyzenhaus, 'State of Emergency', in M. Rosenfeld and A. Sajó (eds), *The Oxford Handbook of Comparative Constitutional Law* (2012) 442, at 443.

[174] For his criticism, see, e.g. W. Sadurski, *Poland's Constitutional Breakdown* (2019).

[175] Sadurski, 'I Criticized Poland's Government. Now It's Trying to Ruin Me', *Washington Post* (22 May 2019); de Búrca and Morijn, 'Open Letter in Support of Professor Wojciech Sadurski', *Verfassungsblog* (6 May 2019).

government-controlled public television station, is suing Sadurski for defamation after he accused the station of 'Goebbels-like' propaganda practices.[176]

The Polish Ombudsman Adam Bodnar is also facing a similar suit brought by *TVP*. Shortly after the mayor of Gdańsk was assassinated, Bodnar made a comment in which he linked the assassination to the poisonous atmosphere of *TVP*'s reporting.[177] The TV station had reported on the mayor's alleged involvement in corruption scandals and his connections to communists or right-wing extremists on an almost daily basis. The court of first instance dismissed the case against Bodnar, but it continues before the Supreme Court.

The proceedings against Igor Tuleya, who has become the figurehead of independent judges, have received a great deal of international attention.[178] Tuleya, a judge at the Warsaw Regional Court, made various decisions that ran counter to the interests of the government. In 2017, he demanded that the public prosecutor's office initiate proceedings for unlawful obstruction of the opposition's work. Instead, disciplinary proceedings were soon brought against him before the pro-government Disciplinary Chamber of the Supreme Court. These proceedings were unlawful; the Court of Justice ruled that the Chamber violates Union law (see 4.6.C). Nevertheless, the Chamber held that it had jurisdiction to decide on Igor Tuleya's judicial immunity. In April 2021, another Chamber of the Polish Supreme Court decided that he need not go to prison, but this has not ended the proceedings against him.[179]

There are further examples of the decay of the rule of law. The Polish Minister of Justice announced that he would initiate proceedings for defamation against legal scholars from the University of Krakow who had criticized proposals in the field of criminal law as unconstitutional.[180] Polish state authorities have also brought numerous civil suits against journalists.[181]

[176] Kublik, 'Auf Linie gebracht: Polens öffentlich-rechtlicher Rundfunk unter PiS-Kuratel', *Osteuropa* (2016) 153. See also the reference to it as a 'government propaganda mouthpiece' by Reporters without Borders, *Poland*, https://rsf.org/en/poland (last visited 11 July 2022). On partisan reporting, see the report of the Organization for Security and Co-operation in Europe's (OSCE's) *ODIHR Limited Election Observation Mission* on the Polish elections of 13 October 2019: OSCE, *Poland, Parliamentary Elections, 13 October 2019: Statement of Preliminary Findings and Conclusions*, 12, http://www.osce.org/odihr/elections/poland/435932 (last visited 11 July 2022).

[177] See the Ombudsman's website, *Information about the Lawsuit Filed by TVP SA and Notified to the CHR Office* (29 February 2013), http://www.rpo.gov.pl/en/content/information-about-lawsuit-filed-tvp-and-notified-chr-office (last visited 11 July 2022).

[178] Tuleya, 'Even in Prison', *Verfassungsblog* (20 November 2020); Werner, 'Kampf um die Unabhängigkeit der Gerichte in Europa: Interview mit Beata Morawiec und Igor Tuleya', *Deutsche Richterzeitung* (2021) 142; European Commission, 2020 Rule of Law Report, Country Chapter on the rule of law situation in Poland, SWD (2020) 320 final, at 7.

[179] Woźnicki, 'Disciplinary Chamber of the Supreme Court Denies the Use of Coercive Measures Against Judge Igor Tuleya', *Gazeta Wyborcza* (23 April 2021).

[180] The Minister of Justice ultimately abandoned this plan. See Grabowska-Moroz, Łakomiec, and Ziółkowski, 'The History of the 48-Hour Lawsuit: Democratic Backsliding, Academic Freedom, and the Legislative Process in Poland', *ruleoflaw.pl* (9 July 2019).

[181] Maciejasz, 'Gag Lawsuits and Judicial Intimidation: PiS Seeks to Turn Courts Into an Instrument of State Censorship', *Gazeta Wyborcza* (26 March 2021).

B. Criminal Liability

In European society, inquiring into the criminal liability of state institutions that persecute political opponents is not fanciful. It can be constructed, in a manner that complies with the rule of law, by combining various elements of European law.

I start with the issue of competence. The Union itself has no penal authority over individuals; only national courts have this, be they a Polish criminal court or a Member State court acting within its international jurisdiction.

While the Union cannot throw anyone into prison, Union law can establish criminal offences, and it can require Member States to prosecute individuals. The Union can even engage in criminal investigations and prosecution, as follows from the competences established in Articles 67, 75, and 82–89 TFEU. These competences have been put to good use: the Council's current compilation on Union criminal law is 1,272 pages long.[182] Accordingly, there can be no doubt that the CJEU can develop case law on criminal matters. Long gone are the times when criminal law, the most intrusive instrument of public authority, was off-limits for the Union, which was considered to lack the requisite democratic legitimacy. This is yet more proof of the transformation of European public law.

There is much Union criminal legislation but not against instrumentalized judges or the politicians who instrumentalize them. Since the principles of Article 2 TEU cannot function as criminal legislation (Article 49(1) of the Charter of Fundamental Rights (CFR)), such judges' criminal liability can only result from Member State law. To use domestic law in such constellations, I suggest connecting the doctrine of effectiveness (see 3.3.C) with the doctrine of the European constitutional core (see 3.1.C). This connection can generate a doctrine of criminal liability that supports European transformative constitutionalism (see 3.6, 4.6.C).

Politically motivated proceedings against critics call for European transformative constitutionalism because they represent a European concern (see 3.6.A). What is happening in Poland violates the essence of the European rule of law with respect to judicial independence as well as the essence of the European freedom of expression. The freedom of government critics 'constitutes one of the essential foundations of a pluralist, democratic society, and is one of the values on which, under Article 2 TEU, the Union is founded'.[183] Since this essence is protected by Article 2 TEU, it is irrelevant that the CFR does not apply to many of these proceedings (Article 51 CFR, see 3.6.B). Though it is true that the CJEU has not yet declared Article 2 TEU to be directly applicable, the combined interpretation of

[182] European Council, *European Union Instruments in the Field of Criminal Law and Related Texts* (2019), https://www.consilium.europa.eu/en/documents-publications/publications/european-union-instruments-criminal-law (last visited 27 June 2022).

[183] In a similar sense, see CJEU, Joined Cases C-203/15 and C-698/15, *Tele2 Sverige* (EU:C:2016:970) para. 93; ECtHR, *Baka v. Hungary*, Appl. no. 20261/12, Judgment of 23 June 2016, para. 158.

Article 2 TEU with another Treaty provision, such as Article 19(2) TEU, has, by and large, the same effect.[184]

In proceedings against government critics or independent judges, national judges must interpret and apply the criminal offences of insult or slander, civil claims for damages, and disciplinary rules in accordance with the European constitutional core (see 3.1.C, 4.6.C). Furthermore, the primacy of Union law prohibits applying national provisions that target government critics, such as Hungarian laws on people working for the Open Society Foundation or the Central European University.[185] These duties apply to judges as well as to other authorities. All public office holders must interpret national law in conformity with EU law and disapply it when their interpretation cannot yield such conformity.[186]

Since national judges must respect the European constitutional core, they must refuse being instrumentalized for the purposes of illegal governmental repression. This puts them in a difficult position because the Polish government has little respect for judicial independence. Here, it might help to involve Europe by implicating the CJEU. Indeed, many Polish courts have initiated preliminary ruling proceedings (Article 267 TFEU) to gain European support. To counteract this, the Polish Minister of Justice has petitioned the captured Polish Constitutional Court to declare such proceedings unconstitutional[187] and has initiated disciplinary proceedings, heard by the new and captured Disciplinary Chamber at the Polish Supreme Court, against referring judges.[188] Similarly, the Hungarian Supreme Court ruled that a district court's reference requesting the CJEU to review the Hungarian judiciary's independence was unlawful.[189]

To support referring judges, I contend that a national court ought to be duty-bound to refer a case to the CJEU in such situations. A reference should be mandatory when the case turns on the European constitutional core. If the duty to refer is violated, the Commission can initiate infringement proceedings, allowing the CJEU to quickly intervene with interim measures.[190] This duty does not yet exist.

[184] In detail, see von Bogdandy and Spieker, 'Protecting Fundamental Rights beyond the Charter. Repositioning the Reverse Solange Doctrine in Light of the CJEU's Article 2 TEU Case-Law', in M. Bobek and J. Adams-Prassl (eds), *The EU Charter of Fundamental Rights in the Member States* (2020) 525.

[185] See CJEU, Case C-78/18, *Commission v. Hungary (Transparency of Associations)* (EU:C:2020:476); Case C-66/18, *Commission v. Hungary (Enseignement supérieur)* (EU:C:2020:792).

[186] CJEU, Case C-378/17, *Minister for Justice and Equality and Commissioner of the Garda Síochána* (EU:C:2018:979) para. 38; Case C-103/88, *Fratelli Costanzo v. Comune di Milano* (EU:C:1989:256) para. 31; Case C-224/97, *Ciola* (EU:C:1999:212) para. 30.

[187] Biernat and Kawczyńska, 'Though This Be Madness, Yet There's Method in't: Pitting the Polish Constitutional Tribunal against the Luxembourg Court', *Verfassungsblog* (26 October 2019).

[188] Act on the Supreme Court of 8 December 2017 (Ustawa z dnia 8 grudnia 2018 r. o Sądzie Najwyższym).

[189] Kúria, Judgment of 10 September 2019, Bt. 838/2019; Bárd, 'Luxemburg as the Last Resort: The Kúria's Judgment on the Illegality of a Preliminary Reference to the ECJ', *Verfassungsblog* (23 September 2019).

[190] See CJEU, Case C-619/18 R, *Commission v. Poland (Independence of the Supreme Court)* (EU:C:2018:852); for detailed reasoning, see Case C-619/18, *Commission v. Poland (Independence of the Supreme Court)* (EU:C:2018:1021).

Deriving it recapitulates some of this book's core propositions and applies them to Article 267(3) TFEU, the most important procedural provision of European public law (see 4.3.B).

Pursuant to the wording of Article 267(3) TFEU, only last-instance courts have a duty to refer. However, the CJEU has extended this duty to lower-instance courts that wish to disapply a provision of Union law they consider unlawful.[191] To justify this seminal extension, the CJEU highlighted its objective of protecting the effectiveness of Union law, the Court's guiding principle since 1963 (see 3.3.C, 4.3.B).

Over the past 10 years, the CJEU has duplicated this guiding principle by adding a genuinely constitutional logic (see 2.6.B) to the well-established functional one. To oppose authoritarian developments in some Member States, the Court now conceptualizes the EU as a union of values. Today, protecting the constitutional principles of Article 2 TEU is, to say the least, as important as protecting the effectiveness of EU law. This justifies treating the two situations equally in procedural terms. Consequently, a Member State court must refer a case whenever it identifies a threat to the European constitutional core (see 4.4.B, 4.6.C), for example, when the government attempts to silence a critic. Today, upholding the union of values against such threats is as important for EU law as controlling the disapplication of one of its provisions. Both decisions require involving the CJEU.

While this doctrine may support independent judges, it will not suffice to save the European rule of law or the freedom of political speech in Poland. Many Polish judges owe their appointment to the government and might act as its political allies. Other judges surely fear the Disciplinary Chamber of the Polish Supreme Court. Hence, many judges might do the government's bidding.

If that is the case, they may be held criminally liable. The same applies to the politicians pulling the strings in the background[192] or other authorities involved, for example, prosecutors. Although this liability is not yet recognized, all doctrines from which it flows are well established. Therefore, the step to it is small, from a doctrinal point of view, even though its political dimension is huge.

The point of departure for this doctrine, which seeks to fight fire with fire, lies in national criminal law. It is a punishable offence in almost all legal orders for public officials seriously and intentionally to exceed their powers.[193] According to Article 231(1) of the Polish Criminal Code, 'a public official who, exceeding his authority, or not performing his duty, acts to the detriment of a public or individual interest

[191] CJEU, Case 314/85, *Foto-Frost* (EU:C:1987:452).

[192] G. Mettraux, *The Law of Command Responsibility* (2009); Schünemann, 'Schrumpfende Basis, wuchernder Überbau. Zum Schicksal der Tatherrschaftsdoktrin nach 50 Jahren', in M. Heinrich *et al.* (eds), *Strafrecht als Scientia Universalis. Festschrift für Claus Roxin zum 80. Geburtstag* (2011) 799.

[193] Canivet and Joly-Hurard, 'La responsabilité des juges, ici et ailleurs', 58 *Revue Internationale de Droit Comparé* (2006) 1049; Cappelletti, '"Who Watches the Watchmen?" A Comparative Study on Judicial Responsibility', 31 *American Journal of Comparative Law* (1983) 1.

shall be subject to the penalty of deprivation of liberty for up to 3 years'.[194] This includes the judicial perversion of justice.[195]

This criminal offence under Polish law can easily be understood to cover and protect the respect for the European constitutional core. It is an established principle of Union law that violations of EU law must be punished comparably to violations of national law.[196] If the law of a Member State criminalizes the perversion of national law, this includes comparable perversions of Union law.

Of course, not every misapplication involves a perversion of justice. Judges may err. They may interpret and apply the law differently than other courts without any consequences. Thus, judges are not accountable except for the most egregious errors, given the separation of powers, judicial independence, and the guarantee of effective legal protection.[197] In Poland, judicial immunity is entrenched in Articles 173, 180(1 and 2), and 181 of the Polish Constitution.[198]

Therefore, *criminal* liability for the perversion of justice must be limited to extreme cases of misconduct. The EU doctrine on *state* liability for judicial malpractice provides guidance. There can be liability only 'where the decision concerned was made in manifest breach of the case-law of the Court in the matter'.[199] Since criminal liability affects the liberty of the deciding judge, the threshold should be even higher. I suggest, therefore, that criminal liability requires not only a manifest but also a serious case of unlawfulness.

I wish to stress that my proposal does not aim to criminalize every refusal to make a reference to the CJEU.[200] This would criminalize many courts, including the *Conseil d'État* and the *Bundesverfassungsgericht* (see 4.4.B). I oppose this criminalization, which would endanger the courts' cooperation. My proposal is much narrower in scope because it aims to protect the European constitutional core. It confines criminal liability to instrumentalized judges and their political masters who undermine democratic society (see 3.1.B, 3.6.B, 5.4.C).

[194] For the English translation of the Polish Criminal Code, see http://legislationline.org/sites/default/files/documents/6a/Poland_CC_1997_en.pdf (last visited 11 July 2022).

[195] For an example of how these facts are applied to judges, see the Polish Supreme Court, Judgment of 30 August 2013, SNO 19/13.

[196] CJEU, Joined Cases C-387/02, C-391/02, and C-403/02, *Berlusconi et al.* (EU:C:2005:270) para. 65; Case C-105/14, *Taricco et al.*, Opinion of AG Kokott (EU:C:2015:293) para. 80; Dougan, 'From the Velvet Glove to the Iron Fist: Criminal Sanctions for the Enforcement of Union Law', in M. Cremona (ed.), *Compliance and the Enforcement of EU Law* (2012) 74.

[197] CJEU, Case C-216/18 PPU, *LM* (EU:C:2018:586) para. 63; ECtHR, *Ramos Nunes de Carvalho e Sá v. Portugal*, Appl. nos 55391/13, 57728/13, 74041/13, Judgment of 6 November 2018, paras 144 ff.

[198] Bodnar and Bojarski, 'Judicial Independence in Poland', in A. Seibert-Fohr (ed.), *Judicial Independence in Transition* (2012) 667, at 716.

[199] CJEU, Case C-224/01, *Köbler* (EU:C:2003:513) para. 56.

[200] On the debate, Rönnau, 'Rechtsbeugung durch (beharrliche) Verweigerung der Pflichtvorlage an den EuGH?', in B. Hecker, B. Weißer, and C. Brand (eds), *Festschrift für Rudolf Rengier zum 70. Geburtstag* (2018) 313.

Criminal liability requires intentional action. Determining intent falls to the national court in charge of the proceedings. Generally, it must prove that the judge was aware of the relevant law and deliberately disregarded it. To protect judicial independence, merely misapplying the law does not prove intent. Intent requires more evidence, and here, EU institutions can play a role. Thus, it may be relevant that a national judge disregarded a CJEU decision that was brought to their attention. Moreover, one can infer intent when the national judge's decision is incompatible with a CJEU ruling in the case at hand. Therefore, the Commission should monitor such proceedings in the Member States and initiate infringement proceedings (Article 258 TFEU).[201] At least judges from second-instance courts could then face a CJEU decision and corresponding criminal liability if they subsequently disrespect it to an individual's detriment. This situation is comparable to when a constitutional court hands down a decision and a criminal judge proceeds to disregard the ruling and sanctions the defendant.

One may object that the crimes I am trying to counteract originate with the government and not with the judges. While this is true, it does not exonerate the judges, let alone justify their actions. If government repression avails itself of the judiciary, the judges involved are jointly responsible. The excuse that a judge had no choice but to cede to the government's pressure must be considered but can mostly be discarded. Maria Mammeri-Latzel shows how much leeway judges had even under the totalitarian regime of national socialism. Accordingly, the government's pressure does not exonerate pliant judges.[202]

Under the current Polish government, criminal proceedings against such judges or their political masters are highly unlikely. But this does not undermine my proposal. No government lasts forever. After its fall, the new majority will have to decide how to fully restore democracy and how to deal with judges who cooperated too willingly with the previous majority. To be sure, opting for criminal law implies a monumental political decision, one that must take much more into account than its lawfulness. But one can hardly deny the relevance of a doctrinal argument that shows how such a decision can comply with the European rule of law. Moreover, it might help the new government muster support from European institutions and, last but not least, European society.[203]

[201] On this possibility, see CJEU, Case C-416/17, *Commission v. France (Advance payment)* (EU:C:2018:811) paras 100 ff.

[202] M. Mammeri-Latzel, *Justizpraxis in Ehesache im Dritten Reich. Eine Untersuchung von Prozessakten des Landgerichts Berlin unter besonderer Berücksichtigung der Ideologie des Nationalsozialismus* (2002) 281 ff.

[203] On the possible objection that the doctrine amounts to victors' justice, see Müller, 'Die Verwendung des Rechtsbeugungstatbestands zu politischen Zwecken', 17 *Kritische Justiz* (1984) 119.

C. *Solange*

The proposed doctrine seeks to support the European constitutional core and activate European society while avoiding the harmonization of domestic constitutional law. Thus, it mediates between European and national identity (see 3.2.C). To deepen our understanding of this crucial feature, I will now frame the proposal in the light of *Solange*, a doctrinal concept that captures much of the *Gestalt* of European public law.

The conjunction *solange* (as long as) became a doctrinal concept on 29 May 1974, in a decision of the *Bundesverfassungsgericht*'s Second Senate known as *Solange I*. In this decision, the Senate accepted most of the CJEU's early transformative case law (see 3.3.C, 4.3.B) but imposed a proviso to protect Germany's constitutional identity and the Court's competence to police it (see 3.2.A, 4.4.B).[204] Much like the related Italian *controlimiti* doctrine,[205] the *Solange* doctrine initially seemed like an instrument of judicial resistance.[206] Over the following decades, however, it transformed into an almost iconic doctrine of cooperative constitutional pluralism (see 4.3.D, 4.4.C).[207] This is largely due to the Second Senate's constructive *Solange II* order of 22 October 1986. Helmut Steinberger, who was assisted by his clerk Rainer Hofmann, was the rapporteur.

However, *Solange II* did not abolish the identity proviso. The latter stands, writes the Court, *as long as* there is no EU catalogue of fundamental rights enacted by a European parliament. Overcoming the proviso would, hence, require granting the European Parliament the power of constitutional legislation. This, in turn, would be anathema to the Second Senate as it would interpret such transfer of power as the revolutionary attempt to forge a European nation, people, or state (see 2.3.A). For that reason, it is essential that the proposed doctrine of criminal liability comply with the Second Senate's *Solange* doctrine. It does so because it avoids constitutional harmonization and only entrenches basic requirements.

At the same time, the doctrinal concept of Solange helps throw into relief the transformation of European public law in its second period. In that period, a European constitutional core (or *identity*) has emerged alongside the Member States' constitutional identity (or *core*). Moreover, it seems that, today, the European core is more threatened by domestic measures than national identity by European

[204] BVerfGE 37, 271, *Solange I*.

[205] Corte costituzionale, sentenza n. 183/1973, *Frontini*, para. 9; sentenza n. 170/1984, *Granital*, para. 7; sentenza n. 1146/1988, para. 2.1; sentenza n. 232/1989, *Fragd*, para. 3.1.

[206] B. Davies, *Resisting the European Court of Justice. West Germany's Confrontation with European Law, 1949–1979* (2012) 188 ff.

[207] M. Wendel, *Permeabilität im europäischen Verfassungsrecht. Verfassungsrechtliche Integrationsnormen auf Staats- und Unionsebene im Vergleich* (2011) 446 ff.; Tzanakopoulos, 'Judicial Dialogue in Multi-level Governance: The Impact of the Solange Argument', in O. K. Fauchald and A. Nollkaemper (eds), *The Practice of International and National Courts and the (De-)Fragmentation of International Law* (2012) 185.

measures. The European core needs entrenchment, and this entrenchment is underway (see 3.6.C, 4.6.C). It can be conceived via a *mirror-image* or *Reverse-Solange* doctrine. Today, European public law provides for the mutual entrenchment of constitutional principles while maintaining constitutional pluralism.

The Reverse-*Solange* doctrine emerged in 2012 to provide a Union law response to authoritarian tendencies in Hungary, especially the decay of media freedom.[208] At the time, much of that decay was perceived to occur outside the scope of Union law because the potential of Article 2 TEU remained insufficiently acknowledged. The doctrine was invented to mobilize that potential as well as the courts against such developments. The doctrine of criminal liability simply follows up on the Reverse-*Solange* doctrine.

The Reverse-*Solange* doctrine introduced a doctrinal way to operationalize—and thus vindicate—Article 2 TEU in court vis-à-vis any Member State conduct. In 2012, that seemed like legal science fiction to most. But much has happened since then, not least that the CJEU started operationalizing Article 2 TEU to combat authoritarian tendencies in 2018 (see 4.6.C). Article 19 TEU, not Union citizenship (as was proposed in 2012), served as the Court's point of departure.[209] Accordingly, the Reverse-*Solange* doctrine has been adjusted.[210]

In 2012, the doctrine's focus lay on the unifying dimension (see 4.3.B) as the objective was to mobilize the courts for entrenching the European constitutional core. Given the CJEU's current jurisprudence, its other dimension, preserving pluralism, has become more significant in the meantime.[211] To this end, the Reverse-*Solange* doctrine only seeks to protect the requirements for membership under Articles 2 and 49 TEU, which explains its focus on systemic deficiencies (see 4.2.C, 4.4.C, 4.6.C). Hence, the doctrine exhibits a very different logic than the EU CFR, whose application to the Member States mainly aims at the uniform application of Union law.[212]

The *Bundesverfassungsgericht*'s *Solange II* decision declares its trust in the European institutions. The Reverse-*Solange* doctrine similarly presupposes trust in the Member States for it establishes the presumption that they respect the

[208] von Bogdandy *et al.*, 'Reverse Solange—Protecting the Essence of Fundamental Rights against EU Member States', 49 *Common Market Law Review* (2012) 489. The co-authors include C. Antpöhler, J. Dickschen, S. Hentrei, M. Kottmann, and M. Smrkolj. On the discussion, see the contributions by D. Halberstam, A. Jakab, J. Komárek, M. Kumm, P. Lindseth, A. Mangold, W. Sadurski, P. Sonnevend, D. Thym, R. Uitz, and A. Wiener in M. Steinbeis, A. Kemmerer, and C. Möllers (eds), *Gebändigte Macht. Verfassung im europäischen Nationalstaat* (2015) 143 ff.

[209] On the case law on Union citizenship (which later became restrictive), see Spaventa, 'Earned Citizenship—Understanding Union Citizenship through its Scope', in D. Kochenov (ed.), *EU Citizenship and Federalism. The Role of Rights* (2017) 204, at 205.

[210] von Bogdandy and Spieker, 'Protecting Fundamental Rights' (n. 185).

[211] On these concerns, see Schorkopf, 'Value Constitutionalism in the European Union', 21 *German Law Journal* (2020) 956.

[212] CJEU, Case C-399/11, *Melloni* (EU:C:2013:107) para. 60; Case C-206/13, *Siragusa* (EU:C:2014:126) para. 32; Case C-198/13, *Julian Hernández* (EU:C:2014:2055) para. 47.

European constitutional core. Mutual trust between all institutions has become a core category of European public law (see 3.3.A).

Yet, eternal vigilance is the price of liberty. This is why this trust is neither blind nor unconditional. All courts retain the power to ascertain whether this presumption still holds in any given Member State. If it is rebutted, they must stand up for European values (see 5.4.B). National courts must involve the CJEU in this process. Only a preliminary ruling proceeding can satisfy the right of the concerned Member State's institutions to be heard (see 4.4.B). Moreover, any such case requires determining the European constitutional core, a task that falls to the Union's supreme court (see 4.4.C).

The *Solange* doctrines, whether under national or EU law, reflect the basic structure of European public law. They articulate and protect the prerequisites for cooperation between legal orders that are closely connected but autonomous. Let us briefly recapitulate the core elements. First, legal order A establishes constitutional requirements for the acts of another legal order (B). A will only comply with B's acts if the latter comply with these requirements. Second, the courts of legal order A can review B's legal acts for compliance. Third, there is mutual trust; it is presumed that B's legal acts meet A's requirements, and the threshold for refuting this presumption is high. This logic also applies between the EU Member States[213] as well as between the Union and the European Convention on Human Rights.[214]

This cooperative logic draws on the *Solange II* order, which inverted the defensive logic of *Solange I*. Pursuant to the *Solange I* decision, *all* German fundamental rights applied vis-à-vis the Union. With the *Solange II* order, the Second Senate abandons this dead end. First, it limits itself to 'essential' standards. Second, it refrains from reviewing EU acts as long as the Union institutions 'generally' guarantee fundamental rights protection that can 'be regarded as essentially equal to the indispensable fundamental rights protection mandated by the Basic Law'.[215] Evincing an even more pluralistic orientation, the Reverse-*Solange* doctrine focuses solely on systemic deficiencies (see 3.6.B, 4.6.C).

[213] Canor, 'My Brother's Keeper? Horizontal Solange: "An Ever Closer Distrust among the Peoples of Europe"', 50 *Common Market Law Review* (2013) 383.

[214] ECtHR, *Bosphorus v. Ireland*, Appl. no. 45036/98, Judgment of 30 June 2005; *Avotiņš v. Latvia*, Appl. no. 17502/07, Judgment of 23 May 2016.

[215] BVerfGE 73, 339, *Solange II*, 375, 386.

6

This Book's Quintessence with Marius Ivaškevičius

Solange teaches us a lot about European public law. It summarizes the basic relationship between its constituent legal orders and articulates the foundational significance of delicate compromises. With respect to European society, it is a testament to the society's capacity to engage in constructive compromise. Hegel, Schmitt, and Böckenförde help us acknowledge the magnitude of this civilizational achievement. And, last but not least, *Solange* underscores the development of a European constitutional core, which represents European public law's key transformation in its second period.

This book has addressed the question of how to understand the process of EU-centred Europeanization from a legal point of view. It has reconstructed how 70 years of Europeanization have given rise to the public law of a European society that, for all its shortcomings, is characterized by pluralism, non-discrimination, tolerance, justice, solidarity and equality between women and men, human dignity, freedom, democracy, equality, the rule of law, and respect for human rights, including the rights of persons belonging to minorities. I believe this is quite an achievement, one that many fail to recognize.

The Lithuanian playwright Marius Ivaškevičius sums up this quintessence in delightfully polemical words. He identifies 'the critics' never-ending chatter about Europe's unsolvable problems and inevitable death' as the greatest of its many problems:

> You've piled up an entire mountain of these problems. It's crushing Europe and obstructing all the good you've gotten from it. But I have disappointing news: This mountain exists only in your grumpy heads. Try on my glasses for a change. What you see through them is also distorted; it shows something too positive [. . .]. But if you look at Europe through my glasses, your eyes will recover, at least a little, because there's so much more light, colour, and will to live.[1]

[1] Ivaškevičius, 'Europa mit den Augen eines Verliebten', *Frankfurter Allgemeine Zeitung* (16 February 2017) 6.

The Emergence of European Society through Public Law. First Edition. Armin von Bogdandy, Oxford University Press.
 DOI: 10.1093/oso/9780198909347.003.0006

Author Index

For the benefit of digital users, indexed terms that span two pages (e.g., 52–53) may, on occasion, appear on only one of those pages.

Subject Index

For the benefit of digital users, indexed terms that span two pages (e.g., 52–53) may, on occasion, appear on only one of those pages.

The manufacturer's authorised representative in the EU for product safety is Oxford University Press España S.A. of el Parque Empresarial San Fernando de Henares, Avenida de Castilla, 2 – 28830 Madrid (www.oup.es/en or product.safety@oup.com). OUP España S.A. also acts as importer into Spain of products made by the manufacturer.

www.ingramcontent.com/pod-product-compliance
Lightning Source LLC
LaVergne TN
LVHW011913200926
848484LV00002B/608
9780198909347